RISKWORK

Riskwork

*Essays on the Organizational Life
of Risk Management*

Edited by
MICHAEL POWER

OXFORD

UNIVERSITY PRESS

Great Clarendon Street, Oxford, OX2 6DP,
United Kingdom

Oxford University Press is a department of the University of Oxford.
It furthers the University's objective of excellence in research, scholarship,
and education by publishing worldwide. Oxford is a registered trade mark of
Oxford University Press in the UK and in certain other countries

© Oxford University Press 2016

The moral rights of the authors have been asserted

First Edition published in 2016

Published in the United States of America by Oxford University Press
198 Madison Avenue, New York, NY 10016, United States of America

British Library Cataloguing in Publication Data
Data available

Library of Congress Control Number: 2016932199

ISBN 978-0-19-875322-3

Preface and Acknowledgements

In May 2014 a small group of risk and organization scholars came together for a workshop to debate risk management as a work process without, as far as possible, the shadow of disaster and deviance hanging over the discussions. The workshop took place in the Centre for Analysis of Risk and Regulation (CARR) at the London School of Economics and Political Science and the chapters in this volume are the results of intense exchanges over two days drawing on many disciplines and theories, but keeping a concrete a grasp of practice in the foreground. Each contribution focuses on what people in organizational settings do when they seek to make sense of, and be accountable for, the normal and everyday management of risk. This is not the tidy, conflict-free world of immaculate risk processing to be found in textbooks and practice guidance. It is rather a fluid and messy world of *riskwork* characterized by the entanglement of varied human and non-human agencies, by emotion and identity work as much as calculation, and by a continuous tension between practice and accountability.

I would like to acknowledge the financial and moral support of colleagues in the Department of Accounting at LSE and, in particular, the administrative expertise and support of Justin Adams, who made organizing this complex event look very easy. More importantly, his efforts allowed me to be a worry-free and fully engaged participant in it. I would also like to thank all the participants, and especially those who made it this far, for being such good sports and tolerating my hands-on approach, both to the event and to the editorial process. And of course, I would like to thank (for the third time in my career) David Musson at Oxford University Press for his support and encouragement for this project. It is also an opportunity to thank him more generally for his immense impact on the field of academic management over a long and influential career which ends in 2016.

One often hears these days that edited books 'don't count'. If that is true, it's a great shame and how it has happened is most likely a long and strange story. The best of these collections—and there are many examples—have the ability to travel across disciplinary boundaries, and create new and exciting fields. They can be 'go to' places to understand where a field currently is, and also show where it might go. Of course there are those who beat the drum of quality and robustness and argue that edited collections are a priori deficient. Edited collections sit outside rankings of 'top' journals and citation metrics and all the many devices of academic evaluation which have currency today. Yet in fact the issue of quality is empirical and cannot be assumed. As academic journals become ever more intellectually conservative, so it also becomes more important to defend the diversity of our scholarly eco-system. The best of edited collections, which allow authors to be a little freer and a little more experimental, can end up as much more than the sum of their parts, and as durable reference points in the academic landscape. I do not dare to presume that *Riskwork* can achieve this kind of impact, not least because it builds largely on existing scholarship and its role is more that of consolidation than innovation. Yet I hope that its chapters have the kind of critical mass and visibility which will make them a useful resource for teaching and research and even, who knows, for the many risk managers out there who are 'natural' constructivists about their work.

Michael Power

London, January 2016

Contents

List of Figures

List of Tables

List of Contributors

Åsa Boholm is Professor of Social Anthropology at the University of Gothenburg, Sweden.

Hervé Corvellec is Professor of Business Administration, Department of Service Management and Service Studies, Lund University, Sweden.

David Demortain is an INRA researcher at LISIS (Laboratoire Interdisciplinaire Sciences Innovations Société), a joint centre of the French Institut National de la Recherche Agronomique (INRA), Université Paris-Est Marne-la-Vallée (UPEM) and Centre National de la Recherche Scientifique (CNRS).

Renuka Fernando obtained a PhD from the London School of Economics and Political Science, and is Head of Financial Governance at the British Council, London, UK.

Michael D. Fischer is Senior Research Fellow in Organizational Behaviour and Leadership, University of Melbourne, Australia, and University of Oxford, UK.

Matthew Hall is Professor of Accounting Monash Business School, Australia.

Cynthia Hardy is Professor of Management at the University of Melbourne, Australia and Cardiff Business School, UK.

Silvia Jordan is Associate Professor of Accounting, University of Innsbruck, Austria.

Lene Jørgensen is a PhD candidate at the University of Stavanger, Norway.

Véronique Labelle is a PhD candidate at HEC Montréal, Canada.

Gerry McGivern is Professor of Organizational Analysis at Warwick Business School, UK.

Steve Maguire is Professor of Strategy and Organization at McGill University, Canada.

Anette Mikes is Professor of Accounting at HEC Lausanne, Switzerland.

Tommaso Palermo is Lecturer in Accounting, London School of Economics and Political Science, UK.

Brian T. Pentland is Professor of Accounting and Information Systems at Michigan State University, USA.

List of Contributors

Michael Power is Professor of Accounting at the London School of Economics and Political Science, UK.

Linda Rouleau is Professor in the Department of Management, HEC Montréal, Canada.

Zsuzsanna Vargha is Lecturer in Accounting and Organization at the University of Leicester, UK.

Maria Zhivitskaya obtained a PhD from the London School of Economics and Political Science and joined Goldman Sachs in 2016.

Introduction

Riskwork: The Organizational Life of Risk Management

Michael Power

In 1976 Barry Turner analysed a variety of disasters and accidents (Turner 1976; Turner and Pidgeon, 1997). He found that these events exhibited very similar patterns, not least missed opportunities to react to warning signs during what he called the 'incubation' period. A few years later, Charles Perrow applied his own prior work on complex organizations to the case of the Three Mile Island nuclear reactor accident in 1979 (Perrow, 1984). Perrow used the case to argue that accidents were somehow a 'normal' feature of large and complex technological systems which were increasingly opaque to human actors.

The work of both Turner and Perrow has been controversial and much debated, both in terms of the former's hindsight bias and the latter's apparent technological determinism. Yet jointly their work established a subfield for subsequent organization-based studies focused on accidents and disasters. Notwithstanding their controversies, the methodological and policy messages of this work embody a common message: disaster analysis, whether by academics or policymakers, needs to look beyond the proximate technical causes of failures and accidents, and pay attention to the role of management practice and values. In short, the origins of disaster should be traced back to the mundane level of organizational life, to climates of tolerance for routine operational errors, to failures in legal compliance, and to weak monitoring and control practices. As Vaughan puts it in the context of the *Challenger* disaster in 1985, 'No extra-ordinary actions by individuals explain what happened: no intentional managerial wrong-doing, no rule violations, no conspiracy. The cause of the disaster was a mistake embedded in the banality of organizational life' (1996: xiv).

It is understandable that the study of risk and risk management in organizations is heavily influenced by disasters; each new one brings both disappointment with the way risk was managed and a search for reform.

These events are often spectacular and headline grabbing, and there seems to be no shortage of them. They generate public enquiries, diagnoses, blame, and post-disaster introspection about what went wrong and how it might have been prevented (e.g. Atkins et al., 2012). Yet, is it possible to analyse risk management practice without this implicit orientation towards failure of some kind? While the prevention of errors, accidents and disasters is the very point of formal risk management, can we bracket this perspective and focus on normal risk processing practices, and how they are constituted by organizational actors and material artefacts?

The chapters in the present volume are commonly motivated to do this and approach risk management as a form of organizational work. Unencumbered by assumptions about 'incubation periods' and missed warnings, the aim of this collection is to reveal more of the day-to-day nature of risk processing activity across a variety of organizational settings and fields. This is not so much a radical break with the preoccupations of disaster theorists but an attempt to pay more attention to the normal, even banal, work routines as Vaughan suggests: 'Organizational encounters with risk and error are not restricted to the sensational cases that draw media coverage when mistakes, near misses and accidents become public. They are, instead, a routine and systematic part of daily organizational life that only occasionally becomes visible to outsiders' (2005: 33).

There is a vast and growing literature on risk and risk management, both practical and academic. This textual expansion mirrors the increased salience of risk management for organizations and governments. Scholars and practitioners know a great deal about the various techniques of risk management—such as diversification, insurance, and scenario analysis (Bernstein, 1996). There have also been many studies of the politics of risk regulation, the organization of risk regulation regimes and the institutional and cultural climates of blame which accompany the management of risk (Hood et al., 2001). Another important intellectual focus has been individual perceptions of, and feelings about, risk (Sitkin & Pablo, 1992; Slovic, 2000). Within these different strands of scholarship risk management is variously conceptualized as a branch of knowledge, as a site for the interplay and competition of interests, as an affective encounter between individuals and dangers, and as part of a regulated 'world of standards' (Brunsson et al., 2000; Power, 2014). And of course, there has been much debate about whether we live in a 'risk society' (Beck, 1992).

Despite this body of scholarly and practical analysis of risk management the normal, non-post disaster, work of organizational actors has received much less attention (exceptions being Czarniawska, 2009; Macrae, 2014 Short & Clarke, 1992; Weick & Roberts, 1993; Weick & Sutcliffe, 2007) Furthermore, risk studies in the shadow of disaster tend to have an epistemic presumption that the negative outcome was in principle foreseeable and avoidable (Downer, 2011). However, each of the chapters in this volume is concerned more with everyday processes rather than 'momentous events

(Powell & Colyvas, 2008: 277). Whether an organization is in an incubation period or not is empirically open in these analyses rather than being a retrospectively applied construct.

This introductory chapter sets the scene and provides a synthesis of the volume as a whole. Overall, the chapters which follow contribute to a field that might be called 'back-office studies' and to a growing body of research on institutional work (Phillips & Lawrence, 2012; Riles, 2011). They provide several rich cases of the situated human effort, in combination with material infrastructure, through which risk management and governance practices come to be constructed. In the next section, this *riskwork*—to coin a term— is positioned within a more general 'turn to work' in management and organization studies. This section is followed by synopses of each chapter according to three thematic clusters: *frameworks, risk identification,* and *affect and persuasion.* The first cluster of chapters addresses the work related to the development and operationalization of formal aspects of risk management: oversight frameworks, risk maps, and key risk indicators. The second cluster of chapters deals with the work involved in identifying and constructing specific 'risk objects'. The third cluster deals with the more agonistic and emotional aspects of riskwork, such as efforts to persuade and enrol organizational actors to manage risk and take it seriously. These chapter synopses are followed by a discussion of their collective contribution to our understanding of riskwork as being: diverse and plural in nature; mediated by material artefacts; and distributed within and across organizations.

THE TURN TO WORK: RISK FROM THE BOTTOM UP

The turn to work in risk management studies continues an earlier 'social turn' in the study of both risk and regulation (Short, 1984) which demanded attention to the social and political dimensions of risk analysis. This social turn in risk studies took many forms. It recognized the importance of values and choice, not simply in risk acceptance but also in risk identification and in the techniques of risk analysis itself, the heartland of rational risk calculation (Boholm & Corvellec, 2011; March & Shapira, 1987). It was in part a critique of expertise coupled to a concern to democratize risk regulation (Jasanoff, 2003; Wynne, 1982). It also saw the emergence of both psychological studies of individual risk perception (Slovic, 2000) and also macro-cultural theories of risk (Beck, 1992; Clarke & Short, 1993; Douglas & Wildavsky, 1983; Power, 2004, 2014). In parallel, the law and society 'movement', and the rise of socio-legal studies of risk and regulation, played an important supportive role in moving from the study of law 'on the books' to law where it happens and is enforced (e.g. Etienne, 2013; Hawkins & Thomas, 1984; Hutter, 1997).

The social turn in risk studies also built on the sociology of everyday life (Adler & Adler, 1987) by examining experiences of risk beyond the workplace, for example, in family life and relationships, in health and ageing, and in leisure activities (e.g. Burgess & Mitsutoshi Horii, 2012; Caplan, 2000; Lupton, 1999; Simon, 2002; Taylor-Gooby & Zinn, 2006; Tulloch & Lupton, 2003). Furthermore, and in reaction to the self-styled technical autonomy of risk analysis, risk studies have both historicized risk (Hacking, 2003; Power, 2014: 379–81) and also recognized that material artefacts and representations of risk play a critical role in reproducing everyday organizational life (e.g. Kalthoff, 2005).

Though different in focus and methodological orientation, these different 'social' pathways within risk and regulation studies share a 'bottom-up' approach to the understanding of risk, rooted in everyday practices within and outside of formal organizations, and informed by analyses of the way human actors make sense of risk in complex environments and in reaction to events (e.g. Gephart, 1993). This bottom-up agenda in risk studies also requires the analysis of organizational and information design issues in risk management. In trying to escape from the focus on disasters, Bourrier (2002) argues that researchers should pay more attention to systems and processes which are 'green' rather than ignored warnings and misdeeds, an agenda already implicit in Vaughan's (1996) analysis of the *Challenger* launch disaster. While Vaughan's concept of the 'normalization of deviance', which emerged from her study of NASA, is largely understood in terms of rule-breaking which is ignored or sanctioned in some way, she also draws attention to the 'incremental expansion of normative boundaries' (1996: 409) which have nothing to do with norm violations in the commonly accepted sense. For Bourrier, this insight supports a critique of post-event analyses by both academics and formal commissions for being too actor focused and unable to surface the causal role played by organizational design issues.

Bourrier suggests that public diagnoses and recommendations are often framed in terms of information deficits, and the need for new reporting requirements, or in general terms of a need to improve 'organizational culture'. In the context of the 2009 financial crisis, she has a point. A great deal of attention and energy has been focused on the cultural causes of the crisis, the ethics and incentives inside banks, and on the need to restore a healthy 'risk culture' (Power et al., 2013; PRA & FCA, 2015). Rather, Bourrier argues that scholars need to examine the normal functioning of organizations and, in particular, changes in crucial organizational patterns and associated changes in social relations as a result of new techniques and ways of working. Rather than deviant normalities or rogue behaviour it is 'the disturbance of social relations [which] greatly impacts the social construction of reliability' (Bourrier, 2002: 177).

Bottom-up studies of risk management in organizations can draw intellectual support from a more general 'turn to work', itself a reaction to the perceived inadequacies of increasing abstraction in organization studies in explaining post-industrial societies (Barley & Kunda, 2001). Barley and Kunda argue that the scholarly focus on new kinds of work and on networks are themselves overstated reactions to post-industrialism, and do not escape 'petrified images of work'. Instead of sloganistic positing of a 'world without boundaries', they call for (a return to) rich descriptions of where and how boundaries are drawn and how the units of analysis for work (projects rather than jobs) and agents (intermediaries rather than workers) may be changing. Methodologically, this requires more participant observation and 'augmented observational capacity'—a feature of many of the chapters in this volume—which is capable of generating new analytic concepts.

According to Barley and Kunda (2001: 89), this refocusing on work has many potential payoffs, such as an enhanced sense of 'communities of prac-tice' as units of analysis in which decision-making or learning are no longer conceived as singular cognitive acts. Indeed, the turn to work potentially reveals the 'flows of choreographed attending' and the grammar of organiza-tion routines (Pentland & Feldman, 2005) which have more to do with situation and accumulated micro-actions than with deliberation. As Phillips and Lawrence (2012: 227) put it, 'one of the powerful effects of adopting a "work lens" is a shift from the outcomes of action to the actors involved and the action itself'.

The work lens is itself hardly new. Sociologies of work reach back at least to the ethnomethodological studies by Garfinkel and colleagues (Garfinkel, 1967, 1986). They observed the skilled reproduction of social and organizational order and elicited the implicit assumptions sustaining that order within the 'accounts' embedded in practical reasoning. While contingent assump-tions and categories become habitualized and exteriorized as objective facts, human actors are also inventive in sustaining a reasonable world of work. Furthermore, as Baccus's (1986b) detailed study of the safety regulation of 'multipiece truck wheels' shows, the situated logics of safety evident in the workplace may be different from top-down regulator logics of safety, yielding different but equally legitimate ways of providing accounts of risk. Indeed, this tension between the formal and the situated underlies many of the chapters in this volume.

Although ethnomethodology was never developed into an 'expansive field' (Powell & Colyvas, 2008: 280) it spawned many variants and has had con-tinuing influence, not least on Weick's sensemaking programme which focuses in part on how the sustaining of identities and reciprocal relations are at stake in habituated practical action. In an analysis which has become foundational for risk studies—the Mann Gulch disaster—Weick (1993) shows how the firefighters who perished had both underestimated the danger and were also unable to adapt their work identities in an increasingly confusing situation. More generally, the sensemaking approach shows how disasters may be situated in the everyday habits of actors who attend to the signs in the environment that conform to their expectations and idiosyncratic logics of work. For risk studies the sensemaking approach requires an emphasis on the cognitive aspects of work, rather than on wilful non-compliance or deviance, and on the systematic patterns in vocabularies which shape the attention of organizational actors (Loewenstein et al., 2012; Ocasio, 2005).

Like Weick, Phillips and Lawrence also emphasize how the 'turn to work' must take account of the increased salience of identity issues in post-industrial societies. Forms of work focused on the production and reproduction of symbols, including those expressing institutional orders, are increasingly prevalent activities in and across organizations, including organized markets (e.g. Zaloom, 2004). For example, many of the major risks facing the post-industrial organizations are legal and reputational, in other words they are a product of the organizational environment itself and require new work forms to manage them more explicitly (Power et al., 2009). From this point of view, practice is not merely the sharing of operational routines across groups of actors but often and simultaneously the performance of socially legitimate activity (Schatzki, 2001) as a kind of institutional risk management. Phillips and Lawrence suggest that this post-industrial entanglement of work identity and social legitimacy issues explains why organizational units which were regarded as marginal to first order production, such as human resources, have become more significant over time. For example, the rise of equal opportunities programmes increased the organizational significance of human resource departments (Dobbin, 2009).

Successive disasters and scandals also increase the organizational significance of risk. Organizational risk management has evolved beyond the purchasing of insurance to become a mode of governing the organization as such via generic templates and categorizations (Power, 2007). Furthermore, risk has become an identity issue as the everyday work of many organizational actors is increasingly articulated in the language of risk (Horlick-Jones, 2005; Power, 2004) while new dedicated roles, such as chief risk officers (CROs) have emerged (Power, 2005). Yet many of the chapters in this volume testify to the fluidity of the interface between dedicated risk functions and others parts of organizations. For example, as Mikes shows in her contribution to this volume, CROs are engaged in continuous and often self-effacing work at the boundary between their formal oversight role and the need to generate relationships and reciprocal support for risk management. Zhivitskaya and Power observe how non-executive directors with risk oversight responsibilities must improvise between their potentially dissonant identities as both overseer and colleague of the executives. And Fischer and McGivern describe an even more fluid identity situation in which patients and medical staff co-produce the management of risk.

It follows that an empirical and theoretical turn to work in risk studies requires methodological agnosticism about who does the work of 'managing' risk and about the boundaries of risk management practice. For example, the sensemaking perspective adopted by a number of chapters suggests that the work of risk identification sits outside, and has a complex relationship to, formal risk management systems, not least in so-called high reliability environments which require habituated forms of attention and mindfulness (Weick & Roberts, 1993; Weick & Sutcliffe, 2007). Furthermore, formal risk management systems may or may not have workstreams to capture and process these constructions of risk by situated actors for whom getting the job done is at least as important as conforming to official norms of safety (Baccus, 1986b; Hutter, 2001).

To repeat, the focus on work means that the very idea of 'risk management' as an institutional category cannot be taken for granted but is continuously 'pulled into' different micro-accounts of organizational work practices by a multiplicity of actors who, from the bottom up, more or less reproduce the category (Powell & Colyvas, 2008). However, following Knorr Cetina (1981), the turn towards an ethnomethodologically inspired micro-sociology of risk management work should not be confused with smallness of focus or the prioritization of individual decision-making. The emphasis is rather on forms of interaction understood as the 'interlocking of intentionalities'. In turn, these intentionalities are not individual acts of rational cognition, but are context-referring, including institutional context, and are defined by forms of reciprocity which make action describable and understandable in the first place. In short, individual purposeful action about risk is not the primary unit of analysis but, as Vargha shows in her chapter, is derived from episodes of situated interaction which are generative of identities and their decision capabilities. This *methodological situationalism* as Knorr Cetina calls it has affinities with Latour's (2005) account of actor–network theory. Importantly, both emphasize the theoretical and empirical significance of technologies of representation and the non-human material artefacts which mediate the sensemaking of actors and are a mechanism by which reciprocal relations and connections between organizational actors are created and sustained in 'action nets' (Czarniawska, 2009).

A micro-sociological focus on technologies of representation parallels studies of the constitutive role of accounting in reproducing organizations as economic entities (Hopwood, 1992). It has also surfaced within the relatively new subfield of social studies of finance which posits that the economy is literally performed through the repeated use of models and related artefacts (Callon, 1998). Millo and Mackenzie's (2003) analysis of options trading provides a very specific case of performativity in which the options market increasingly conforms to theories of it. Via the 'theory' of options pricing, a mathematized risk management model generates the world of its own applicability. Though not quite examples of this kind of pure performativity, the chapters by Jordan and Jørgensen on risk maps, and Hall and Fernando on risk indicators show directly how these specific technologies of representation are positioned within, and are generative of work practices. Such technologies are also accounts of work in Garfinkel's sense and constitute work identities (Jordan et al., 2013). Like accounting statements, risk maps and risk indicators produce the organizational facts of risk which become reciprocally embedded in the intentionalities of actors. One cannot be understood without the other.

This broad micro-sociological point of view with its many sources and variations defines the space of the chapters that follow and their common focus on the work of managing risk, on *riskwork*. In contrast to the implied unity and coherence of risk management as a category, the idea of riskwork makes no presumptions of coherent practice and directs attention to the actions and routines through which organizational actors makes sense of risk, of themselves and their roles, and collectively try to enact institutional scripts. Against the often implicit epistemological assumption in many risk studies that risk management is a form of *knowledge*, grounded in statistical thinking, and conducted as punctuated episodes of calculation, the focus on riskwork is agnostic about what counts as the management of risk. From this point of view, risk management practice, and the ability to package it and make it visible and institutionally acceptable must be understood as an *outcome* of varied forms of riskwork rather than a starting point or presumption.

The studies of riskwork which follow can be positioned as part of a larger, if widely dispersed, genre of *back-office studies*. 'Back office' here is intended in two senses. The first is the literal distinction between front and back office which is in common use in financial institutions. Back office in this sense seems to denote something like infrastructure, namely the administrative and regulatory activities which are conditions of possibility for trading and even for markets themselves to exist (Riles, 2011). The everyday life of this 'back office' is an object of scholarly attention by anthropologists, organization theorists, and science studies specialists. And this work creates an understanding of back office in the second sense, reaching back to Goffman's (1959) 'back stage' of face-to-face practice, of the work that creates order and representations of orderliness, the work by which rational organizational narratives of risk, control, and governance come to be assembled and exported to different audiences. There are useful affinities between Goffman's back stage and Foucault's notion of an apparatus (Hacking, 2004; Power, 2011); both are characterized by a kind of unobservability which is essential to their role in constructing common sense. It follows that back office/stage analysts must read the signs of that which is normally unseen (Baccus, 1986a: 7–8).

Finally, a focus on riskwork does not ignore the salience of disasters and spectacular events. This would be unwise on historical grounds since risk management practices evolve in the wake of accidents and scandals mediated by public enquiries and new forms of regulation. However, the turn to work requires a provisional bracketing of the disaster bias, however difficult, in order to bring to the surface the assumptions that sustain the practice of risk management. Such a bracketing enables the link to accidents to be recast as a series of *ex ante* enquiries without any hindsight bias. In other words, for each of the chapters which follow it could be asked whether the bottom-up analysis of riskwork reveals that the organization or field is in an incubation period or not, and whether the normality on show is somehow potentially or actually deviant or not. These are of course much harder questions to answer than in the case of post-disaster analysis for two main reasons. First, the question of incubation or deviance at any particular time is a function of the different values which constitute the 'culture' of managing risk, and is therefore more contestable ex ante than in retrospective analyses. Second, it may be the case that such questions cannot be answered on epistemic grounds; certain kinds of failure may not in principle be knowable in advance (Downer, 2011).

The chapter summaries which follow are clustered in terms of their orientation to one of three themes. The first theme concerns the work involved in generating and sustaining many of the *formal* components of risk management practice: risk frameworks, risk maps, key-risk indicators, and models of risk oversight such as the 'three lines of defence'. The second theme concerns the kinds of work and routines involved in producing and attending to *risk objects* themselves, involving implicit value judgements in combination with technologies and instruments. The third theme addresses the affective dimension of riskwork and the *conflicts and emotions* at stake, including network-building and identity issues, which give risk management from the bottom up its human and visceral character.

FRAMEWORKS AND DESIGNS

The practical field of risk management is heavily populated by frameworks and designs which have been widely institutionalized, which project a rational image of practice and which prescribe processes and metrics. Yet the history of the formation of such frameworks and devices, the work involved in negotiating and producing them, is relatively under-researched (Hayne and Free, 2014; Power, 2007: ch. 3). In Chapter 1, David Demortain examines the production of a risk management framework which has provided the template and organizing reference point for many subsequent formalizations of risk management. He focuses on a small group of actors within an ad hoc committee created by the US National Academy of Science (or National Research Council). Their task was to advise on the organization of regulatory agencies, such as the Environmental Protection Agency, and particularly on their use of science. The work of the committee to develop a generic framework and a kind of 'pure' procedure for risk management presented the challenge of mediating and representing three different bodies of expertise and associated outlooks, namely: the *scientific* measurement and calculation of environmental or health risks; the economic calculation of *costs and benefits* of regulatory action; and the demands for transparency and *accountability* to audiences and constituencies of the agency. The chapter highlights the competences, resources and political context of this work to develop a generic framework for decision-making, which was subsequently highly influential.

Demortain's argument emphasizes the effort involved to achieve the genericization, rationalization, and portability of risk knowledge. As the case of the EPA shows, frameworks acquire normativity as they become progressively purified of local and seemingly idiosyncratic elements. The echoes of this history can still be discerned within contemporary frameworks for so-called enterprise-wide risk management despite their apparent naturalization, a naturalization reinforced by both professional and academic pedagogy. Demortain also uses the case of the EPA to explain why some frameworking efforts are more successful than others.

In Chapter 2 Silvia Jordan and Lene Jørgensen deal with another readily familiar and highly institutionalized element of the risk landscape—the risk map. Risk maps are widely used by organizations and governments. They represent and rank 'risk objects' as diverse as cost overruns, health and safety concerns, environmental damage, and reputational risks on a Cartesian coordinate system defined by the dimensions of probability and impact . This chapter studies the everyday work of constructing, revising, and drawing upon risk maps in an inter-organizational project in the Norwegian petroleum industry, specifically a project to upgrade two gas-processing plants. Based on three years of participant observation, Jordan and Jørgensen reveal the processes by which risk maps are developed and the day-to-day issues and challenges which actors encounter when using this risk representation technology. For example, actors express concerns about the 'blinding' effect of the 'traffic light' grading of risks, the tendency to focus on short-term rather than longer-term objectives, and the pseudo-commensuration of qualitatively different types of risk objects on risk maps. Yet for all these difficulties the risk map is also regarded as useful by project participants, and something which facilitates both inter-organizational collaboration and assurance, as well as supporting the execution of the project through its different phases and gateways.

In Chapter 3 Matt Hall and Renuka Fernando deal with a related and important component of the risk management armoury—risk metrics and indicators. Indeed efforts to measure and communicate risk characterize a core feature of its history, from the formation of probability theory to the present day (Bernstein, 1996). However the organizational context for Hall and Fernando's analysis is one where risk measurement is relatively new

The discourse of risk has been a prominent feature of policy debate about the operation of non-governmental organizations (NGOs), particularly those NGOs working in conflict situations and/or seeking to provide care for, and services to, vulnerable persons. Yet this discourse has tended to focus on headline-making events, such as misdeeds stemming from cases of fraud, financial misreporting, and corruption, along with operational failures related to threats to human security from dangerous environments. Although very important, this focus on public failure has meant that relatively little attention has been directed towards the day-to-day practices of risk measurement and management in NGOs. This is an important omission because it is at the level of everyday practices that employees influence (positively or negatively) the incidence and severity of headline-making events.

Hall and Fernando analyse two types of riskwork drawing on empirical data from a study of a large UK-based international development NGO. The first involves the work to develop *key risk indicators* to measure legal compliance and security management across its developing country operations. The second focuses on the use of risk matrices and templates (including risk maps) to understand and document threats to human security facing volunteers and staff. A central theme of the analysis is the inherent tension created by the formalization of risk management. On the one hand, key risk indicators and risk templates can provide helpful guidance and reassurance to operational staff and senior decision-makers. On the other hand, they also potentially displace meaningful action by focusing attention on ensuring compliance with mandated procedures. Hall and Fernando also demonstrate the challenges of trying to centralize risk measurement and management across a geographically and culturally dispersed organization.

In Chapter 4 Maria Zhivitskaya and Mike Power analyse the nature of the work involved in practices of risk *oversight* by boards of directors. They examine the way members of board risk committees in UK financial services operationalize their risk oversight responsibilities in the post-financial crisis environment. Based on interviews during 2014 with a small number of senior risk committee chairs at major financial institutions, the chapter reveals the sensemaking work of these actors as they negotiate the meaning of their independent oversight role in the face of its inherent ambiguity, and how they try to construct a working distinction between management and oversight. For these organizational actors, their independence is not an absolute property of their role but a flexible attribute which is used strategically to manage complex relationships, both with regulators and with executive management. The case of risk committee members and chairs discussed in this chapter is of more general interest to corporate governance studies and the problem of 'gatekeeper' independence (Coffee, 2006).

Zhivitskaya and Power show that so-called independent directors engage in continuous and skilled boundary work to maintain their identity and legitimacy at the management–oversight interface. Sometimes they are distant from management, more formal and regulation-focused, and sometimes they are close, supportive and collaborative. This account of the continuous negotiation of an ambiguous role seems to constitute the very nature of risk oversight, an activity which is itself risky and problematic for its proponents. The work of risk oversight emerges as a distinctive kind of capability for maintaining the 'stable instability' of a role which must be both executive-facing and yet not-executive.

In summary, these four chapters provide accounts of the work involved in very different settings of producing and reproducing some of the formal components of risk management. These components exert a normative power over actors for whom compliance and conformity are complex and effortful accomplishments. An important input into the processes which operationalize these frameworks is risk identification, which is the point at which risk objects become real and factual for organizations and their members. The chapters which follow are all concerned with risk identification, but not in the positivistic sense of identifying clearly defined, pre-existing risks. Rather, each of them displays the work involved, and the values at stake, in processes which both identify and construct risks for organizational attention.

NEGOTIATING RISK OBJECTS AND VALUES

In Chapter 5 Åsa Boholm and Hervé Corvellec build on their relational theory of risk (Boholm & Corvellec, 2011) to explore risk identification processes in organizations. This involves teasing out the relationship between *risk objects* (Hilgartner, 1992)—i.e. things which cause harm, and *objects at risk*—i.e. things which are valued and may be harmed. Their essential thesis is that risk objects threaten the fundamental values embedded in objects at risk, but these values are often invisible in conventional risk identification processes. Drawing on the example of railway planning in Sweden, the chapter shows the varied kinds of 'valuation work' involved in risk identification and risk management by public agencies, planners, and companies, and the activity involved in identifying values at risk and in developing corresponding action to weaken the relationship understood to exist between threat and value (Boholm, 2009; Boholm, Corvellec, & Karlsson, 2011; Corvellec, 2010). The case shows how riskwork is embedded in the mundane contingency of organizational activities aimed at identifying, assessing, managing, and communicating threats to valued resources.

In Chapter 6 Steve Maguire and Cynthia Hardy examine the different ways in which chemical risks arising as a by-product of economic and technological progress are being managed in three case studies. They focus on the 'discursive work' in which the meaning of risk is constructed in multiple actor settings and becomes attached to objects (Maguire & Hardy, 2013). This approach is well suited to exploring chemical risks, which are characterized by scientific uncertainty, divergent interpretations of ambiguous data, contestation among scientific disciplines, and plural conceptions of the public interest.

Maguire and Hardy distinguish between three risk scenarios and their respective workstreams in Canada. First, regulatory organizations manage *established* risks (e.g. carcinogenicity, toxicity to aquatic organisms) which stem from known hazards associated with existing practices. Second, organizations develop different forms of work to deal with *emerging* risks (the example being endocrine disruption and associated negative developmental, reproductive, neurological, or immune system effects) which stem from novel hazards that are in the process of becoming linked causally to practices in the field. The work involved in managing emerging risks is different to that of established risks, involving more scope for contestation about scientific methods and epistemology. Third, organizations work to *eliminate* risks altogether through the substitution of hazardous practices with alternatives known to be safer—how Canadian organizations are engaging with 'green chemistry' is the example in this case.

Maguire and Hardy's comparative analysis of different kinds of riskwork in the chemical industry illustrates the discursive co-constitution of risk objects, their regulatory workstreams, and their patterns of distributed agency. Taken together the three cases or scenarios suggest two ideal-typical forms of discursive riskwork: normalizing, e.g. managing according to accepted guidelines, and problematizing, e.g. where the very nature of the risk object to be managed is in question, as is the attitude of different actors to it.

In Chapter 7 Tommaso Palermo also addresses the work within organizations to identify and capture risks for further processing. He asks the following questions: when and how do organizational actors feel free to 'speak up' and report a risk? What kinds of instruments enable such risk reporting and how does their operation define a certain way of working with risk as a form of 'risk culture'? It is well known from psychological studies of risk that risk identification and assessment are fraught with potential biases and these issues are compounded when risk reporting and incentives for 'speaking up' are also involved. Palermo explores these issues by drawing on empirical work at a large airline in which (a) notions of a 'just culture' were promoted to solve the incentives problem combined with (b) a sophisticated safety reporting system (SRS) to enable easy risk identification, capture, reporting, and analysis. The 'just culture' has the status of a widely touted motif and aspiration but it also becomes hard-wired and operationally expressed by the SRS.

Palermo suggests that this commitment to a 'just culture' creates a distinctive style of riskwork in the organization. On the one hand there is a concerted effort by management to promote an atmosphere of trust via the principle of a just culture, in order to encourage and incentivize staff to be the front-line identifiers of safety risk objects. On the other hand, the SRS is designed to make the 'work' of this kind of risk reporting as easy as possible for staff, via mobile technology and similar methods. However, this facilitation role of the SRS is necessarily in the context of a highly forensic system that also does not allow any 'corners to hide'. The technology of the SRS enables the collective identification and production of safety risk 'facts' in the airline for further processing and investigation if necessary. It is disciplinary in the sense that the commitment to the SRS is a necessary condition of being an organizational member of the airline. It also contributes to a distinctive interactive control style between staff and the technology which captures safety-relevant facts. At the heart of the SRS is a human–machine interface—a *technoculture* as Palermo puts it—which conditions risk identification.

In Chapter 8 Zsuzsanna Vargha deals with the work involved in a different kind of risk identification and capture technology, namely the interaction between financial advisers and their clients, and the regulatory requirement to assess clients' so-called Attitude to Risk (ATR). The chapter shows how ATR is produced from the work of a face-to-face advising process, in two contrasting cases. For one wealth manager, the risk preferences of clients 'emerge' from the routine classificatory work that constitutes financial planning. Experienced advisers weave the client's life story and financial strategy fluidly, drawing conclusions from one to the other. Risk preferences come to be embodied and represented in graphical planning work done jointly with the client.

This discursive–visual practice of 'discovering' client ATRs led to conflict with the UK financial regulator. The advisers argued that financial planning is necessarily interactive and cannot be formalized. Clients came to trust the advisor in this process and revealed their social–financial situation. In essence, Vargha shows that some wealth managers defend conversation as a better, more accurate, 'truth-producing' method than a formal series of questions which may impede the revelation process. However, in the second case of a large retail bank, standardized ATR questionnaires are used. The risk preferences of the client emerge not from extended interaction with an expert but through the act of the customer filling out the questionnaire.

Both these cases show that ATR is not a pre-existing property of the consumer to be extracted and matched with investments. It is situationally constructed in the encounter with the adviser and related technology. Yet only in one of these cases does ATR emerge as an auditable and regulatory fact capable of defence. In the other case the riskwork to produce the ATR is characterized by a struggle to defend the fluidity of interactions with clients against the use of standardized tests to define the suitability of advice. In both cases the adviser works hard to match the client to the profile of a risk-taking liberal consumer. In this way, the ATR process is not only one of controlling advisers, as regulators see the process, it also *responsibilizes* individuals as investors, implying that they must accept the risky investment outcomes associated with their ATR profile.

In Chapter 9 Brian Pentland is concerned with the different kinds of riskwork involved in managing information security in a world where technology is changing the space of possible risk objects. As digitization continues to transform business and our personal lives, a new sphere for imagining risk has been created. The chapter draws on the narrative networks framework as developed by Pentland and Feldman (2007) to model the dynamics of organizational routines. Narrative networks provide a convenient way to summarize central tendencies in complex patterns of action such as those involved in risk identification. A narrative network can be visualized as a kind of decision tree, because it represents action pathways through possible events. In principle, each pathway can be assigned a probability. However, before one can quantify such a network, Pentland argues that it must be *constructed*. That is, actors articulate sets of stories (pathways) about the future; each pathway reflects a possible chain of actions.

The analytical and empirical challenge is how organizations and actors construct these observed narrative pathways in a world where new kinds of events (risk objects) are being created, where old kinds of events are being made obsolete, and where the connections between events are being redefined (enabled/constrained) by new technology. Different kinds of riskwork emerge from the narrative networks approach. For example, one focuses on the development of awareness by organizational actors of a network of possibilities—i.e. how supposedly safe pathways in that network can become dangerous. Another involves the control work designed to limit and manage these different pathways. And a third is more existential involving personal decisions about whether and how to interact with technology, e.g. 'should I click on that?'

In summary, it is clear from these five chapters that the work of risk identification is much messier than textbooks and frameworks lead us to believe. Risk identification is not simply moderated by the psychology of individual risk perception. Rather, the chapters show how perceptions are embedded in collective processes of assembling risk objects for identification and action. These processes are contingent on values, on specific technologies and devices, and on discourses for representing and talking about risks. Indeed, risk perceptions are likely to be the very thing at stake in, and a contingent outcome of, the activities described in each of these five chapters (see Hilgartner, 1992).

CONFLICT, EMOTION, AND PRACTICE

It is a short step from recognizing the value-laden nature of risk object identification and construction to a realization that conflict and emotion also play a role in the constitution of risk management practice within organizations. In Chapter 10 Véronique Labelle and Linda Rouleau report the results of a study conducted at a mental health hospital, mixing participant observation at multidisciplinary meetings and interview-based data. They observe the way that professionals, managers, and patients engage, individually and collectively, in practices related to safety risks. Labelle and Rouleau identify four general kinds of riskwork in play which are often conflicting: regulative–normative work to display conformity to templates and best practices; techno-scientific work to operationalize and materialize approaches to risk; political work to build networks and negotiate risk ownership; interpretative work with patient everyday concerns. These four types of riskwork range across formal and informal kinds of risk management, and their respective demands must be managed skilfully by actors. The chapter shows how medical staff cope with, and make sense of, these different and often conflicting logics in their day-to-day routines, and how this work influences the way that safety risks are addressed at the organizational and institutional levels.

Continuing the medical theme, in Chapter 11 Michael Fischer and Gerry McGivern take Labelle and Rouleau's category of interpretative work as their main focus, specifically by emphasizing the emotional dimension of riskwork. Based on access to a very distinctive setting—a democratic therapeutic community (DTC)—they argue that clinical riskwork may be the most intimate and affect-laden form of risk management, involving the handling of human subjects and embodied subjectivities. Yet prevailing notions of clinical risk management obscure the inherently ambivalent and potentially conflicting relationships between the intimacies of clinical riskwork on the one hand, and ideals of professional detachment on the other. There are many accounts of defences, anxieties, and, above all, detachment from the clinical handling of sickness, injury, and death, which reinforce ideals of professional distance. Yet Fischer and McGivern's empirical analysis of clinical encounters reveals intersubjective entanglements to be at the heart of such work. Animated by affect, these relational entanglements are not outside of, but become materially embedded in, technologies of risk management such as the regular DTC risk report. Indeed, the materiality of routines, scripts, and facts are readily imbued with emotions, values, desires, and fantasies; they may be strategically deployed, refashioned, and undermined in the unfolding of relational entanglements. Paradoxically, this backstage work, ostensibly hidden from much external scrutiny, is one that is intimately understood and experienced by human actors in their day-to-day riskwork and continually overflows the 'cool' logic of formal frameworks.

In Chapter 12 Anette Mikes tracks the evolution of the role of two chief risk officers (CROs), and the tools and processes which they have implemented in the name of Enterprise Risk Management in their respective organizations.

Over a number of years, at both firms, risk management was transformed from a collection of acquired 'off-the-shelf' tools and practices into a seemingly inevitable and tailored control process. In the first case of an electricity company, the CRO facilitates continuous *risk talk* (see Vera-Sanso, 2000) via workshops and face-to-face meetings over ten years. He succeeds in orchestrating the creation and proliferation of a new language (that of risk management), and established processes that bring business people together from diverse places and hierarchical levels. This *risk talk* seems to be a necessary condition for the formal elements of risk management to become accepted in the organization.

The second case, focuses on a CRO, who initially tried and failed to create linkages of permanence and significance between the 'conventional' COSO-prescribed ERM tools (similar to those championed by his counterpart above) and the business lines. After a period of searching, the CRO settled on a less conventional risk-identification tool, scenario planning, and facilitated its transformation over two years from an ad hoc future-gazing exercise into a widely accepted and a seemingly self-evident element of the annual business planning process.

The two cases highlight how the role of the CRO may be less about the packaging and marketing of established risk management ideas to business managers, and more about the facilitation and internalization of a specific type of 'risk talk' as a legitimate, cross-functional vocabulary of business. In both cases, facilitation involved a significant degree of humility and *emotional work* on the part of the CRO, to offset limited formal authority and meagre resources. Their skill was to build an informal network of relationships with executives and business managers, which allowed them to resist being stereotyped as either compliance champions or as a business partner (see also Hall et al., 2013, 2015; Mikes, 2011).

Overall, this final cluster of three chapters completes the movement of *Riskwork* from the formal front stage of practice—the frameworks and protocols which characterize risk management texts and training manuals—to the back stage of negotiation, network building, emotional commitment, entanglement with representational devices, and the inevitable everyday conflicts of organizational life. Along the way, temporarily stable risk objects emerge as the 'cool' outcomes of 'hot', affect- and value- laden identification practices.

ISSUES IN THE MICRO-SOCIOLOGY OF RISK MANAGEMENT

One of the key messages from the chapters taken as a whole is that riskwork varies greatly by field, and by the kinds of actors involved and the technologies they employ. There remains analytical work to be done to develop useful typographies which are faithful to this variety. Riskwork may reflect different 'calculative cultures' (Mikes, 2009; Power, 2007) but this captures only one dimension of variability; there may also be different emotional and technical intensities to the work of risk management, which are as salient in the construction of practice. Labelle and Rouleau in this volume inductively derive four categories of riskwork, yet they also recognize that these are hardly mutually exclusive and actors will be engaged in different 'types' of work at the same time. For example, while there is no doubt that riskwork takes place in the shadow of regulation and may be explicitly driven by it, as in the case of the work of risk committees in the UK financial services sector, equally there are degrees of flexibility in the orientation towards rules, and in some cases, like that of ATR discussed by Vargha, outright resistance by some actors. Regulatory and advisory environments will therefore shape riskwork, but never deterministically.

Resources and organizational starting points will also be important contingent factors and there is considerable path dependency to riskwork within organizations (Woods, 2009). In addition, variations in accepted conceptions of risk objects and objects at risk will generate variations in riskwork across many dimensions, not least in terms of a contrast between routine and regularized forms of work and those which essentially demand improvisation and deeply internalized capabilities, such as in the case of fire-fighting. In this volume we also see how organizational actors develop a variety of ways of engaging with institutionalized devices and artefacts like risk maps and risk indicators which, although not legally regulated in the narrow sense of the term, nevertheless exert a field-level normative force over practice routines. So an important dimension for further research on riskwork concerns the nature of its normative climate and the specific mix of legal, regulatory, and local logics of practice. Riskwork is neither purely implementation nor local improvisation, but encompasses hybrid forms of work within different normative registers (Miller et al., 2008), not least accountability and auditability requirements. In the postscript to this collection, I deal more explicitly with this issue.

The plural and hybrid nature of riskwork is also evident when we try to isolate its techno-scientific features and focus on the production of analyses, risk registers, and related technologies of risk representation. From a number of the contributions, it is clear that the instruments through which riskwork is conducted play a major role in constructing and maintaining the visibility of risk objects. Indeed, this work of making visible is itself often invisible, being carried on in the shadow of more formal templates and procedures, but essential to the operating reality of those procedures. Riskwork is the work of making risk management 'work' but it is plural and often experimental as many chapters suggest (see also Tekathen and Dechow, 2013). For example Mikes shows that the 'humble' CRO works at making risk management into an organizational fact and reference point for others, but in an unobtrusive kind of way. Labelle and Rouleau reveal the subtle and ad hoc nature of this kind of experiential riskwork, as do Zhivitskaya and Power in their chapter on how non-executive directors create the fragile reality of risk oversight. All of this experimentation is blended with politics, the network-building and alliance construction which may or may not be crowded out by institutional pressures to conform to immaculate representations of work.

These 'political' aspects of riskwork reveal not just the play of competing interests that might be visible in other studies. As Fischer and McGivern show, this politics and its strategies to persuade and enlist others, is deeply affective and emotional in form. The humble CROs of Mikes's chapter also make emotional appeals to other organizational actors. The ongoing analysis of riskwork therefore requires attention to organizational dramatologies underlying rational techniques, stagings of risk which are emotionally laden (Fenton-O'Creevy et al., 2010). In these dramatologies, making sense of risk objects and executing strategies to acquire and diffuse attention to them are intertwined. Rather than some cool process of information exchange in the name of 'transparency', emotion pervades the ground level of risk governance where concepts such as 'comfort' have more currency than rational calculation (Pentland, 1993) and where questions of value and objects at risk are often suppressed or taken for granted. Even the production of compliance and audit trails to document riskwork are premised as much on anxiety and fear in the face of possible blame as they are on rational demands for supporting evidence (Guenin-Paracini et al., 2014).

Finally, the chapters suggest that riskwork is essentially *collective* and distributed in nature rather than a series of punctuated calculative acts. This collective effort is oriented largely towards the production of assurance about risk and the creation of images of managerial and regulatory control (see Chapters 2–4). However, the boundaries of this collective effort are fuzzy and do not solely reside within risk management departments or even within formal organizational boundaries. For example, Labelle and Rouleau, Vargha, and Fischer and McGivern all show how patients and clients are also involved in riskwork within hospitals and wealth management firms respectively.

The collective nature of riskwork requires a form of analysis which does not start or end with defined notions of what risk management or risk managers are. As noted earlier, the idea of *riskwork* reflects a sensitivity to the 'mangle' (Pickering, 1993) of risk management practice and to the manner in which the management of risk is a hybrid (Fischer & Ferlie, 2012; Miller et al., 2008) continually being made by many different kinds of actor, both human (including external advisers who are notably absent from this volume), and non-human as we saw most clearly in the chapters by Palermo and Vargha. From this point of view, the boundary between what is and what is not risk management is something that is *produced* by riskwork. For example, Jordan and Jørgensen allude to the interconnections between different management systems—such as quality control, accounting, and marketing. It follows that the study of riskwork must pay close attention to the wider ecology of organizational functions in which different kinds of work are entangled, rather than assuming the 'organization chart' view of discrete systems, disciplines, and functionalities.

In conclusion, the chapters in this volume reflect the extension and consolidation of two research agendas. One is to continue the work of connecting risk studies to mainstream organization and management studies (e.g. Czarniawska, 2009: 1; Gephart et al., 2009). In this respect there are certainly gaps in this volume both methodological and substantive. For example the temporality (Langley et al., 2013) of riskwork processes is at best implicit, and sociological studies of insurance work are conspicuous by their absence (see Ericson & Doyle, 2004; Jarzabkowski et al., 2015). The other, related, agenda is to analyse the routine work of managing risk without the shadow of accidents and disasters hanging over it. From this point of view, whether the observed practices, forms of sensemaking, and related artefacts to produce order characterize an 'incubation period' or not is an open question. As Vaughan (2005) has noted, close attention to organizational routines for handling risk and for dealing with anomalies, provides the opportunity for addressing this question *ex ante* rather than *ex post*, and for grounding the answer in a detailed understanding of normal, everyday riskwork and the structures and instruments that shape it. One thing is for sure, the studies of riskwork represented in this volume are not about the good or bad 'implementation' of risk management norms and accepted practices. This is not a book to promote best practices and the chapters are not implementation studies in disguise. And yet, sustained micro-sociological studies of the everyday life of risk management in organizations, of the kind represented in the chapters which follow, are not a bad place to start when considering practice reform.

REFERENCES

Adler, P. & Adler, P. (1987). Everyday Life Sociology. *Annual Review of Sociology*, 13, 217–35.
Atkins, D., Fitzsimmons, A., Parsons, C., & Punter, A. (2012). *Roads to Ruin: A Study of Major Risk Events: Their Origins, Impact and Implications*. London: AIRMIC.
Baccus, M. (1986a). Sociological Indication and the Visibility of Real World Social Theorizing. In H. Garfinkel (Ed.), *Ethnomethodological Studies of Work* (pp. 1–19). London: Routledge.
Baccus, M. (1986b). Multipiece Truck Wheel Accidents and their Regulations. In H. Garfinkel (Ed.), *Ethnomethodological Studies of Work* (pp. 20–59). London: Routledge.

Barley, S. & Kunda, G. (2001). Bringing Work Back In. *Organization Science*, 12(1), 76–95.

Beck, U. (1992). *Risk Society—Towards a New Modernity*. London: Sage, 1992.

Bernstein, P. (1996). *Against the Gods: The Remarkable Story of Risk*. London: John Wiley and Sons.

Boholm, Å. (2009). Speaking of Risk: Matters of Context. *Environmental Communication: A Journal of Nature and Culture*, 3(2), 335–54.

Boholm, Å. & Corvellec, H. (2011). A Relational Theory of Risk. *Journal of Risk Research*, 14(2), 175–90.

Boholm, Å., Corvellec, H., & Karlsson, M. (2011). The Practice of Risk Governance: Lessons from the Field. *Journal of Risk Research*, 15(1), 1–20.

Bourrier, M. (2002). Bridging Research and Practice: The Challenge of 'Normal Operations' Studies. *Journal of Contingencies and Crisis Management*, 10(4), 173–80.

Brunsson, N., Jacobsson, B., & Associates (Eds) (2000). *A World of Standards*. Oxford: Oxford University Press.

Burgess, A. & Mitsutoshi Horii (2012). Risk, Ritual and Health Responsibilisation: Japan's 'Safety Blanket' of Surgical Face Mask-Wearing. *Sociology of Health and Illness*, 34(8), 1184–98.

Callon, M. (1998). Introduction: The Embeddedness of Economic Markets in Economics. *Sociological Review*, 46(S1), 1–57.

Caplan, P. (Ed.) (2000). *Risk Revisited*. London: Pluto Press.

Clarke, L. & Short, J. (1993). Social Organization and Risk: Some Current Controversies. *Annual Review of Sociology*, 19, 375–99.

Coffee, J. (2006). *Gatekeepers: The Professions and Corporate Governance*. Oxford: Oxford University Press.

Corvellec, H. (2010). Organisational Risk as It Derives from What Managers Value: A Practice-based Approach to Risk Assessment. *Journal of Contingencies and Crisis Management*, 18(3), 145–54.

Czarniawska, B. (Ed.) (2009). *Organizing in the Face of Risk and Threat*. Cheltenham, UK: Edward Elgar.

Dobbin, F. (2009). *Inventing Equal Opportunity*. Princeton, NJ: Princeton University Press.

Douglas, M. & Wildavsky, A. (1983). *Risk and Culture*. Berkeley, CA: University of California Press.

Downer, J. (2011). 737-Cabriolet: The Limits of Knowledge and the Sociology of Inevitable Failure. *American Journal of Sociology*, 117(3), 725–62.

Ericson, R. & Doyle, A. (2004). *Uncertain Business: Risk, Insurance and the Limits of Knowledge*. Toronto: University of Toronto Press.

Etienne, J. (2013). Ambiguity and Relational Signals in Regulator/Regulatee Relationships. *Regulation & Governance*, 7(1), 30–47.

Fenton-O'Creevy, M., Soane, E., Nicholson, N., & Willman, P. (2010). Thinking, Feeling and Deciding: The Influence of Emotions on the Decision Making and Performance of Traders. *Journal of Organizational Behavior*, 32(8), 1044–61.

Fischer, M. & Ferlie, E. (2012). Resisting Hybridisation between Modes of Clinical Risk Management: Contradiction, Context, and the Production of Intractable Conflict. *Accounting, Organizations and Society*, 38(1), 30–49.

Garfinkel, H. (1967). *Studies in Ethnomethodology*. Cambridge, UK: Polity Press.

Garfinkel, H. (Ed.) (1986). *Ethnomethodological Studies of Work*. London: Routledge.

Gephart, R. (1993). The Textual Approach: Risk and Blame in Disaster Sensemaking. *Academy of Management Journal*, 38(6), 1465–514.

Gephart, R. P., Van Maanen, J., & Oberlechner, T. (2009). Organizations and Risk in Late Modernity. *Organization Studies*, 30(2–3), 141–55.

Goffman, E. (1959). *The Presentation of Self in Everyday Life*. Garden City, NY: Doubleday.

Guénin-Paracini, H., Malsch, B., & Marché-Paillé, A. (2014). Fear and Risk in the Audit Process. *Accounting, Organizations and Society*, 39(4), 264–88.

Hacking, I. (2003). Risk and Dirt. In R. Ericson (Ed.), *Risk and Morality* (pp. 22–47). Toronto: Toronto University Press.

Hacking, I. (2004). Between Michel Foucault and Erving Goffman: Between Discourse in the Abstract and Face-to-Face Interaction. *Economy and Society*, 33(3), 277–302.

Hall, M., Mikes, A., & Millo, Y. (2013). How Experts Gain Influence. *Harvard Business Review*, 91(7), 70–4.

Hall, M., Mikes, A., & Y. Millo (2015). How do Risk Managers Become Influential? A Field Study of Toolmaking in Two Financial Institutions. *Management Accounting Research*, 26, 3–22.

Hawkins, K. & Thomas, J. (Eds) (1984). *Enforcing Regulation*. Dordrecht: Kluwer-Hijhoff.

Hayne, C. & Free, C. (2014). Hybridized Professional Groups and Institutional Work: COSO and the Rise of Enterprise Risk Management. *Accounting, Organizations and Society*, 39(5), 309–30.

Hilgartner, S. (1992). The Social Construction of Risk Objects: Or, How to Pry Open Networks of Risk. In Short J. F. & L. Clarke (Eds), *Organizations, Uncertainties and Risk* (pp. 39–53). Boulder, CO: Westview Press.

Hood, C., Rothstein, H., & Baldwin, R. (2001). *The Government of Risk: Understanding Risk Regulation Regimes*. Oxford: Oxford University Press.

Hopwood, A. (1992). Accounting Calculation and the Shifting Sphere of the Economic. *European Accounting Review*, 1(1), 125–43.

Horlick-Jones, T. (2005). On 'Risk Work': Professional Discourse, Accountability and Everyday Action. *Health, Risk and Society*, 7(3), 293–307.

Hutter, B. (1997). *Compliance: Regulation and Enforcement*. Oxford: Clarendon Press.

Hutter, B. (2001). *Regulation and Risk: Occupational Health and Safety on the Railways*. Oxford: Oxford University Press.

Jarzabkowski, P., Bednarek, R., & Spee, P. (2015). *Making a Market for Acts of God: The Practice of Risk-Trading in the Global Reinsurance Industry*. Oxford: Oxford University Press.

Jasanoff, S. (2003). (No?) Accounting for Expertise. *Science and Public Policy*, 30(3), 157–62.

Jordan, S., Jørgensen, L., & Mitterhofer, H. (2013). Performing Risk and the Project: Risk Maps as Mediating Instruments. *Management Accounting Research*, 24, 156–74.

Kalthoff, H. (2005). Practices of Calculation—Economic Representations and Risk Management. *Theory, Culture & Society*, 22(2), 69–97.

Knorr-Cetina, K. (1981). Introduction: the Micro-Sociological Challenge of Macro-Sociology: Towards a Reconstruction of Social Theory and Methodology. In

K. Knorr-Cetina and A. Cicourel (Eds), *Advances in Social Theory and Methodology: Toward an Integration of Micro- and Macro-sociologies* (pp. 1–47). New York: Routledge & Kegan Paul.

Langley, A., Smallman, C., Tsoukas, H., & Van de Ven, A. (2013). Process Studies of Change in Organization and Management: Unveiling Temporality, Activity and Flow. *Academy of Management Journal*, 56(1), 1–13.

Latour, B. (2005). *Reassembling the Social*. Oxford: Oxford University Press.

Loewenstein, J., Ocasio, W., & Jones, C. (2012). Vocabularies and Vocabulary Structure: A New Approach Linking Categories, Practices, and Institutions. *Academy of Management Annals*, 6, 41–86.

Lupton, D. (1999). *Risk*. London: Routledge.

Macrae, C. (2014). *Close Calls: Managing Risk and Resilience in Airline Flight Safety*. London: Palgrave/Macmillan.

Maguire, S. & Hardy, C. (2013). Organizing Processes and the Construction of Risk: A Discursive Approach. *Academy of Management Journal*, 56(1), 231–55.

March, J. G. & Shapira, Z. (1987). Managerial Perspectives on Risk and Risk Taking. *Management Science*, 33, 1404–18.

Mikes, A. (2009). Risk Management and Calculative Cultures. *Management Accounting Research*, 20(1), 18–40.

Mikes, A. (2011). From Counting Risk to Making Risk Count: Boundary Work in Risk Management. *Accounting, Organizations and Society*, 36, 226–45.

Miller, P., Kurunmaki, L., & O'Leary, T. (2008). Accounting, Hybrids and the Management of Risk. *Accounting, Organizations and Society*, 33(7–8), 942–67.

Millo, Y. & Mackenzie, D. (2003). Negotiating a Market, Performing Theory: The Historical Sociology of a Financial Derivatives Exchange. *American Journal of Sociology*, 109(1), 107–45.

Ocasio, W. (2005). The Opacity of Risk: Language and the Culture of Safety in NASA's Space Shuttle Program. In W. Starbuck & M. Farjoun (Eds), *Organization at the Limit: Lessons from the Columbia Disaster* (pp. 110–21). Oxford: Blackwell.

Pentland, B. T. (1993). Getting Comfortable with the Numbers: Auditing and the Micro-Production of Macro-Order. *Accounting, Organizations and Society*, 18(7–8), 605–20.

Pentland, B. T. & Feldman, M. (2005). Organizational Routines as a Unit of Analysis. *Industrial and Corporate Change*, 14, 793–815.

Pentland, B. T. & Feldman, M. (2007). Narrative Networks: Patterns of Technology and Organization. *Organization Science*, 18(5), 781–95.

Perrow, C. (1984). *Normal Accidents: Living with High Risk Technologies*. New York: Basic Books.

Phillips, N. & Lawrence, T. (2012). The Turn to Work in Organization and Management Theory: Some Implications for Strategic Organization. *Strategic Organization*, 10(3), 223–30.

Pickering, A. (1993). The Mangle of Practice: Agency and Emergence in the Sociology of Science. *American Journal of Sociology*, 99, 559–89.

Powell, W. & Colyvas, J. (2008). The Microfoundations of Institutions. In R. Greenwood, C. Oliver, K. Sahlin, & R. Suddaby (Eds), *Handbook of Organizational Institutionalism* (pp. 276–98). London: Sage.

Power, M. (2004). *The Risk Management of Everything*. London: Demos.

Power, M. (2005). Organizational Responses to Risk: The Rise of the Chief Risk Officer. In B. Hutter & M. Power (Eds), *Organizational Encounters with Risk*, (pp. 132–48). Cambridge: Cambridge University Press.

Power, M. (2007). *Organized Uncertainty: Designing a World of Risk Management*. Oxford: Oxford University Press.

Power, M. (2011). Foucault and Sociology. *Annual Review of Sociology*, 37, 35–56.

Power, M. (2014). Risk, Social Theories and Organizations. In P. Adler, P. du Gay, G. Morgan, & M. Reed (Eds), *The Oxford Handbook of Sociology, Social Theory and Organization Studies: Contemporary Currents* (pp. 370–92). Oxford: Oxford University Press.

Power, M., Palermo, T., & Ashby, S. (2013). *Risk Culture in Financial Organizations: A Research Report*. London: Financial Services Knowledge Transfer Network/CARR.

Power, M., Scheytt, T., Soin, K., & Sahlin, K. (2009). Reputational Risk as a Logic of Organizing in Late Modernity. *Organization Studies*, 30(2/3), 165–88.

PRA & FCA (2015). *The Failure of HBOS plc (HBOS): A Report by the Financial Conduct Authority and the Prudential Regulation Authority*. London: Bank of England.

Riles, A. (2011). *Collateral Knowledge: Legal Reasoning in the Global Financial Markets*. Chicago, IL: University of Chicago Press.

Schatzki, T. (2001). Introduction: Practice Theory. In T. Schatzki, K. Knorr-Cetina, & E. von Savigny (Eds), *The Practice Turn in Contemporary Theory* (pp. 1–14). London: Routledge.

Short, J. (1984). The Social Fabric of Risk: Toward the Social Transformation of Risk Analysis. *American Sociological Review*, 49(6), 711–25.

Short, J. & Clarke, L. (Eds) (1992). *Organizations, Uncertainties and Risks*. Boulder, CO: Westview Press.

Simon, J. (2002). Taking Risks: Extreme Sports and the Embrace of Risks in Advanced Societies. In T. Baker & J. Simon (Eds), *Embracing Risk: The Changing Culture of Insurance and Responsibility* (pp. 177–207). Chicago, IL: University of Chicago Press.

Sitkin, S. & Pablo, A. (1992). Reconceptualizing the Determinants of Risk Behaviour. *Academy of Management Review*, 17(1), 9–38.

Slovic, P. (2000). *The Perception of Risk*. London: Earthscan.

Taylor-Gooby, P. & Zinn, J. (Eds) (2006). *Risk in Social Science*. Oxford: Oxford University Press.

Tekathen, M. & Dechow, N. (2013). Enterprise Risk Management and Continuous Realignment in Pursuit of Accountability: A German case. *Management Accounting Research*, 24, 100–21.

Tulloch, J. & Lupton, D. (2003). *Risk and Everyday Life*. London: Sage.

Turner, B. (1976). The Organizational and Interorganizational Development of Disasters. *Administrative Science Quarterly*, 21(3), 378–97.

Turner, B. & Pidgeon, N. (1997). *Man-Made Disasters*, 2nd edition. London: Butterworth-Heinemann.

Vaughan, D. (1996). *The Challenger Launch Decision.* Chicago, IL: University of Chicago Press.

Vaughan, D. (2005). Organizational Rituals of Risk and Error. In B. Hutter & M. Power (Eds), *Organizational Encounters with Risk* (pp. 33–66). Cambridge: Cambridge University Press.

Vera-Sanso, V. (2000). Risk-Talk: The Politics of Risk and its Representation. In P. Caplan (Ed.), *Risk Revisited* (pp. 108–32). London: Pluto Press.

Weick, K. E. (1993). The Collapse of Sensemaking in Organizations: The Mann Gulch Disaster. *Administrative Science Quarterly,* 38(4), 628–52.

Weick, K. & Roberts, K. (1993). Collective Mind in Organizations: Heedful Interrelating on Flight Decks. *Administrative Science Quarterly,* 38(3), 357–81.

Weick, K. & Sutcliffe, K. (2007). *Managing the Unexpected: Resilient Performance in an Age of Uncertainty.* San Francisco, CA: John Wiley & Sons.

Woods, M. (2009). A Contingency Theory Perspective on the Risk Management Control System within Birmingham City Council. *Management Accounting Research,* 20(1), 69–81.

Wynne, B. (1982). *Rationality and Ritual: The Windscale Inquiry and Nuclear Decisions in Britain.* London: British Society for the History of Science.

Zaloom, C. (2004). The Productive Life of Risk. *Cultural Anthropology,* 19(3), 365–91.

1

The Work of Making Risk Frameworks

David Demortain

Risk management is a field that is replete with models, frameworks, and schemes of all kinds. These frameworks constitute the reality of risk management, discursively at least. Models provide a language and frame for speaking about risk management as well as a way of evidencing its presence in organizations. It is against the background of what models prescribe that we are able to evaluate and rank the risk management in organizations. When something has gone wrong, such as in the case of a major failure, models provide a framework for diagnosis. And often we respond to disasters by amending models.

More specifically, regulatory agencies for health and environment have recourse to risk management frameworks in the form of coherent sets of principles and criteria that frame their decisions. Such principles provide for diagnosis, multidisciplinary quantitative assessment of the risks, stakeholder engagement, and the re-evaluation of risk management itself in a continuous cycle when necessary (Power & McCarty 1998; Jardine et al. 2003).

This chapter analyses the origins of the risk assessment–risk management framework, which is commonly traced to a specific report: *Risk Assessment in the Federal Government: Managing the Process* (RAFG) produced by the US National Research Council (NRC) (NRC, 1983).[1] The chapter has one key question in mind: what kind of work underpins the construction and institutionalization of a framework? This question is motivated by the particular properties of a management framework. First, it is a standard, or 'agreed-upon rule' to produce an object (Bowker & Star, 2000). Second, it is generic: it has a

---

[1] Risk assessment in health and environmental regulation is the subject of multiple publications by different scholars: lawyers, scientists, historians as well as specialist risk researchers. Early contributions on this topic include Jasanoff (1994) and an informative retrospective study and synthesis is provided by Rodricks (2007). A similar sociological perspective on risk analysis as a managerial and government tool is presented in Demortain (2012), Boudia (2014), and Boudia & Demortain (2014).

template-like form that makes it portable and tolerates, in fact identifies, various options to perform the same thing. Finally, it is integrated: it generally provides for the complete description of a world, its agents, and the associations between them—an organizational ontology of sorts. These attributes very much explain why frameworks diffuse, but they make the very designing of such an object puzzling. What did the experts that produced the report specifically do to succeed in creating a generic organizational ontology in their particular situation and position?

In what follows, I first provide a description of the content, impact, and context of the report. The second section then details by whom and how it was composed. The third section analyses the kind of work involved in creating a framework successfully, highlighting not only the task of codifying and abstracting knowledge of organizational processes, but also the work of representing and mediating the various organizational constituencies that will be part of the framework, in the very process of designing it.

RISK ASSESSMENT IN THE FEDERAL GOVERNMENT: MANAGING THE PROCESS

When interviewed, one of the authors of RAFG stated that 'Nobody reads National Academy of Science reports'. But RAFG, published in March 1983 and commonly referred to as the Red Book, is a little different to other reports by the US NRC. It is allegedly the most popular, the most requested report ever issued by the academies. There is even a celebration of the anniversary of its publication.[2]

Like all NRC reports, the report was written in response to a solicitation from a client institution, in this case the United States Congress. The requirement was to clarify the analytic part of the regulatory decision-making process. In addition NRC was charged to investigate whether assigning risk assessment functions to a dedicated institution in the federal government, separate from specific regulatory agencies like the Food and Drug Administration (FDA), the Environmental Protection Agency (EPA) or the Occupational Safety and Health Administration (OSHA), would remedy the alleged distortion or politicization of science by regulatory agencies.

---

[2] In 1993, for the ten-year anniversary of its publication, a major conference was organized to critically review its recommendations about science and policymaking. Approaching the twentieth anniversary, a reunion of its authors was organized, leading to the publication of a special issue of the journal *Human & Ecological Risk Assessment* (issue 5 of volume 9, 2003). The NRC itself organized another reunion for the 25th anniversary of the report in 2008—a repetition of the dinner it organized on 28 February 1983 to launch the report.

RAFG is a neat, well-written, and highly readable report that provides key definitions in its very first pages:

Regulatory actions are based on two distinct elements, risk assessment, the subject of this study, and risk management. Risk assessment is the use of the factual base to define the health effects of exposure of individuals or populations to hazardous materials and situations. Risk management is the process of weighing policy alternatives and selecting the most appropriate regulatory action, integrating the results of risk assessment with engineering data and with social, economic, and political concerns to reach a decision.

Risk assessments contain some or all of the following four steps:

  – Hazard identification: the determination of whether a particular chemical is or is not causally linked to particular health effects.

  – Dose-response assessment: the determination of the relation between the magnitude of exposure and the probability of occurrence of the health effects in question.

  – Exposure assessment: the determination of the extent of human exposure before or after application of regulatory controls.

  – Risk characterization: the description of the nature and often the magnitude of human risk, including attendant uncertainty. (p. 3)

In RAFG, these definitions are represented in a general diagram, depicting key operations and mechanisms in shaping regulatory decisions (see Figure 1.3).

The primary impact of RAFG is in codifying the meaning of 'risk assessment'. RAFG defines risk assessment as the product of the definition of the danger at stake (hazard identification), an estimate of its frequency (hazard characterization), and a measurement of different populations' exposure to this hazard (exposure assessment), leading to a synthetic estimate of risk (in the sense of a measurement of the danger's probability, gravity, and distribution: or risk characterization).

This definition had a major impact in structuring a nascent scientific field. For example, the most important textbook on toxicology, one of risk assessment's constitutive disciplines, uses this four-step structure to define risk assessment. A great number of individual academic papers also adopt this structure to risk assessment, most of the time citing RAFG as the origin of it. Food microbiologists, GM risk assessment specialists and students of nano-materials safety have all adopted the structure (König et al., 2004; Notermans et al., 2002). In 1995, the Office of Research and Development of the EPA reorganized its numerous laboratories in four broad directions, corresponding to the operations in the Red Book (Patton & Huggett, 2003). Most regulatory agencies that perform risk assessments describe the process and content of their documents in the terms of the fourfold scheme that was first presented in RAFG.

The second major impact of the report was to rethink the relation between science and policy in terms of the categories of 'risk assessment' and 'risk management'. Armed with the above definitions, the report argues that the main political problem in risk decision-making is not whether and how 'science' should inform 'policy' (or the opposite), but a practical issue of making sure that choices pertaining to the analysis of hazards on the one hand, and to regulatory strategies on the other hand, are made transparently (hence distinguished from one another) but also in full awareness of one another. Risk assessment and risk management are in dialogue, but also transparently distinguished from one another. This rule is most important for what the report calls 'risk assessment policy', that is the models and assumptions that risk analysts choose to apply.[3] In the words of recommendation A in the report:

> regulatory agencies [should] take steps to establish and maintain a clear conceptual distinction between assessment of risks and consideration of risk management alternatives; that is, the scientific findings and policy judgments embodied in risk assessments should be explicitly distinguished from the political, economic and technical considerations that influence the design and choice of regulatory strategies. (NRC 1983: 7)

This recommendation had a massive impact,[4] and almost instantly so. The impact is illustrated by the immediate reaction of William Ruckelshaus, who had just been reappointed Administrator of the EPA by President Reagan. Upon receiving the report, Ruckelshaus decided that the distinction between risk assessment and risk management provided a good way to explain the mission and procedure of the EPA: to reduce risks for the public, and to be transparent about the use of science (Ruckelshaus, 1983). Various guidelines were developed inside the agency to institute analytical processes to inform decisions by the administrator and his deputy administrator. The terms risk

---

[3] Quite originally, the report argues that there is politics in risk-based decision-making throughout the process, both in risk assessment and in risk management. This is explicitly stated on page 49 of the report, and was recalled by the authors at various occasions, for instance by Rodricks in his 1983 testimony before the Committee on Agriculture of the House: 'One central point [in the report] is that, while subjective judgments that have policy implications – particularly on the degree of conservatism that should be applied in areas of scientific uncertainty – may be an inherent part of risk assessment, certain other types of policy considerations, such as the economic importance of a substance, should not be permitted to influence risk assessments.' In short: there is politics or elements of policy throughout the regulatory decision-making process, but some are classified as ingredients to assess risks, others to manage them. But both are equally political, which is why neither can claim to have the upper hand over the other. Jasanoff (1992, 1994) accuses the report of being ambiguous in its treatment of policy, but conflates the two meanings of policy that the report distinguishes.

[4] More so than the two other recommendations: Recommendation B concerns the development and use by regulatory agencies of what is termed 'uniform inference guidelines', namely the texts that detail the policy assumptions that were applied in the risk assessment. Recommendation C advises the federal government to create a central 'board' for risk assessment methods, whose function would be, among other things, to review the guidelines adopted by regulatory agencies, and make sure they are in keeping with advancing scientific knowledge in the area.

assessment and risk management were used to neatly distinguish between the work and roles of different people and services inside the organization. Similar reorganizations based on these two categories of work occurred elsewhere around the world, notably in Europe starting in the second half of the 1990s (Demortain, 2009, 2012).

So, the description of decision-making as a compound of risk assessment and risk management processes, the components of risk assessment and the principle that the policy inherent in risk assessment should always be explicated, were put at the heart of what became a highly influential and widely diffused 'risk assessment–risk management framework'. This way of conceptualizing the elements of riskwork can be traced to RAFG.

A TIME FOR FRAMEWORKS

The report was written by an expert panel of the NRC, which had been established to respond to the question of whether regulatory agencies dealing with chemical hazards should retain competences and capacities to perform risk assessment.

The issue of the assessment of risks of chemical substances, particularly carcinogenic risks, was particularly controversial in the US. In the 1970s, cancer policy took the form of a search for a generic methodology covering 'the whole class of chemical carcinogens' (Rushefsky, 1986: 209).[5] This search revealed a number of complicated scientific and medical questions. Chemical substances that might cause cancer were seen as very diverse.[6] Not only were the exact amount of carcinogenic substances unknown, the evaluation of their carcinogenicity was and remains a difficult exercise. Carcinogen identification is not an exact science, and is on the contrary full of controversy and politics. No definitive scientific proof is available to say whether a test on animals— very often the only available evidence for chemicals—is fully predictive of what would happen in humans. Hence, it is a matter of choice to trust animal tests or not. Similarly, no definitive agreement exists on whether cancer effects are triggered at low levels of exposure, or not. Here there is also a question of choice, namely whether to hold on to that assumption or not.

---

[5] The connection between health (oncologists, epidemiologists or toxicologists) and engineering sciences is one of the things that made possible the formal creation of a science and professional society for risk analysis (Rip, 1986).

[6] Some were active as medicines, others as pesticides, food additives or industrial chemicals present in the atmosphere of plants...i.e. substances regulated by various agencies through different criteria of what is hazardous or not. These substances also have diverse molecular structures. Some can cause cancer rapidly, others only through chronic exposure. Yet cancer is the thing to tackle.

Several groups competed at the end of the 1970s to standardize the response to these tricky scientific questions. First, regulatory agencies, particularly the recently created EPA and OSHA, engaged in the work of developing guidelines for cancer risk assessment to stabilize their choices on each of these issues. These guidelines proved to be 'exceptionally controversial' (Rushefsky, 1986). They were judged to be either too precautionary or too neglectful of potential risks. Regulatory agencies were perceived as disguising in scientific terms what was essentially a policy choice of waging war on cancer and on cancer-causing chemical substances. In addition, a cross-agency group named the Inter-Regulatory Agency Liaison Group (IRLG), tried to develop common guidelines. But, again, the group was accused of not admitting its policy biases and of hiding them within arcane technical choices (Landy et al., 1994).

Another proposal stemmed from the American Industrial Health Council (AIHC), which was created in the autumn of 1977 by Shell, Procter & Gamble, and Monsanto, and gathered 130 chemical companies as a vehicle for the industry to respond and to counter these guidelines. This proposal marked a shift towards more generic and procedural solutions, that is, towards frameworks that do not provide substantive criteria of what is carcinogenic, but prescribe who is to determine such criteria. In a memo dated October 1979, the industry group developed its vision that the scientific and objective task of identifying whether a substance is carcinogenic or not should be separated or insulated from regulatory agencies. They proposed a threefold process, beginning with the qualitative determination of existence of a hazard, followed by the performance of the most probable quantitative risk estimation, concluding with the determination of the degree of control. The group argued that the first two steps should be handled by a central risk assessment board, a sort of 'science court', separate from the regulatory agencies.

The AIHC claimed that its proposal was aligned with yet another document and proposal, that of the Office of Science and Technology Policy (OSTP) of the White House. Several staff members of the OSTP, the assistant administrator included, had effectively issued a report in which a two-stage approach was advocated: first research, then assessment of the significance of the risk and of the benefits, by regulatory agencies (Calkins et al., 1980). In operational terms, the framework contained three steps: 'identification' of carcinogenic substances and 'characterization' of their risks by scientists, followed by the act of 'control'—the preserve of regulatory bodies.[7]

---

[7] A number of other proposals and guidelines were edited on top of those of AIHC and OSTP. In February 1980, Representative Wampler proposed a bill in which the creation of a central independent panel of scientists was suggested, to review the scientific basis for particular regulatory initiatives of agencies. In June 1981, the Office of Technology Assessment published a report that reviews previous proposals, and put forward yet another framework (OTA, 1981): a three-step framework of hazard identification, hazard evaluation, risk evaluation (or assessment), concluded by risk management.

In proposing generic step-like frameworks for decision-making on top of criteria for deciding on what is causing cancer, the AIHC and the OSTP were incorporating the typical way of thinking of emerging risk research. The search for comparative risk assessment methods had animated the nascent risk analysis community in the US in the 1970s. In 1972 for instance, the Committee on Public Engineering Policy, under the aegis of the National Academy of Engineering, picked up on ideas of physician Chauncey Starr (published in *Science* in 1969—Starr, 1969) and developed the *benefit–risk assessment* of technologies. The National Academy of Science's Committee on Science and Public Policy (COSPUP) was working at nearly the same time on risk–cost–benefit calculation methodologies. Yet another committee was created in 1979 at the NRC, entitled the Committee on Risk and Decision-Making. The statistician and decision scientist Howard Raiffa chaired it. While it failed to gather consensus on any concrete recommendations, this committee contributed to the thinking around the respective roles of 'assessment', 'evaluation', and 'control' of risks, and the organization of their interactions in concrete regulatory practice (NRC, 1982).

The political tactic of the AIHC was to have the National Academies of Science endorse the superiority of a staged approach and the evacuation of analytic work from regulatory agencies. To that end, AIHC representatives engaged in simultaneous lobbying of the National Academies of Science and of Congress and the Senate. Both responded positively. The Subcommittee on Agriculture and Related Agencies of the Senate Committee on Appropriations approved the allocation of $500,000 for a study on risk assessment, 'to assess the merits of institutional sharing of scientific functions through the separation of the objective risk assessment process from the regulatory process per se' and 'to consider the feasibility of unifying the different functions of risk analysis'.[8]

THE WORK OF MAKING THE FRAMEWORK

The request for a study on the analytic part of the regulatory decision-making process was passed to the NRC (the operating arm of the National Academies of Science).[9] Expectations were high—the study was mentioned in the national press on numerous occasions between 1981 and 1983. For the NRC staff, the

[8] Report no. 96-1030, Agriculture, Rural Development and Related Agencies Appropriation Bill 1981, Archives NAS–NRC Executive Offices Organization. Projects proposed: Risk Assessment and Federal Regulation Policies.
[9] This branch of the Academies takes care to organize the production of reports for those institutions that have turned to the Academies 'for advice'. The current tag line of the Academies is 'The National Academies—Where the Nation Turns for Independent, Expert Advice'.

request behind the study was transparent. It was 'to evaluate the "science court" idea'.[10]

Composing the Committee

The Board on Toxicology and Environmental Health Hazards (BOTEHH) of the NRC worked on establishing the panel to do the study. People were selected to represent the following subfields of expertise: Risk assessment policy, Risk assessment, Law, Economics, Decision analysis, Political science/ organization theory, Psychology/perceived risk, Epidemiology, Biostatistics, Oncology, Public, Industry, Basic science/other. The assembling of experts from these different subfield categories illustrates the way that NRC did not generally seek to eliminate all biases in the individuals it selected. Rather, it looked to compose a committee in which the mild biases and attachments of people would cancel out each other. In the NRC tradition, authority and neutrality are less properties of individuals than outcomes to be achieved through collective deliberations. The committee as a whole must appear as credible, authoritative, and speak with one voice. This subtle functioning gives committee chairs a key role, and also opens up the possibility for the outright failure of committees.

The Committee on the Institutional Means for Assessment of Risks to Public Health (hereafter 'the Committee') eventually comprised fourteen people. Five members provided academic expertise in environmental health and toxicity testing. The chair, Stallones, was an epidemiologist from the University of Texas and specialized in cardiovascular and neurological diseases. Morton Corn was an industrial hygienist from Johns Hopkins University, and a specialist in workplace safety risks related to aerosol particles. He was also the former administrator of one of the agencies with considerable interest in the study, the Occupational Safety and Health Administration (1975–7). Vincent Dole was a professor of medicine, a member of the Institute of Medicine (another branch of the National Academies of Science) and a researcher in biochemistry. He is, and was already, mostly known for his research on heroin addiction understood as a metabolic process. Kenny Crump was a mathematician and biostatistician, who had developed a reputation in the field of environmental health and regulation for his method of extrapolation from low dosage of chemicals to high dosage—a method used by the EPA at the time. Elizabeth Weisburger from the National Cancer Institute brought her knowledge of oncology and carcinogenic substance identification.

---

[10] Source: interview with author.

Two members of the Committee were identified as specialists in the emerging science of risk assessment. Warner North was a young up-and-coming decision scientist, and early developer of applications of this science to environmental and health issues. By his own admission, he was a protégé of Raiffa and other pioneers in decision science. When the study began, he had already looked at such things as the process of making decisions about air pollution or chemicals-related risks both through his own research and also through his participation as a consultant to NRC committees. He had formed his own consultancy, Decision Focus, which he founded after leaving the Stanford Research Institute—Stanford University's contract research branch. The second risk research expert was Paul Slovic, a psychologist and pioneer in risk perception research, at the time a research consultant based at Decision Research. Slovic and North knew each other, since Slovic had worked with the behavioural psychologist and economist Amos Tversky, who interacted intensively with the Stanford Research Institute.

The Committee included a lawyer and two political scientists. The lawyer was Richard Merrill, from the University of Virginia School of Law. From 1975 to 1977, he was the Chief Counsel of the FDA. He was also a member of the NRC BOTEHH. Terry Davies, a political scientist and early researcher on environmental policy, was a member of the group that Nixon consulted in order to decide to create a federal environmental agency in 1970. He was based at the think tank *Resources for the Future* at the time of joining the Committee. Ted Greenwood was an assistant professor of political science at MIT, on leave at the OSTP between 1977 and 1979, whose research on regulatory agencies informed the committee. One should add that the NRC staff project director, Larry McCray, who played a major role in preparing the ground for the Committee deliberations, analysing materials and writing reports, was also a political scientist—incidentally also from MIT and a good friend of Ted Greenwood.[11]

A smaller subset of two had a mixed scientific and administrative profile. Joseph Rodricks, a biochemist and toxicologist by training (Ph.D., University of Maryland), was at the FDA between 1969 and 1980, ending his career there as FDA's Deputy Associate Commissioner for Health Affairs from 1977 to 1980. Before joining the Risk Assessment Committee, he had left the FDA to establish a private risk assessment consultancy. Gilbert S. Omenn was a medical doctor and geneticist. When the Risk Assessment Committee was established, he had just ended a four-year stint in the federal government, first as deputy science adviser of Carter and deputy administrator of the OSTP (the

---

[11] Greenwood emphasizes McCray's role in the following terms: 'Larry interacted with Reue [the chair] a lot. And the selection of witnesses, the structure of meetings, all those things which have a big influence on outcomes of these kinds of exercises, Larry played a big role in. But mostly in the drafting and organizing of the documents. But also simply in the thinking' (source interview with the author).

administrator being Frank Press, who in 1981 became president of the national academies and of the NRC), and later deputy administrator of OMB (Office of Management and Budget)—on leave from the University of Washington in Seattle. He also had experience in government as White House Fellow (1973–4), serving as the assistant to the head of the Atomic Energy Commission. Omenn had the interest, expertise, and competence in government to serve as chair of the Risk Assessment Committee. Press thus chose him for this role in July 1981, a couple of months before the actual commencement of the work.

Two less vocal people on the Committee included Franklin Mirer and H. Michael Utidjian, selected to represent the 'public' and the 'industry' respectively.[12] Frank Mirer was originally a chemist and toxicologist, having spent time as Ph.D. candidate and postdoctoral researcher at the Harvard School of Public Health. He joined the Risk Assessment Committee as the head of the health and safety department of the United All Workers Union. He was mostly interested in occupational health chemical safety standards, and the activity of OSHA (Occupational Safety and Health Administration). Utidjian was the corporate medical director of the chemical company American Cyanamid.

Stallones, Corn, Crump, Dole, and Weisburger were designated by Davies as the 'science camp': those people from biology broadly speaking who were most likely to defend the idea that risk assessment is science, and that science is objective and not influenced by 'values' (Davies, 2003). Davies, Greenwood, North, Merrill, and Slovic formed the 'social science group', or the 'values side' and were considered to be those who would be initially more inclined to defend the view that risk assessment is a mix of scientific and political values. The committee was thus evenly balanced in terms of initial biases or orientations.

Beyond the inherent diversity of backgrounds and differences in views on the science-policy and science court debate, the Committee was unique in that a majority of members had some exposure to, or even experience in, administrative and regulatory affairs, either as political analysts, consultants, or members of staff of these agencies or of the federal government. This probably gave a particular centre of gravity to the group. McCray recalls that

> I think the thing I liked most was that...we really knew what was going on in agencies. That's unlike other committees I have seen. I always say to my colleagues that we need practitioners...This committee was different because people really knew about agencies. Rodricks, Merrill, Omenn...these are people who really respected government.[13]

---

[12] These are the categories used in NRC documents.
[13] Source: interview with the author.

Answering the Charge

The Committee first convened in October 1981. Immediately after the first
meeting, the decision was made to change the chairman. The meeting had
revealed that Omenn would be inclined to push the particular 'two-stage'
framework he had developed at the OSTP a few years back, which was
inappropriate in a committee that was supposed to review proposals and
elaborate a common vision from scratch. Omenn was replaced as chairman
by Stallones. The concrete work of writing the report began immediately and
by December 1981, an outline was already available, with chapters assigned to
various people. In January, key literature from the emerging specialists of risk
research had been circulated. Kenny Crump had communicated two of his
recently written chapters on statistical extrapolation. Slovic shared a copy of
Lawrence's (1976) *Of Acceptable Risk*, a book that claimed that safety is not
just an objective reality that can be captured with numbers, but one that
depends on the social acceptability of the risk in question.

The collective position of the Committee on the 'science court' idea
crystallized early on. Most people knew why and how regulatory agencies
work, and were clear about what was at stake politically in these organizations. The deregulation and anti-environment agenda had emerged
slowly under Carter, but was now—in 1981—powerfully driven by the
new Reagan administration. Regulatory agencies like EPA and OSHA
specifically were under regular and fierce attacks. The Committee developed a subtle positioning towards these political debates. On the one hand,
people were strongly aware of them, if not part of the debates directly. On
the other hand, they suspended their views and interests to do the job the
Academies had given them, namely to evaluate a proposal and to suggest
new, workable, accepted recommendations. No member of the Committee
proposed extreme views about social regulation, whether for or against. In
short, the external political controversies were not played out inside the
Committee.

The open discussion among members of the group led them rapidly to
reject the science court proposal on the grounds of its being too impractical for
regulators and too disruptive of their functioning. Instead of discussing this
controversial institutional option, the Committee adopted a more empirical
approach, by surveying how various agencies were organized to produce and
use scientific data, and by identifying the pros and cons of each organization.
Those who worked on the survey were not the natural or medical scientists of
the Committee, but a lawyer and two political scientists: Merrill, Davies, and
Greenwood. In parallel, the project director McCray, a political scientist,
surveyed the mechanisms for institutional separation and the current agency
practices. The review showed that there were considerable variations across
regulatory agencies both in the kind of science they used and in the way they

used it. Some used in-house scientific departments, others drew on the expertise of external national research institutes. No organization seemed better in terms of producing more credible regulatory decisions. There seemed to be no single 'best' organizational solution for the use of science in regulatory decision-making processes.

The (brief) evaluations of the science court idea and the empirical review of organizational arrangements were combined with a third line of collective work by the Committee: the identification and naming of both generic and specific activities that comprise regulatory decision-making in environment and health.

Definitional Work

The group admitted from the outset that definitions were missing that might enable simple agreement across the table about what risk assessment meant and where it belonged. The definitional work required would be a way to manage different viewpoints inside the Committee, where contradiction, or conflict, was evident. People with a background in biological sciences were not accustomed to consider that scientific practice, even for regulatory purposes, might be informed or underpinned by values, implicit or explicit. But others in the group did think along those lines and the issue was not swept aside, but addressed head-on. The question of what was science and what was policy within risk assessment was debated openly inside the group, leading eventually to a collective endorsement of the view that the science involved in risk assessment is intertwined with some type of policy judgement. The progression towards that argument and its associated definitions was slow. Various proposals for defining terms were drafted between meetings, and discussed or tested during those meetings. Figures 1.1, 1.2 (two successive drafts of the framework developed by the committee), and 1.3 (the representation of the framework published in the final report; NRC 1983) show that there were several stages to that progression, and three notable moves.

The first move is the semantic *generification* of risk assessment, under which four, until now, clearly defined and distinct operations, were progressively subsumed. The notions of 'risk assessment', 'risk assessment policy', of the 'analytic process', and so on, already existed in the bureaucratic or scientific discourse. But a diversity of definitions and schemes coexisted (Lave, 1982; OTA, 1981). In documents of the EPA pre-dating RAFG, for instance, risk assessment is but one type of assessment that coexists alongside 'hazard assessments', 'exposure assessments', and 'health assessments'. It was not a *generic* category under which exposure and hazard assessments could be subsumed. In the report of the Raiffa committee (NRC, 1982), 'assessment' is always twinned with 'evaluation'. Figures 1.1, 1.2, and 1.3 show that the specific contribution of RAFG is to have promoted, or generified,

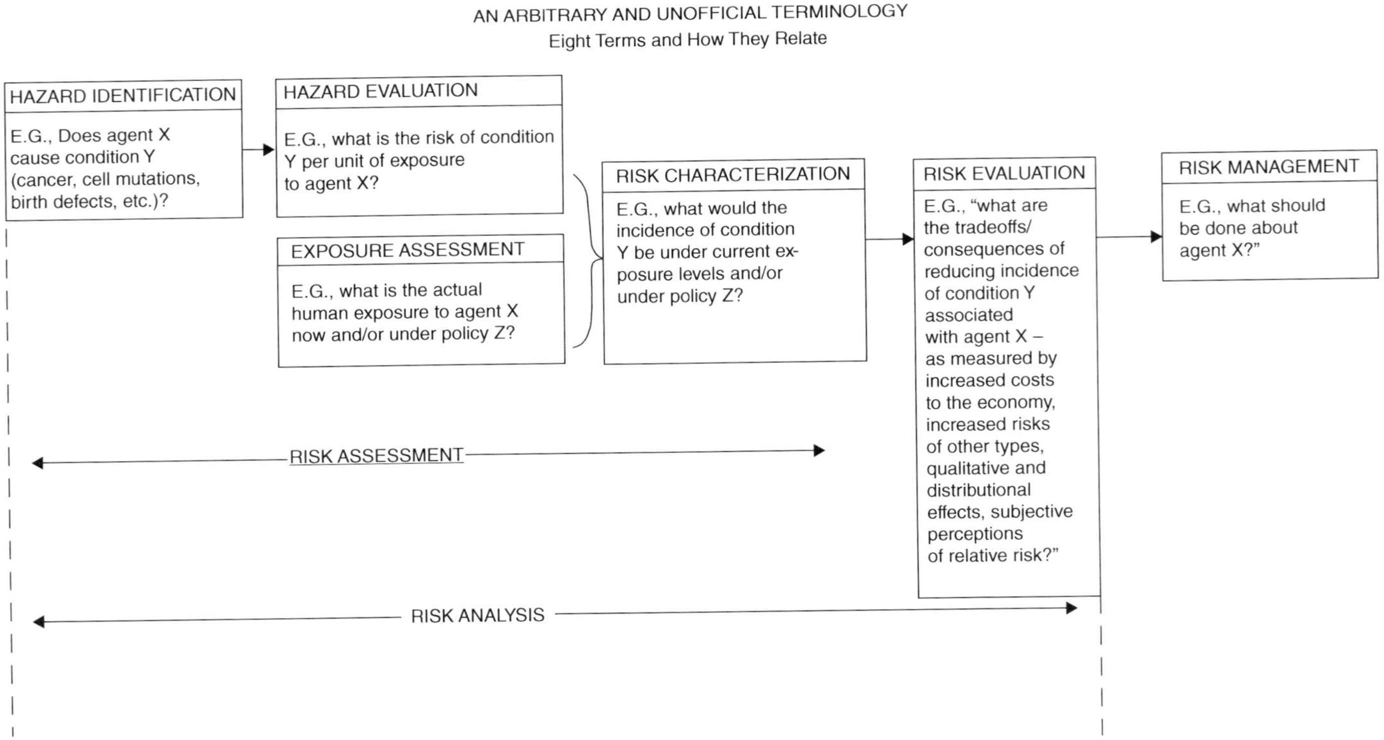

AN ARBITRARY AND UNOFFICIAL TERMINOLOGY
Eight Terms and How They Relate

HAZARD IDENTIFICATION
E.G., Does agent X cause condition Y (cancer, cell mutations, birth defects, etc.)?

HAZARD EVALUATION
E.G., what is the risk of condition Y per unit of exposure to agent X?

EXPOSURE ASSESSMENT
E.G., what is the actual human exposure to agent X now and/or under policy Z?

RISK CHARACTERIZATION
E.G., what would the incidence of condition Y be under current exposure levels and/or under policy Z?

RISK EVALUATION
E.G., "what are the tradeoffs/ consequences of reducing incidence of condition Y associated with agent X – as measured by increased costs to the economy, increased risks of other types, qualitative and distributional effects, subjective perceptions of relative risk?"

RISK MANAGEMENT
E.G., what should be done about agent X?"

RISK ASSESSMENT

RISK ANALYSIS

Figure 1.1. An arbitrary and unofficial terminology

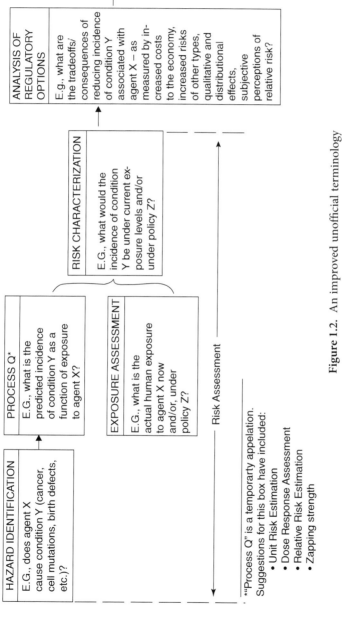

AN IMPROVED UNOFFICIAL TERMINOLOGY
Seven Terms and How They Relate

HAZARD IDENTIFICATION

E.G., does agent X cause condition Y (cancer, cell mutations, birth defects, etc.)?

PROCESS Q*

E.G., what is the predicted incidence of condition Y as a function of exposure to agent X?

EXPOSURE ASSESSMENT

E.G., what is the actual human exposure to agent X now and/or, under policy Z?

RISK CHARACTERIZATION

E.G., what would the incidence of condition Y be under current exposure levels and/or under policy Z?

ANALYSIS OF REGULATORY OPTIONS

E.g., what are the tradeoffs/ consequences of reducing incidence of condition Y associated with agent X – as measured by increased costs to the economy, increased risks of other types, qualitative and distributional effects, subjective perceptions of relative risk?

ANALYSIS DECISION

E. g., what should be done about agent X?

Risk Assessment

*"Process Q" is a temporarty appelation. Suggestions for this box have included:
• Unit Risk Estimation
• Dose Response Assessment
• Relative Risk Estimation
• Zapping strength

Figure 1.2. An improved unofficial terminology

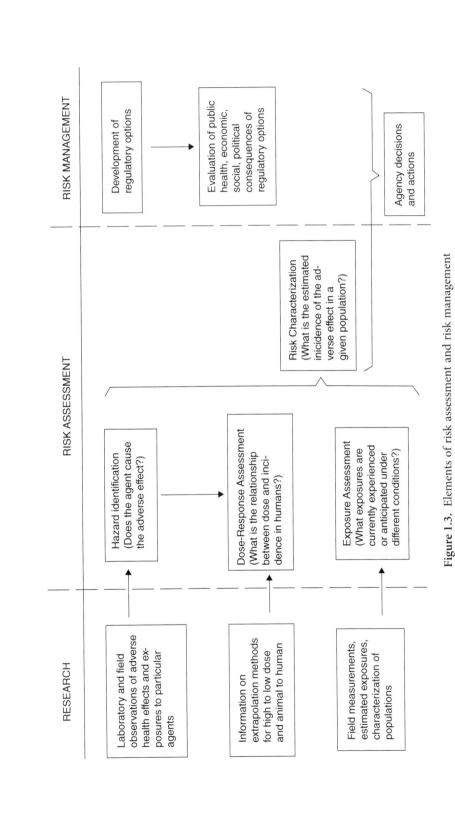

Figure 1.3. Elements of risk assessment and risk management

the notion of risk assessment. Four clearly delineated operations, corresponding to well-identified disciplinary expertise, were defined as the four specific steps to populate the rubric of risk assessment. Generification also provided a way to hold together the necessary stress on quantification of risk but also to preserve the narrative-based interpretation of risk and risk characterization, something for which Omenn pushed.

The second move (somewhat surprising for a Committee that was meant to focus on risk assessment) was its invention of a generic notion of 'risk management'. Until then, that term either referred to an engineering exercise involving the design of systems to render them less risky, or was so broad that it was useless as an organizational category. The Committee focused the definition of risk management on the notion of policy alternatives based on various analyses and evaluations (e.g. of benefits, costs, and social values), or 'the process of weighing policy alternatives and selecting the most appropriate regulatory action, integrating the results of risk assessment with engineering data and with social, economic, and political concerns to reach a decision' (NRC, 1983: 3), much in the way the AIHC or members of the nascent risk analysis community were starting to use the notion. As a consequence, risk management became a broader category than 'risk control' or 'decision and action', and a recognizable, autonomous activity. As the report makes clear, the distinction between risk assessment and risk management 'closely parallels' the distinction that the OSTP report made, three years before, between a stage of identification and characterization of chemical substances, and a second stage of evaluation of regulatory options. But, in RAFG, the linearity of the sequence is somewhat minimized: a regulatory decision is now depicted as the product of two activities of risk assessment and risk management running in parallel, not the end sequence of a linear process starting with assessment.

RAFG thus effectuates an important and innovative terminological construction, in which regulatory decision-making in the face of risk ceases to be represented as a linear process of 'science' that informs 'policy', but is now the product of two concurrent activities, namely 'risk assessment' and 'risk management'.

The third move, which results from the first two, is the squeezing out of the controversial notion of 'risk evaluation'. In previous NRC reports, but also in public discourses, values had consistently been a bone of contention and the main problem in the concrete allocation of tasks and responsibilities for decision-making. Who, in current organizational and regulatory design terms, would qualify as an 'evaluator' as mentioned in previous expert reports, such as that of the NRC Committee on Risk and Decision-Making? The work that the Risk Assessment Committee did on the vocabulary unlocked this problem by simply dropping the term 'value'. It became redundant in the architecture of risk assessment and risk management, and was replaced in the definition of risk assessment as involving a choice among different

Riskwork

possible 'assumptions'.[14] The political dimension of risk decision-making is
covered by the symmetrical notions of risk assessment and risk management.
Both activities are now conceptualized as similar in that they grapple with
uncertainty—hence their common denomination as processes with 'risk' as
their object. In previous schemes, uncertainty was supposed to have been dealt
with and eliminated during a prior scientific stage. Now, risk assessment and
risk management cover the political aspects of dealing with risk and this takes
away the need, at least provisionally,[15] to speak of values altogether.

The definitions were laid out in the first chapter of the report, drafted by
Warner North and fully written by the NRC staff. Armed with these terms, the
group then focused on the 'tricky issue'[16] of how to handle the relationship
between risk assessment (RA) and risk management (RM), and between
science and policy. The remainder of the report thus addresses the interplay
between RA and RM, notably through the use of guidelines (chapter II, drafted
by Rodricks) to clarify the respective territories of politics and of science in the
process, and the organizational arrangement of these interactions (chapter III,
drafted by Merrill).[17] In the end, the Committee refrained from imposing a
single organizational template. It did not get involved in the design of local
applications of a general scheme. It adhered to a more high-level discourse,
working on the associative relationship between RA and RM.

In summary, by working to create and elaborate a list of fundamental terms,
the group effected a move from the representation of the calculation of risk as
a 'rigid formula',[18] to a depiction of it as a process instead. The process-based
terms form what could be called an institutional thesaurus. The terms in
that lexicon have an associative relationship (RA and RM) or a hierarchical
one (risk assessment as the generic term for the specific operations of hazard
identification, dose–response assessment, and so on). The terms can be combined to shape the process of risk regulation. The thesaurus serves to index,
flexibly, different types of policy contents, and to distinguish how and when to
employ them to shape a regulatory decision. What the resulting report says, in
essence, is that the management of these contents is more important than the
actual allocation of tasks and powers to one institution or the other. It is this
generic and flexible character that proved so influential at the EPA and other
regulatory agencies in the reorganization of their processes and missions.

---

[14] That word 'value' appears only three times in this 191-page report. RAFG goes for a
different, arguably less prescriptive term: 'assumption(s)' (twenty-two occurrences). Fo
Shrader-Frechette, the report could very well have used a more normatively explicit term like
'methodological value judgement' (Shrader-Frechette, 1995).
[15] Subsequent discussions in the field of risk assessment and risk management revolved
around the need to attend to the political aspect of risk decisions through more explici
communication with audiences and the public, or the incorporation of publics in the proces
of making decisions, through deliberative arrangements (NRC, 1989, 1996; Stern et al., 2009).
[16] Source: interview with the author.   [17] Chapter IV details all ten recommendations.
[18] Source: interview with the author.

FRAMEWORKING

The preceding narrative shows that the Committee had no intention of producing a harmonized scheme for decision-making about the risks specifically of potentially carcinogenic substances. According to McCray, the construction of the definitions that eventually composed the framework 'was really an internal thing'. At no stage did the group have the explicit ambition to design a formal framework, even though this is what the Red Book is now known for. There was also no intention, let alone mandate, to standardize the practice of regulatory agencies based on that scheme. Ironically, what would later be constitutive of the renowned framework were the working definitions that the group designed for itself. The more substantive recommendations— that is, what was specifically advanced as a contribution to the institutional and political debate—were not ultimately applied in a straightforward way. Paraphrasing McCray, one could say that 'the famousness of the report', and the subsequent durability and influence of the categories that it elaborated, is almost an accident.[19]

Still, what the Committee produced in this report is something that resembles a framework: it is rule-like, generic and describes a coherent system for making decisions. This is an indication that the Committee generated the conditions and the work that was necessary for the subsequent diffusion and institutionalization of a framework. To analyse the emergence of diffusible organizational institutions, new-institutionalist scholars speak of 'institutional work' (Lawrence & Suddaby, 2006). Pertaining to this institutional work is the action of transforming local knowledge 'into a reified, commercially valuable form presented as objective, ahistorical and having universal principles' (Suddaby & Greenwood, 2001: 938), or knowledge commodification. It comprises knowledge codification and abstraction—two items that are helpful to capture what happened in the Committee.

Knowledge codification is the fact of making experience explicit (Suddaby & Greenwood, 2001: 938). The group used its own collective experience of the assessment of hazards and substances, and the making of regulatory decisions by regulatory agencies. It did so because it faced the need to clarify its own experience and meanings. The group empirically reviewed various ways of making those decisions or organizational arrangements. It worked from the bottom up, finding ways of describing these arrangements comparatively. That Rodricks and Omenn had played leading roles in the composition of cancer risk assessment frameworks could only add to this experience.

Knowledge commodification also involves 'abstraction': converting experience into more universal and portable form (Suddaby & Greenwood,

---

[19] Source: interview with the author.

2001: 939). The neat definitions, the graphs and tables presented in the report, but more importantly the semantic generification of the various notions involved, enabled this kind of abstraction. The group invented a finite set of terms, which I have characterized as a thesaurus, which systematically conveys a set of activities and practices and their interrelations. The number of notions included in this terminology was limited (indeed the Committee evolved towards a smaller number of fundamental notions to describe the decision-making process) to those that were most universal. And they chose to associate them with a notion of risk, rather than speaking about chemical substances in general, or of particular chemicals. Strikingly, the group did not consider the evaluation of particular substances and did not review past controversies, such as the recent decisions on asbestos or benzene. It did not try to stabilize criteria for carcinogenicity, but remained abstract. The group did not drill down into the substantive detail of how to do a dose–response assessment. The terms adopted finally apply well beyond the class of cancer-causing chemical substances, the original object of concern. In that vein also, the group decided not to prescribe a particular organizational arrangement for any one regulatory agency in particular, and opted instead for more incremental improvements based on the suggested thinking. The portability of the categories that the group coined was all the greater as they had already emerged in previous work and reports, and gained popularity. As noted above, they selected from pre-existing categories, such as 'risk characterization'. They defined risk management in the way certain people and groups started to approach it, establishing distance from a stricter engineering meaning of the term.

Abstraction is intimately linked to the work of proceduralizing decision-making. In effect, the Committee abstracted regulatory decision-making from the substance of particular controversies. It seemed to adopt a Simonian perspective of opting for procedural rationality, where no common substantive rationality is achievable (Simon, 1969). Instead of defining carcinogenicity substantively, the Committee suggested ways of defining a carcinogenic substance. Instead of dealing with these uncertainties itself, the Committee suggested that an inherent part of decision-making is the necessary explication of uncertainties by the decision-making actors themselves. Instead of defining the substance of the appropriate science, or prescribing whether a conservative policy has more or less merits, the group tried to clarify the processes by which agreement on such questions can be fostered. Here, the shared decision-oriented perspective of the group seems to have played an important role (Boudia & Demortain, 2014).

Knowledge commodification in Suddaby and Greenwood's sense does not cover the work of constructing an ontology, as the Committee did by constructing a class of actions and identities (assessment (in its various components), management), and of associations between these classes. This work is however crucial in creating a framework, particularly in disputed fields such as risk regulation. Risk-based decision-making is a diverse field, which involves a variety of potentially conflicting communities: scientists (and different kinds of scientists at that), lawyers, bureaucrats, and so on. Through risk-based decision-making, what is being commodified is knowledge of how those people should work together. It only works if the framework appears relevant and legitimate simultaneously to this heterogeneous set of people and audiences—those that are meant to work together in the framework—to achieve their differentiated goals. Several elements of the work of the Committee pertain to the kind of ontology modelling that is at stake here.

The group mainly worked on the 'analytical part' of the decision-making process (in the terms of the initial charge) or 'risk assessment', but they also defined what lies beyond risk assessment. They consolidated a category to capture it: 'risk management'. They did not define and order its specific operations as they did for risk assessment. In doing so, not only did they respect their charge, and thus remained within their mandate and legitimacy perimeter. But they still named its components, and also identified its ideal-typical logic of choosing between alternative policy courses (the 'weighing of policy alternatives'). More importantly, they defined risk management in a relational way, vis-à-vis risk assessment and other aspects, as an element of a system for making decisions. This was performative in essence, because, with this move, administrators and bureaucrats in regulatory agencies saw their own jurisdiction, which was highly disputed in regulatory scientific controversies around chemicals, recognized and given the 'imprimatur' of the Academies (to use a term that many participants themselves used).

The work of modelling an organizational ontology also appears in the fact that the group tested various definitions of the essential components of risk-based decision-making. The work was iterative, as shown by the changes between the various graphs produced along the way. The Committee functioned like a laboratory, in which the various possible positions in the real world debate were recreated on a smaller, more manageable, scale. The composition of the Committee was in that respect crucial. It included representatives of the various views and audiences that take part in the science-policy and risk controversies outside. The two typified positions regarding science—as socially constructed and imbued with policy positions, or as objective and independent—coexisted within the group. The various interests or stakes involved in the science-policy debate were also present in the group, since scientists based in regulatory agencies, bureaucrats, academics, industries, environmental groups, and trade unions were all represented inside the Committee.

The Committee experienced, at the very beginning of its work, difficulty in collaborating, given this internal diversity. But it also provided the possibility of replicating the political controversy and the various stakes that existed externally at a smaller scale within its own membership. Codifying, generifying, or modelling was in short a response to these difficulties and potential conflicts, and to the external controversies that they replicated. The members of the group did not speak for those external groups and views, but could be used to imagine these groups' reaction to various proposals. The composition of the group also allowed for experimentation, politically speaking, with the acceptability of an institutional design.

CONCLUSION

One of the key interrogations behind the study of riskwork is whether or not one can detect in its very content and form the seeds of malfunctions and failures—without waiting for those to arrive. This is as imperative as it is difficult with frameworks, which are seldom proved wrong. Disasters are rarely attributed to the fact of having followed a formal framework. The claim that a disaster could have been avoided had frameworks been better implemented is more frequent.

Frameworks can fail, however, to do what they are functionally supposed to be doing—i.e. coordinate various functions and sources of information to improve consistency and precision in addressing risks across an organization. As Mikes (2012) observes, frameworks are the object of a struggle to codify risk management, and some may rise while others decline. I have focused on the work performed in one particular place, which is generally regarded as the origin of the risk assessment–risk management framework: the Committee on the Institutional Means for Risk Assessment of the US NRC, to understand the conditions in which a framework, or elements of a framework, may prevail.

I have highlighted here a number of conditions and resources that seem conducive to this: a collective capacity to commodify knowledge, deriving in this case from the application of a decision-aiding perspective and an ability to think in terms of process; an ability to insert one's contribution into a longer history of codification, and build on elements of already genericized and tested managerial knowledge; finally, and perhaps more importantly, a laboratory-like, experimental setting in which propositions can be put on trial. The elements that were coined in this experimental setting travelled well because the work to ensure that the rules would survive contestation by one or the other audience had already been done. The internal diversity of the group functioned as an initial trial for the framework, which made it resistant to subsequent trials and controversies in the wider world.

Approaching this committee as a particular setting—as an institutional design laboratory—helps us to analyse the success but also the limits of frameworks at the point of design. Frameworks result from the modelling of intra-organizational diversity, of its components, and of associations between them. They successfully emerge where the diversity that is modelled in the framework is represented in the very site in which it is designed and in its content—rather than simply in the networks and channels that are used to diffuse an already packaged model (Haynes & Free, 2014). The corollary is that whatever isn't represented or translated in the design may potentially become the object of later and alternative codification, which relates to two main things in this case: the public, the values that are represented across the public and the deliberative processes by which they are attended to in public decision-making; the objectives and needs of policymakers. Both of these aspects would be taken up in subsequent reports of the NRC, explicitly aimed at complementing or going beyond the Red Book (NRC, 1996, 2009).

There is thus a fine line between success and failure in the work of making frameworks. In this particular case, the Committee could very well have failed by the inability of the members of the group simply to communicate with each other and to engage in the elaboration of a common view. In fact, there was a real possibility that this would happen. NRC's Al Lazen, *ex post facto*, wrote to the chair with the following words of gratitude: 'How you got a consensus out of such a vocal and diverse group will always be something of a mystery to me – but I'm not knocking it!'[20] The letter is anecdotal, but the meaning is not: it captures the risk of forgetting the actual reality that is being modelled in the framework, and the inherent difficulty of this implicitly political work.

REFERENCES

Boudia, S. (2014). Managing Scientific and Political Uncertainty. In S. Boudia & N. Jas (Eds), *Powerless Science?: Science and Politics in a Toxic World* (pp. 95–112). Berghahn Books.

Boudia, S. & Demortain, D. (2014). La Production d'un Instrument Générique de Gouvernement. Le 'Livre Rouge' de l'Analyse des Risques. *Gouvernement & Action Publique*, 3(3), 33–53.

Bowker, G. & Star, S. (2000). *Sorting Things out: Classification and Its Consequences*. Cambridge, MA: MIT Press.

Calkins, D. R., Dixon, R., Gerber, C., Zarin, D., & Omenn, G. (1980). Identification, Characterization, and Control of Potential Human Carcinogens: A Framework for Federal Decision-Making. *Journal of the National Cancer Institute*, 64(1), 169–76.

Davies, J. (2003). The Red Book Committee: Creative Conflict. *Human and Ecological Risk Assessment: An International Journal*, 9(5), 1113–18.

Demortain, D. (2009). Standards of Scientific Advice. Risk Analysis and the Formation of the European Food Safety Authority. In J. Lentsch & P. Weingart (Eds), *Scientific Advice to Policy Making: International Comparison* (pp. 141–59). Berlin: Barbara Budrich.

---

[20] Letter of David Lazen to Reuel Stallones, 18 April 1983.

Demortain, D. (2012). Enabling Global Principle-Based Regulation: The Case of Risk Analysis in the Codex Alimentarius. *Regulation and Governance*, 6(2), 207–24.

Hayne, C. & Free, C. (2014). Hybridized Professional Groups and Institutional Work: COSO and the Rise of Enterprise Risk Management. *Accounting, Organizations and Society*, 39(5), 309–30.

Jardine, C., Hrudey, S., Shortreed, J., Craig, L., Krewski, D., Furgal, C., & McColl, S. (2003). Risk Management Frameworks for Human Health and Environmental Risks. *Journal of Toxicology and Environmental Health Part B: Critical Reviews*, 6(6), 569–718.

Jasanoff, S. (1992). Science, Politics and the Renegotiation of Expertise at the EPA. *Osiris*, 7, 195–217.

Jasanoff, S. (1994). *The Fifth Branch: Science Advisers as Policymakers*. Cambridge, MA: Harvard University Press.

König, A., Cockburn, A., Crevel, R., Debruyne, E., Grafstroem, R., Hammerling, U., Kimber, I., Knudsen, I., Kuiper, H., & Peijnenburg, A. (2004). Assessment of the Safety of Foods Derived from Genetically Modified (GM) Crops. *Food and Chemical Toxicology*, 42(7), 1047–88.

Landy, M., Roberts, M., & Thomas, S. (1994). *The Environmental Protection Agency: Asking the Wrong Questions from Nixon to Clinton*. Oxford University Press.

Lave, L. B. (1982). *Quantitative Risk Assessment in Regulation*. Washington, DC: Brookings Institution.

Lawrence, T. & Suddaby, R., (2006). Institutions and Institutional Work. In S. Clegg, C. Hardy, T. Lawrence, & W. Nord (Eds), *Handbook of Organization Studies*, 2nd edition (pp. 215–54). London: Sage.

Lawrence, W. (1976). *Of Acceptable Risk: Science and the Determination of Safety*. Los Altos, CA: William Kaufman.

Mikes, A. (2012). The Struggle to Codify Risk Management. *Risk & Regulation*, 24(4), 18–19.

Notermans, S., Barendsz, A., & Rombouts, F. (2002). The Evolution of Microbiological Risk Assessment in Food Production. In M. Brown & M. Stringer (Eds), *Microbiological Risk Assessment in Food Processing* (pp. 5–44). Cambridge: Woodhead Publishing & CRC Press.

NRC (1982). *Risk and Decision Making: Perspectives and Research. Committee on Risk and Decision Making*. Washington, DC: National Academies Press.

NRC (1983). *Risk Assessment in the Federal Government: Managing the Process*. Washington, DC: National Academies Press.

NRC (1989). *Improving Risk Communication*. Washington, DC: National Academies Press.

NRC (1996). *Understanding Risk: Informing Decisions in a Democratic Society*. Washington, DC: National Academies Press.

NRC (2009). *Science and Decisions: Advancing Risk Assessment*. Washington, DC: National Academies Press.

OTA (1981). *Assessment of Technologies for Determining Cancer Risks from the Environment*. Washington, DC: US Government Printing Office.

Patton, D. & Huggett, R. (2003). The Risk Assessment Paradigm as a Blueprint for Environmental Research. *Human and Ecological Risk Assessment: An International Journal*, 9(5), 1137–48.

Power, M. & McCarty, L. S. (1998). A Comparative Analysis of Environmental Risk Assessment/Risk Management Frameworks. *Environmental Science and Technology*, 32(9), 224A–31A.

Rip, A. (1986). The Mutual Dependence of Risk Research and Political Context. *Science and Technology Studies*, 4(3), 3–15.

Rodricks, J. V. (2007). *Calculated Risks: Understanding the Toxicity and Human Health Risks of Chemicals in Our Environment*, 2nd edition. Cambridge and New York: Cambridge University Press.

Ruckelshaus, W. (1983). Science, Risk and Public Policy. *Science*, 221(4615), 1026–8.

Rushefsky, M. E. (1986). *Making Cancer Policy*. New York: SUNY Press.

Shrader-Frechette, K. S. (1995). Evaluating the Expertise of Experts. *Risk*, 6, 115.

Starr, C. (1969). Social Benefit versus Technological Risk. *Science*, 165, 1232–8.

Stern, P., Wilbanks, T., Cozzens, S., & Rosa, E. (2009). Generic Lessons about Societal Responses to Emerging Technologies as Involving Risks. *Working Paper ORNL/ TM-2009/114*. Oak Ridge National Laboratory, Oak Ridge, Tennessee.

Suddaby, R. & Greenwood, R. (2001). Colonizing Knowledge: Commodification as a Dynamic of Jurisdictional Expansion in Professional Service Firms. *Human Relations*, 54(7), 933–53.

2

Risk Mapping

Day-to-day Riskwork in Inter-Organizational Project Management

Lene Jørgensen and Silvia Jordan

In this chapter, we study the everyday riskwork involved in practices of constructing, drawing upon and revising risk maps. The case setting is an inter-organizational project in the Norwegian petroleum industry.[1] Our study is situated against the background of the widespread use of risk maps in practice, academic criticism of the risk mapping technology and enterprise risk management (ERM) rationales more generally, and the relative lack of empirical accounts of risk representation practices. Risk maps have been described as typical technologies of ERM (Mikes, 2009; Power, 2004, 2007; Woods, 2009) and 'risk-based policy making' (Rothstein & Downer, 2012), and they have been reported to be highly popular in diverse fields of practice (Collier, Berry, & Burke, 2007). While ERM guidelines such as COSO (2004) propose risk maps as 'good' instruments for setting risk appetite levels and for assessing and ranking diverse types of risks, some authors characterize this technology as imprecise and unduly simplifying (e.g., Cox, 2008; Rommelfanger, 2008). Furthermore, as simple, visual overview instruments, risk maps may be prone to be used primarily as tools for reputation management. That is, they may be used to testify to external constituencies that an accepted risk management system is in place, while organization-internal actors may not regard them as particularly useful for their work (Power, 2007). The widespread use of risk maps in practice may thus primarily be due to their usefulness as auditable overview instruments particularly for senior management.

---

[1] The empirical sections of this chapter represent an adaptation and extension of the empirics presented in Jordan et al. (2013).

To date we have only very few detailed empirical accounts of how risk maps are actually developed and used in specific contexts (Boholm, 2010; Rothstein & Downer, 2012). This chapter thus seeks to give an account of risk mapping in action, highlighting the day-to-day issues and challenges that actors encounter when engaging in risk mapping, and the ways in which risk maps are enacted to facilitate organizational action and to serve particular ends. We focus our analysis on two interrelated risk mapping rationales that were prominent in the inter-organizational project management context under investigation: (1) producing mutual reassurance; and (2) testifying to efficiency and synergy. For each of these rationales, we illustrate the work involved in producing and using risk maps in this context. In particular, we argue that a fair amount of 'work' concerns the definition and evaluation of a limited set of broadly defined risks. We find that processes of producing such broadly defined 'top ten' risks on risk maps often depart from the calculative rationale espoused in general framework and internal governance documents. In doing so, they facilitate certain types of organizational action, such as testifying to project management efficiency and providing mutual reassurance. In these regards, the question of *when* a risk is represented as an event plays a significant role in the life of risk maps in this specific context.

The remainder of the chapter is structured as follows. We first introduce the context of the studied inter-organizational project. We then move on to describe the observed risk mapping practices and rationales in this context. We conclude by discussing our findings, and by outlining avenues for future research.

STUDY CONTEXT

The studied inter-organizational upgrading project is situated in the Norwegian petroleum sector that—in line with the European gas market more generally—is characterized by the separation of ownership, operatorship, and production.[2] The studied upgrading project aimed at replacing technical systems in two gas processing plants due to ageing, lack of replacement parts, and the risk of a technical breakdown. The project thus had economic, technical, and safety motivations and was considered to be of high priority at the same time as it was linked to several dangers and risks. Three key actors were involved in the upgrading project. First, the *Owners* supervise and finance the project, acting as 'gatekeepers' responsible for approving the investments and the project's continuation through the various project phases'. Second, the

---

[2] Detailed information on the organization of the Norwegian petroleum sector can be found at the Norwegian Petroleum Department <www.npd.no/en/Publications/Facts/Facts-2011>.

project is supervised by the *Operator* who is responsible for the gas transportation infrastructure. Third, the *Technical Operations Company* (TOC) runs the plants on a daily basis and is responsible for implementing the technical solutions in the course of the project.

These three actor groups collaborate on a regular basis and have institutionalized a broad set of documents, blueprints, and regulations to manage inter-organizational projects. One prominent blueprint is shown in Figure 2.1 and represents the prevailing understanding of 'project phases' separated from each other by 'decision gates' that have to be passed. The proclaimed aim of the first project phase, the *Feasibility* phase, is to elaborate different possible solutions and to evaluate them with regard to their technical, economic, and HSE (health, safety, and environment) feasibility. In the *Concept* phase, further information is collected in order to select one solution ('concept') which is then to be further defined (detailed engineering plans, scheduling, cost estimates, assigning responsibilities, etc.) in the *Definition* phase. In the final *Execution* phase, the planned solution is carried out, e.g. the obsolete systems are replaced by alternative systems. To enter each of these phases, the owner organization has to officially approve that a 'decision gate' has been passed. Our analysis focuses on the last three project phases shown in Figure 2.1 which were carried out between autumn 2009 and summer 2012.

Each project phase is formally organized into the same 'milestones' that are regulated and proceduralized by various documents. One important milestone is the delivery of the 'decision gate support package' which consists of a collection of standard documents that TOC is required to complete, giving an account of the project content and status. This report is reviewed by the Operator who creates their own version which is then presented in the Independent Project Review (IPR)—a two-day audit involving all three actor groups as well as external 'facilitators' with the aim of evaluating the extent to which the requirements for this project phase have been met. If the proposal to pass the decision gate is approved by the owners, the project formally enters the next phase. Several internal and inter-organizational meetings are organized in addition to these milestones, such as 'monthly meetings' and 'risk workshops' between TOC and Operator, and internal 'risk reviews' within TOC and the Operator.

National regulations and guidelines (PSA, 2013, 2014), internal risk management guidelines (D-TOC-02, D-TOC-03, D-TOC-08, D-OP-01, D-OP-02, D-OP-03) and project management guidelines (D-TOC-01, D-TOC-04,

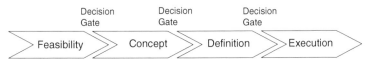

Figure 2.1. Blueprint of project phases (D-TOC-1)

D-OP-04) consistently stress a 'risk-based approach'. According to these guidelines, the setting of objectives, planning, coordinating, and controlling activities shall all be linked to risk assessment. Both the Operator and TOC state in their general governance documents that they follow an ERM approach (D-OP-2, D-OP-3, D-OP-05; D-TOC-05, D-TOC-08). These documents stress that risk management should be a continuous process applicable to all activities and all systems. Furthermore, they specify that risk management should be an integrative exercise by means of which risks within various areas such as HSE, Operational/Technical, Strategies/Objectives/Plans, Public Issues, and Finance/Cost should be managed. These general documents are complemented by a set of specific project risk management guidelines which repeat these risk areas and specify the risk management process and associated risk management tools (D-TOC-01, D-TOC-04). In both general governance and project risk management documents, risk maps are presented as an important risk assessment and communication tool.

Risk maps represent risks within a matrix format, graphically indicating their probability of occurrence and their potential impact. Placing risks on the map creates a ranking of risks according to their criticality and intervention urgency, often visually reinforced by means of traffic lights. The traffic light colours create different zones of acceptability on the map. Green is usually associated with 'risk acceptable, no action required', amber with 'risk acceptable, risk reducing action should be implemented if economically feasible', also described as 'ALARP – As Low As Reasonably Practicable', and red with 'risk not acceptable' (e.g., Renn, 2008). Figure 2.2 shows an ideal-type risk map template as presented within TOC's project documentation.

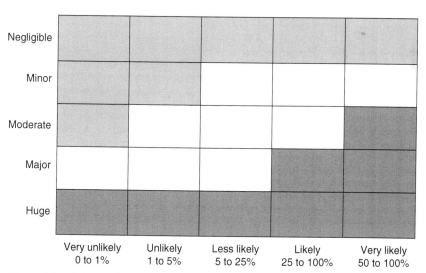

Figure 2.2. Risk map format as represented in TOC's monthly report (D-TOC-06)

Risk maps are also one device among other management tools that are included in various project governing documents. They are an integrated part of the risk module of the software system PIMS (Project Information Management System) and they are prescribed by standard documents such as those to be completed within the decision support packages.

In order to facilitate the ranking of qualitatively different risks, risk management governing documents provide impact tables that operationalize the impact categories from 'negligible' to 'huge' impacts for different types of objectives at risk. For instance, impact categories are specified in terms of monetary variation for financial/cost risks as compared to different degrees of injuries and accidents for HSE risks, or number of days by which the project is at risk of being delayed for schedule risks. Probability categories are specified by the risk map design itself, as is visible in Figure 2.2 where five categories from 'very unlikely' to 'very likely' are represented along with probability percentage ranges (e.g. 0–1 per cent = 'very unlikely'). Governance documents do not give any formal guidance, however, as to how such probabilities should be established for different types of potential impacts.

Interestingly, it is difficult to identify a formally accepted purpose and ideal use of risk maps in this context. In internal regulations and procedures, the necessity and relevance of identifying, representing and managing risks is explicated vaguely with reference to an 'enterprise-wide risk management approach', so as 'to make sure that our operations are safe, and to reach our corporate goals in compliance with our requirements' (D-TOC-5). The particular rationale for using risk maps as a specific tool of risk representation is presented in governing documents in terms of increasing the efficiency of reporting and supporting internal decision-making (D-TOC-3). Emphasis is also placed on their relevance for complying with external accountability requirements.

RISK MAPPING PRACTICES

In line with the different risk areas defined in the governance documents, project members sought to represent risks to various project objectives on the risk map. In the first risk meeting in the beginning of the project, members of the Operator and TOC started with a brainstorming of opportunities and risks based on their experience with similar projects. In this process, the risks were categorized according to the different impact arenas such as cost, HSE, operational/technical, and public issue impacts. Based on this brainstorming, project subgroups within the Operator and TOC then developed their own risk registers, discussing the concrete labels and the relevance in terms of impact and probability of a set of risks within their area of responsibility (e.g., HSE risks). The construction and update of risk maps in the project then required the selection of the ten most 'exigent' risks out of these 'lower-level' registers, the discussion of potential additional risks, and the placement of identified risks on the risk map.

During the upgrading project, both TOC and the Operator constructed their own risk maps and were required to constantly review and update these maps. TOC also received monthly risk maps from their EPC (Engineering, Procurement, Construction) contractor. Reviews of risk maps took place in meetings attended by representatives of different project subdisciplines like HSE, costing, and engineering. The Operator updated its risk map every six months during a 'risk review' that was also attended by TOC representatives. The Operator was dependent on TOC to receive risk information, since TOC was handling the daily operations and the technical upgrading of the plants on behalf of the Operator and the owners.

In these reviews, project management teams from the Operator and TOC met for a one-day session that was facilitated by a member of the Operator's project department. Guided by the facilitator, the participants went through each of the existing risks on the map, discussed their current status and decided on whether and how these risks should be moved on the map. After discussing the existing risks, the facilitator asked the participants towards the end of the risk review for any newly emerging risks in the project or any other important issues that had not yet been addressed. During these meetings, the participants often came to agree on the placement of the risks relatively quickly. When debates arose, they often concerned the adequacy of descriptions of the mapped risks. For instance, with regard to the risk 'interfaces at site', questions were posed such as, 'What exactly had we intended with this risk? Does this concern the interface between different projects or between different divisions?' Other discussions in these meetings revolved around the scope of the risks, i.e. whether the mapped risks concerned only one or both plants included in the project, and whether the risks concerned the specific project or the general operations. In this regard, Operator representatives sought to keep the risk map clear from issues that were, in their view, not directly related to the project, so as to avoid additional work and costs. Over the course of the project, the originally placed risks tended to stay on the map, and only few risks were added to it.

Within TOC, monthly risk reviews were held by TOC's project team and a facilitator from a central Quality and Risk Department located in another city. As in the semi-annual risk reviews described above, the facilitator was an expert in handling the risk management software (the risk module within the PIMS) who was also experienced in chairing risk reviews. These risk reviews started with the TOC project team going through the risk map reported from the EPC contractor. The explicit purpose of this process was both to ensure that EPC has control over the project, and also to see whether EPC has identified risks that TOC should include in their own map. After reviewing EPC's risk map, they turned to their own risk map and went through each represented risk. Most discussions concerned their partly divergent under-standings of each risk and the mitigating actions linked to each risk. Lastly the project management team discussed whether the placing of a risk should be altered. Like the semi-annual Operator's risk reviews, there was generally little movement of the risks. The risks on the risk map were highly aggregated and often contained several related risks each associated with several mitigat-ing actions. The status of the mitigating actions for each risk often differed, i.e. mitigating actions were often not yet completed, and new mitigating actions were defined. The outcome was therefore generally to keep a risk in the same location or to move it just slightly. The result of the risk review was an updated risk map that was reported as part of the monthly report delivered to the Operator before the monthly inter-organizational meeting between the Operator and TOC. Risk maps also became part of the decision gate support package at the end of each project phase.

During the project, risk mapping involved frequent discussions of the project risk status and mitigating actions, but was not primarily used as a tool to spur critical discussion of emerging threats in the inter-organizational setting. At times risk mapping was even regarded as impeding attention to relevant risks. Criticism was voiced as risks tended to be defined in rather abstract terms, to be oriented towards short-term objectives, to stay on the map over time and to converge over plants, projects, and organizations.

Nevertheless, many project members saw risk mapping in this inter-organizational setting as a relevant activity which should not be discarded, and did not regard it as a mere box-ticking exercise. In what follows, we focus on two exemplary ways in which risk maps were put to use in the course of the project: (1) producing reassurance; and (2) testifying to efficiency and synergy, and we illustrate the work that is involved in making risk representation matter in these regards.

THE PRODUCTION OF REASSURANCE
AND CONFIDENCE

Informed by institutionalist approaches on legalization and litigation mental-ity (Bies & Tyler, 1993; Meyer, 1983; Scott, 1994; Sitkin & Bies, 1993), the role of documentation and procedures for producing comfort in control processes has long been stressed in critical auditing and risk management work (Pentland, 1993; Power, 1997, 2003, 2007). On this view, organizations may engage excessively in documentation and proceduralization in order to comply with ambiguous laws and to insure themselves against potential blame through defensive audit trails.

We observed that a few project members stated that risk maps were used primarily in order to comply with regulative requirements and to insure against potential blame. Such 'insurance' activity was seen as necessary, but problematic as it took away attention and time from what were considered to be more relevant activities. An engineer at TOC, for instance, was particularly vocal in his concern over the inclusion of perceived unnecessary risks in the map. Since regulations recommended accounting for a broad mix of different types of risk in risk representation, he felt that the technical risks which he considered as most complex and relevant in the upgrading project became under-represented in favour of other risk types such as HSE risks (I-TOC-02).

However, although risk mapping in the project complied with industry regulations that ask for comprehensive risk assessment, defensive protection against external blame was not a pervasive theme in risk mapping conversations. Producing reassurance through risk mapping was rather related to building the confidence of distributed project members in each other's commitment to 'the project'.

In this regard, project members referred to risk maps often in terms of relevant proceduralized reporting milestones, as a bureaucratic road map which gives structure to the inter-organizational work and allows the project to 'move forward' as long as the risk picture remains tolerable. Risk maps that do not feature red risks signal to project members that the project is 'alive', in a 'healthy state', and will not come to a halt, since identified threats are 'under control'. A TOC project member described the relevance of risk maps for inter-organizational cooperation with regard to the production of confidence as follows:

It will help their [the other organizations'] decision process, of course. They can see that we've made a good risk assessment around this project, and that will help them in their decision process.

I: In what way?

They increase their confidence. We're talking about confidence. How confident are we that we're going to perform the work within the right time, within the right budget, without any injuries? ... Then they can confidently go to their manager and say, 'TOC has done a good job here. We're confident that we're going to come within the budget frame.' Then their management team will go up to the owners and say, 'We're confident that they've done a very good job. They've looked at all the aspects. Of course, things could pop up totally unexpectedly but we're confident that they've assessed the situation properly' ... So, they're confident that they can go up and say, 'We need this amount of money to install this item.' ... If we haven't followed the guidelines or haven't followed the documentation exactly, this might pop up and they'll say, 'We're not confident with this. I think we need to go back and make a reassessment. We've got to design again.

Stop the project. We're not going to sanction this project. We're not going to deliver money.' (I-TOC-01)

Confidence and commitment to the project by different actors in this inter-organizational collaboration is thus progressively constructed and sustained by the delivery of standardized assessments and reports, including the risk map. If the report is not complete, 'if we haven't followed the documentation exactly', this would prompt suspicion of owner representatives and might delay the project's progress through the 'decision gate'. As Kalthoff (2005) in his analysis of credit risk calculations in banks argues, symbolic machines such as risk calculations and models imply a shift from truth to 'correctness'. Accordingly, what is primarily assessed by the Operator and Owner representatives is whether TOC had followed the inter-organizational reporting guidelines and completed all the documentation correctly. Delivering the risk map in the expected format, embedded correctly in the monthly report, thus represents commitment and confidence of the reporting party, at the same time as it creates confidence in the receiving party. As such, the risk map was a kind of 'hygiene factor' for project stakeholders.

TOC followed the same logic when dealing with contractors and sub-contractors. Throughout the project, incomplete documentation and reporting from suppliers was discussed as being related to several risks and was one of the hottest topics in almost every meeting, both in intra- as well as in inter-organizational meetings. In these discussions, trust and lack of trust were voiced and directly coupled to incomplete documentation and reporting. In some cases, worries over incomplete documentation resulted in audits, in other cases, particularly when contractors and sub-contractors delivered incomplete reports, TOC and the Operator interpreted this as a sign of 'risk' and included such 'incomplete (sub)contractor documentation risk' in their risk maps, often classified as the most significant ones on the map, and linked these risks to a number of mitigating actions. While these risks were regarded as significant, project members interestingly had some difficulties in categorizing them with regard to the common impact categories of cost, schedule, (technical) quality, HES, and reputation. They thus either left the category column simply blank or they assigned several categories, such as 'cost' as well as 'schedule' to such documentation risks (D-TOC-07).

Reassurance is thus not based on the belief in true and precise representation, but rather in the signal through the map, and complete documentation more generally, that project participants have been engaged in some kind of risk discussion and are competent project partners. This is not only a defensive activity vis-à-vis potential external scrutiny, but also a process of 'choice' through which participants become committed to action and 'create and sustain a belief in the wisdom of the action chosen, thus in the enthusiasm required to implement it' (March, 1987: 161). If regularly delivered risk maps create some kind of mutual belief in each other's thorough risk reviewing and project management procedures, and if identified risks move over time towards the green zone on the map, this helps to create a sense of 'the project moving forward without unnecessary halt', as one interviewee put it (I-OP-00).

Corresponding to the production of reassurance within the project through comprehensive and gradually improving risk maps, we observed the practice of defining inclusive risks that summarized a few more concretely defined risks under abstract categories. Thus, risk mapping often did not imply a simple selection of the top risks as ranked in existing subgroup risk registers. For instance, 'functionality of the system' on the Operator's risk map, was defined as a risk which comprised several different uncertainties as to whether the new technical system to be implemented in the project would work at least as well as the current system operating at the two plants. Interestingly, such overview categories tended to be defined in terms of 'objectives at risk' (e.g., technical functionality) rather than in terms of 'risk to an objective'. A TOC employee who worked with quality management and risk management in projects explained the relevance of mapping 'objectives at risk' as follows:

> The risks shall reflect the targets, and this coupling is very important. I certainly use this very consciously. Whenever I have the opportunity, I use risk manage- ment to market the targets. The targets are not necessarily equally understood, it easily gets dynamic. Someone can think that the target is at one place, then it changes, then you think the target is somewhere else, so you have to get the picture [risk map] out there and repeat it. When we have run these base-line updates and management updates, I have always made my own package on risk management, where I have repeated the targets in order to get alignment around them, that it is the targets we see risk against, that it is this that we steer towards in the project. (I-TOC-5)

Practised in this way, the risk map rendered relevant project objectives visible rather than particular risks to these objectives.[3] While this was seen as a useful tool to remind various project members of the main project objectives and reassure the various parties that these targets are being pursued, the particu- larities of threats to these objectives disappeared from sight.

Other constructed risks did refer to risk events rather than objectives at risk, but their abstract definition in many cases implied an unclear relationship to a particular project objective. 'Interfaces at site', for instance, referred to risks emanating from other projects that are conducted in parallel at the plants to be

---

[3] In line with this observation, Hirschhorn (1999) describes how 'primary risk', the felt risk of choosing the wrong primary task, often creates ambiguity. In order to manage this primary risk, it becomes relevant to clarify the figure–ground relationship between focal and less focal tasks. In our example this is supported by rendering objectives visible on the map rather than risks to these objectives.

upgraded, as well as from the necessity to continue plant operation while undertaking the technical upgrade. A wide range of risks and related objectives at risk can fall under this category, such as technical problems, project delays, unexpected costs and increased danger for plant personnel. By means of such inclusive risk definitions, a wide variety of risks and objectives at risk can be covered on the map, providing reassurance that risk assessment has been comprehensive.

With such abstract and inclusive risk definitions, it becomes difficult (and/ or unnecessary) for project members to use probability and impact scales in order to assess and place a risk on the map. If a particular risk comprises several types of objectives at risk, no individual impact and probability of its occurrence can be identified for this risk object. The colour coding of risk maps that produces a third dimension of the risk criticality is 'useful' in the face of such difficulties, as it allows actors to position more or less broadly defined risks in relation to each other without necessarily calculating specific impacts and probabilities. In line with Boholm's (2010) study on risk assessment in railway planning, we often observed the practice of classifying risks along the red–amber–green typology, establishing impact and probability categories only post hoc as a result of a risk's placement on the map. This practice was particularly visible in the end of risk reviews when risk maps were updated. In these discussions, project members very rarely used the impact matrix as a tool for supporting their decisions to move risks on the map. Equally rarely did project members analyse the status of the related mitigating actions in order to decide whether or not to move risks. Since each of the mapped 'top ten' risks typically related to several subcategories of risk and thus to many different mitigating actions which would all be in different states of completion, it became difficult to use an analysis of mitigating actions in order to alter the risk map. Instead, alterations of the risk maps were often performed in a rather ad hoc manner, involving little discussion and rather swift agreement within the team. While this could be interpreted as a 'misuse' of risk maps, these practices make sense with regard to the explicitly defined purpose of risk maps as tools for 'efficient compliance' (D-TOC-3) and with regard to the related rationale of mutual reassurance of project members.

The rationale of producing reassurance was to some extent linked to the project managers' responsibility for the risk map. Each organization's project manager had the overall responsibility for the project and for project reports. Members in the different subdisciplines had considerable autonomy for managing risks within their area of responsibility, but when it came to the project's risk map, the project manager had the final word. Several informants pointed to the fact that risks considered as serious in their respective disciplines (engineering, HSE, cost, schedule, reputation), were not considered as part of the top ten project risks on the risk map (I-TOC-02, I-TOC-05). These risks did not get included in the map, as the project manager was keen to signal that he was in control of the project and the tasks he had been assigned. Any apparent trouble (indicated by newly emerging red risks on the map) could reflect back on him as the project manager. Such concerns came up in observed meetings and were also voiced in interviews. According to some project members, these concerns could also result in a reluctance to map risks as red (I-TOC-05). Informants argued that this was more usual some time ago, and that it is now more common and accepted practice to mark risks as red. However, while positioning risks in the red zone has become more accepted in the early stages of the projects, the project manager sometimes made a point of mapping some risks as red at first, so as to be able to later move them towards the green zone in order to show that all problems had been successfully dealt with (I-TOC-05). We can see here a time component with regard to the mapping and expected interpretation of 'red risks'. In the course of the project, it seemed to become increasingly more difficult for actors to flag emergent risks as 'red risks' and/or to individually include them as part of the 'top ten' risks in the first place. In this regard, the risk map can be seen to serve as a 'rationalisation machine' that is enacted to legitimize and justify actions that have already been decided upon (Burchell et al., 1980). However, we did occasionally observe that actors classified risks as red, even at later stages of the project, if they wanted to bring another actor group to act on a particular issue. This concerned for instance identified risks of 'incomplete documentation' by contractors and subcontractors. In these instances, the risk map's predominant use was transformed from a 'rationalisation machine' to an 'ammunition machine' (Burchell et al., 1980).

From an ideal-typical risk management perspective brought forward by guidelines such as COSO (2004), the evaluation of a risk should not depend on when a risk is identified. In the studied project management context, however, riskwork did involve the consideration of time. This is particularly interesting since risk maps themselves do not explicitly represent time. Contrary to other project management and planning tools, risk maps seem to be rather timeless, similar to geographical maps (of e.g. a particular coastline). As critical geographers (e.g., Monmonier, 1996; Wood, 2010) indicate, time is nevertheless a crucial component of maps, as (mapped) space emerges as the product of synchronization and the closure of movement. That is, timing concerns are central when producing maps (e.g. the time period taken to perform geographic measurements, the time period for which the map is intended to be used, etc.), but such timing is not visible in the resulting map as such. As Wood (2010: 96) notes, 'We cannot squeeze time out of the map, only onto it'. We would argue that this applies not only to geographic maps, but also very much to risk maps. The work that is involved in producing and using risk maps in projects, to some extent, has to do with squeezing time onto the map and making a seemingly 'timeless' map work within particular short- or longer-term perspectives of project actors. The risk map seems to be timeless in the sense that it does not explicitly specify time periods, for instance, whether the mapped risks are considered for short-term or long-term impacts, or whether considered risk events may have different effects if they occur at the same time or at separate times. The map presents a somewhat static 'risk landscape' at a particular moment in time. In the course of a project, actors are very much concerned with timing issues, such as scheduling and coordinating activities, and achieving certain milestones set for specific periods of time. In order to render risk maps useful as a project management tool, project members therefore added a time dimension to the map that was not visible in the risk map results, but rather in the risk mapping conversations when constructing the map.

We observed different ways in which project members dealt with time concerns when producing risk maps. Most explicitly, time entered the picture when 'schedule' risks, specifying risks of project delays, were identified and placed on the map and when risk mitigating actions, related to the mapped risks described in additional documents, were given a particular deadline. With most risks, the time component was not visible in the risk map result, but became an object of discussion when producing and updating risk maps.

In this regard, reassurance through the risk map so as to move the project jointly ahead can be linked to the practice of aligning the map's time horizon with 'project phases' as represented in Figure 2.1. The relevant time horizon to be taken into account when updating risk maps became an object of disagreement in the course of the project. While some held the view that risks to long-term project objectives should be considered, i.e. impacts of the technical upgrade on the long-term technical functioning, safety etc., others started to promote a narrower view on risks to the objectives of the respective project phase. One of the defined objectives of a project phase was to move the project into the next phase, i.e. to get approval by the owner organization. Evidently, 'objectives at risk' and consequently the risks to be considered as most relevant differ with such divergent time perspectives taken. The following episode exemplifies such divergent understandings.

In a risk meeting of the Operator during the Definition phase of the project, a discussion arose over the HSE risk of working under the condition of limited space during the plants' upgrade, which would take place in the Execution phase. Project members had different opinions on: (1) whether this risk should be mapped and addressed already in a stage of the project in which no 'phase-specific' objectives would be impacted by that risk; and (2) how to place this risk if it gets represented, i.e. which colour category should be assigned:

PROJECT MEMBER (PM) 1: This [risk 'HSE in limited space in a live plant'] would be a risk during the operation/execution phase.

PM 2: This risk map should be for the definition phase. What are the procedures in [the Operator] related to this?

PM 3: I have also wondered about that.

PM 4: It is possible to include risks for the whole project period.

PM 3: Our focus must be on this phase.

PM 4: We must assess the criticality of the risks, and this can change through the different phases.

PM 3: It is not even sure we will make it to the 4th [Execution] phase.

PM 2: Shall we mark it as red now?

PM 4: In this phase it is not red.

PM 2: I think we have different philosophies and practices on this. (M-OP-11)

The main argument for placing only phase-specific risks on the risk map was that such a focused picture would allow for concentrating project activities towards the main objective of this phase which is to proceed to the next phase, whereas the main argument against this position was that risks and action plans should be identified as early as possible so as to prevent them from impacting *overall* project objectives. As to the colour coding, some argued for categorizing this risk as a red risk because no risk reducing activities have yet been implemented, while others argued it should be marked as green, since it was not critical in the current project phase. The arguments for 'breaking' risk maps down to project management phases and concentrating on shorter time frames are in line with the map's use as a reassuring bureaucratic road map that enables the project to move ahead through the phases and 'across' the 'decision gates'.

As the meeting excerpt above shows, the production of reassurance was not a frictionless activity. In addition to struggles over the definition of time horizons, project members also criticized risk maps as being too abstract, rendering it difficult to understand what lies behind each risk bubble. On several occasions, actors got frustrated with represented risks on the map that they couldn't make sense of, as over time they forgot the broader context and meaning of the represented risk, or couldn't interpret it because someone else, not present at the current meeting, had been originally responsible for placing that risk. In a monthly risk meeting in TOC an engineer voiced the confusion that can arise from these overview categories:

> There are too many things connected to this risk, I didn't know what to do with it [move the risk or leave it in the same position on the map], I had to wait for this meeting today to clear it up. (M-TOC-07).

When such interpretive difficulties became explicit in meetings, they were discussed in order to seek further clarification or to specify mitigating activities, but these discussions did not result in the definition of less comprehensive and more concrete risks. Rather, the originally broadly defined risks tended to stay on the map over the course of the project. Thus, repeatedly, discursive work needed to be performed during the course of the project in order to establish links between abstractly defined 'risks' on the map and activities intended to manage these risks. Discursive work basically consisted of conversations by means of which project members made sense of mapped risks by establishing relations to prior discussions and activities that were not visible on the map itself (see also Chapter 6 this volume). Along with the practice of excluding longer-term risks, abstractly defined risks seem to impede the recognition and mitigation of emerging risks. From the perspective of mutual reassurance, however, such practices can be made intelligible: abstractly defined and short-term oriented risks were useful in their comprehensive outlook and the possibility to move risks progressively towards the green zone without the need (and possibility) to neatly measure the performed changes in probabilities and impacts.

The rationale of inter-organizational reassurance was also visible when certain risks got excluded from the map because they were regarded as 'dangerous' to report. The perceived danger was related to offending another actor group and disturbing the relationship by officially naming and thus 'bringing to life' risks that result from the actions of another actor group. The Operator, for instance, did not feel comfortable with officially identifying TOC's ability to prioritize the project as one of the Operator's project risks, although this was considered to be one of its major risks for a short period in that particular project phase. Both in meetings and in interviews, actors referred to the non-representation of this type of risk as a relevant face-saving activity within inter-organizational cooperation, with justifying statements like 'You can't flash this right in their face' (I-TOC-4), 'That would be very provocative' (I-OP-1), and 'We don't have a tradition of doing it like that' (I-Op-1). One Operator representative explained the problem of 'contentious' risk representation in an interview as follows:

> The point is that you have to look at what setting you're going to use it [the risk map] . . . If you're showing a cooperation partner a risk that the cooperation is bad, then I think what you're doing is actually helping the risk become a reality. So, in some respects, I've also seen ones where we don't think the sponsors [the owners] will approve the project. We will not put that on a risk matrix that we show to the sponsor, because that will just [pause] 'You're not expecting us to approve it'. So, I think the risk register will have a certain amount of, let's say, political correctness about it, depending on where it's to be shown. (I-OP-2)

Hence, the building of confidence was a reflexive matter of constructing confidence in the project by demonstrating confidence in one's own as well as the partners' activities. This was particularly pronounced when risk maps and documents were prepared in intra-organizational meetings for inter-organizational settings. There was a focus on making the information as unproblematic as possible. In many meetings we observed TOC working on formulations that would reassure the Operator. This could in some cases mean that details were removed or details were added in the related documents. What they thought the Operator would think of the information was motivating these processes. Exactly the same happened when the Operator prepared documents for the owners. They made careful choices about wording and about how much detail to provide. The rationale for this was voiced in terms of being able to avoid discussions and difficult questions in inter-organizational meetings and avoid overlong meetings. The selection of the information provided in the documentation was thus strongly characterized by efforts to reassure the receiving partners rather than trigger their suspicion or invite critical discussions. Such filtering in processes of 'translation' and 'editing' has been characterized as an essential feature of governance at a distance (see Latour, 1987; Robson, 1992; Sahlin-Andersson, 1996).

TESTIFYING TO EFFICIENCY AND SYNERGY

The creation of abstract and inclusive risks—often defined as 'objectives at risk'—was not only used as a means to mutually reassure project members and external constituencies that a comprehensive risk assessment process has been undertaken, but also as a means to merge risk representations over plants and projects. Synthesizing risk mapping in these ways was a visual means to testify to the proclaimed synergy effects and the efficiency of (portfolio) project reporting and management.

The merging of risk maps occurred at several levels. First, we observed a tendency of the Operator to take over the risks as represented in TOC's map when creating the Operator's own risk map, thus partly converging TOC's and the Operator's risk maps into a single project risk map. Second, risk maps were chosen to be identical for both plants to be upgraded, i.e. the same *types* of risks were mapped for both plants in which technical systems were to be updated. Dealing with upgrading two different plants in the same project was frequently justified with reference to generated synergy effects. Such synergy was not clearly operationalized, e.g. in a specified amount of cost savings. However, the fact that the same risk maps were used for these different undertakings was referred to as evidence that project management synergies could be achieved. Two separate, but nearly identical risk maps managed by the same team would, in contrast, be time consuming, confusing, and pose challenges for documentation and updating of the maps. Thus, 'synergy' was made visible by means of identical risk maps.

While all actor groups defended the practice of using a common risk map, they did at times express concern about one of the plants (located geograph-ically where most of the project team of TOC is situated and close to the Operator's location) receiving more attention than the other plant (where actually most of the work was to be done). Project members did not explicitly relate this perceived imbalance to the use of common risk maps, although identical maps can imply that the specificities of the 'neglected' plant do not get mapped. By using identical project risk maps as a means to make the proclaimed synergy effects visible, the risk map gave 'the project' a recognizable outlook, and was also used to legitimize the way the project was organized.

The practice of merging maps over the two locations (plants) in the project is situated in the context of broader 'project portfolio' practices in this context. Managing projects in project portfolios entails that the same project team handles several projects which are given a common overarching name. Such portfolio management practices seem to be highly motivated by cost concerns. Dividing management cost between different projects is considered a huge opportunity in this context (M-TOC-02). If you have a stand-alone project, especially a small one, the management costs would be a considerable part of the total costs, which would be regarded as a risk (cost risk). This was also the case for the studied project, where concerns over management costs were often voiced and discussed and, after having started as a stand-alone project, two more projects were added into the portfolio as the project progressed. Many project members saw drawbacks of such portfolio management, as is illustrated by the quotes below:

> When the projects are out of sync, it becomes problematic to report in cases where the documentation is common for the projects, for instance in decision gate support packages. (M-TOC-04)

> Portfolio management is the biggest problem we have within risk management. It is a nightmare. Not only do you compare apples with apples or bananas with apples, but there are boats, rocks, time, everything in one soup, big and tiny issues, process risks, case risks and god knows what. When you aggregate the risks from the different projects, or the individual projects come with input on risk, there could be a red risk in the projects, but this does not necessarily mean anything for the portfolio as such, while still being potentially important for the totality. Then you can ask yourself what consequence matrix you shall use when you design the risk map. This is not an easy matter... The problem is that you mix projects together with very different character when it comes to size, phases and challenges. (I-TOC-05)

As these quotes illustrate, mapping risks for complex project portfolios was considered as problematic for the definition, evaluation, and accountability of risks. However, in spite of the frequently voiced problems with portfolio management, it had become a common way of organizing projects in this context which influenced the way in which risk maps got used. The justifications for portfolio management included cost benefits, enhanced communication and collaboration between the team members who were jointly allocated to similar projects, and efficiency gains to be realized in booking joint meetings and in organizing milestones, meetings, reports, and documentation jointly in one package. Representing synergy by means of using common risk maps was thus part of a larger portfolio management practice where efficiency seemed to be the predominant rationale that impacts upon all parts of project management, including risk mapping and risk management more generally.

Some actors perceived these practices as problematic in terms of insufficient updating and lack of critically engaging with the specific risks that each organization, plant, and project is exposed to. Generally, the criticism and worry over possible neglect did not change the general tendency of mapping rather abstract, overview risks and merging risk maps across different organizations. However, some actors sought to use the risk map itself to counteract perceived problems of neglecting the specificities of plant and projects when risk maps were merged. The Operator, for example created a risk called 'neglect of [plant B]' on their risk map during the concept selection and the definition phases of the project. Riskwork, in this case, thus comprised counteractions to risks being perceived to be caused by risk (portfolio) management practices themselves. This exemplifies how different actors used risk reporting tools in rather diverse ways. That is, while rationales of testifying to efficiency and of creating mutual reassurance were rather pronounced in the observed context, we could also see actors drawing upon the same tools to somewhat counteract these rationales and to draw attention to the perceived shortcomings of these risk management practices.

CONCLUSION

In this chapter, we have focused on the ways in which risk maps were produced and used in inter-organizational project management. Actors perform a great deal of work when producing, adapting, and using risk maps. Such riskwork is not primarily to do with conducting sophisticated numerical transformations. Rather, in order to make risk representation through risk maps relevant to the different actors, project management actors performed a variety of discursive transformations. The 'selection' of the 'top ten' risks to be represented on the risk map was characterized by processes of generalization and abstraction, particularly when risk maps became merged across plants, organizations, and projects. Actors repeatedly argued over the concrete ways in which these generalizations should be best performed (e.g., whether to define 'objectives at risk' or 'risk to objectives', whether to define risks to short-term or longer-term objectives). There were different rationalities at play in this process, such as the use of risk maps to remind distributed project actors of the main targets, the use of risk maps to cautiously evaluate different courses of action, the use of risk maps as means of mutual reassurance so as to move the project jointly ahead, and the use of risk maps as a mechanism to represent and testify to efficiency and synergy. In the observed project management context, the latter two rationales were rather prominent. Following these rationales, it makes sense to produce comprehensive maps, to orient risks towards short-term objectives, and to avoid the mapping of red risks at later stages of the project. From other points of view, of course, these practices appear rather problematic and several project members criticized them and sought to counteract them by means of alternative uses of risk maps. Implementing, counteracting, or reconciling different risk representation rationalities thus required actors to consider several issues beyond the formal calculations of impacts and probabilities when producing and using risk maps. For instance, risk mapping was influenced by considerations of the time frame of a risk, and by considerations of potential reactions by risk map recipients (will they ask difficult questions, will they further fund the project, will they be offended, etc.?).

More generally, we would argue that this case exemplifies how riskwork often is not characterized by straightforward, coherent practices, but crucially involves more or less explicit struggles over the reconciliation of different rationales such as producing reassurance, reporting efficiency, accountability, critical reflection, and the cautious imagination of alternative futures. In the inter-organizational project context addressed in this chapter, rationales of reassurance and efficiency often came to dominate other rationalities, suppressing a focus on the complex interaction of different risks, on long-term impacts, and on emerging risks.

In addition to risk maps there are many artefacts and inscriptions that may be implicated in practices of reassurance and that testify to the project management's efficiency and synergy, such as meeting protocols, time schedules, and documentary audit trails. However, in contrast to long lists of protocols, time schedules, or technical specifications, the risk map diagram provides a comprehensive project image that can be understood 'immediately', even without knowing on what concrete information the map is based and which mitigating activities are undertaken by whom at a particular moment in time. As such, the visual, non-calculative overview character of this technology provides it with a certain meta-position amongst a wider ecology of inter-related practices.

This chapter has provided only a glimpse of the work involved in producing and using risk maps. Future research could produce more detailed accounts of risk mapping practices by following the concrete transformations of particular risks on risk maps over time, across different managerial levels and across different organizations (e.g., subcontractors, contractors, etc.). Future studies could also investigate the use of risk maps in different contexts so as to analyse under what circumstances particular risk mapping rationalities come to dominate over others. Empirical studies could focus in more detail on how risk mapping practices influence decisions on resource allocation. With their combined focus on the two dimensions of impact and probability, risk maps may engender tensions in this regard, as impact requires measures to mitigate it and probability requires measures to reduce it and avoid risk crystallization. Finally, we think that studies could investigate how different risk map designs (e.g. the chosen scaling), as well as particular ideals of how 'normal' risk maps should look, influence their use.

REFERENCES

Bies, R. & Tyler, T. (1993). The Litigation Mentality in Organizations: A Test of Alternative Psychological Explanations. *Organization Science*, 4(3), 352–66.

Boholm, A. (2010). On the Organizational Practice of Expert-based Risk Management: A Case of Railway Planning. *Risk Management*, 12(4), 235–55.

Burchell, S., Clubb, C., Hopwood, A., & Hughes. J. (1980). The Roles of Accounting in Organizations and Society. *Accounting, Organizations and Society*, 5(1), 5–27.

Collier, P., Berry, A., & Burke, G. (2007). *Risk and Management Accounting: Best Practice Guidelines for Enterprise-wide Internal Control Procedures*. Oxford: Elsevier/CIMA Publishing.

COSO. (2004). *Enterprise Risk Management—Integrated Framework: Application Techniques*. New York: Committee of Sponsoring Organizations of the Treadway Commission.

Cox, L. A. (2008). What's Wrong with Risk Matrixes? *Risk Analysis*, 28(2), 497–512.

Hirschhorn, L. (1999). The Primary Risk. *Human Relations*, 52(1), 5–23.

Jordan, S., Jørgensen, L., & Mitterhofer, H. (2013). Performing Risk and the Project: Risk Maps as Mediating Instruments. *Management Accounting Research*, 24(2), 156–74.

Kalthoff, H. (2005). Practices of Calculation: Economic Representations and Risk Management. *Theory, Culture & Society*, 22(2), 69–97.

Latour, B. (1987). *Science in Action. How to Follow Scientists and Engineers through Society*. Cambridge, MA: Harvard University Press.

March, J. G. (1987). Ambiguity and Accounting: The Elusive Link between Information and Decision Making. *Accounting, Organizations and Society*, 12(2), 153–68.

Mikes, A. (2009). Risk Management and Calculative Cultures. *Management Accounting Research*, 20(1), 18–40.

Meyer, J. (1983). Organizational Factors Affecting Legalization in Education. In J. Meyer & W. R. Scott (Eds), *Organizational Environments: Ritual and Rationality* (pp. 217–32). San Francisco, CA: Jossey-Bass.

Monmonier, M. (1996). *How to Lie with Maps*, 2nd edition. Chicago, IL: University of Chicago Press.

Norwegian Petroleum Department. (2011). <www.npd.no/en/Publications/Facts/Facts-2011> (accessed on 1 July 2012).

Pentland, B. T. (1993). Getting Comfortable with the Numbers: Auditing and the Micro Production of Macro Order. *Accounting, Organizations and Society*, 18(7), 605–20.

Power, M. (1997). *The Audit Society: Rituals of Verification.* Oxford: Oxford University Press.

Power, M. (2003). Auditing and the Production of Legitimacy. *Accounting, Organizations and Society,* 28(4), 379–94.

Power, M. (2004). *The Risk Management of Everything. Rethinking the Politics of Uncertainty.* London: Demos.

Power, M. (2007). *Organized Uncertainty: Designing a World of Risk Management.* Oxford: Oxford University Press.

PSA (Petroleum Safety Authority Norway) (2013). Regulations Relating to Health, Safety and the Environment in the Petroleum Activities and at Certain Onshore Facilities (the Framework Regulations). Petroleum Safety Authority Norway, Norwegian Environment Agency, Norwegian Directorate of Health, Norwegian Food Safety Authority. <www.psa.no/framework-hse/category403.html>

PSA (2014). Guidelines Regarding the Framework Regulations. Same issuing authority. Last revision 2014. <www.psa.no/framework/category408.html>

Renn, O. (2008). *Risk Governance. Coping with Uncertainty in a Complex World.* London: Earthscan.

Robson, K. (1992). Accounting Numbers as 'Inscription': Action at a Distance and the Development of Accounting. *Accounting, Organizations and Society,* 17(7), 685–708.

Rommelfanger, H. (2008). *Risikoaggregation in der Praxis. Beispiele und Verfahren aus dem Risikomanagement von Unternehmen.* Berlin: Springer.

Rothstein, H. & Downer, J. (2012). 'Renewing Defra': Exploring the Emergence of Risk-based Policymaking in UK Central Government. *Public Administration,* 90(3), 781–99.

Sahlin-Andersson, K. (1996). Imitating by Editing Success: The Construction of Organizational Fields. In B. Czarniawska & G. Sevón (Eds), *Translating Organizational Change* (pp. 69–92). Berlin, New York: Walter de Gruyter.

Scott, W. R. (1994). Law and Organizations. In S. Sitkin & R. Bies (Eds), *The Legalistic Organization* (pp. 3–18). Thousand Oaks, CA: Sage.

Sitkin, S. & Bies, R. (1993). The Legalistic Organization: Definitions, Dimensions, and Dilemmas. *Organization Science,* 4(3), 345–51.

Wood, D. (2010). *Rethinking the Power of Maps.* New York: Guilford Press.

Woods, M. (2009). A Contingency Theory Perspective on the Risk Management Control System within Birmingham City Council. *Management Accounting Research,* 20 (1), 69–81.

Internal Risk Management Guidelines/Procedures

D-TOC-02: Risk Management. Function Requirement (2009)

D-TOC-03: Risk Management. Work Process Requirements (2010)

D-TOC-05: The TOC Book (2009)

D-TOC-06: All 'monthly reports' delivered by TOC during the upgrading project

D-TOC-08: Guideline: Compliance and Leadership (2013)

D-OP-01: Risk and Opportunity Management (first version 2005, revised in 2008)

D-OP-02: Risk Based Methodology for Integrity Assessment of Gas Pipeline (2010)

D-OP-03: HSE Risk Analyses and Acceptance Criteria (first version 2007, revised in 2008)

D-OP-05: Long Range Plan and Budget and Business plan 2011–2014 (2010)

Internal Project Management Guidelines/Procedures

D-TOC-01: Project Development (2010)

D-TOC-04: Risk Management in Projects (2010)

D-OP-04: Project Governance Process (2007)

3

Beyond the Headlines

Day-to-day Practices of Risk Measurement and Management in a Non-Governmental Organization

Matthew Hall and Renuka Fernando

Risk has long been a prominent feature in the operation of non-governmental organizations (NGOs), particularly those NGOs working in conflict situations and providing care for, and services to, vulnerable persons. Discussions of risk in NGOs have tended to focus on headline-making events, such as misdeeds stemming from cases of fraud, financial misreporting, and corruption, along with operational failures related to threats to human security from dangerous or threatening environments. Although important, this focus has meant that relatively little attention has been directed towards the more day-to–day practices of risk measurement and management in NGOs. This is an important omission because it is through the everyday practices of employees in NGOs—their riskwork—that they can influence (positively or negatively) the incidence and severity of headline-making events.

This chapter analyses two types of riskwork, drawing on empirical data from a study of a large UK-based international development NGO. The first is the use of risk matrices and templates to understand and document threats to human security facing volunteers and staff. The second is risk measurement, whereby the NGO sought to develop key risk indicators to measure legal compliance and security risk management across its developing country operations. A central theme of the analysis in this chapter is the inherent tension arising from the formalization of risk management: on the one hand, risk templates and key risk indicators can facilitate talk and provide helpful guidance and reassurance to operational staff and senior decision-makers; on the other hand, they can also potentially serve to displace meaningful action by focusing undue attention on ensuring compliance with mandated procedures.

RISK MANAGEMENT IN NGOs

For NGOs, perceptions of risk management are affected by headline-making events. Cases of fraud and corruption, such as the CEO of the United Way of America stealing $1.2 million in 1992, or that of an accountant employed by Save the Children accused of sexual harassment, adversely impact the public trust invested in NGOs (BBC, 2009; Cordery & Baskerville, 2011; Hendricks et al., 2008). Such instances of fraud and corruption, though isolated, nevertheless affect the wider reputation of NGOs. For example, after NGOs, such as the Holy Land Foundation for Relief and Development and Benevolence International Foundation, were linked to financing 9/11, Islamic NGOs faced greater scrutiny of their financial accounts and had difficulties raising funds (FBI, 2003; Othman & Ameer, 2012). In such circumstances, risk management has been presented as a way of detecting fraud and corruption by identifying risks associated with staff sourcing, financial accounting, and reputation (Othman & Ameer, 2012). However, discussions of risk in the NGO sector extend beyond corruption and fraud. For NGOs, there are different faces of risk management which include both financial and social dimensions.

Risk management in the context of NGOs is driven and framed by their social mission. For example, NGOs focused on emergency relief enrol diverse government, institutional, and community stakeholders into social initiatives by presenting scientific evidence supporting the benefits of 'risk preparedness' and 'risk mitigation' (Christoplos et al., 2001). In addition, discussions around risks can be used specifically to engage vulnerable or excluded actors (Izumi & Shaw, 2012). The United Nations (UN) and Red Cross, for instance, promote a community-based disaster risk-reduction approach which supports community resilience, and involves establishing risk committees in communities, artisan training courses for safe rebuilding, and local disaster drills (Kafle & Murshed, 2006).

Definitions and discussions of risk also inform the content of institution-wide and individual training, especially for NGOs operating in conflict zones (Merkelbachm & Daudin, 2011). In this vein, there are efforts to standardize and centralize training in security risks through international agencies. For instance, the UN introduced training principles entitled 'Minimum Operational Security Standards' which were applicable to all UN stations in 2002. Standards and personnel training programmes presented the risks which are inherent in field environments and directed attention to building up personnel risk resilience by providing an 'interpretative framework and guide to action within the mind of the aid worker' (Duffield, 2011: 461). In addition to standards around risk security, though not specific to NGOs, general guidance on strategic-, rather than event-focused-, risk management has been provided by ISO 31000 on risk management (Merkelbachm & Daudin, 2011). These

shifts from event-specific actions towards the development of sectoral standards is consistent with the widespread emergence of generic decision-making
frameworks and guidelines seeking to standardize and routinize the criteria
and procedures used to manage risk (Chapter 1, this volume).

The way in which standards and frameworks present risk shapes how
clients and beneficiaries can be identified. For instance, the social protection
unit of the World Bank introduced social risk management (SRM) for analysing 'income risk' of the poor. Factors such as household consumption,
access to services, and market shocks were framed as factors contributing to
levels of 'riskiness' around poverty. To manage income risks, three strategies
were proposed: prevention (reducing the occurrence of the risk), mitigation
(modifying risks), and coping (relieving impact) (Holzmann & Jorgensen,
1999). Parallel to SRM, social workers advocated that factors such as personal
experiences, neighbourhoods, and socio-demographic characteristics (i.e. race,
class, age, etc.) determined the probability of risks faced by potential clients
(Fraser et al., 1999). As with SRM, these attributes serve as a springboard for
making sense of risks and seek to recast the qualities of communities as risks
faced by the poor, clients, and beneficiaries. These practices are consistent
with the expansion of risk management into new domains of social life
(Power, 2004).

As part of conversations around risks and the field of risk management,
financial and strategic threats are also discussed. For example, staff traits have
been used to predict the likelihood of fraud within NGOs, where staff characteristics such as age and gender, and the set-up of control mechanisms,
signal organizational risk exposure (Holtfreter, 2008). Aside from the detection of financial issues, risk management is also associated with NGO financial
sustainability. For instance, revenue streams reliant on single sources, such as
the government, pose 'funding risks' (Tyminski, 1998). Similarly, the make-up
of financial accounts—adequate equity and reserves, revenue concentration,
low administration costs and low operating margins—indicate the risk
of NGO financial vulnerability (Tuckman & Chang, 1991). According to
Wilson-Grau (2003), risks may be 'positive' opportunities for strategic thinking, and uncertainty around risks are a source of innovation. Furthermore, by
linking strategic thinking to risk management there is an improvement in: an
NGO's exchange of information; ability to act; potential for delegation; and
use of judgement (Wilson-Grau, 2004).

Even with such wide-ranging discussions about risks facing NGOs, little is
understood about how organization goals are translated into regular routines
through risk management (Gallagher & Radcliffe, 2002). This chapter will
provide insights into how the introduction of templates and the formulation of
indicators around risks directs daily risk management. This link is important
because templates and indicators can represent the translation of ideas about
risk into daily practice. The chapter will also examine how, on the one hand

the formalization of risk management through templates and indicators can serve to facilitate risk assessments, discussion, and analysis. On the other hand, there is a danger that such formalization and codification over time can take priority over the provision of advice and decision-making support to operational staff.

METHOD AND CONTEXT: VOLUNTARY SERVICE OVERSEAS IN SRI LANKA

The data for this chapter are drawn from a larger field study of Voluntary Service Overseas (VSO) (see Chenhall, Hall, & Smith, 2013, 2015; Hall, 2015), a UK-based non-governmental international development organization that works by (mainly) linking volunteers with partner organizations in developing countries. VSO was founded in 1958 in the UK in order to send school-leavers to teach English in Commonwealth countries that were considered underdeveloped (Bird, 1998). Initially, volunteers were 18-year-old high school graduates, but now comprise mainly 30-year-old-plus experienced professionals. Volunteers typically work according to a capacity-building approach, being involved in a wide range of initiatives such as job training, organizational development, and advocacy. Each year VSO recruits approximately 1,500 volunteers to take up placements in one of the over forty developing countries in which they now operate. Data were collected from interviews, meetings, and participant observation, along with internal and publicly available documents, during the period 2008–13 in Sri Lanka.

VSO has been working in Sri Lanka for over three decades. In Sri Lanka, VSO operations and staff had to be sensitized to the political and social turmoil of the country's civil conflict. Since 1983, the Tamil Tigers of Eelam (LTTE) fought for a separate Tamil homeland, an ambition which directly confronted government rule in the north and east of Sri Lanka. For NGOs in Sri Lanka, direct commentary or engagement with separatist elements and communities were problematic for the government (Dibbert, 2014). In addition, concerns over staff and volunteer safety in conflict zones were foremost. For example, known as the 'Muttur Massacre', in 2006 seventeen staff from Action Contre la Faim, a French NGO, were shot in the war-torn city of Muttur, Sri Lanka (Apps, 2008). This incident is consistent with the perception that violence against NGO staff and volunteers has increased, especially in conflict zones (Fast, 2007). As such, part of understanding risks faced by staff and volunteers is examining operations and field activity within a country's political context.

VSO's primary mode of operation, involving international volunteers working in a variety of developing country contexts, generated many risks related to personal security and operational activities. For example, there were many security risks for volunteers associated with living in a foreign country, sometimes in conflict or heightened security situations. A wide variety of operational risks were also evident, ranging from political unrest, natural disasters, poor governmental relations, inability to access areas of a country, and infrastructure issues such as reliable electricity and internet access. Although staff and volunteers had always undertaken actions to 'manage' such risks during the course of their daily work, VSO had recently put in place specific mechanisms to define, identify, and document risks. This move towards the formalization of risk management at VSO reflects broader efforts to codify risk management in NGOs (e.g. ACCA, 2014) as well as in the public and for-profit sectors (see Chapters 1 and 2, this volume). For instance, a handbook—*VSO Sri Lanka Safety & Security Policy*—the first of its kind at VSO, was issued in 2008. This handbook was part of partner, staff, and volunteer inductions to 'ensure that there is a common understanding of security risk management' (see Table 3.1).

Table 3.1. Key risk processes from the *VSO Sri Lanka Safety & Security Policy Handbook*

Process	Example of Action
Defining security and risk concepts	Included definitions of security, risk, and security risk management. For example, security risk management 'concerns management and individual staff/volunteer action, including but not limited to the establishment of security policies and procedures, designed to reduce the risks to VSO, its staff and volunteers, programmes and partners, from security threats in the operating environment'.
Providing examples of possible risks to staff/ volunteers which are consistent with definitions of risks in the handbooks	List of possible threats linked to staff/ volunteer vulnerability and exposure to risks, such as arrest, abduction, landmines. grenade attacks, sexual violence, etc.
Identifying and reducing risks to ensure the personal safety of staff/volunteers	Outline of four 'Core Security Values' 1. Primacy of life and personal well-being 2. Right to say no 3. Need to share information 4. Responsibility for yourself and for others
Linking values/expectations around risk to context specific procedures	Four levels of documentation: VSO's Global Security Policy followed by a VSO Security Manual, a Country Security Plan and Location Specific Security Plans
Making staff/volunteer responsible for risks	An established administrative structure responsible for risk (Country Director, Risk Team, and field-based Security Focal Points) and personal responsibilities of staff/ volunteers to be aware/report on risks noted.

These changes at VSO motivated us to examine how the daily work of staff and volunteers would be affected by the introduction of more formal methods for assessing and recording risks, such as policies, templates, and indicators. In particular, we focus on two practices that were introduced to formalize risk management. The first concerns the formalization of day-to-day risk management work in templates and other documents used by volunteers and VSO staff, particularly as part of assessing security and operational risks in developing country operations. The second relates to attempts to develop performance indicators related to risk and security as part of a wider effort at VSO to measure the quality of performance in country programmes.

MANAGING RISKS WITH TEMPLATES

Historically, risk management had been the province of staff working in the country programme office, with little or no input or formal requirements from head office in London. This began to change around 2005, when VSO issued a lengthy (48-page) security policy addressing 'issues involved in managing the security of volunteers and VSO staff in country'. Part of this policy involved the provision of a variety of templates to be used as part of risk assessment and management. As we detail below, over time these templates became more prevalent, being used to make risk assessments for volunteer placements and to assess the risk of the country programme office as a whole.

Volunteers had always been responsible for their own personal security, and this was still reinforced by the security policy: 'the primary manager of a volunteer's everyday health safety and security management is...the volunteer'. Notwithstanding this, volunteers were increasingly encouraged to document their risk assessments in the form of an individual risk template each volunteer would complete, typically after two months of being in their placement.

Figure 3.1 reproduces the template that volunteers would complete for their risk assessment. For example, under the 'Threat & initial risk assessment' column, a female volunteer working in Sri Lanka as a mental health professional, identified 'harassment', such as 'verbal and non-verbal abuse' and 'inappropriate sexual behaviour', as a threat and assigned an initial assessment of 'high risk'. She then documented a variety of mitigation procedures, such as 'ignoring verbal comments' and sitting 'next to a female or family when using public transport'. As a result, she concluded that the final risk assessment of harassment was as a 'medium risk'.

Threat & initial risk assessment	Threat Assessment	Risk	Detail	Mitigation procedures / risk management	Final risk assessment / residual risk

Figure 3.1. Risk plan and mitigation template

Documenting risks in the template could help volunteers to think about risks in a structured way, particularly in relation to the identification of risks, their potential significance, and what mitigating procedures might be available. But there appeared to be little follow-up activity after the template had been completed, as it was typically sent to the relevant programme manager for filing. In particular, the same female volunteer, when discussing the risk template, commented how it was a 'lot of paperwork and a lot of reporting' and that she had 'written a lot' and 'it takes a lot of time'. In this way, the template seems to have been directed at the recording and reporting of risks and played little role in facilitating talk about risks between the volunteer and the programme manager. This resonates with the way in which excessive emphasis on risk formats can potentially limit and constrain 'risk talk' (see Chapter 12, this volume).

A similar procedure was increasingly being employed to assess and document risks facing the country programme as a whole. Under the purview of the country director, programme offices would first use a risk matrix (see Figure 3.2) to identify risks and make an assessment of their 'likelihood' and 'impact' along a scale of low, medium, and high, producing a 3x3 risk matrix. For example, for the VSO Sri Lanka programme office, three risks were identified as both high impact and high likelihood: the potential for the government to 'refuse visas to international volunteers/ staff', concerns about 'significant restrictions on access to VSO partners and field operations' due to the security situation in Sri Lanka (which at the time of this research was nearing the end of the civil war), and concerns over 'intermittent interruption to communications such as telephone and internet in Colombo or at a national level'. Risks identified as both high in likelihood and impact were then subject to further attention using the Figure 3.1 template. For example, Figure 3.3 shows the further assessment that was made of the risk of refusal of visas to international volunteers/staff and potential mitigation strategies. This led to the 'Final risk assessment/

IMPACT	HIGH			
	MEDUIM			
	LOW			
		LOW	MEDIUM	HIGH
			LIKELIHOOD	

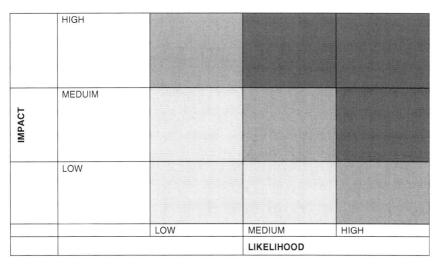

Figure 3.2. Risk assessment matrix

Threat & initial risk assessment	**Threat assessment**	**Risk**	**Detail**	**Mitigation procedures / risk management**	**Final risk assessment/ residual risk**
Refusal of visas to international volunteers and staff **High risk**	Government refuses visa approval for international volunteers & staff	The risk is that we would no longer be able to work through international volunteers in Sri Lanka and would need to either close the programme or rely on alternative interventions	GoSL [Government of Sri Lanka] have advised VSO that continued approval of visas is dependent on VSO exploring the recruitment and placement of Sri Lankan nationals in overseas programmes.	VSO has developed close institutional and personal relationships with the relevant Department in GoSL (NGO Secretariat) that should allow for greater flexibility/negotiation.... but the PO [Programme Office] needs greater corporate support in addressing this threat.	**Medium to high risk**

Figure 3.3. Illustration of risk plan and mitigation document from Sri Lankan programme office

residual risk' being lowered from its initial rating of high to a 'medium to high risk'.

As was the case with the individual risk assessments, the use of the templates for the country programme were considered useful in helping staff and volunteers to think about the variety of risks they faced and to identify steps towards potential mitigation. But they also imposed considerable work on the programme office staff in particular, usually in the form of making risk assessments and writing it up according to the template. For example, the Sri Lankan office templates totalled over twenty pages of text and analysis. In addition, the Sri Lankan country director also identified two further concerns with completing and using the template as the main approach to risk management.

The first concern related to getting 'information about risks'. He noted it was important to get 'multi-source information' and 'triangulation' of information. To help obtain information on risks the country director participated in a fortnightly security meeting with security officers of other international NGOs working in Sri Lanka. Although this meeting was helpful in providing a forum to discuss risks with NGO colleagues, he felt that security issues were particularly difficult for him to assess, as he personally did not have a background in security, unlike other members of the security meeting whom he stated were typically 'ex-army or security people'. Further, as the programme office staff numbered around twelve people, there was no single person dedicated to security issues, with responsibility therefore falling on the country director himself. This situation suggests that the template does prompt some discussion about risks between the country director and NGO colleagues. However, it is rather brief and limited, owing to a lack of expertise in security issues, and a lack of both time and other staff involved in risk management issues who could potentially act as a sounding board for the country director to discuss and talk about risk assessments.

The second concern related to the primary focus on documenting risks rather than dialogue and discussion. The country director commented how having discussions with somebody about his own security and operational risk decisions was very important in order to validate his assessments and 'spread responsibility for decision-making'. In this case, documenting risks in the template (e.g. see Figure 3.3) could have provided a setting whereby staff could participate in discussions regarding risk assessments and decisions facing the country programme. But the country director further commented that the global security adviser, a position recently created at VSO's head office in London, was typically not available to have these more substantive discussions about risk issues that arose when completing the template, and as such there was a tendency for such roles to 'enforce systems rather than provide support'. In addition, as noted above, staff in the country office did not have the time or expertise to devote to risk discussions. Consistent with this view, the programme office documented in their risk matrix that dealing with the identified threat from visa issues required 'greater corporate [head office] support in addressing this threat'. Yet, at least during the period of this research, such support was not forthcoming. We now turn to examine further efforts to formalize risk management in the form of performance indicators.

DEVELOPING PERFORMANCE INDICATORS TO ASSESS RISK

In 2007 VSO began to develop a performance measurement tool to measure the performance of each of its country programmes on an annual basis. This tool, which came to be known as the Quality Framework, included a common set of standardized indicators attempting to measure performance across a variety of 'elements' thought to make up a quality programme office at VSO, such as volunteer engagement, financial management, funding, and innovative programming (see Chenhall et al., 2013 for further details). Risk was also considered an important aspect of quality, with Element 12 of the Quality Framework consisting of 'Legal and policy compliance and risk management'. As shown in Figure 3.4, two indicators were developed within this element to address risk management.

The first indicator (12.1) concerned whether the programme office had any outstanding audit actions related to legal compliance from the most recent internal audit. Unlike other indicators comprising the Quality Framework, indicator 12.1 was only scored as either a 4, in the case of zero outstanding audit actions, or as a 1, where the programme office had at least one out-standing audit action. The second indicator (12.2) was designed to assess progress in developing and implementing a security and risk management plan by the programme office. This indicator addressed progress in developing a risk management plan, as well as assessing whether the programme office had passed its latest security test.

Despite the variety of security and operational risks facing programme offices (as outlined above), the two indicators seem to only address aspects of risk management involving the production of formalized procedures. This is perhaps not surprising as they are relatively easy to measure, relating to highly visible products of risk management, such as internal audit reports and risk plans, which can be checked and compared across different country programmes. In contrast, there are no indicators to assess how well country programmes made actual decisions about risk issues or events, or the quality of its risk management systems—perhaps the most

Riskwork

Key performance indicators	Performance range guide		Possible means of verification	PO KPI result & supporting info
12.1 *Number of outstanding category A and B internal audit actions for PO action relating to legal compliance*	High 4	0 outstanding action	Internal audit report in the 'Summary of Findings' section	1 4
	3	It is only possible to score 4 or 1!		
	2			
	1	>1 outstanding action		
	Room for development			
12.2 *Security Risk management plans signed off and implemented and tested according to country's main security risks (e.g. avian flu, security, natural disasters etc)*	High 4	A clear security management plan is in place and updated more than annually, risk assessments are carried out at least annually for each risk environment in the country and the last annual security plan was passed	Risk management plans	1 2 3 4
	3	All components of a security risk management plan are present and implemented and the last security test was passed		
	2	Components of a Security risk management plan are in place and implemented, but failed the last test		
	1 **Room for development**	Security risk management plan in development		

Figure 3.4. Indicators related to risk management in VSO's Quality Framework

critical work of all. But these risk management activities are typically more difficult to measure and capture in management tools, particularly as they relate to a stream of ongoing actions that do not produce visible products that can be checked and compared.

The formalization of risk performance in the indicators in element 12 was, to some extent, helpful for programme offices. For example, a programme office scoring 1 on each risk indicator in its 2009 Quality Framework report reflected on what had gone wrong in the prior year and spelled out what action would be taken to improve matters, such as prioritizing the development of the security risk management plan and listing specific actions to be undertaken to address poor financial management. The use of the indicators and the formalization of action plans in the Quality Framework helped programme office staff to think about and discuss current performance in this area, and to develop actions plans for the future in order to improve performance. Importantly, unlike the use of the risk templates, the Quality Framework process provided explicit space and support for programme staff to discuss scores and action plans (including those related to risk management), providing a situation where documentation was (at least to some extent) able to facilitate talk about risks.

But generating the scores for the indicators was in some ways problematic, particularly in relation to the role to be played by local or contextual information in determining the appropriate score for the indicators. As shown in Figure 3.4, indicator 12.1 refers to the presence of category A and B internal audit actions still outstanding from the most recent internal audit. A problem arose, however, due to the timing of internal audits, which were typically conducted every three years. As such, it was possible that the situation 'on the ground' had changed substantively since the last audit but was yet to be officially acknowledged. This was problematic for scoring indicator 12.1 in situations where a programme office had dealt with all of the issues from the last internal audit, but were aware their situation had since changed. Should they comply with the wording of the indicator and record a score of 4, or should they put strict definitions aside and acknowledge the presence of (undocumented) concerns with a score of 1?

This issue arose in a meeting of regional directors in May 2009, where a regional director noted how, for one country he supervised, they had provisionally assigned a score of 1 to indicator 12.1, even though they had no actions outstanding from the last internal audit. This was because he, and the staff in that country, were aware of issues that had arisen that would now be viewed as category A and B risks if an internal audit were to take place. The regional director said he and his team knew there were concerns (for example, a lack of segregation of duties) and wanted to note the issues now in the Quality Framework 'rather than having an audit to tell us that'. He then asked the other regional directors at the meeting: 'if I know that there are A and B risks without having an audit to show it, should I score them appropriately? I shouldn't say we don't have an audit so I can't score it?' The other regional directors agreed it is an issue worth thinking about but concluded it was too late to include in that year's Quality Framework scoring as most countries had already scored indicator 12.1 according to the internal audit results, rather than any other relevant information.

Another issue concerned interpretation of the scores for the risk indicators, particularly in relation to longitudinal comparisons. For example, in 2009 it was reported that the 'overall performance on element 12 declined, with 17 countries reporting the same score as 2008, 9 reduced and 4 increased'. On the surface, this appears to represent a lower standard of risk management performance compared to the prior year. However, in interpreting these scores, the global security adviser commented 'it is possible that from the security perspective, the slight downward trend is not evidence of deterioration in performance, but a result of better awareness of corporate standards in security management, enabling a more precise score'. He suggested that as programme offices became more aware of risk and security issues and what good practice looks like, this had resulted, in effect, in the use of a tougher standard for determining scores and hence performance on the indicator overall appears to have declined.

This example indicates an important issue regarding the interpretation of risk indicators, particularly regarding who is involved in this process and their expertise. As shown in the example, very different conclusions can be drawn from risk indicators depending on the level of expertise and knowledge of the interpreter. For example, the global security adviser, who had intimate knowledge of security issues, drew the conclusion that risk performance had not deteriorated, even though the raw scores seemed to suggest this. In contrast, for people who may not be familiar with the background conditions influencing the risk indicator scores, such as VSO senior managers not versed in the details, it would be relatively easy (and understandable) to take the scores at face value and form the view that risk performance had indeed deteriorated in 2009. This indicates that the issue of who interprets risk indicators is a very important one, and suggests, in the first instance, that involving staff who have expertise in the underlying substantive issue (such as security in this case) is likely to be important for drawing appropriate conclusions and implications from risk indicators. It also highlights the potential risks involved in attempting to interpret risk indicators free of, or without, adequate reference to the contexts in which those indicator scores were produced.

TENSIONS OVER THE FORMALIZATION OF RISK MANAGEMENT

Beyond the completion of templates and the scoring of risk indicators, a more general concern related to a tension about what aspects of risk management were given attention by head office staff at VSO. Day-to-day in-country security and risk management was primarily the responsibility of each programme office, and they felt more support and assistance in this area from head office was required. For example, several programme offices noted in their Quality Framework report that support received from head office staff, particular the global security adviser, had been very welcome. One country noted 'it is good to know that VSO has finally recruited a security person that can support and provide advice to programme offices on security-related issues', and another country stated that the 'The visit in May 2008 by VSO's Security Management Advisor has helped [the programme office] to withdraw from [an area of the country with security problems] which later proved to be a correct decision.'

However, although there were some positive reports, many countries noted a general lack of feedback and support in relation to day-to-day risk management activities. Programme offices expressed frustration, for example, about the length of time they needed to wait for feedback and support from head office staff. Programme offices noted 'we haven't yet received any feedback from [head office] on the security test so we cannot say whether or not we have met the expectations' and 'We are yet to receive feedback on our handling of the emergency procedures testing carried out at the start of March. This might be helpful for our learning.' This lack of feedback was compounded by the fact that

programme offices were often of the view that they spent a lot of time performing tasks necessary to comply with directives or policies from head office, such
as carrying out required security tests, developing risk management plans, and
scoring the indicators in the Quality Framework. This is despite the security policy
issued by VSO head office warning that: 'procedures and guidelines do not replace
the need for good judgement, constant monitoring and analysis of the situation'.
In this way, staff tended to view the formally mandated risk management
requirements as controlling rather than supporting their day-to-day riskwork,
with the focus on documenting risks and complying with mandated procedures
'crowding-out' opportunities for discussion and the provision of direct advice and
support (see Frey and Jegen, 2001).

Not surprisingly, programme offices also wanted more resources and capacity to help them deal with risk and security issues. For example, the Malawi
programme office noted in its Quality Framework report that 'the audit
recommendations were so many that they were overwhelming for many
staff, it would be an idea that if a programme office has such a lot to sort
out that extra roving capacity is given to work on it'. Similarly, the Cambodia
programme office noted 'the biggest daily risk in our programme is associated
with riding motorbikes [and] still seems to have little attention despite the
survey and several e-mail exchanges about helmets etc. It would be great to see
more support in this area from [head office].' In both cases the requested
support from the programme offices was not forthcoming. Although resourcing is always an issue for NGOs, typically short on funds, this lack of support
at least in part appears to stem from the tension, noted earlier, over what
aspects of risk management were being given priority. This was neatly captured in the comment from the Sri Lankan programme office:

> The appointment of a Global Security Advisor has been a welcome source of
> support for [programme offices] working in insecure environments…there is an
> emerging sense that the role is becoming more focussed on enforcing policy and
> reporting, rather than providing advice, support and a 'sounding board' for those
> involved in managing security.

This statement suggests that the limited resources available to support and
assist programme office staff in risk management were increasingly perceived
as being devoted to the production of formal plans and procedures rather than
to the provision of much needed day-to-day advice and support.

DISCUSSION

In this chapter we have examined the risk management efforts of an NGO,
focusing in particular on the production and use of risk matrices, templates,

and indicators as part of attempts to bring more formalization to risk management practices. The findings reveal that in some instances formalization in the form of templates and indicators is seen to help risk management, primarily by prompting staff to think about risk assessments and mitigation practices and by providing a structured process in which this can take place. In addition, the manner in which staff act within designated frameworks suggests that the visual aspects and boundaries set in templates play a role in making sense of the possibilities for riskwork. In this case, templates can construct 'risk objects' to be acted upon within VSO and its wider network (see Jordan et al., 2013). For example, as noted earlier, the separation of 'Threats & initial risk assessment' from the mitigation procedures column in a volunteer risk assessment template provided a structured guide for a volunteer to articulate 'harassment' as a risk. The volunteer's identification of harassment within one column served as a prompt for thinking through and filling in the remainder of the table. In this example, the layout and order of the template shaped the volunteer's perception and thought process around risk. The potential of visual templates to affect actors and action is consistent with Jordan et al.'s (2013) analysis of risk maps. It also resonates with the way the visual dynamic of matrices can help actors to conceptualize risks in a more formal way (Pollock & D'Adderio, 2012).

The findings also highlight, however, how risk management can become focused on its own codification in plans and policies (such as templates and indicators) rather than on providing (much desired) advice and decision-making support to front-line staff. An overarching theme emerging from the analysis was the potential for the formalization of risk management to 'crowd out' other types of risk management activities and other forms of risk knowledge, particularly where resource and time constraints force (at least some) prioritization of how much time and effort can be devoted to formal versus informal risk management activities. This suggests that efforts to document and record risks can affect how different types of riskwork are prioritized in organizations. In this way, risk management activities can become primarily focused on standardized procedures that are codified and thus more easily auditable in order to demonstrate 'sound' risk management (Huber & Scheytt, 2013; Power, 2007: ch. 6) but may leave little room for the actual discussion and management of risks themselves (Power, 2009).

The use of risk templates could have provided opportunities for discussions and support, but it was not accompanied by the provision of adequate time and resources to enable the risk discussions that could have taken place during the completion of the template. This indicates that a primary focus on documenting risks (in this case via the template), without accompanying efforts to formalize the necessary resources, time, and space, will tend to 'crowd in' the completion of documentation as the prime product of risk management, and 'crowd out' opportunities for such documentation, such as the template, to facilitate the desired but all too infrequent discussions and dialogue about risks (see Frey & Jegen, 2001). That is, in an environment where staff time is limited (or at least somewhat restricted), formalizing risk management can lead front-line staff to (deliberately or unwittingly) prioritize the production of policies, templates, matrices, and other documents ahead of actual risk management activities. This is reinforced where head office support for risk management is increasingly directed towards compliance with, and delivery of, risk management documents as opposed to support for day-to-day risk management activities. It suggests, somewhat paradoxically, that the provision of extra resourcing, in the form of centralized risk management experts (such as the global security adviser), could actually hinder risk management efforts where those resources are primarily devoted to the production of, and ensuring compliance with, risk management plans and policies.

The formalization of risk management also has the potential to crowd out other forms of risk management knowledge. The concerns over how to score indicator 12.1 illustrate how the formalization of risk performance in a performance indicator generates questions over, and even uncertainty about, the status of other pertinent risk information not necessarily captured by or reflected in the formal risk management system. That is, significant events or activities occurring since the last internal audit were clearly relevant pieces of information to inform risk assessments, but the necessity of specifying the parameters of the risk indicators (in this case, the presence of category A and B actions) means that there are, at the very least, questions about whether and how such information should be disclosed, as opposed to a presumption of its inclusion in risk discussions. Perhaps even more striking in this case, such information was not captured as part of the risk performance in the Quality Framework and so was not even available for consideration of overall risk and security assessments. This suggests there is a danger that the necessity to codify and formalize information about risks can lead to a situation where such information is the only (or most important) knowledge that counts. Again somewhat paradoxically, codifying and formalizing risk management has the potential to hinder risk management efforts by limiting opportunities for (and even delegitimizing) other types of risk management knowledge. This resonates with the way in which more formal and standardized approaches to risk management can direct organizations to focus on conformance and the avoidance of blame, potentially leading to the ignorance of (often highly salient) knowledge not fitting neatly into these predefined formats (see Huber & Scheytt, 2013; Power, 2007).

On a practical level, the chapter suggests the need for risk practitioners to place more explicit focus on the activities and actions accompanying risk documentation processes. It invites an awareness of how documenting and recording risks can affect how different types of risk management work are prioritized, particularly where formal risk management processes can intrude upon (rather than facilitate) day-to-day activities. The following questions can help to prompt reflection on how to avoid a singular focus in risk management on the production and completion of templates and indicators: when completing risk templates, reports, and indicators, is sufficient time and space dedicated towards discussion of risks amongst staff? Are adequate financial and other resources available to facilitate discussion and feedback? Are risk specialists available to assist front-line staff with queries and concerns raised by the formal risk documentation process? What activity is accorded higher priority: the provision of ongoing advice and support to facilitate risk discussions, or the production and completion of risk documentation?

This chapter provided insight on how VSO sought to measure risk and align expectations and practices around riskwork from their head office to the field. To communicate definitions and frameworks for understanding risk, matrices, templates, and indicators played a vital role. For staff, filling in indicators, matrices, and templates as well as the emphasis on formal frameworks in discussions solicited reflections around risk, yet also misplaced other forms of informal communication. More pointedly, such interplay between formal and informal dimensions noted in this chapter raises questions about how 'risk' as a concept and object in an NGO gains visibility and actionability for management and employees.

REFERENCES

ACCA (2014). Charities SORP 2015. <http://www.accaglobal.com/ubcs/en/discover/cpd-articles/corporate-reporting/charities-sorp15.html> (accessed 23 January 2015).

Apps, P. (2008). Report Details Sri Lanka Aid Massacre, Blames Forces. <http://www.reuters.com/article/2008/04/01/idUSL31705107._CH_.2400> (accessed 14 October 2014).

BBC (2009). Child Charity Worker Admits Rape. London. <http://news.bbc.co.uk/1/hi/england/london/8119511.stm> (accessed 5 May 2014).

Bird, D. (1998). *Never the Same Again: A History of VSO.* Cambridge: Lutterworth Press.

Chenhall, R., Hall, M., & Smith, D. (2013). Performance Measurement, Modes of Evaluation and the Development of Compromising Accounts. *Accounting, Organizations and Society*, 38, 268–87.

Chenhall, R., Hall, M., & Smith, D. (2015). The Expressive Role of Performance Measurement Systems: A Field Study of a Mental Health Development Project. *Accounting, Organizations and Society*, in press.

Christoplos, I., Mitchell, J., & Liljelund, A. (2001). Re-framing Risk: The Changing Context of Disaster Mitigation and Preparedness. *Disasters*, 25(3), 185–98.

Cordery, C. & Baskerville, R. (2011). Charity Transgressions, Trust and Accountability. *Voluntas*, 12, 197–213.

Dibbert, T. (2014). Sri Lanka's NGO Clampdown. <http://foreignpolicy.com/2014/07/25/sri-lankas-ngo-clampdown> (accessed 16 October 2014).

Duffield, M. (2011). Risk-Management and the Fortified Aid Compound: Everyday Life in Post-Interventionary Society. *Journal of Intervention and Statebuilding*, 5, 37–41.

Fast, L. (2007). Characteristics, Context and Risk: NGO Insecurity in Conflict Zones. *Disasters*, 31(2), 130–54.

Federal Bureau of Investigation (2003). Testimony of John S. Pistole, Counterterrorism Division, Terrorism Financing: Origination, Organization, and Prevention. 31 July 2003. <http://www.fbi.gov/news/testimony/terrorism-financing-origination-organization-and-prevention> (accessed 13 April 2014).

Fraser, M., Richman, J., & Galinsky, M. (1999). Risk, Protection, and Resilience: Toward a Conceptual Framework for Social Work Practice. *Social Work Research*, 131–43.

Frey, B. & Jegen, R. (2001). Motivation Crowding Theory. *Journal of Economic Surveys*, 15(5), 589–611.

Gallagher, M. & Radcliffe, V. (2002). Internal Controls in Nonprofit Organizations: The Case of the American Cancer Society, Ohio Division. *Nonprofit Management and Leadership*, 313–25.

Hall, M. (2015). Crafting Compromises in a Strategising Process: A Case Study of an International Development Organisation. *Financial Accountability and Management*: forthcoming.

Hendricks, M., Plantz, M. C., & Pritchard, K. J. (2008). Measuring Outcomes of United Way-Funded Programs: Expectations and Reality. *New Directions for Evaluation*, 119, 13–35.

Holtfreter, K. (2008). Determinants of Fraud Loss in Nonprofit Organisations. *Nonprofit Management & Leadership*, 45–63.

Holzmann, R. & Jorgensen, S. (1999). Social Protection as Social Risk Management: Conceptual Underpinnings for the Social Protection Sector Strategy Paper. *Journal of International Development*, 1, 1005–27.

Huber, C. & Scheytt, T. (2013). The Dispotif of Risk Management: Reconstructing Risk Management after the Financial Crisis. *Management Accounting Research*, 24, 88–99.

Izumi, T. & Shaw, R. (2012). Role of NGOs in Community-Based Disaster Risk Reduction. In R. Shaw (Ed.), *Community-Based Disaster Risk Reduction* (ch. 3). Bingley, UK: Emerald Group Publishing.

Jordan, S., Jørgensen, L., & Mitterhofer, H. (2013). Performing Risk and the Project: Risk Maps as Mediating Instruments. *Management Accounting Research*, 24(2), 156–74.

Kafle, S. K. & Murshed, Z. (2006). *Community-Based Disaster Risk Management for Local Authorities*. <http://www.unisdr.org/files/3366_3366CBDRMShesh.pdf> (accessed March 2016).

Merkelbachm, M. & Daudin, P. (2011). From Security Management to Risk Management: Critical Reflections on Aid Agency. European Interagency Security Forum. <http://www.eisf.eu/resources/item/?d=4834> (accessed 15 April 2014).

Othman, R. & Ameer, R. (2012). Institutionalization of Risk Management Framework in Islamic NGOs for Suppressing Terrorism Financing: Exploratory Research. *Journal of Money Laundering Control*, 17(1), 96–109.

Pollock, N. & D'Adderio, L. (2012). Give Me a Two-by-Two Matrix and I Will Create the Market: Rankings, Graphic Visualisations and Sociomateriality. *Accounting, Organisations and Society*, 37(8), 565–86.

Power, M. (2004). *The Risk Management of Everything: Rethinking the Politics of Uncertainty*. London: Demos.

Power, M. (2007). *Organized Uncertainty: Designing a World of Risk Management*. Oxford: Oxford University Press.

Power, M. (2009). The Risk Management of Nothing. *Accounting, Organizations and Society*, 34, 849–55.

Tuckman, H. & Chang, C. (1991). A Methodology for Measuring the Financial Vulnerability of Charitable Nonprofit Organisations. *Nonprofit and Voluntary Sector Quarterly*, 20(4), 445–60.

Tyminski, R. (1998). Reducing Funding Risk and Implementing a Fundraising Plan: A Case Study. *Nonprofit Management & Leadership*, 8(3), 275–85.

Wilson-Grau, R. (2003). The Risk Approach to Strategic Management in Development NGOs. *Development in Practice*, 13(5), 246–9.

Wilson-Grau, R. (2004). Strategic Risk Management for Development NGOs: The Case of a Grant-maker. *Journal of Diplomacy and International Relations*, 5(2), 125–35.

4

The Work of Risk Oversight

Maria Zhivitskaya and Michael Power

> The corporate governance of large banks was characterised by the
> creation of Potemkin villages to give the appearance of effective control
> and oversight, without the reality ... both the financial crisis and conduct
> failures have exposed very serious flaws in the system of board oversight
> of bank executives and senior management.
>
> (UK Parliament, 2013: 335)

The global financial crisis which began in 2008 had many immediate causes
but one theme is recurrent in diagnostic discourses: the failure of governance
and culture in general, and risk oversight in particular. As Anderson et al.
(2014: 19) put it, 'firms that were previously lionized as corporate exemplars,
such as Citibank, Deutsche Bank, Royal Bank of Scotland and UBS, revealed
widespread weaknesses in how boards undertook the oversight of risk in their
enterprises'. These inadequacies of risk oversight were in turn traced to two
factors, namely (a) the limited time that boards spent focusing on risk, and
(b) the lack of relevant expertise on the part of the board members involved:
'Many boards and senior managements of financial firms neither understood
the characteristics of the new, highly complex financial products they were
dealing with, nor were they aware of the aggregate exposure of their companies'
(de Larosière, 2009: 10).

Accordingly, the work board risk committees in financial services came
under the spotlight and efforts were made to clarify risk oversight as something different from risk management. For example, the consultants Protiviti
define the risk oversight process as 'the means by which the board determines
that the company has in place a robust process for identifying, prioritizing,
sourcing, managing and monitoring its critical risks' (Protiviti, 2013). Risk
management, in contrast, is different. It is 'what management does, which
includes appropriate oversight and monitoring to ensure policies are carried
out and processes are executed in accordance with management's selected

performance goals and risk tolerances' (Protiviti, 2013). Yet despite regulatory pressure to improve risk oversight, the difference between oversight and management is inherently ambiguous and challenging for the actors at the heart of the process, namely the independent or non-executive directors (NEDs) of financial companies.

This chapter addresses the role of NEDs who serve on the risk committees of major financial institutions and seeks to understand how they operationalize the post-crisis emphasis on risk oversight. How do they make sense of this distinctive and peculiar category of riskwork, namely their own work of risk oversight? The data in the chapter are based on extended interviews during 2014 with twelve very senior NEDs of significant financial institutions based in the UK (see Appendices 4.1 and 4.2 at the end of this chapter). Although this is numerically a small number and comprises mainly chairs of risk committees, as high-profile leaders their views are likely to provide representative insights into the work of conducting risk oversight. The next section provides a brief overview of the institutional background and history of NEDs and risk committees. This is followed by four sections based on the interview data and organized according to the four main overlapping themes which emerged: how NEDs on risk committees make sense of their role; how they construct the distinction between management and oversight; how their work is shaped by their relationships with regulators; how they make oversight work through their relationships with management. The chapter concludes with an analysis of these findings in the light of existing studies of NEDs. It concludes that many of the tensions and trade-offs associated with the risk oversight role are only imperfections when compared to an idealized and unrealistic image of what it could be, one which tends to be promoted by regulators and advisers. Rather, we suggest that the role of oversight is in fact *essentially constituted* by these trade-offs which necessitate the creation and balancing of multiple relationships. NEDs are engaged in continuous boundary work (Mikes, 2011), in the sense of operating with and across the fuzzy boundary between oversight and management. Because they constantly work at stabilizing that which is unstable, we argue that the concept of oversight is essentially relational and processual, and not primarily a function of formal structures and static ideals of independence.

THE RISE OF THE NON-EXECUTIVE DIRECTOR

According to Millstein and MacAvoy (1998: 12), 'The evolution of boards from managerial rubber-stamps to active and independent monitors has been in large part the result of efforts to address or avoid serious performance problems associated with managerial entrenchment.' They suggest that since the 1990s US boards have generally become more closely aligned with share-holder interests. Similarly, in the UK, the Cadbury report in 1992 was 'explicitly designed to improve internal control mechanisms, based on the assumption of a relationship between internal control, financial reporting quality and corporate governance' (Spira & Page, 2003: 646). Independent directors are central to these changes in governance philosophy and to the expanded role of board subcommittees for audit, remuneration, and appointments (nomination committees). For the last two decades there has been an increased emphasis in both the regulatory sphere and in academic thinking on directors' independence (Clarke, 2007; Eisenberg, 1999; Lin, 1995). Over time this has led to a growing proportion of independent directors on boards of US public companies 'from approximately twenty percent in 1950 to approximately seventy-five percent in 2005' (Gordon, 2007: 1465). These directors, NEDs in the UK, are by definition outsiders and part-timers facing significant information asymmetries in relation to management, yet with no apparent diminution of regulatory responsibility.

NEDs are agents of a distinctive regulatory style which is 'not to control the corporation with more regulation from the outside, but to encourage the development of a transparent inner space for self-regulatory capacity' (Power, 1999, 2000: 1). In particular, NEDs as members of audit committees and, in the financial sector, risk committees are intended to oversee the quality of internal control and risk management, and thereby contribute to the 'self-governance of the organisation' (Spira & Page, 2003: 655).

These arrangements came under further pressure for change following the financial crisis. In 2009 The Walker review in the UK recommended that banks and other financial institutions (BOFIs) should establish board-level risk committees in addition to audit committees. While many already had such dedicated risk committees at board level, others had tended to subsume risk within the mandate of the audit committee. Walker argued that audit committees were backward-looking while risk committees had to have a forward-looking view of risk: 'the audit committee has clear responsibility for oversight and reporting to the board on the financial accounts and adoption of appropriate accounting policies, internal control, compliance and other related matters... This vital responsibility is essentially, though not exclusively, backward-looking' (Walker, 2009: 92). Notwithstanding the artificiality of this distinction, it motivated close regulatory attention to risk committees and their members.

The precise terms of reference for risk and audit committees vary across firms. By way of an illustrative example, Table 4.1 summarizes the position as disclosed at Morgan Stanley which shows some overlap between the two committees and emphasizes their respective oversight roles.

One of the key divisions of labour between the two committees in this example concerns the oversight of regulatory and economic capital management, stress

Table 4.1. Risk versus audit committee charters at Morgan Stanley (2014)

Risk Committee:[1] Oversight of:	Both	Audit Committee:[2] Oversight of:
Risk Tolerance	Risk Management	Relationship w/Independent Auditor
Capital, Liquidity, Funding	Coordination with Management	Internal Audit Department and Internal Controls
Chief Risk Officer	Coordination with Other Board Committees	Financial Statements, Audit, and Disclosure
		Compliance with Legal and Regulatory Requirements

[1] *Source*: Risk Committee Charter (as amended 13 May 2014) <https://www.morganstanley.com/about/company/governance/pdf/rcchart.pdf?v=20140513> (accessed 5 March 2106).
[2] *Source*: Audit Committee Charter (as amended 31 October 2014) <http://www.morganstanley.com/about/company/governance/auditcc> (accessed 5 March 2106).

testing, and liquidity management. In recent years, recovery and resolution plans (colloquially known as 'living wills') have also become a major area of responsibility. Importantly, some NEDs serve as members on both committees and the terms of reference of the two committees are treated as a rough guide rather than followed in their pure form. As one NED observed 'I've been chair of a risk committee for several years and I don't look at the terms of reference' (Interviewee_02), while another NED amplified that point further by explaining that communication with regulators and others in the field is much more useful than the terms of reference. Furthermore, while audit committees have defined expertise requirements in terms of accounting, and are served by the internal and external auditors, the expertise requirements for risk committees are less clear and there is no equivalent of the internal audit function. For this reason, NEDs on risk committees face different challenges in making sense of their roles than in the case of audit committees.

MAKING SENSE OF AN AMBIGUOUS ROLE

NEDs were very conscious of the difficulties of making forward-looking judgments based primarily on internal information: 'You join the dots between the different bits of information and figure out...a kind of total view of the company' (Interviewee_02). For this reason they often sought to combine internal and external sources of relevant information by attending conferences, reading the financial press, leveraging experience on other boards, as well as having many informal chats with the chief risk officer

(CRO) and her staff. NEDs continually emphasized the importance of face-to-face interaction in fulfilling their role:

> You cannot do it by emails, in my view, you can't do it by emails and quantitative data, you actually have to be out in the business, you have to learn what's going on and you have to build a broad perspective from many different sources, be they regulators, be they investment analysts, be they academics and what is happening in the economy and where the emerging risks are. (Interviewee_06)

Other NEDs put more emphasis on the value of their intrinsic knowledge when evaluating the various complexities of the business:

> Essentially it's a role where you use your instincts and emotional intelligence probably more than you use sort of rational IQ. Because you're always... you know, you have less than perfect information, you're always less well informed than the management. (Interviewee_06)

Both these comments suggest that NEDs work hard to overcome the information asymmetry between themselves and management while accepting its inevitability. Many of the NEDs interviewed in 2014 had also internalized the 'three lines of defence' (TLD) as a conceptualization of governance and oversight in general, and as a way of positioning the risk function for which they have oversight responsibilities:

> Fundamentally I think the Risk Committee has to get comfortable with the CRO and the Risk function and be in accord with what they're doing, agree that that's the right way to run the second line of defence... and provide the challenge to the risk function and the CRO. (Interviewee_05)

Indeed, the justification of the TLD structure and governance structures more generally is to create a separation of powers in which different functions monitor and challenge the assumptions and actions of management, and each other. Yet paradoxically the creation of a risk committee may also lull boards into thinking that they have delegated responsibility for risk:

> I chair the risk committee and, you know... in the main board, there's almost a sense of relief that they don't have to worry about these issues because the chair of the risk committee is worrying about them. And it's very easy to get into that mindset. (Interviewee_05)

Overall, given a mix of information asymmetry, regulatory pressure, and the unintended effects of internal structures, NEDs on UK risk committees in 2014 were feeling their way within an emerging responsibility for risk oversight which contained a number of tensions. Not least among these tensions were those involved in making sense of, and constructing, their relationship with management and, by implication, the difference between management and oversight.

CONSTRUCTING THE DIFFERENCE BETWEEN
MANAGEMENT AND OVERSIGHT

Even though in theory NEDs have no management role, in practice, due to their knowledge and experience, as well as the increasing expectations placed on them by regulators and shareholders, it can be difficult for them to remain entirely separate from the management process. Their role is to oversee management, but the fuzzy borderline in the spectrum between 'oversight' and 'execution' is not always clear, and is affected both by dynamics within the firm and by regulators. As one interviewee explained his struggle:

> The regulators now expect you to be far more closely involved in the business than you were before. So the line itself between accountability and the traditional role of the non-exec on the board and the management has shifted and finding your place in that is very difficult. (Interviewee_12)

And, indeed, when asked about their role, interviewees' answers ranged from absolutely no intervention in managerial jobs to a recognition of having to step in and manage when needed. One NED described her role as 'nose in, fingers out' (Interviewee_02). This basic viewpoint was echoed by another NED:

> One of the biggest challenges is to be challenging, understand the business, understand the people...but then not get involved in the execution. (Interviewee_08)

However, while acknowledging that he had no actual management power, another NED pointed to the importance of influence in discharging the job:

> I have no management role. As a Board Risk Committee you have no management role. You cannot take a decision...everything is governance and oversight. And you use influence and respect I guess and the positional power to get management to do stuff. (Interviewee_06)

Despite the apparent clarity of consulting statements, a clean working distinction between management and oversight was more challenging for NEDs who have been, or are, senior executives themselves. For example, one NED was a CRO in one firm before taking on this role within the risk committee of another, and pointed out the inherent difficulty of transitioning from a high-level management role into a NED oversight role:

> If you step back from being a hands-on manager and you simply just want to step in and, say, be prescriptive, you have to be very careful not to be prescriptive in areas that are management responsibility. You can suggest, you can encourage. (Interviewee_09)

It seems from many of these comments as if oversight is predominantly defined negatively as 'not management' i.e. not taking decisions, not executing. The waters are further muddied when extreme circumstances necessitate the

NEDs to take a more hands-on role. The NED is an overseer who may by default become a manager:

> You would only intervene and manage if there was an absolute crisis and something was going wrong. And what you really have to do if the executive are not managing the organization effectively, you have to decide whether with appropriate advice and coaching and whatever it might take, you can get them to manage the place effectively. If you can't, you have to change them. I mean that's ultimately what you have to do as a non-executive. (Interviewee_08)

Furthermore, even if a NED has successfully defined her oversight role, this may not always be easy to sustain due to other external pressures. It takes a lot of work to remain standing back from management:

> There's a little bit of a drift in financial services for the non-execs almost to be given executive responsibilities. It's almost as though there are times when you're almost...an executive. You can't be an executive, you cannot be an executive. (Interviewee_04)

Another related tension arose as a result of the need for NEDs to balance their role as colleagues with executives in a unitary board structure with their emerging oversight responsibilities. In the United States where boards tend to be mainly composed of independent directors and the CEO, it clearly has, and is easier to maintain, an explicit oversight role distinct from management. This is less the case in the UK where NEDs are equal colleagues of executive members of a board, with shared responsibility for both the strategic decisions and the overall success of the company. Yet NEDs are also a part of the oversight of management—and very explicitly so in the case of regulated firms—not least in evaluating the performance of senior executives. Some interviewees were particularly conscious of the need to balance being critical and being supportive. For example:

> It's very important not to try to second-guess the executive...you have to go there, you're there to operate governance which means challenge and it means sometimes criticism. But it's also about encouragement and development. (Interviewee_05)

To summarize, no 'standard' definition of the NED risk oversight role emerged from the interview data. Rather, the picture is one of seasoned professionals working to balance a number of competing pressures along the borderline between management and a more distant oversight role, between being a colleague and being the ultimate policeman of the executive, and between being enough of a generalist to identify broader risk issues which might be relevant to the company while remaining enough of a specialist to understand the risk profile of the organization with the required depth. This 'impossible job', as one interviewee described it, is compounded by the complexity of the NED relationship to the regulator.

MAKING OVERSIGHT WORK: NEDs AND REGULATORS

MZ: How often do you meet with the PRA?
Interviewee: As often as they want.

As outlined in the previous section, NEDs find themselves having to balance a number of factors in defining their relationship with management, but they must also do the same in relation to regulators. In part, this is because the relationship with the regulator can be regarded as aligned with accountability to shareholders:

> You can only discharge your responsibility to shareholders by having a good and compliant . . . not compliant in the sense of agreeing with everything that they say but compliant in the sense of obeying rules, relationship with the regulator. So one follows naturally from the other. (Interviewee_04)

Yet the financial crisis showed that the regulator is not actually an agent of the shareholder in the same way as NEDs, and will have different statutory responsibilities which may override the interests of specific shareholders, such as securing financial stability or protecting retail customers. Furthermore, the influence of regulators on NEDs and on risk committees has grown in recent years to be substantial:

> Until the financial crisis the regulator was an element, one among many elements. They were clearly there, everybody respected the role of the regulator but they were not . . . I'm trying to find the right word . . . The word omnipresent comes to mind. (Interviewee_01)

This increased regulatory attention also means that there are heightened expectations and pressures on the NEDs. For example, one interviewee pointed out that:

> I think there's a danger of expectations that you know, the regulators are full-time, the non-execs are part-time but in a way that interaction will generate more and more expectation on the non-execs as agents of the regulators to do more and more. (Interviewee_02)

Yet this perception of increased regulatory influence was not always negative:

> It is easy to emphasize what is difficult about the new system, and to be frustrated by the demands of regulators. But, overall, the introduction of a risk committee has sharpened the Board's focus on what is going on in the business, and improved its understanding of how vulnerable the bank is to outside events. So it must be seen as a net positive, in spite of everything. (Interviewee_12)

Some NEDs also saw regulators as potential partners in reducing the information asymmetries they faced:

> They're a great source of information. And fundamentally, you are on the same side as the regulator. (Interviewee_06)

The same respondent also saw value in the more active approach now taken by regulators in the UK, and explained that this approach helps both communication and discussion between the NEDs and regulators:

> The regulators have got more assertive which I think is a good thing... Because they should have the courage of their convictions and they should be willing to have a discussion with you... they should be willing to say this is what we think. (Interviewee_06)

Yet for all these informational advantages, NEDs expressed concerns that regulators were now using them as a means to achieve their own specific objectives, such as consumer protection. More generally, there were concerns about the implications of closer engagement with regulators not just for the traditional accountability relationship to shareholders but also for the nature of interactions on the board between executives and non-executives. One interviewee thought that the quasi-reporting line to regulators increased the ambiguity of their role and created suspicion between the two categories of director:

> And then it's inevitable that you feel you have a sort of... duty to the regulator as well because you're almost like a mini regulator inside the organization and yet you're kind of a colleague of the execs, so you're sort of in and out as it were. (Interviewee_02)

In fact, this particular interviewee went further by arguing that a direct link between NEDs and regulators could be fatal to the traditional unitary board model operated in the UK:

> It's like putting a nail into the unitary board idea. So the non-execs, if they had more contact with the regulators they'd be increasingly perceived as part of that world by the execs. And that would be not good for... board unity. (Interviewee_02)

This concern was echoed by another NED:

> there's a slight tendency for the regulators to pit the executives and the non-executives almost against each other... it's as though you're sitting on opposite sides of the table. And I think that's an unhealthy thing. (Interviewee_04)

However, other NEDs had less experience of a cosy relationship with the regulator and saw the relationship as increasingly confrontational in nature:

> The regulators have definitely moved from trusting you to the not trusting you. They're much more judgemental about individuals. They're requiring much higher levels of technical, financial competence. (Interviewee_03)

Importantly, not only do regulators implicitly and explicitly want more from NEDs, they also want proof that they are discharging the oversight role. Specifically, regulators want to see concrete examples (in minutes and other documents) of differences in view between the NEDs and the executive. Such differences would be proof that the NED 'challenge' function is working. Because what happens within the boardroom has a limited audit trail, the self-estimation of board effectiveness can be seen as an example of 'black boxing' (Gendron & Bédard, 2006: 214). So regulators in the UK have introduced a requirement for the boards to demonstrate 'evidence of challenge' via 'minutes and sitting in and observing Board and Committee meetings' (Deloitte, 2013). However, NEDs see this approach and the demand for evidence as a misunderstanding by regulators of the way in which a board and its committees function:

> The moment you make an outcome into a target you get some perverse effects. So…that has led to people being very concerned about questions they ask…in board meetings [and] that [they] are actually minuted. I can perfectly understand where they're coming from, boards should be very challenging and therefore they want evidence of it. But the very evidence process is something which can distort…(Interviewee_02)

Another interviewee was even more forthright. The evidence of challenge envisaged by regulators as a sign of a successful board would in fact be evidence of its failure:

> The problem is that the regulators equate challenge as being a row. And actually that's rubbish: if you get to having a stand-up row in the boardroom you've failed, almost certainly. (Interviewee_06)

Yet another interviewee explained why the regulatory approach to challenge reflected a poor understanding of the dynamics of collective governance frameworks. Indeed, it was evident from the interviews that demonstration of the evidence of challenge as an indicator of success was regarded as deeply simplistic because it suggests that management proposes things in the boardroom without prior consultation and it is up to NEDs to reject them. In practice, however, considerable negotiation happens outside these meetings. Moreover, if that is not how problems are resolved, it would not be a mature board:

> [FSA] once they asked me in an interview, 'How often do you turn back the proposal from the management and ask them to go away and redo it?' And I said 'Well I would regard that as a failure, that's not how boards should work. I shouldn't be sitting one side of the table and the executive sitting the other and interviewing the management and receiving a paper by surprise and saying well you know, this isn't good enough, go away and redo it. That's not the way mature, adult stuff happens.' (Interviewee_04)

But there was also a more nuanced view from one NED. He noted that although it is not entirely unreasonable for the regulators to look for evidence of challenge, cultural factors made this more problematic in the UK context than elsewhere, perhaps given the polite and consensual way in which board meetings are conducted in this particular country. The question of whether this was a better or worse way of reaching tough decisions was left open:

You can easily write notes of meetings full of biff-baff. What do they mean by challenge? Having a big row with somebody is not helpful, it's not constructive, it's not going to get their confidence in you...Challenge is really asking somebody the one question they hadn't thought about and doing it in a way that they then go away and think about it and come back with something constructive. There's also a stylistic thing, there's a cultural thing as well; I mean we have incredibly forthright conversations in [another country] that I really don't think you would have in a UK board, it's just the culture there. (Interviewee_08)

While not all interviewees agreed with the need for evidence of challenge by the regulators, NEDs generally acknowledged that regulators are right to require the boards to be challenging. Indeed, as a chair of a risk committee in an insurance firm suggests:

A lot of boards and board chairmen still don't really want people on their boards who are going to be challenging. I mean they really don't. On two of the boards I was hired on, the chairman said 'I'm hiring you despite that I've been told you're very challenging'. (Interviewee_08)

To summarize, the interview data suggest that the regulatory relationship has affected, and even disturbed, the balance between NEDs and senior executives in UK financial services. This has created more uncertainty for NEDs about their role, and created a more complex environment of accountabilities for them as they seek to make risk oversight into an operational reality for the risk committees of which they are members. At the heart of this operational reality is another key relationship, namely the ability of NEDs to work with executive management in general and the CRO and her staff in particular.

MAKING OVERSIGHT WORK: NEDs AND MANAGEMENT

I have a good relationship with the chief risk officer; it's horses for courses...I work together with him and his team very closely indeed. I have separate meetings with them and I'm kind of chief coach but also chief challenger...I think they would trust me to come and tell me about a problem, which is very, very important.

(Interviewee_08)

Although in practice there are many types and levels of interaction between directors and management, both within and outside the boardroom, the relationship between non-executives on the risk committee and the CRO is nonetheless central. All of the NEDS interviewed saw this relationship and the establishment of mutual respect and trust as essential to being a successful chair of a risk committee. A proxy for the quality of that relationship with the CRO could be the frequency of meetings and interactions which go beyond those of the formal risk committee meetings.

> Formally I would see him one-on-one at least once a month. In reality I would see him probably once a fortnight/once a week. I'd certainly speak to him at least once a week.... A good chair of the risk committee has a great relationship with the chief risk officer. You have to build a relationship of trust. (Interviewee_06)

Open channels of communication between the CRO and the committee were regarded as crucial, not least because NEDs were sensitive about the danger of being kept in the dark and uninformed about problems and disputes within management. They saw the CRO as their 'eyes and ears' within the company structure:

> I don't think I could imagine myself sitting on a board in a company where there was any sort of mistrust or secrets going on between the executives and the board. (Interviewee_05)

The issue of building and maintaining relationships extended not only to the CRO but also to his senior team who might be closer to key issues facing the board risk committee. These interactions were regarded as opportunities for NEDs to learn more about risk in the business and to make the committee more effective:

> So I interact with the CRO and I interact with the people who work for him, the risk team . . . It's always helpful to have informal contacts with other members of the executive because I think when you have conversations with them about how they're reacting to what the CRO is doing or what the risk department is doing, you can get a much better more-rounded view of how things are working out . . . It's not about spying on the chief risk officer but it's about just getting another perspective. (Interviewee_05)

By developing these relationships, chairs of risk committees typically saw it as their role to attempt to head off disputes, which might otherwise surface in the risk committee or at the board:

> You don't want to embarrass the executives if there are mistakes or you don't want to show off or anything, so there are some things I would just ring up the CRO and ask a question or say something's wrong, you just don't do that in a meeting. You want the meetings to be productive. (Interviewee_02)

The importance of relationship building naturally extends beyond the CRO and his team to that of other executive functions and levels, particularly as NEDs recognize that their risk committees are likely to be kept informed more fully—and respected more—if: (1) they are seen as performing a useful function; and (2) are not trying to duplicate or replace the management process:

> Trying in a sense to make the discussion more strategic than procedural, which is really difficult. It's really difficult because you will be drawn into, especially in a regulated industry, a lot of talk about our compliance processes and our documentation processes. That's an inevitable part of that world. And you know, that will crowd out the strategic discussion. So it's a real balancing act but I think it's sort of... personal respect is important for the committee in its role, you've got to put it in a position of respect. (Interviewee_02)

These reflections suggest that the risk committee should really perform a kind of high-level strategic risk role which does not conflict with management but provides a forum for risk managers to raise detailed concerns. In different ways, NEDs articulated this balancing act at the boundary between supporting and motivating management and providing more critical strategic oversight.

> There's numbers but in the end organizations are bundles of human beings. And if you don't get the right human beings and you don't motivate them in the right way, you're not going to get the right outcomes. You can have sexy models coming out of your ears but in the end human beings are very, very clever and they will get round them. So if you're not motivating people properly, if you haven't got them engaged in the sort of vision or whatever you want to call it, then all these models eventually will be circumnavigated. (Interviewee_08)

More generally, NEDs defined the success of their role more in terms of managing and sustaining complex relations—motivating and encouraging the CRO and her team as noted above—but also legitimizing their own position in relation to other members of the board and executive management:

> I would define [success] as acquiring the respect of the business you know, the top team and other people. And really feeling you've acquired that. Really feeling you know the business. Unfortunately when you really do that they chuck you out because it's the nine-year rule. (Interviewee_02)

But while NEDs were conscious of their own need to be credible, they also tended to see success as something achieved through the quality of the relationships built by the NEDs collectively:

> Good non-executives hunt in packs... it's groups of them rather than individuals [which] is when they're most successful. (Interviewee_06)

This perceived value of collegial decision-making among NEDs is also manifested through their ability to interact effectively outside the boardroom in support of the formal interactions:

> So you have to be able to not quite build alliances, that implies too formal a situation, but you have to be able to work with people effectively to test whether what you're believing is right. (Interviewee_06)

This collective concept of successful oversight is also relevant to regulatory debates about board capability and diversity noted earlier in this chapter. Here the likely trade-off involves balancing members possessing deep industry experience with those having other backgrounds and skills.

> You need to have people that have been experienced...that have worked in industries and have a depth of knowledge in at least one or two businesses, so not superficial knowledge but a depth and have very senior level jobs in one or two different businesses/industries. (Interviewee_09)

Yet despite these different conceptions of, or proxies for, success, many NEDs also acknowledged the difficulty of proving their effectiveness, and of being sure about the quality of decision-making and risk management in the business:

> You're never quite sure what contribution you make because risk management's kind of the dog that doesn't bark...if you do your job well, fewer bad things happen. But who's to say whether they would or they wouldn't have? It's quite difficult to attribute success, it's difficult to measure success. (Interviewee_03)

In the absence of solid evidence applicable to their own roles, NEDs tended to emphasize their personal experience and the importance of judgement by the people who directly manage risks in the business. Underlying this is an important construction of risk oversight as something that influences the quality of risk management indirectly rather than being a kind of diluted form of risk management.

To summarize: NEDs saw the construction and maintenance of relationships with key executives in risk and beyond as being an essential component of their capability. Indeed, it follows that capability is not only a function of individual knowledge and expertise but is necessarily relational. The relationships are also multidimensional, requiring NEDs to be sometimes close and supportive, and sometimes distant and evaluative. Importantly, the former is seen as a necessary part of being able to do the latter credibly. Potentially this requires us to rethink the very idea of oversight, with its implicit binary hierarchy of overseer–overseen and to suggest that oversight is continuously constructed by NEDs as a network of relationships. We consider this further in the final section.

DISCUSSION AND CONCLUSION

The overall picture that emerges from the interview material is that, whatever the aspirations of policymakers and regulators to improve something called 'risk oversight' in financial organizations, the enactment of that aspiration by NEDs on risk committees is riddled with tensions and trade-offs. As we have seen, they are required to be independent overseers of executive management with little guidance as to how this independence might be realized other than by being 'challenging'. This problem of the gap between policy aspiration and lived reality is of course not confined to NEDs and is relevant to all control agents of different kinds who experience role conflicts. For example, in the context of internal auditors, there is a 'difficulty of applying an idealized conception of independence and purist governance principles to practice' (Roussy, 2014: 237). Indeed, regulatory systems implicitly assume that both independence and competence can be optimized, rather than, as the data in this chapter suggest, requiring trade-offs against one another. Furthermore, as a form of work, risk oversight is constructed *in situ* through the creation of relationships which are essential for information gathering but which only increase the situated complexity of the role, including in particular the accountability 'tightrope' between serving regulators and fulfilling the duties of a unitary board.

The NEDs interviewed accepted in principle that they should stay at the level of oversight, but could only conceptualize this negatively as not doing the job of management. Consequently they found it hard to articulate the nature of their success as risk committee members, with a tendency to focus on the indirect effects of encouraging and supporting the risk function. The NEDs built 'their organizational awareness and influence through contacts with executive directors, managers and other non-executives beyond the boardroom' (Roberts et al., 2005: S7). But this necessity creates a fundamental tension for the practice of risk oversight. As Roberts et al. (2005) put it, 'the role of the non-executive is to both support executives in their leadership of the business and to monitor and control their conduct' (Roberts et al., 2005: S11). NEDs are always working to combine both these roles in practical ways but, 'The contrast of oversight and support poses an important concern for directors and challenges them to maintain what can become a rather delicate balance' (Daily, Dalton, & Cannella, 2003: 375). Or as Roberts et al. (2005) suggest, there are three linked sets of characteristics that NEDs should embrace. They should be: 'engaged but non-executive', 'challenging but supportive', and 'independent but involved' (Roberts et al., 2005: S6).

It is as if the NEDs interviewed in this chapter and those in previous studies are involved in delicate boundary work of a specific kind, but not so much in the traditional sense of clearly demarcating management from non-management (oversight) activity as we might expect. Rather, they make that boundary fluid enough for them to operate seemingly on both sides of it when it suits. Thus, in the case of risk committee NEDs:

what might be a hindrance to creating a distinct expert group—one kind of boundary-work—can be a help in crossing organizational boundaries in order to 'get things done' in the business lines—another kind of boundary-work. While the first approach appears to be more effective in creating an independent and distinct expert function, its practitioners seem to have limited relevance to (or lack the ambition to participate in) the discussion of non-measurable strategic uncertainties. (Mikes, 2011: 4)

From this point of view we can say that oversight is produced both as practice and as *continuous problem* from boundary work of a distinctive kind, namely of subtly being on both sides of the management–oversight boundary.

Yet, this complex boundary spanning activity and its associated trade-offs and tensions creates a degree of role-ambiguity (Kahn et al., 1964) for NEDs which they have to internalize. Like any organizational actor, they need to work at establishing and maintaining their credibility and relevance in the internal management landscape (Hall, Mikes, & Millo, 2015; Chapter 12, this volume). Yet the very scope and depth of the riskwork of NEDs is a continuous problem, despite recommendations that oversight should focus on key risks which are material and strategic. The scope of the agenda of a board risk committee is potentially very great—every conceivable risk facing the business might be included. This creates a difficulty of 'depth' for NEDs, namely to decide which issues deserve more detailed attention and analysis in the form of a so-called 'deep dive'. But how deep can NEDs go before they are caught 'offside' in the territory of operational management?

Some of the role ambiguity of NEDs stems from the need to negotiate plural accountabilities. Not only are there 'very different potentials of remote accountability to investors and face-to-face accountability within the board between executive and non-executive directors' (Roberts et al., 2005: S11), but for the NEDs in UK financial services the regulator is also a focal and real point of accountability. So it is not just within public administration that accountability is a 'multifaceted concept fraught with ambiguity' (Salamon, 2002: 524). NEDs in financial services organizations are constantly working individually and collectively to balance these multiple accountabilities.

In conclusion, the interview data together with prior literature suggest that the tensions facing NEDs in discharging the role of risk oversight are inherent and fundamental rather than a transitional feature of new regulatory expectations. For this reason we might define the expertise of a good NED as precisely the ability to manage these tensions, to do boundary-spanning work, to create a zone for oversight activity without being confined to it, and to work hard at independence from management on some occasions and less hard on others. Far from being the imperfection it seems when compared to official accounts of governance and immaculate structures such as the 'three lines of defence', this model of the continuous negotiation of an ambiguous role seems to constitute the very nature of risk oversight, an activity which is itself risky and problematic. From this point of view, the NEDs interviewed for this chapter are fascinating as actors for whom the work of risk oversight emerges as a distinctive kind of capability, namely of maintaining the 'stable instability' of a role which is both executive-facing and yet not-executive.

APPENDIX 4.1

INTERVIEW PROTOCOL FOR NEDs

About the Role

What are the main challenges of being a non-executive director?
What does it mean to be a successful NED?
To whom are you responsible?
How do you balance oversight and management roles?
What can the board risk committee accomplish and for whom?

Relationship with the CRO

What are the reporting lines between you and the CRO?
Do you feel that executive management support you in your non-executive role?

Quality of Information

What do you want to achieve with the information you are getting?
Some organizations have adopted a three lines of defence model of governance.
 What are your thoughts about it? [What output do you see from the three
 different lines? What reports are you getting?]
Do you think the information you get is sufficient to perform your role?
How do you get confidence that you are seeing the organization as it is?
What specific information is particularly useful for your job?
How much influence do you have over the information you get? How do you deal
 with the level of granularity of information that you receive?

APPENDIX 4.2

LIST OF INTERVIEWEES

Code #	Date	Firm	Position
Interviewee_1	7 May 2014	Top 10 Bank	Chair Risk Committee
Interviewee_2	8 May 2014	FTSE100 Insurance	Chair Audit Committee
Interviewee_3	20 May 2014	FTSE200 Insurance	Ex-CRO, Risk Committee member
Interviewee_4	12 May 2014	Top 10 Insurance	Chairman
Interviewee_5	29 May 2014	Top 10 Insurance	Chair Risk Committee
Interviewee_6	30 May 2014	FTSE100 Insurance	Chair Risk Committee
Interviewee_7	25 May 2014	European Retail Bank	Chair Risk Committee
Interviewee_8	6 June 2014	FTSE100 Bank	Chair Risk Committee
Interviewee_9	27 May 2014	Top 10 UK Bank	Chair Risk Committee
Interviewee_10	10 June 2014	Top 10 Bank	Member Risk Committee
Interviewee_11	23 June 2014	Top 10 Bank	Member Risk Committee
Interviewee_12	18 July 2014	Top 10 Bank	Chair Risk Committee

108   *Riskwork*

REFERENCES

Andersen, T. J., Garvey, M., & Roggi, O. (2014). *Managing Risk and Opportunity: The Governance of Strategic Risk-taking.* Oxford: Oxford University Press.

Clarke, D. C. (2007). Three Concepts of the Independent Director. *Delaware Journal of Corporate Law*, 32, 73.

Daily, C. M., Dalton, D. R., & Cannella, A. A. (2003). Corporate Governance: Decades of Dialogue and Data. *Academy of Management Review*, 28(3), 371–82.

De Larosière, J. (2009). *The High Level Group on Financial Supervision in the EU: Report.* Brussels: European Commission. <http://ec.europa.eu/finance/general-policy/docs/de_larosiere_report_en.pdf> (accessed 6 March 2016).

Deloitte. (2013). Internal Audit in Insurance Breakfast Briefing. September.

Eisenberg, M. A. (1999). Corporate Law and Social Norms. *Columbia Law Review*, 95(5), 1253–292.

Gendron, Y. & Bédard, J. (2006). On the Constitution of Audit Committee Effectiveness. *Accounting, Organizations and Society*, 31(3), 211–39.

Gordon, J. N. (2007). The Rise of Independent Directors in the United States, 1950–2005: Of Shareholder Value and Stock Market Prices. *Stanford Law Review*, 95(65), 1465–568.

Hall, M., Mikes, A., & Millo, Y. (2015). How Do Risk Managers Become Influential? A Field Study of Toolmaking in Two Financial Institutions. *Management Accounting Research*, 26, 3–22.

Kahn, R. L., Wolfe, D. M., Quinn, R. P., Snoek, J. D., & Rosenthal, R. A. (1964). *Organizational Stress: Studies in Role Conflict and Ambiguity.* Oxford: Wiley.

Lin, L. (1995). Effectiveness of Outside Directors as a Corporate Governance Mechanism: Theories and Evidence. *Northwestern University Law Review*, 90, 898–976.

Mikes, A. (2011). From Counting Risk to Making Risk Count: Boundary-work in Risk Management. *Accounting, Organizations and Society*, 36(4), 226–45.

Millstein, I. M. & MacAvoy, P. W. (1998). The Active Board of Directors and Performance of the Large Publicly Traded Corporation. *Columbia Law Review*, 98(5), 1283–322.

Power, M. (1999). *The Audit Society: Rituals of Verification.* Oxford: Oxford University Press.

Power, M. (2000). *The Audit Implosion: Regulating Risk from the Inside.* London: ICAEW.

Protiviti (2013). Board Risk Oversight. <http://www.protiviti.com/en-US/Pages/Board-Member-Risk-Oversight.aspx> (accessed 5 March 2016).

Roberts, J., McNulty, T., & Stiles, P. (2005). Beyond Agency Conceptions of the Work of the Non-executive Director: Creating Accountability in the Boardroom. *British Journal of Management*, 16(s1), S5–S26.

Roussy, M. (2014). Welcome to the Day to Day of Internal Auditors: How Do They Cope with Conflicts? *Auditing: A Journal of Practice and Theory*, 34(2), 237–64.

Salamon, L. M. (2002). *The Tools of Government: A Guide to the New Governance.* Oxford: Oxford University Press.

Spira, L. F. & Page, M. (2003). Risk Management: the Reinvention of Internal Control and the Changing Role of Internal Audit. *Accounting, Auditing & Accountability Journal*, 16(4), 640–61.

UK_Parliament (2013). Parliamentary Commission on Banking Standards Report. June. <http://www.parliament.uk/business/committees/committees-a-z/joint-select/profes sional-standards-in-the-banking-industry/publications> (accessed 5 March 2106).

Walker, D. (2009). *A Review of Corporate Governance in UK Banks and Other Financial Industry Entities*. London: HM Treasury.

5

The Role of Valuation Practices
for Risk Identification

Åsa Boholm and Hervé Corvellec

Risk identification is widely acknowledged as an essential component of risk management (e.g. Cooper et al., 2014). However, how risk identification is understood derives from how risk is conceived. If risk is understood as an observer-independent fact, it follows that risk identification will focus on establishing causal circumstances that can potentially produce adverse outcomes. But, if risk is understood to be an observer-*dependent* mode of addressing the uncertainties and contingencies that characterize life, identification will consist of unfolding from a particular point of view what is considered to be a risk or not.

In the present chapter, we adopt a relational theory of risk (Boholm & Corvellec, 2011) that builds on the second of these two views of risk to show that evaluation practices—i.e. how and why people attach value to things, play a key role in risk identification.

The relational theory of risk draws on sociological and anthropological insights that understandings of risk are situated in specific social contexts. Conceptions of risk draw on knowledge, values, and concerns that are embedded in livelihoods and imprinted on individuals by social institutions, historical experience, and collective identity (Boholm, 2003, 2015; Caplan, 2000; Grätz, 2009; Mairal, 2003, 2008; Sjölander-Lindqvist, 2005; Stoffle & Arnold, 2003; Stoffle & Minnis, 2008). Far from being abstract and disembodied constructs, risk conceptions are associated with everyday practices and cultural assumptions that vary from group to group, place to place, and time to time (Shaw, 2000).

More specifically, Boholm & Corvellec (2011) build on Hilgartner's (1992: 40) analysis that 'particular risks include at least three conceptual elements: an object deemed to "pose" the risk, a putative harm, and a linkage alleging some form of causation between the object and the harm' (emphasis in original). To characterize an object as 'risky', two conditions must be met: the thing under consideration has to be constructed as an object; and a linkage has to be established between this object and a putative harm. Objects should be understood in a broad sense. They can be natural phenomena, such as lightning, technological, like a cell phone, cultural, such as the virginity of girls, or behavioural, such as smoking. The relational theory of risk (Boholm & Corvellec, 2011) suggests that risk is a cognitive schema, a cultural model of a domain of knowledge (Strauss & Quinn, 1997: ch. 3) that constructs relationships between objects in terms of a potential threat to the value embedded in objects at risk.

Three elements are central to this schema. First, there are risk objects, identified as potentially dangerous. Dangerousness is a matter of potentiality: a risk object might incur damages only under contingent circumstances (Corvellec, 2011). And not all the characteristics of risk objects are equally salient. Whether one speaks of dogs, guns, nuclear waste, competitors, the evolution of technology, or of a piece of new legislation, the identification of a risk object implies fronting some characteristics that are hazardous under some circumstances and downplaying others which are not. The dangerousness of risk objects results from a circumstantial framing.

Second, there are objects at risk, identified as being endowed with value, that are considered at stake. Objects at risk embody worth, for example life, nature, principles, or money, but also include chief executive officers, companies, or nations. Like risk objects, objects at risk are not a given; rather, they are defined when indexed with worth. While risk objects are construed around characteristics of potential destruction, objects at risk are construed around characteristics of appeal and importance, weight and significance. The value understood to be associated with an object at risk can potentially be degraded, stained, reduced, diminished, or even lost. A key characteristic of an object at risk is that its worth is circumstantial and contextual, and therefore merits protection from various potentially harmful influences, for example by adequate riskwork.[1]

Third, relationships of risk build on connections and associations (van Loon, 2002) that are established by means of conjectures, probabilistic models, laboratory tests, narratives, or other means. A relationship of risk establishes a contingent relationship, answering the question 'What if?' (Ravetz, 1997): relationships of risk rest on hypothesized conditions, courses of events, and consequences (Corvellec, 2011), but they are also causal. It is not sufficient to claim a relationship of convenience, similarity, or proximity. A relationship of risk must establish that the risk object actually has a

---

[1] The notion of Object-at-Risk (OaR) may seem similar to the notion of Value-at-Risk (VaR) (e.g. Dowd, 1998). There is indeed a similarity in the sense that both OaR and VaR rest on imagining a potential loss in value arising from an adverse event. But there is also a major difference. Whereas VaR is a probabilistic *measure* of the potential loss of a financial portfolio, OaR refers to the *object* itself that carries this loss. Moreover, this object need not be financial.

potential to threaten the object at risk. It has to establish a relation of causality between the two. How and possibly why the risk object threatens the object at risk needs to be spelled out in order to establish a relationship of risk. For example, one needs to show how and why a legislative change threatens a company's business model or key success factor. Scientific understanding and expertise therefore assumes a privileged position in societal risk management (Jasanoff, 1999).

Our purpose in this chapter is to show, using a relational understanding of risk, how risk identification as a form of riskwork, connects risk objects, objects at risk, and relationships in an assemblage where each element gains identity from being put in conjunction with the other. Something becomes a risk object when put in a relation to an object at risk. Constructing risk is a craft which relies on expertise, expectations, and social roles embedded in particular organizational settings. Our contention is that valuation practices are an essential ingredient of this craft.

ON VALUATION

Several authors have noted that value is central to the concept of risk (Boholm & Corvellec, 2011; Hansson, 2010; Möller, 2012; Rescher, 1983; Shrader-Frechette, 1991). For example, Rescher (1983: 31) observes that 'there is no risk assessment without normative *evaluation*' (emphasis in original). Similarly, Rosa (1998: 28) defines risk as 'a situation or event where something of human value (including humans themselves) has been put at stake and where the outcome is uncertain', and Aven and Renn (2009: 2) claim that 'risk refers to uncertainty about and [the] severity of the consequences (or outcomes) of an activity with respect to something that humans value'.

However, acknowledgement of the essential role of value for risk takes us only halfway into understanding risk identification. As valuation studies (e.g. Beckert & Aspers, 2011; Berthoin Antal, Hutter, & Stark, 2015; Helgesson & Muniesa, 2013; Muniesa, 2011) have made clear, value is neither objective nor subjective. Value is an outcome of intricate social processes of identification, definition, hierarchization, and calculation that condition preferences in more or less determined ways. Therefore, if one wishes to understand what value stands for, one needs to unfold the social practices of valuation that determine, explicitly or implicitly, what is worth being considered as an object of care and why this is the case (Horlick-Jones, 2005).

The observation that valuation processes are intrinsically social, dating back to the early days of social science, noted by pioneers such as Durkheim (1991 [1893]), Mauss (2000 [1902]), Weber (& Whimster) (2008 [1921–2]), and Tarde (1902), has found a renewed interest in economic sociology (e.g. Beckert & Zafirovski, 2010) and economic anthropology (e.g. Carrier, 2005; Wilk & Cliggett, 2007). For example, *The Worth of Goods* edited by Beckert & Aspers (2011) provides several examples of how definitions of value result from social processes with individual and organizational practices at their core.

Beckert and Aspers (2011) suggest that value is diverse, and that there is no generally agreed-upon exchange rate for translating one scale of value into the other. However, as Appadurai (1986) notes, even if there are differences between how stakeholders define value, for example between the 'environmental' scale and 'economic' scale, this does not necessarily prevent them from communicating about value and trading objects of value. Value is inevitably a matter of judgement and attitude: something that derives from the preference of actors. Preferences are not exogenous (Bourdieu, 1979), as mainstream neoclassic economic theory assumes; they are embedded in the social psychology of desire, the non-decidability of meaning, and the dynamics of organizational and managerial practice. It is not always clear where criteria to assess value come from, how they relate to the object under consideration, or how they develop into taken-for-granted conventions (e.g. Hennion, 2015). But it is clear that managerial practice has the ability to establish such criteria in terms of organizational norms and turn them into tools for decision-making. Or, rather, as Stark (2009) claims, at the core of managerial practice is an ability to create ambiguity and uncertainty about what is valuable so that the coexistence of multiple principles of evaluation provides managers with sizeable opportunities for ventures of their choice.

Beckert and Aspers (2011) show that valuation is a multifaceted organizational practice that draws on hearsay, legal assessment procedures, as well as mathematical algorithms when trading in derivatives. Valuation processes draw on organizational modus operandi (Corvellec, 2009, 2010), rhetorical traditions (Sauer, 2003), historical commitment (Vaughan, 1996), mindfulness (Weick & Sutcliffe, 2007), modes of accountability (Dekker, 2007), and communitarian commitments (Boholm, Corvellec, & Karlsson, 2011; Gherardi & Nicolini, 2000). Depending on organizational practice, valuation is something that organizational actors actually do (Heuts & Mol, 2013). Valuation is embedded in the everyday dynamics of organizational life. It is a situated collective achievement, not an individual subjective outcome. Individual cognitive frames shape, and are shaped by, collectively validated preferences so that organizational and managerial practices condition and subtend what individuals consider as being of worth. Valuation reflects agreements as well as trade-offs or conflicts among actors about what matters. It is an activity that takes place over time, and that is as much attuned to past experience as it is to scenarios about the future or a sense of the present. It is this organizational practice, in the specific case of risk identification, that the case study in this chapter will portray.

CASE STUDY: RAILWAY PLANNING IN SWEDEN

Institutional Framework

At the time of this study, 2007–8 in Sweden, the Rail Administration[2] was responsible for the railway system, including the rail track, the signal system, and the provision of electric power to trains. Trains themselves are operated by companies (e.g. the former state monopoly, regional companies, Veolia, and cargo carriers) which hire rail capacity from the Rail Administration.

Schematically, the procedure for railway planning unfolds as follows. It starts with an investigation phase aimed at identifying possible routes and comparing them in terms of costs, benefits, risks, technical requirements, environmental impact, and other possible effects and consequences. The investigation phase involves substantial consultation with the regional county board(s), municipalities, potential stakeholders, and members of the public. It results in a proposal that must include an analysis of socio-economic costs and benefits and show how the railway line corresponds to the national transportation policy goals.

Next comes the railway planning phase. This phase involves a detailed plan of the decided route, including the exact design of bridges, tunnels, barriers, and road crossings. The railway plan must include considerations of safety regarding future train traffic, specification of constructions, construction processes, and facilities (such as working roads or locations for storage of excavated masses), as well as legal, organizational, technical, and economic issues. Swedish regulation of railway planning requires that the Rail Administration makes a systematic assessment of the operational and environmental risk involved in its projects. Correspondingly, the Rail Administration issued risk management rules (Banverket, 2008) and a handbook (Banverket, 2006) that spell out how risk management should be conducted.

Apart from a detailed characterization of all technical elements of the new railway line, information on risk identification, and risk management strategies, the railway plan must show that all property rights and land use matters have been legally settled. It must also account for the mandatory consultations held with the public, real estate owners who are affected by the project, municipalities, and regional boards. And it must present an Environmental Impact Assessment (EIA) that needs approval by the county board, or if they refuse, the Swedish government must approve it, which would cause substantial delays to the project.

---

[2] Two years later, in 2010, the Rail Administration ceased as an independent government authority. Today the Swedish Transport Administration is responsible for planning the transport system for road and rail traffic, and for maritime shipping.

Despite providing stakeholders with certain legal rights, Swedish railway planning adheres to a technocratic regulatory style of consensual negotiation between the state, political interests, and elite stakeholders, but public participation is limited (Löfstedt, 2005). Continuous reconciliation of a multitude of interests therefore proves to be a major task for railway planning officials who must negotiate diverging regulatory issues and stakeholder interests, and who must adapt general rules and standards to contextual practical working agreements regarding complex socio-technical arrangements (Johansson, 2012).

Planning for Upgrading a Track Section

In 2004, the Swedish government decided to upgrade railway capacity on the Norway–Väner Link north of Göteborg by doubling track rail, dimensioned for high-speed trains. The new railway line promised to reduce travel time, offer more frequent departures, present new commuter stations, and provide diverse environmental benefits. The building of the track began in 2009, and the new Göteborg–Trollhättan railway line was inaugurated in December 2012.

Between March 2007 and mid-autumn 2008, Boholm attended all twenty-three planning meetings for a subsection of the route, located in a rural area south of the city of Trollhättan, 90 kilometres north of Göteborg. The meetings included the Rail Administration internal project meetings, the project's reference group meetings with stakeholders such as the county board, the municipality of Trollhättan, the regional public transport company, and the Road Administration, and one public consultation meeting with the general public as part of the exhibition of the railway plan (October 2007). All meetings were documented by field notes written during observation. Data also include internal documents, minutes, official reports, Rail Administration handbooks and standards, and informal discussion (including asking questions) with officials, planners, designers, and consultants. This case study was part of a larger research project on risk in public transportation carried out together with Corvellec.

The planning project was managed by a Rail Administration project leader responsible for the project's budget and schedule. This project leader was in charge of coordinating the in-house expertise on economic matters, environmental control, quality, information, procurement, safety, and traffic. Railway planning is an information intensive activity. It requires numerous investigations into geology, hydrogeology, groundwater, ecology, wildlife, landscape, property, building materials, technical design, existing roads, and traffic. Calculations of economy, time, safety, construction stability, logistics, and mass balance were essential to project management, in particular to rule out inconsistencies and unwanted consequences. Railway planning thus depends on external consultants who are contracted for a number of tasks, including: fine-tuning the spatial location of the railway line; the design of the signal system and the contact cables; the design of bridges, tunnels or over- or under-crossings with roads; environmental impact assessment and various legally mandatory investigations. Ensuring that consultants fulfil their contractual commitments is a key task of the project manager.

IDENTIFYING VALUES AT STAKE AND RISK OBJECTS

The Risk-identifying Exercises

A series of meetings was dedicated to the identification and management of risk. A one-day meeting was held at the beginning of the project (March 2007) to identify and assess risks relevant to the railway planning stage. This risk identification meeting brought together about fifteen project members, consultants, and Rail Administration officials, representing a variety of specialist competencies. It was the first stage in the preparation of the mandatory risk management plan. The project leader introduced the objectives of the meeting. When the participants introduced themselves, it transpired that eight came from the Rail Administration (expert support, technical coordination, and real estate), and seven were consultants, two of whom worked under (or with) the lead consultant. Competencies in the group included environmental impact assessment, geotechnology, contaminated soil management, construction, real estate property, tunnel building and tunnel security, and bridge design.

After a joint introduction to the concept of risk, defined as the product of consequence and probability, and to how the Rail Administration views risk assessment, the group was divided into two subgroups. Each participant was asked to write down on sticky notes the risks that he or she could identify, and then describe what the Rail Administration called the domains of consequence of this risk—whether it pertains to time, economy, quality of delivery, environment, work environment, societal trust in the Rail Administration, or 'third party or parties'. Each subgroup was assigned the task of a risk assessment and the two subgroups were to jointly categorize each individually identified risk as red, yellow, or green.

The instruction immediately gave rise to questions among the participants regarding which risks were relevant to the identification exercise and which were not. The question was asked: 'What about risks that the Rail Administration cannot influence?' Traffic risks and circumstances relating to weather conditions were brought up as examples of risks that were beyond control in the planning process: 'What about the planning stage in relation to the building stage? If it rains a lot, is that a risk that should be counted?' Answering these questions, an official from the Rail Administration explained that the focus should be on what the project planning could influence, and that experience from earlier projects therefore was important.

Another meeting was held three weeks later (April 2007) with fewer participants: the project leader, the co-coordinators of the consultants, and the quality coordinator from the Rail Administration. The sticky notes were compiled into a list of 125 different risks that were entered into the Rail Administration's risk management planning document template. This template contained several columns. One column listed the risk items, specifying their domains of consequence: one for a quantified estimation of the consequence that the risk presents and one with an estimated probability of the risk. The document also had columns for management actions, indicating who is considered to bear the responsibility for the risk, and the date for the latest update of the information about this risk. The magnitude of risk was calculated as the product of consequence and probability, and since both consequence and probability were measured on scales ranging from 1 to 5, the highest possible risk estimate is 25 and the lowest is 1.

The purpose of the April meeting was to provide an assessment of which risks may be involved and to present prevention measures for each risk or type of risk. The project leader suggested that the group should quickly go through the list to see whether anything had been forgotten. Questions arose as to how the risks should be sorted. After some remarks she said that 'risk estimates are very subjective'. Someone suggested merging two risks into one, and the quality co-coordinator answered that merging risks could in some cases make them clearer and easier to follow. The list was read through and commented upon, but with little discussion about specific risks. After the risk list was reviewed, the group discussed how the measures could be described and whether a name of a specific person should be entered in the responsibility column. Someone noted that the important thing was for the process to be traceable so that it would be clear how the group had worked. The discussion was mainly about how to comply with the formal requirements for the risk management planning document, for example with action plans and checklists. The discussion was also about how this document was going to be used. At a later project meeting (May 2007), the project manager presented the risk management plan. At that time it contained eighty-six identified risks.

The brainstorming exercise at the initial March 2007 meeting, in particular, showed how railway planners identify, understand, and negotiate risk. Our observations of the exercises in risk identification showed how riskwork is a dynamic social process of evaluation practice revolving around the detection, characterization, and agreement on values and potential threats. The next section shows how risk identification work entails dealing with a variety of issues such as accidents and contingencies, lack of competence, regulatory obstacles, interfering authorities, technical limitations, traffic problems, and resource uncertainty.

Risk Identification Work

In what follows we focus on a number of themes that emanated from the risk identification exercises. To separate risk issues written down by the planners on the sticky notes from what was said during the discussions, we use the following typographic conventions: risk items written on the sticky notes are indicated within *[square brackets]*; statements made during discussions are identified within *'quotes'*.

Matters 'Out of Control'—Accidents and Contingencies

The planners made considerable effort to address matters that they understood to be 'out of control' but could have a vital impact on the building of a railway line due to the complex causal conditions for such work. The planners were acutely aware that even with the minutest and most prudent planning, it was unrealistic to believe that all negative events that might possibly occur could be foreseen. An external and crucial 'matter out of control' which was repeatedly referred to during the discussions of the March 2007 meeting was weather: the two risks [exceptional weather causes delays] and [construction area is flooded] were discussed a lot. One specialist argued that these risks were not very probable, but another expert countered that 'natural catastrophes are becoming more frequent' and that 'this is a fact'. It was suggested that the probability was a 2 for these risks. One planner pointed out that a small river in the area had been flooded recently and asked about the consequences of such an event. Someone answered that 'this is a question about the solicitation process. How did that look?' The discussion continued and one participant noted that the water level in Lake Vänern (Sweden's largest lake) could be a risk and this gave rise to questions such as: 'Can this risk be made clear in the procurement documents?' 'Can water flows be specified?'

The discussion moved to the sharing of economic responsibilities between the Rail Administration and, for example, construction companies in case of weather-related emergencies: 'At what point does the contracting authority take over costs from the contractors?' Then a discussion followed about what was referred to as 'correct pricing', and the comment that 'contractors might speculate in weather!' Someone suggested that 'maybe the consequence is a 4' but it was unclear what this suggestion referred to. The discussion on weather-related risk continued and a question was raised about how such things were managed 'on the oil rigs in the North Sea'. Someone asked what would happen if there was a '100-year wave every 10 years'. Then the weather-related discussion shifted to storms and a question was raised as to whether storms had 'the same probability' as heavy rain or sea waves.

A question was asked about the practical matter of how to approach a flooded workplace area. In connection with that, one expert argued that 'storms are more temporary than floods. You have to shut down and floods last longer.' The discussion on weather rambled on and ended by broad comparisons with serious flooding cases in Sweden and elsewhere: 'What about Arvika?[3] Or Bangladesh?'

Other matters discussed from within an 'out of control' interpretation frame were construction risks such as [landslide during building], [the failure of the bridge foundation], [landslide in Slumpån with ecological disaster], and [collapse in tunnel, concrete leaks into mountain shaft]. A general comment that was made in connection with these risks was that construction problems had to be distinguished from environmental problems. The risk [mountain ground work fails and there is a collapse in a tunnel] was given as an example. A question was then raised about probability and the discussion continued with the questions 'Shall we not start with probability?' and 'is this usual?', and although it was not clear to which one of the noted risks the speaker referred, an expert answered that 'it has occurred' and pointed out, as a comparison, that '[collapses] are more common within the Road Administration'. The probability was set at 2 and no one protested. The discussion continued and an expert posited that 'there is a difference between bridges and tunnels' and that 'a bridge has a probability of 5 and a tunnel of 2'. No one protested and another of the construction experts agreed to the suggested figures.

Discussion on the identified risks continued [landslide in Slumpån] and [Slumpån is affected by process water]. The Rail Administration environmental expert stated that these risks had major consequences. The project leader suggested that the risks should be subdivided to make clearer what was collapsing: 'fundaments of the old bridge, or land masses?'. It was agreed that the consequences would be major, commanding a consequence of 5, but that this probability was more difficult to assess. No one had an answer and it was suggested that the risk should be classified as a 'yellow' (with a middle-size risk estimate) with a probability of 3. The project leader then asked 'can we agree on this?'. Someone thought that the probability was too high, since 'such things occur several times every month but there are protection measures'. The identified risk [landslide and collapse during building] gave rise to a question as to whether this was caused naturally by a collapse of the ground due to the high volume of water. Somebody noted that the identified risks could result in loss of public trust in the Rail Administration. The Rail Administration environmental expert mentioned that a landslide had already

---

[3] A medium-sized Swedish city affected by a catastrophic flood when in 2000 the water levels from the nearby lake reached 3 metres above normal.

occurred in a nearby stream, and if that were to happen during the building phase, it could be interpreted as being caused by the Rail Administration's construction activities. One participant asked about a probability and noted that 'such things will happen again'.

Mistakes and Lack of Competence

Another theme identified during the risk identification exercises relates to human and organizational failure. In the discussions of the March 2007 meeting, the identified risks [ill-conceived planning] and [lack of competence] were met with the question (as usual) 'What about probability?' which gave rise to laughter and a lively discussion. It was observed that this was 'a likely risk but also likely that it will be managed' and that 'there is a tremendous uncertainty in project planning—a guessing competition' and that '[no matter how] good a job one does, there is always big uncertainty'. It was further noted that 'things will always happen!'. The group agreed on a 4 for probability. It was argued that mistakes and lack of competence was a 'significant risk' and that it was particularly important that it was managed properly by means of 'internal control'. An economic dimension was involved here, since the participants recognized that appropriate and qualified skills in railway planning costs money. Someone remarked that 'the contracting authority has run public procurements before, and you get what you pay for'. The consequence is rated high, a 5.

About the risk [poor competence of private contractors, for example, consultants], someone commented that 'If the consultant does not think correctly, everything can be affected'. It was also noted that 'competence is a combination of knowledge and experience'. One participant argued that the risk of poor competence was small; another asked whether this risk might vary from one group of actors to another. A question was raised as to whether there was a difference between the contracting authority (i.e. the Rail Administration) and the contractor in terms of necessary competence in railway planning. During the discussion, someone pointed out that there was an interaction between the contracting authority and the contractor and that these had differing interests. It was underscored that the probability that a contractor had poor competence was low, but that the consequences were devastating if this were to prove to be the case. The probability that the contractor lacked competence was agreed to be 2. The consequence was set to 5.

Some participants expressed concerns about contractors' incompetence, inability, or even neglect. Others countered that insufficient performance of contractors could also derive from incorrect, inadequate, and insufficient steering by the Rail Administration. The relationship between the Rail Administration and the contracted builders or consultants was seen as crucial and rather sensitive. Several emphasized that the Rail Administration's ability to steer contractors was only indirect because they steer through procurement and contracts. Contractors can always fail. Likewise, contracts can prove to be faulty or inadequate. So the Rail Administration officials had no other choice but to trust the contractors (Kadefors, 2004). Railway planners are acutely aware that contractual control and steering have limits and give rise to a considerable degree of uncertainty. Furthermore, the Rail Administration planners also recognized that 'outside' society (such as the media, the public, other authorities) may not regard the division of responsibility between the public and the private actors in the same way as they do. Faults of a contractor have a potential to 'overflow' and to damage the reputation of, and trust in, the Rail Administration. Thus, what has been identified in the literature as 'reputational risk' (Power et al., 2009) is a salient theme within the risk identification process.

Regulatory Obstacles and Interfering Authorities

Another risk identified concerned the relationships between the project and its social environment, including local property owners, external government authorities, municipalities, and the county board. There are numerous restrictions in terms of administrative rules and legal standards that can have a decisive impact, causing time delays and cost increases for a railway project. Government agencies have diverging interests, for example, regarding environmental protection, heritage conservation, and safety standards. Therefore, they were identified by the planners as potential threats to the implementation of the new railway line. For example, one risk identified and discussed at the brainstorming meeting in March 2007 was that of [finding previously unknown archaeological remains]. It was recognized that such discoveries had caused difficulties for other projects before. It was noted that there were actually plenty of archaeological remains in the area where the new railway line was to be built. There were jokes about this risk and someone commented that the Swedish National Heritage Board (the government authority in charge of the preservation and protection of the historic environment) did not have an adequate inventory of archaeological sites and that therefore findings could turn up unexpectedly. Other risks within this theme were [an archeologically sensational discovery is made] and [a new species of bird or plant is discovered]. The rationale behind these risks was that the legislation about archaeological heritage and nature conservation could come into play if new discoveries were made. The planners agreed that these risks had a low probability, graded as 1. The fact that there were boglands in the south of the route that were not very well investigated was then discussed, alluding to the fact that the actual knowledge about the area was still limited and that some new species could turn up eventually. The consequence of such risks was rated high, namely 5. Someone asked how such risks could affect trust in the Rail Administration since it might suggest that the authority had done a poor job at the investigation stage. The environmental controller added that biotopes worthy of protection were going to be carefully investigated but remarked that a consequence might be that the public would become engaged in the planning process. The group agrees on 3 for probability and 4 for consequence for [loss of trust in the Rail Administration].

Technical Limitations and Traffic Problems

Technical coordination and traffic disturbances, construction problems, and construction logistics in relation to ongoing road and rail traffic during building were recurrent themes during the risk identification exercises. Risks that were identified and discussed at the March 2007 meeting and belong to this category are [connecting different branches of technology like rail, signal, power line], [assisting power into a functional whole], and [project boundaries in relationship to the rail line that remains in operation]. As usual, the first question was about probability. There was no clear answer and someone commented that a complication could be that 'documents are incompatible'. An additional complication was that there was going to be construction work on a congested road which crossed the railway. Someone asked: 'Are these risks two different risks or do they belong together?' Focus then turned to the risks that [road and rail are going to be simultaneously trafficked], and [traffic over Slumpån on the existing railway bridge]. Answering the question 'what is the risk of traffic problems?' someone commented that it would be 'complex to build and difficult to plan'. Building would be difficult since it would be necessary to make adaptations to the existing railway. The question was raised: 'What about probability for Slumpån?'. The answer was that this 'will depend on where the bridge will be located'. The probability was estimated at 4 and whether it should be 5 was discussed. 'At Velanda, it is possible to plan but the probability will depend on the exact location of the line.' What about probability? Nobody seemed to know, and it was said that [traffic problems] 'can occur'. The probability 3 was then suggested.

As to the identified risk that [different technologies do not form a functioning whole] the participants acknowledged that the railway planning stage was important and that 'a few things might have been missed' and that 'coordinated examination must be accomplished'. There then followed the usual question about probability: one answer was that this could happen but that it was something that could be managed: 'the consequences are not very big. But can be very high if it happens on the Inauguration Day!' Nobody, however, seemed to think that this was very likely, and the probability scores of 2 and 3–4 were accordingly suggested. Someone argued that the consequences 'depend' since the risk was not so complex technically, but there were other complications; the risk was then categorized as medium sized, thereby having little significance. The group was asked to decide on a consequence estimate and they settled for 3, with the comment 'which does not lead to any action'.

Resource Uncertainty—Matters of Economy and Expertise

Various factors such as continuity of staff, funding, and internal priorities within the agency were recurrent themes of concern. From a project perspective, decisions made at higher administrative levels could imply that priorities change, and as a consequence so would allocated resources. Another concern related to the financing of later stages of building, when it came to various costs for compensation to stakeholders or restoration work. One set of issues referred to the contractor and especially to the lack of competition in the market among contractors. This was identified as a risk of escalating cost. During the discussions at the March 2007 meeting, the noted risk that [project participants quit] gave rise to a lively discussion. This risk was related to the broader concerns with time and economy, and the consequence was rated as a 4.

Two other risks were identified together [too few contractors leads to high prices] and [too few contractors due to too many restrictions], and a participant commented that 'this is interesting' and 'a consequence of the procuring process'. It was argued that 'a robust market for contractors' was needed. It was also suggested that the Road Administration and Rail Administration should coordinate their procurements better. Someone questioned this, and asked 'What market are we talking about? For tunnels? This is a Nordic market and what about the region?' and, on the assumption that this market was actually very small, the following observation was made: 'You can't squeeze blood from a stone'. Then one participant asked: 'What about the probability for this risk?' The answer supplied was that it 'depends on the procuring authority that can mitigate the risk'. The score of 3 was suggested. What about consequence? 'The cost can easily exceed 30 million' but this figure was objected to as being far too low. 5 was settled on as the consequence rating.

CONCLUDING DISCUSSION: RISK IDENTIFICATION AS THE ORGANIZATIONAL PRACTICE OF VALUATION, STARTING WITH VALUE AND WORKING INSIDE-OUT

These glimpses into risk-identifying practices in railway planning show how, to a great extent, riskwork is intuitive and experience based. Although risk identification and assessment is orchestrated according to a formal risk management protocol, the process is guided by practical reasoning based on a blend of expertise with fragmentary, intuitive, anecdotal, narrative, and socially situated knowledge. Experts draw on their past experience and heuristic conjectures to produce apportionments, hierarchies, bargaining, and qualified guesswork. There is only a nominal resemblance to the formalistic rationality of risk identification techniques and procedures. Understanding risk and risk management work is embedded in more or less explicit organizational practices (Corvellec, 2009), and is shaped by social trust among actors, their respective understanding of the institutional context, collaborative intentions, and a sense of mutual responsibility (see also Boholm, 2013a, 2013b).

In particular, risks are clearly not identified independently of their management—contrary to a cornerstone of formal risk management (e.g. Royal Society, 1992). Rather, risks are identified in the context of how actors understand and anticipate their control of elements deemed crucial to the project (Boholm, 2010). Keeping control over the factors understood to condition the success of the project—e.g. budget, schedule, feasibility, possible vetoes, political support, societal worth—surface as a recurrent concern and a way of structuring discussions.

As predicted by the relational theory of risk (Boholm et al., 2011; Boholm & Corvellec, 2011, 2014), actors focus on the potential threats to values deemed to be critical to the success of their project. Actors keep building relationships between, on the one hand, matters pertaining to insufficient competence, mistakes, violations of contractual agreements, inefficient technical coordination, traffic disturbance, construction problems, and problems in construction logistics, and, on the other hand, matters pertaining to the continuity of staff, available technical expertise, actual and future funding, collaborative stakeholders, and Rail Administration priorities. Riskwork begins with situated valuation processes to establish vested value-meriting protection measures. Valuation practices are therefore at the core of risk identification since it is when risk objects are connected to a value at stake that risk emerges as a meaningful organizational category. Since actors consider time, cost, and quality to be essential values, they focus on what may incur delay, unforeseen expenses, and insufficient performance. Risk identification and assessment rest on collective definitions of potential threats to what matters.

As the present case illustrates, the activity of ascribing value is produced together by actors through managerial activities. Examples of such activities are formal or informal interactions, choices or the absence of decisions, heated debates or consensual agreements, and calculations or rules of thumb. Valuation activities are encapsulated in memos, tables, standards, slogans, contracts, and other inscriptions that enable them to act at a distance (Lowe, 2001; Robson, 1992). In particular, the production of a common inscription in the form of a risk register or map requires and facilitates negotiations across perspectives and organizational members, for example, to assess the relevance of a norm or associate a red, yellow, or green colour to a specific risk. In this sense, the main performance of risk maps may be to enforce communication even when communicative premises are weak (see also Chapter 2, this volume). Practically, but even metaphorically, risk-mapping exercises bring actors to the same table, even if they come from different domains of expert knowledge, or from different hierarchical levels, and even if they all read the map in idiosyncratic ways.

Valuation is an organizational practice embedded in organizational history, culture, and mission, but also in routines and rules of thumb. It is this practice that determines what, at the end of the day, comes to be identified as a risk or not. And, correspondingly, risk identification has its origin in situated judgements about what is of worth and thus a legitimate object of protection. Riskwork can employ objective measures of threats or systematic evaluations of consequences but only after a value at stake has been identified. The starting point involves exercises in practical rationality to establish collective judgements of worth.

If one accepts the position that a potential threat becomes a risk only when attached to something that is of value, as suggested by Boholm & Corvellec (2011), the origin of risk will therefore not be found in external threats but in internal conceptions of value. Riskwork starts with an inside-out activity, where value serves as the heuristic basis for searching out what may constitute a risk, rather than an outside-in activity that consists only in imagining the possible negative consequences of threats.

A relational understanding of risk thus brings with it an invitation to riskworkers to reflect on what is held as of value and why. We have good reasons to assume that most riskworkers have quite clear ideas about value in many cases, in particular when life or money are at stake, but that in other cases their assumptions are less clear. They may not always be fully aware of the practical consequences of the socially flexible character of valuation, to the extent that others not only can have other ways to value things, but that priorities and hierarchies of value often prove to be less stable than admitted. A practical recommendation to riskworkers would therefore be to bring their own valuation processes under systematic critical supervision. Here are three simple questions that organizational participants and others can ask: what are we holding as valuable? Why are we holding this in esteem? Where does this esteem come from? There are indeed good strategic reasons for asking why one is holding, for example, the company brand or a budget in esteem so that any threat to them is considered as a risk to be identified and managed.

Based on our findings, we would also suggest more critical reflection upon what currently established valuation processes mask or downplay. Valuation processes are also devaluation processes in the sense that hierarchies are set up where certain objects are held as more valuable than others. For example, a public administration that gives top priority to economic considerations might downgrade public service, reliability, or sustainability, to mention other possible orders of worth. The question of what cannot be seen or imagined due to established taken-for-granted assumptions opens the way for critical reconsideration of the rationale(s) for organizational activities. An enquiry into why an actor is heralding this and not that as a risk prompts a critique of prevailing organizational sense-making and the social order in which it is embedded. From our perspective, the most important lesson for riskwork is for actors to remain clear about what they hold as being of value and why.

REFERENCES

Appadurai, A. (1986). Commodities and the Politics of Value. In A. Appadurai (Ed.), *The Social Life of Things: Commodities in Cultural Perspective* (pp. 3–63). Cambridge: Cambridge University Press.

Aven, T. & Renn, O. (2009). On Risk Defined as an Event where the Outcome Is Uncertain. *Journal of Risk Research*, 12(1), 1–11.

Banverket (2006). *Banverkets Riskhantering: Handbok* [Rail Administration Risk Management Handbook], HK06-967/AL20, 1 July.

Banverket (2008). *Riskhantering i Banverket* [Risk Management in the Rail Administration], F07-14965/AL20, 1 February.

Beckert, J. & Aspers, P. (Eds) (2011). *The Worth of Goods: Valuation and Pricing in the Economy*. Oxford: Oxford University Press.

Beckert, J. & Zafirovski, M. (2010). *International Encyclopedia of Economic Sociology*. London: Routledge.

Berthoin Antal, A., Hutter, M., & Stark, D. (Eds) (2015). *Moments of Valuation: Exploring Sites of Dissonance*. Oxford: Oxford University Press.

Boholm, Å. (2003). The Cultural Nature of Risk: Can There Be an Anthropology of Uncertainty? *Ethnos: Journal of Anthropology*, 68(2), 159–79.

Boholm, Å. (2010). On the Organizational Practice of Expert-Based Risk Management: A Case of Railway Planning. *Risk Management—An International Journal*, 12(4), 235–55.

Boholm, Å. (2013a). From within a Community of Planners: Hypercomplexity in Railway Design Work. In S. Abram & G. Wiskalnys (Eds), *Elusive Promises: Planning in the Contemporary World* (pp. 57–76). New York and Oxford: Berghahn Books.

Boholm, Å. (2013b). Messy Logic. Organisational Interactions and Joint Commitment in Railway Planning. In C. Garsten & A. Nyqvist (Eds), *Organisational Anthropology: Doing Ethnography in and among Complex Organisations* (pp. 169–86). London: Pluto Press.

Boholm, Å. (2015). *Anthropology and Risk*. London & New York: Routledge.

Boholm, Å. & Corvellec, H. (2011). A Relational Theory of Risk. *Journal of Risk Research*, 14(2), 175–90.

Boholm, Å. & Corvellec, H. (2014). A Relational Theory of Risk: Lessons for Risk Communication. In J. Arvai & L. Rivers (Eds), *Effective Risk Communication* (pp. 6–22). London: Earthscan.

Boholm, Å., Corvellec, H., & Karlsson, M. (2011). The Practice of Risk Governance: Lessons from the Field. *Journal of Risk Research*, 15(1), 1–20.

Bourdieu, P. (1979). *La Distinction: Critique Sociale du Jugement*. Paris: Éditions de Minuit.

Caplan, P. (Ed.) (2000). *Risk Revisited*. London: Pluto Press.

Carrier, J. G. (Ed.) (2005). *Value: Anthropological Theories of Value*. Cheltenham: Edward Elgar.

Cooper, D. F., Walker, P., Raymond, G., & Grey, S. (2014). *Project Risk Management Guidelines: Managing Risk with ISO 31000 and IEC 62*. Chichester: Wiley.

Corvellec, H. (2009). The Practice of Risk Management: Silence Is Not Absence. *Risk Management—An International Journal*, 11(3–4), 285–304.

Corvellec, H. (2010). Organisational Risk as It Derives from What Managers Value: A Practice-Based Approach to Risk Assessment. *Journal of Contingencies and Crisis Management*, 18(3), 145–54.

Corvellec, H. (2011). The Narrative Structure of Risk Accounts. *Risk Management*, 13(3), 101–21.

Dekker, S. (2007). *Just Culture: Balancing Safety and Accountability*. Aldershot: Ashgate.

Dowd, K. (1998). *Beyond Value at Risk: The New Science of Risk Management*. Chichester: Wiley.

Durkheim, É. (1991 [1893]). *De la Division du Travail Social*. Paris: Presses Universitaires de France.

Gherardi, S. & Nicolini, D. (2000). The Organizational Learning of Safety in Communities of Practice. *Journal of Management Inquiry*, 9(1), 7–18.

Grätz, T. (2009). Moralities, Risk and Rules in West African Artisanal Gold Mining Communities: A Case Study of Northern Benin. *Resources Policy*, 34(1–2), 12–17.

Hansson, S. O. (2010). Risk: Objective or Subjective, Facts or Values. *Journal of Risk Research*, 13(2), 231–8.

Helgesson, C.-F. & Muniesa, F. (2013). For What It's Worth: An Introduction to Valuation Studies. *Valuation Studies*, 1(1), 1–10.

Hennion, A. (2015). Paying Attention: What Is Tasting Wine About? In A. Antal Berthoin, M. Hutter, & D. Stark (Eds), *Moments of Valuation: Exploring Sites of Dissonance* (pp. 37–56). Oxford: Oxford University Press.

Heuts, F. & Mol, A. (2013). What Is a Good Tomato? A Case Study of Valuing in Practice. *Valuation Studies*, 1(2), 125–46.

Hilgartner, S. (1992). The Social Construction of Risk Objects: Or, How to Pry Open Networks of Risk. In J. Short & L. Clarke (Eds), *Organizations, Uncertainties, and Risk* (pp. 39–53). Boulder, CA: Westview Press.

Horlick-Jones, T. (2005). On 'Risk Work': Professional Discourse, Accountability, and Everyday Action. *Health, Risk and Society*, 7(3), 293–307.

Jasanoff, S. (1999). The Songlines of Risk. *Environmental Values*, 8(2), 135–52.

Johansson, V. (2012). Negotiating Bureaucrats. *Public Administration*, 90(4), 1032–46.

Kadefors, A. (2004). Trust in Project Relationships—Inside the Black Box. *International Journal of Project Management*, 22(3), 175–82.

Löfstedt, R. (2005). *Risk Management in Post-Trust Societies*. Basingstoke, UK: Palgrave Macmillan.

Lowe, A. D. (2001). 'Action at a Distance': Accounting Inscriptions and the Reporting of Episodes of Clinical Care. *Accounting Forum*, 25(1), 31–55.

Mairal, G. (2003). A Risk Shadow in Spain. *Ethnos: Journal of Anthropology*, 68(2), 179–91.

Mairal, G. (2008). Narratives of Risk. *Journal of Risk Research*, 11(1–2), 41–54.

Mauss, M. (2000 [1902]). *The Gift: The Form and Reason for Exchange in Archaic Societies*. New York: Norton.

Möller, N. (2012). The Concepts of Risk and Safety. In S. Roeser, R. Hillerbrand, P. Sanding, & M. Peterson (Eds), *Handbook of Risk Theory: Epistemology, Decision Theory, Ethics, and Social Implications of Risk* (pp. 56–85). Berlin and Heidelberg: Springer.

Muniesa, F. (2011). A Flank Movement in the Understanding of Valuation. *Sociological Review*, 59, 24–38.

Power, M., Scheytt, T., Soin, K., & Sahlin, K. (2009). Reputational Risk as a Logic of Organizing in Late Modernity. *Organization Studies*, 30(2–3), 301–24.

Ravetz, J. R. (1997). The Science of 'What-If?'. *Futures*, 29(6), 533–9.

Rescher, N. (1983). *Risk: A Philosophical Introduction to the Theory of Risk Evaluation and Management*. Lanham, MD: University Press of America.

Robson, K. (1992). Accounting Numbers as 'Inscription': Action at a Distance and the Development of Accounting. *Accounting, Organizations and Society*, 17(7), 685–708.

Rosa, E. (1998). Metatheoretical Foundations for Post-Normal Risk. *Journal of Risk Research*, 1(1), 15–44.

Royal Society (1992). *Risk: Analysis, Perception and Management*. London: Royal Society.

Sauer, B. J. (2003). *The Rhetoric of Risk: Technical Documentation in Hazardous Environments*. Mahwah, NJ: Lawrence Erlbaum.

Shaw, A. (2000). 'Conflicting Models of Risk': Clinical Genetics and British Pakistanis. In P. Caplan (Ed.), *Risk Revisited* (pp. 85–107). London: Pluto Press.

Shrader-Frechette, K. S. (1991). *Risk and Rationality: Philosophical Foundations for Populist Reforms*. Berkeley, CA: University of California Press.

Sjölander-Lindqvist, A. (2005). Conflicting Perspectives on Water in a Swedish Railway Tunnel Project. *Environmental Values*, 14(2), 221–39.

Stark, D. (2009). *The Sense of Dissonance: Accounts of Worth in Economic Life*. Princeton, NJ: Princeton University Press.

Stoffle, R. & Arnold, R. (2003). Confronting the Angry Rock: American Indians' Situated Risks from Radioactivity. *Ethnos: Journal of Anthropology*, 68(2), 230–48.

Stoffle, R. & Minnis, J. (2008). Resilience at Risk: Epistemological and Social Construction Barriers to Risk Communication. *Journal of Risk Research*, 11(1–2), 55–68.

Strauss, C. & Quinn, N. (1997). *A Cognitive Theory of Cultural Meaning*. Cambridge: Cambridge University Press.

Tarde, G. (1902). *Psychologie économique*. Paris: Felix Alcan.

van Loon, J. (2002). *Risk and Technological Culture: Towards a Sociology of Virulence*. London: Routledge.

Vaughan, D. (1996). *The Challenger Launch Decision: Risky Technology, Culture, and Deviance at NASA*. Chicago, IL: University of Chicago Press.

Weber, M. & Whimster, S. (2008 [1921–2]). *Economy and Society: The Final Version*. London: Routledge.

Weick, K. E. & Sutcliffe, K. M. (2007). *Managing the Unexpected: Resilient Performance in an Age of Uncertainty*. San Francisco, CA: Jossey-Bass.

Wilk, R. R. & Cliggett, L. (2007). *Economies and Cultures: Foundations of Economic Anthropology*. Boulder, CO: Westview Press.

6

Riskwork

Three Scenarios from a Study of Industrial Chemicals in Canada

Steve Maguire and Cynthia Hardy

Risk is a powerful and pervasive frame for contemporary organizations (Hardy & Maguire, 2016). Risk is generally accepted as the probability of adverse effects on human life, health, property, or the environment, which can be managed if the likelihood of the harm or hazard occurring and the nature and magnitude of its effects can be accurately assessed. As a result, organizations invest a considerable amount of time and money in trying to identify and manage a wide range of risks (Power, 2005). In the case of industrial chemicals in Canada, on which this chapter focuses, the risks are particularly important because chemicals have become part and parcel of everyday life. They are 'integrated into nearly all industrial processes and commercial products and now constitute the primary material base of society' (Wilson & Schwarzman, 2009: 1203). The presence of industrial chemicals in virtually every product we use means that individuals are exposed to them on a daily basis, often involuntarily and without their knowledge. Exposure to hazardous chemicals has been linked to a range of chronic diseases, including cardiovascular disease, Parkinson's and Alzheimer's diseases, diabetes, asthma, and cancer (Cooper et al., 2011). Hazardous chemicals also harm the environment, damaging wildlife and reducing populations of birds and other species (WHO/UNEP, 2012). These chemicals cannot be easily contained. For example, chemicals used in regions around the globe migrate to the Canadian Arctic where they accumulate and adversely affect both humans and wildlife, thousands of kilometres away (Environment Canada, 2013). The ability of chemicals to travel in water and air means that it is impossible to confine their effects within national or jurisdictional boundaries.

The health and environmental risks associated with industrial chemicals can result in considerable economic and social costs. The World Health Organization estimates that toxic chemicals may be responsible for more than 8 per cent of all deaths globally, as well as accounting for a significant portion of healthcare costs (Prüss-Ustün et al., 2011). Chronic diseases account for over 60 per cent of Ontario's healthcare budget alone and, across Canada, they affect millions of individuals and cost billions of dollars (Cooper et al., 2011). At the same time, these chemicals make a major contribution to our economy, and employ large numbers of individuals. Canada's chemicals and plastics sector generated revenues of $60 billion in 2010 (Government of Canada, 2013) and, globally, the industry is worth over C$3 trillion (Pike Research, 2011).

It is not surprising, then, that the risks associated with industrial chemicals are of considerable concern to governments, business, and non-governmental organizations (NGOs) alike. In this chapter, we examine three different kinds of risk *scenario*. The first risk scenario concerns the need to address 'established' risks, which stem from hazards that are widely recognized and which have been causally linked to particular practices or products, usually through significant and mainly uncontroversial scientific study. To examine this risk scenario, we study the implementation of Canada's Chemicals Management Plan, which has contributed to the recognition of Canada as a world leader in identifying and acting on chemical risks that are believed to be well established. Second, organizations must also develop ways to deal with 'emerging' risks, which stem from hazards that are perceived to be novel or unfamiliar, and which are only starting to be recognized by some, but not all, members of scientific and other communities. The challenges of emerging risks are greater than those of established risks as they involve considerably more scope for contestation over scientific methods and epistemology. To examine this risk scenario, we study how Canadian organizations are, under the Chemicals Management Plan, grappling with a controversial risk associated with so-called 'endocrine disrupting' chemicals. Third, organizations can try to 'eliminate' risks altogether, by substituting practices or products understood as being hazardous with alternatives believed to be non-hazardous. To examine this risk scenario, we examine how Canadian organizations are engaging with 'green' chemistry—a set of technologies that the US National Research Council describes as essential to sustainable development.

Our aim in this chapter is to explore the nature and complexity of the different kinds of riskwork undertaken by a range of organizations in relation to each of these scenarios in the context of industrial chemicals in Canada. By 'riskwork', we refer to the practices through which organizations ascertain the 'existence' of, and respond to, risk. We also show how riskwork includes particular forms of 'discursive work', by which we refer to the production, distribution, and consumption of texts (Phillips & Hardy, 2002). We show how the nature of this discursive activity differs according to the scenario in question, thereby making an important contribution to the existing work on risk which has, for the most part, failed to distinguish the different challenges associated with the three scenarios.

We begin by introducing our conceptualization of risk, which is based on risk as a discursive construction rather than an objective phenomenon. We then examine each risk scenario and explore the riskwork undertaken by the various organizations involved. Finally, from this analysis we are able to propose a general model of riskwork.

THE DISCURSIVE CONSTRUCTION OF RISK

We consider risks to be discursively constructed (Jasanoff, 1998) in that it is through different discourses that risks get represented, articulated, and made into meaningful objects for intervention (Maguire & Hardy, 2013). Discourses are constitutive, rather than descriptive, of reality 'through the way they make sense of the world for its inhabitants, giving it meanings that generate particular experiences and practices' (Phillips et al., 2004: 636). A discursive approach does not deny that individuals are adversely affected by particular objects, activities, and events (in our case, industrial chemicals), but it does emphasize that risks are made 'real' through language and practices underpinned by professional and scientific expertise and techniques intended to determine and measure the objective existence of risk (Hardy & Maguire, 2016). Discourses provide a language for talking about a given topic, creating bodies of knowledge—about risk in our case—that are believed to be 'true' (Foucault, 1979). They also construct subject positions whose occupants are understood to have particular rights to speak and act (Maguire & Hardy, 2009) in relation to the topic—i.e. risk.

In adopting this discursive approach we are interested in how meanings related to risk are attached to particular objects through the construction of 'three conceptual elements: an object deemed to "pose" the risk, a putative harm, and a linkage alleging some form of causation between the object and the harm' (Hilgartner, 1992: 40). In particular, we explore the riskwork of multiple organizations as they struggle over divergent interpretations of ambiguous data, competing scientific paradigms, different objectives, and diverse conceptions of the public interest in each of the risk scenarios.

THREE RISK SCENARIOS

In this section we present three risk scenarios facing organizations in the field of industrial chemicals in Canada, show how they present different challenges, and describe the discursive work undertaken by different organizations in relation to each scenario.

Riskwork and Established Chemical Risks

Organizations often engage with 'established' risks, by which we mean that the hazard is familiar and its causal connection to some entity is generally recognized to exist. In Hilgartner's (1992) terms, a harm has been established and causally linked to an object, as a result of which the object's status as a 'risk object' is widely accepted by the network of actors of which it is a part. This typically occurs when well-researched hazards have been causally linked over time to existing practices or products through scientific study, and controversy has been laid to rest. By measuring and calculating the magnitude and probability of harm under a range of different circumstances through scientific study, actions can be proposed and taken to avoid or reduce the risk before it materializes (Gephart et al., 2009). In this way, unknown and unpredictable hazards are transformed into predictable, calculable risks that can be controlled (Beck, 1992). In practice, however, established risks are not always so straightforward. Individuals must contend with incomplete information and scientific uncertainty, as well as with divergent judgements about what constitutes an acceptable level of risk (Maguire & Hardy, 2013).

To explore riskwork in the context of the scenario of established risks, we focus on the Chemicals Management Plan, which was introduced within the regulatory framework of the 1999 Canadian Environmental Protection Act (CEPA). CEPA required the categorization of all its 23,000 'legacy' chemicals—chemicals in use that were 'grandfathered' when more stringent chemical regulations and testing requirements were introduced. This categorization identified some 200 chemicals that the government was predisposed to treat as 'CEPA-toxic'—i.e. based on what was known about them it seemed likely that these chemicals would meet the guidelines for toxicity stipulated in the Act.[1] These chemicals were then put into a programme known as the *Challenge* in order to ascertain whether they did pose risks. Many of these risks were considered to be established in so far as hazards had been well researched and were widely accepted, such as in the case of carcinogenicity, neurotoxicity, and mutagenicity. The final conclusion was guided by submissions from

---

[1] Article 64 of CEPA states that 'a substance is toxic if it is entering or may enter the environment in a quantity or concentration or under conditions that (*a*) have or may have an immediate or long-term harmful effect on the environment or its biological diversity; (*b*) constitute or may constitute a danger to the environment on which life depends; or (*c*) constitute or may constitute a danger in Canada to human life or health'.

business, NGOs, and individuals, based on a weight of evidence approach and the precautionary principle.[2]

The *Challenge* was managed by two government departments—Health Canada and Environment Canada—which worked together to assess twelve batches of twelve to twenty chemicals according to strict timelines. For each chemical, a Draft Screening Assessment Report was produced. If the draft report proposed that a chemical was toxic, then a Risk Management Scope document was produced which summarized the issues and invited business organizations, NGOs, and the public to comment. These comments were summarized in the Summary of Public Comments and factored into the Final Screening Assessment Report, which may or may not have confirmed the original conclusion. If the Final Screening Assessment Report concluded that a chemical was not CEPA-toxic, no further action was taken. If a chemical was found to be toxic, various actions could be taken, following further public consultation, 'to control a chemical's research and development, manufacture, use, storage, transport and/or ultimate disposal' (Government of Canada, 2010).[3] Throughout these processes, information on a chemical's properties, hazards, uses, releases to the environment, and routes of exposure to humans was collected and analysed by staff at Health Canada and Environment Canada, and peer-reviewed by external scientists. The government also solicited advice on specific questions from the *Challenge* Advisory Panel, which consisted of twelve members selected for their knowledge and expertise.

The case of vinyl acetate monomer (VAM) provides an example of the specific discursive riskwork associated with carcinogenicity, which is widely accepted as a well-established hazard implicated in chemical risk. VAM is an industrial chemical used to manufacture a wide variety of polymers, and is found in paints, adhesives, and personal care products in the form of residue from the manufacturing process. Scientific findings suggested that long-term exposure to vinyl acetate could cause a carcinogenic response (Vinyl Acetate Council, 2009), as a result of which VAM was included in the *Challenge*. The Draft Screening Assessment Report, released in May 2008, stated that VAM was toxic to humans based on a conclusion that it had a 'non-threshold' mode of action—i.e. there is a possibility of harm to human health at any level of exposure (Environment Canada & Health Canada, 2008). A sixty-day public comment period followed, during which twenty-eight submissions were received from industry organizations, individual companies, and NGOs. Many

---

[2] The former involves integrating multiple measures or bodies of evidence from prior studies, taking into consideration their strengths and weaknesses. The latter affirms that the 'lack of full scientific certainty shall not be used as a reason for postponing cost-effective measures to protect the environment and human health' (Government of Canada, 2009).

[3] Chemicals could be added to the Priority Substances List for further assessment, or to the Toxic Substances List, in which case the government had to prepare a Proposed Risk Management Approach to address the risks, such as regulations, guidelines, and codes of practice.

of these submissions argued that VAM had a 'threshold' mode of action—i.e. only exposure above a threshold level was considered to be harmful.

The government subsequently accepted that VAM did have a threshold mode of action and, consequently, consulted data about exposure scenarios. It finally concluded that the threshold exposure level had not been met—i.e. Canadians were not exposed to VAM at sufficiently high levels for it to constitute a danger to human health. Therefore, VAM did not meet the CEPA criteria for toxicity. In drawing this conclusion, the government consulted the *Challenge* Advisory Panel on whether it agreed that the weight of evidence and application of precaution supported this conclusion (Government of Canada, 2008b). The Panel agreed that it did. Accordingly, the Final Screening Assessment Report reversed the finding of the draft report and, instead, concluded that VAM was *not* toxic. As a result, no Proposed Risk Management Approach document was required, and the file on VAM was closed with a summary of these processes posted on the government's website.

Our analysis (see Maguire & Hardy (2013) for a more detailed account) identified the extensive use of *normalizing* practices in the riskwork carried out by the government. These practices included *referencing*, where accepted scientific knowledge and methods are applied with reference to extant research, scientific experts, and other jurisdictions; *anchoring*, where current activities are related to past activities, decisions, experience, and/or precedents, and continuity is emphasized; *categorizing*, where clearly bounded categories are used, from which certain actions follow—i.e. if X then Y; and *sequencing*, where actions are temporally sequenced through pre-established timelines, charts, flow diagrams, etc. We refer to this emphasis on the application of 'normal' science and adherence to accepted organizational routines as *normalizing* riskwork.

In the case of VAM, government texts contained extensive referencing to other scientific texts. The conclusion of the draft assessment was also explicitly anchored in a long-standing policy that established a general precedent: any chemical categorized as a non-threshold carcinogen was automatically deemed to be toxic to humans. Hence, the initial categorizing of VAM as having a non-threshold mode of action led directly to the initial conclusion of the Draft Screening Assessment Report that VAM was toxic.

It was not only the government that engaged in normalizing riskwork. So, too, did other actors, including individual companies, industry associations, and scientists. For example, industry submissions to the public consultation referenced a report published by the European Union that challenged the argument that VAM had a threshold mode of action (EU, 2008). The government had referenced an earlier, unpublished version of the European Union report (EU, 2007) in the Draft Screening Assessment Report, but had dismissed its conclusions because of the unofficial status of this text (Government of Canada, 2008b). In response to extensive referencing to the published report in the public submissions, the government acknowledged that new information had come to light regarding VAM's mode of action. It went on to reference the published EU report more than fifty times in the Final Screening Assessment Report. In re-categorizing VAM's mode of action as now being a threshold one, new sequencing required that studies of exposure (also referenced in industry submissions) be taken into account. These studies indicated that exposure levels were lower than the threshold for harm. The final conclusion was, therefore, that VAM was not toxic at current exposure levels and therefore there was no need for any risk management measures.

Established risks, as in the case of VAM, are constructed through riskwork that revolves around normalizing practices. Collective understandings exist as to accepted 'facts', models, categories, and their consequences, as well as methods for generating and validating knowledge. The rules of the 'risk game' (Slovic, 1998) are understood and shared. By referencing scientific research, anchoring in past organizational practice, categorizing with accepted rules of inclusion and exclusion, and sequencing according to predetermined steps, the riskwork of multiple actors helps to ensure that the authority and applicability of a shared body of risk knowledge is reproduced; and the credibility of scientific experts is reaffirmed. In this way, risk is constructed through a nexus of pre-existing texts, such as scientific articles, policy documents, and risk assessments from other jurisdictions, which reflect the uncontested outcomes of discursive work carried out in the past. In fact, the status of the body of risk knowledge is sufficiently taken for granted that conclusions about the risk object's status are deemed legitimate, even in cases where decisions are completely reversed, as with VAM. The fact that VAM went from an object constructed as risky to one that was subsequently constructed as one that did not pose risks was not controversial and generated no outcry from NGOs. The normalizing riskwork carried out for VAM resulted in a straightforward change in focus—from determining VAM's mode of action as a carcinogen to measuring levels of exposure to it—due to sequencing routines flowing directly from the re-categorizing of VAM as a threshold (instead of non-threshold) carcinogen between the publication of the draft and final screening assessments. In Hilgartner's terms, the linkage between harm and object was severed through the concept of exposure, showing the discursively constructed nature of even 'established' risks.

Riskwork and Emerging Chemical Risks

Organizations also face a second scenario—'emerging' or novel risks that arise when unfamiliar hazards that are not widely recognized or accepted, and which are only in the early days of becoming causally linked—often tenuously—to particular practices or products. In this regard, it is the *construction* of the risk object that is emerging within the network of actors of which it is a part, as it gains wider attention from some of these actors, albeit that others contest its status as a risk object. Emerging risks involve considerably more scope for struggles over scientific methods and epistemology than established risks. Information concerning the risk is ambiguous (Ash & Smallman, 2008), posing interpretive challenges as actors try to navigate 'a context rich with weak or equivocal signs of potential problems' (Macrae, 2007: 2). The applicability of extant risk knowledge and the appropriateness of particular paradigms and research methods are more likely to be questioned (Maguire & Hardy, 2013). As a result, divergent opinions arise regarding the very nature and existence of a hazard, let alone how best to calculate the likelihood of its magnitude and occurrence (Beck, 1992). Our study of riskwork in the case of emerging risks also concerns the Chemicals Management Plan and the *Challenge* but, in this instance, a different chemical is involved—bisphenol A (BPA).

BPA is used in baby and water bottles, sports equipment, lenses, CDs, and DVDs. Some scientific findings suggested that BPA is an endocrine disruptor—i.e. a chemical that interferes with hormones to cause reproductive, developmental, neural, or other problems. Whereas the risks associated with carcinogens have been researched for decades and are widely accepted in both scientific and lay communities,[4] those associated with endocrine disruption are more recent and controversial. The hazards of endocrine disruption only started to be documented in the 1990s (Colborn et al., 1996). Knowledge about it, as well as causal links to legacy chemicals, is still accumulating; and much of it is contested. Endocrinologists believe endocrine-disrupting chemicals cause significant harm to humans and the environment, but other scientists do not. As a result, there is notable uncertainty as endocrinologists and traditional toxicologists lock horns in a 'paradigm war' as to whether any risk exists at all, criticizing each other's methods for either overstating or understating the hazard (Fagin, 2012). Meanwhile, NGOs have mounted well-publicized campaigns to draw attention to their claims of BPA's adverse effects. At the same time, industry players such as the American Chemistry Council have invested heavily in attempts to dispel these claims, which they refer to as 'myths'.

---

[4] We acknowledge that the risks associated with what are considered to be carcinogens have not always been so widely accepted as, for example, in the struggle over tobacco. This reinforces the importance of a constructionist approach to risk. In the 1950s, the risks of smoking were emerging and only decades later did they become established, in the sense that we use these terms. There is no definitive state when a risk is irreversibly 'established' in an objective way— witness the current debate over climate change, despite many saying that the science is clear on the matter. It is therefore more helpful to see risks as in a process of 'becoming' (Maguire & Hardy, 2013). Nonetheless, for analytical purposes, it is possible to distinguish between risks that are widely accepted as established and those that are in the earlier stages of becoming risks, as we show in this chapter.

Compounding this problem is the particular vulnerability of subpopulations most affected by endocrine disruption, such as fetuses and infants, which makes even small risks unacceptable to the public.

BPA, like VAM, was part of the *Challenge*. In March 2008, shortly before the publication of the Draft Screening Assessment Report, the Challenge Advisory Panel was asked by the government to comment on the use of weight of evidence and precaution in drawing the conclusion that BPA was toxic. The Panel agreed that, 'the weight of evidence and the application of precaution support the conclusion reached by Health Canada' (Government of Canada, 2008a). The following month, the draft Report was published, concluding that BPA was toxic to both humans and the environment, and proposing that it be added to the Toxic Substances List. It was followed by a sixty-day public comment period during which twenty-one submissions were received from industry organizations, NGOs, public health organizations, and individuals. In October, the Final Screening Assessment Report confirmed that BPA constituted a potential danger in the form of neurological effects in the early stages of a child's development, even at relatively low exposure levels. The Proposed Risk Management Approach, published the same month, outlined a proposed ban on baby bottles, initiating another sixty-day public comment period, which saw the receipt of fifteen submissions. In June 2009, the Government announced that BPA would be added to Schedule I of the Hazardous Products Act to allow for the prohibition of the advertisement, sale, and importation of baby bottles containing BPA. In March 2010, this ban was implemented, making Canada the first country in the world to restrict products containing BPA. The ban did not close the file on BPA since the government continued to carry out activities related to other potential risks. As of August 2010, Environment Canada was monitoring BPA and studying landfills to examine the potential for environmental damage over the life cycle of products containing BPA; while Health Canada was working with the food-packaging industry on the implementation of voluntary measures to reduce levels of BPA in infant formula products due to packaging materials used.

In comparing BPA with VAM, we noted that, although there was clear evidence of normalizing in the case of BPA, other practices were also prominent. They included *particularizing*, where a case was made for unique considerations or special treatment. For example, BPA was singled out as the only chemical in the *Challenge* to warrant its own link from the government's chemicals management portal and its own 'fact sheet' and 'frequently asked questions'. There was also significant evidence of *questioning*, where uncertainty and incompleteness of information were highlighted. In the final report, the term 'uncertainty' was mentioned twenty-eight times in 107 pages, compared to only four times in 47 pages in the case of VAM. The heading 'Uncertainties in Evaluation of Risk to Human Health and Identification of Research Needs' was followed by the statement: 'There are a number of uncertainties related to evaluation of risk to human health' which, in turn, was followed by seven bullet points in each of which the term uncertainty/ uncertainties appeared at least once. In other words, uncertainty as to BPA's toxicity was foregrounded. In contrast, the final Report for VAM had only one heading mentioning 'uncertainties', which was followed by two paragraphs with no bullet points, and in which the word uncertainties was mentioned only once. The government also emphasized the importance of *innovating*—i.e. developing novel methods and using new approaches to deal with this chemical, and *pluralizing*, involving stakeholders other than scientists and government officials in risk assessment and management.

In sum, the government, endocrinologists, NGOs, and the public constructed BPA as an exceptional case: one in which there was considerable uncertainty regarding its toxicity for a particularly vulnerable subpopulation. This situation—the fact that BPA *might* cause harm to infants and children—led the government to conclude it had an obligation to act, even if it meant doing so independently of other regulatory jurisdictions, and to take the lead in restricting BPA. In doing so, it acknowledged that decision-making had to combine scientific evidence, including findings that were uncertain or contested, with societal concerns. We refer to the ensemble of these practices as *problematizing* riskwork, which we define as 'the reflexive acknowledgement of potential inadequacies in knowledge, discontinuity in organizational activities, and the use of open-ended deliberations as a basis for action' when addressing risk (Maguire & Hardy, 2013: 240).

It is our contention that, in order to take action on emerging risks, problematizing riskwork is required because of the tenuous status of risk knowledge. The authority and applicability of the body of risk knowledge is contested. What constitutes relevant knowledge; how to produce it; and what to do with it are up for grabs, such that the rules of the broader risk game, in which decisions about individual risk objects are situated, are more fluid as a result of challenges to the dominant paradigm (from toxicology, in the case of BPA) by an alternative one (from endocrinology, in the case of BPA). Problematizing riskwork therefore includes extensive, contemporaneous *discursive work* as struggles *over* the paradigm intensify, obliging actors to respond on multiple fronts and on the basis of equivocal information. In the case of BPA, a great many more texts were produced, distributed, and consumed than in the case of VAM. These texts were longer, there were more of them, and they involved far more questioning of authors' legitimacy, basic 'facts', causal models, and methods for generating and validating knowledge. It was not only the government that engaged in such discursive work. The manufacturers and users of this chemical were also active, albeit promoting different points of view. For example, the American Chemical Council established a number of different websites, all explicitly stating that BPA was safe. NGO texts were equally numerous and voluminous in making counterclaims to those of business. Scientists also engaged in considerable discursive work: there are thousands of publications on BPA, including major reviews of scientific studies by a range of different agencies from around the world, many of which emphasize uncertainty as to its negative effects on health and the environment.

Riskwork and Eliminating Chemical Risks

The third risk scenario arises when organizations take actions to eliminate 'known' risks through the substitution of practices or products believed to be hazardous with alternatives that are believed to be safe, on the grounds that it then becomes possible to avoid the need to manage risk altogether. This scenario is less common, as organizations appear far more likely to attempt to reduce risk to a level deemed 'acceptable' than to try to eliminate it altogether, since the latter often implies the rejection of dominant risk paradigms and transformational change in technologies, which may involve 'unknown' risks (Nakayachi, 2000). Nonetheless, risk elimination remains a goal for some organizations, as in the case of green (or sustainable) chemistry.

Green chemistry is 'the design of chemical products and processes that reduce or eliminate the use or generation of hazardous substances' (Anastas & Warner, 1998: 1). It aims to substitute the use of chemicals that are believed to be associated with particular risks with alternative substances that are intended to be 'benign by design' (Maguire & Bertels, 2012). Green chemistry is a 'design philosophy' (Mulvihill et al., 2011) with the aim of preventing health and environmental problems associated with industrial chemicals by intervening 'at the molecular level' (Maguire et al., 2013: 298). It is premised on the idea of taking action with the aim of eliminating hazards, which stands in stark contrast to traditional approaches to chemical risk management which accept that hazardous substances are a feature of industrialized economies and therefore emphasize limiting exposure to them in order to reduce risk (Maguire et al., 2013). Focusing on exposure tends to result in regulatory bans on chemicals being relatively rare and typically narrow (e.g. BPA is banned in baby bottles but still available for use in food can linings). If, on the other hand, the hazard can be eliminated, there is no need to limit or regulate exposure. Green chemistry also embraces market forces rather than regulation to deal with chemical risks, and is promoted as 'an innovative, non-regulatory, economically driven approach toward sustainability' (Manley, Anastas, & Cue, 2008: 743). The market value of such technologies is growing significantly, although it remains a small proportion of the global chemical industry (Pike Research, 2011).

The substitution of perchloroethylene (perc) with carbon dioxide (CO_2) in dry-cleaning processes is an example of a green chemistry innovation aimed at eliminating risk (Manley et al., 2008). Dry-cleaning relies on solvents, the most common of which has been perc. Existing scientific findings indicate that perc is hazardous to human health (as a carcinogen and a neurotoxin) and the environment (as a soil contaminant that is also toxic to aquatic organisms) (SUBSPORT, 2013). Its use in dry-cleaning therefore not only results in hazardous waste, but also potentially adversely affects workers in dry-cleaning facilities, as well as people whose homes are in the vicinity of these facilities. Traditional approaches to chemical risk management emphasize reducing the risks posed by perc to a level deemed acceptable by limiting exposure through, for example, dry-cleaning machinery design, facility controls, and handling procedures. In contrast, green chemists propose eliminating the risks identified by existing research, and have gone on to conduct further research to identify suitable alternatives and develop them into viable technologies (Sutanto, 2014), based on the absence of hazards and their effectiveness as dry-cleaning solvents. The aim has been to find a suitable substitute to meet the needs of dry-cleaners and their customers and, at the same time, 'advance inherently safer chemicals and products, consistent with the principles of green chemistry' (SUBSPORT, 2013).

In the case of perc, CO_2 has been identified as a viable alternative: it becomes a liquid solvent under high pressure, is non-flammable, non-corrosive, non-toxic, occurs naturally in the environment, and is available on a large scale (Sutanto, 2014). It performs well in terms of effectively cleaning garments and the technology is available. One drawback is that, while CO_2 is both cheap and plentiful, the cost of a CO_2 dry-cleaning machine is high. However, in the long run, green chemists argue that it will save dry-cleaners money by eliminating the hazardous waste disposal and regulatory costs associated with perc. In adopting this approach, green chemists hope to leverage market forces to promote the voluntary abandonment of a hazardous technology by dry-cleaners, thereby eliminating health and environmental risks. The first dry-cleaning plant using CO_2 technology opened in North Carolina in 1999 (Wentz et al., 2001), and CO_2 has since replaced perc in other dry-cleaning businesses in the US and Canada, although adoption has not been as swift or comprehensive as hoped; the majority of dry-cleaners still use perc.

The success of perc and other green chemistry initiatives rests on a reformulation of the definition of 'success' in implementing chemical processes. Traditionally, success was measured in terms of maximizing the yield of a desired chemical product while minimizing costs, without regard to whether the desired chemical product or manufacturing process was found to be hazardous or not.[5] Increasingly stringent environmental regulations in

---

[5] Except insomuch as there are additional costs associated with using or producing hazardous substances.

the 1970s gave greater prominence to new evaluation criteria for industrial chemical processes. In the 1990s, the US Pollution Prevention Act further refined success in terms of 'pollution prevention' and the EPA developed a formal Green Chemistry Program that set as its goal the 'source reduction' of pollution.

We see evidence of riskwork intended both to clarify and legitimate this approach to risk. For example, the Presidential Green Chemistry Challenge awards were created in 1997 to recognize successful attempts to apply green chemistry principles. The Green Chemistry Institute (GCI)—a non-profit organization—was also created in 1997, with the mission of advancing green chemistry research and education. Members of the nascent profession engaged in research and teaching, organizing conferences and editing books (Woodhouse & Breyman, 2005). The field's first textbook (Anastas & Warner, 1998) was written, elucidating twelve principles to guide the research and development of new chemical products and processes that could eliminate chemical risks. Three prestigious Canada Research Chairs were established in green chemistry at McGill, Queen's, and Brock universities in 2003; the first green chemistry course in Canada was launched at McGill University around this time; and a series of high-profile international conferences on green chemistry were held (Li & Jessop, 2004). In this way, green chemistry has become increasingly accepted within the scientific discipline of chemistry in Canada and the US (as well as in many other countries around the world), with dedicated journals, conferences, and professional associations.

Over time, collaboration between green chemists and other actors increased. In addition to securing a place within the scientific discipline, there has been closer cooperation with industry and government. For example, in 2001, the GCI, which had academic, government, and industry stakeholders, allied itself with the American Chemical Society (ACS), becoming fully integrated in 2005 as the ACS Green Chemistry Institute (ACS GCI) (Matus, 2009). The Canadian Green Chemistry Network (CGCN) was launched in 2002, bringing together more than forty academic chemists, as well as researchers from Canada's National Research Council and two ministries, Natural Resources Canada and Environment Canada. A Canadian Green Chemistry Forum was created within the Chemical Institute of Canada, which is the umbrella organization for three Canadian scientific societies (for chemistry, chemical engineering, and chemical technology).

In comparing this risk scenario with the others, we can make a number of observations. First, in striving to eliminate risks, green chemists draw on the existing body of risk knowledge to identify a 'known' risk for elimination, as well as to evaluate the suitability of alternatives. Therefore, much of the riskwork revolves around normalizing practices that are associated with conventional, quantitative risk assessment. There are, then, parallels with the established risk scenario. However, this riskwork is different in so far as it also involves discursive work to reformulate the *goals* of this normalizing riskwork. Second, like the emerging risk scenario, the risk object is identified by actors not centrally located in the field who must engage with more dominant players—in this case green chemists vs. regular chemists. However, instead of an adversarial relationship as there was between endocrinologists and toxicologists, there is far more evidence of collaboration as green chemists have inserted themselves into mainstream chemistry organizations and structures. Consequently, a significant amount of discursive work goes into symbolizing scientific legitimacy through textbooks, principles, etc., and locating a place for green chemistry within mainstream chemistry.

DISCUSSION AND CONCLUSIONS

Our three case studies show differences in riskwork depending on which scenario faces the organizations in question. This allows us to propose a more general model of riskwork in different risk scenarios, as summarized in Table 6.1.

In the case of risks that appear established, the riskworkers are embedded in the dominant paradigm and occupy central and highly institutionalized positions in a field in which actors have come to share understandings of risk. The riskwork is routine and institutionalized—standardized practices of risk assessment and management are initiated by central actors according to normalized methods and procedures, and based on assumptions that the risk object is identifiable through the use of these models and techniques that measure it as a function of hazard and exposure. It includes relatively little contemporaneous discursive work to construct risk objects because riskworkers, who occupy well-accepted subject positions such as regulators, scientists etc., draw on extensive discursive work undertaken in the past. Any struggle among these actors occurs within the dominant paradigm that underpins the incumbent body of risk knowledge. It arises in relation to individual risk objects and is resolved through further application of normal routines. Riskwork of this nature is therefore likely to reproduce the status quo with incremental change in practices. As a result, the incumbent body of risk knowledge is reproduced, while new risk knowledge will tend to develop incrementally along a continuous trajectory with incumbent subject positions continuing to be privileged.

In the case of risks that appear to be emerging, riskwork is likely to be initiated by actors embedded in an alternative paradigm and occupying peripheral positions in the field that are not, at least initially, recognized as legitimate by central, dominant actors. The riskwork is likely to be novel and conflictual as peripheral actors focus on problems with the incumbent body of

Table 6.1. Comparing riskwork in three scenarios

Scenario	Established risks	Emerging risks	Eliminating risks
Example	VAM: risk assessment and management in Chemicals Management Plan	BPA: risk assessment and management in Chemicals Management Plan	Perc: risk elimination via Green Chemistry innovations
Who are the riskworkers?	Actors embedded in the dominant paradigm, who occupy central and highly institutionalized positions in the field	Actors embedded in an alternative paradigm, who occupy peripheral positions in the field that are not recognized as legitimate by central, dominant actors	Actors embedded in a nascent paradigm, who occupy peripheral positions in the field that are not recognized as legitimate by central, dominant actors
What is the nature of riskwork?	Practices to ascertain and address risk are routine and institutionalized: riskwork is initiated by central actors according to normalized methods and procedures	Practices to ascertain and address risk are novel, conflictual: riskwork is initiated by peripheral actors who focus on problems— i.e. they question the appropriateness of the incumbent body of risk knowledge and advocate alternative methods and procedures	Practices to ascertain risk are routine and institutionalized, but practices to address risk are novel and collaborative: riskwork is initiated by peripheral actors who focus on solutions— i.e. they accept the incumbent body of risk knowledge but suggest alternative trajectories for its development
What is the nature of discursive work?	Little contemporaneous discursive work because riskworkers draw on discursive work undertaken in the past; struggle occurs within an established paradigm underpinning the incumbent body of risk knowledge, arises in relation to individual risk objects, and is contained	Extensive contemporaneous discursive work by riskworkers to legitimize the alternative body of risk knowledge and delegitimize the established one; struggle occurs over competing paradigms and appropriateness of the incumbent body of risk knowledge, and is significant	Extensive contemporaneous discursive work by riskworkers to legitimize new subject positions within the incumbent body of risk knowledge; some struggle occurs over the direction in which the incumbent body of risk knowledge should evolve
How is the risk object conceptualized?	Risk object is assumed to be identifiable with existing models and techniques for measuring risk as a function of hazard and	Risk object is assumed not to be identifiable with existing models and techniques for measuring risk as a function of hazard and	Risk object is assumed to be identifiable with existing models and techniques for measuring risk as a function of hazard and

	exposure; emphasis on reducing exposure to hazard	exposure; emphasis on alternative models and techniques to identify risk	exposure; emphasis on eliminating hazard via hazard-free alternatives
What are the effects?	Incumbent body of risk knowledge is reproduced; new risk knowledge continues to develop incrementally along a continuous trajectory; incumbent subject positions continue to be privileged	Incumbent body of risk knowledge is undermined; alternative body of risk knowledge is developed; new subject positions become legitimated; incumbent subject positions are disrupted	Incumbent body of risk knowledge is reproduced; new risk knowledge develops along a discontinuous trajectory; new subject positions become legitimated; incumbent subject positions are not disrupted

risk knowledge. Riskworkers attempting to construct a risk object argue that it is not recognized by dominant actors because existing models and techniques are based on inappropriate understandings of hazards and causal relationships. To solve this problem, they propose new methods and approaches associated with the alternative paradigm they advocate. Extensive contemporaneous discursive work by riskworkers is required to legitimize the alternative paradigm and delegitimize the dominant one, as a result of which significant struggle occurs over competing paradigms and the appropriateness of the incumbent body of risk knowledge. In the case of industrial chemicals, a long-standing mantra of 'the dose makes the poison' underpins traditional toxicology—i.e. the greater the exposure to a hazardous chemical, the greater its negative effects. However, many endocrinologists dispute this assumption, arguing that endocrine-disrupting chemicals can pose greater risks at low doses as compared to higher ones because their dose–response curves are 'non-monotonic'.[6] Such new knowledge is incompatible with existing risk knowledge. As a result, riskwork serves to undermine the incumbent body of risk knowledge and disrupt incumbent subject positions, while an alternative body of risk knowledge is developed and new subject positions are legitimated.

In the case of eliminating risks, riskwork is also undertaken by actors who occupy peripheral positions in the field which are, at least initially, not recognized as legitimate by central, dominant actors. Riskwork is novel not so much in terms of practices to ascertain risk but in terms of those to deal with risks. The incumbent body of risk knowledge is accepted—the risk object is assumed to be identifiable with existing models and techniques for measuring risk as a function of hazard and exposure. In our case, the existing

---

[6] They do not follow a linear relationship.

body of risk knowledge allowed green chemists to ascertain that perc was hazardous. However, riskworkers place a different emphasis on how to deal with that risk—rather than restrict exposure to perc, they proposed that it be substituted with CO_2. Also, in contrast to the case of emerging risks, riskwork is collaborative, bringing together peripheral and central actors. Extensive contemporaneous discursive work is required by riskworkers to legitimate their new subject positions within the frame of the incumbent body of risk knowledge and in relation to dominant actors; and to advocate a new direction in which this risk knowledge should evolve through, in our case, the creation of a bona fide scientific sub-discipline. As a result, the incumbent body of risk knowledge is reproduced, although it develops along a discontinuous trajectory, and new subject positions become recognized as legitimate but without disrupting incumbent subject positions.

In sum, we have examined three case studies to explore the risks associated with the use of industrial chemicals in Canada, with a view to understanding better the riskwork undertaken by organizations in the context of three different scenarios: an apparently established risk in the case of VAM, which was ultimately assessed as non-toxic as part of the Chemicals Management Plan; emerging risks in the case of BPA, which led to restrictions on baby bottles, also as part of the Chemicals Management Plan; and eliminating risks in the case of perc, which green chemists have sought to substitute with CO_2 in dry-cleaning. We find that the riskwork carried out in each scenario is quite different in terms of which organizations conduct riskwork, how they conduct it, how they conceptualize risk objects, the nature of the discursive work they are required to do, and the effects their riskwork has on the incumbent body of risk and dominant subject positions. This has allowed us to propose a more general model of the three scenarios. We acknowledge that we have presented the scenarios in the form of 'ideal types' and it is likely that there is some overlap among them. Nonetheless we hope that our work will encourage other researchers to explore these different scenarios in more depth and in relation to other fields where the risks in question are posed by objects other than chemicals.

ACKNOWLEDGEMENT

The authors gratefully acknowledge the support of the Australian Research Council (DP160101088 and DP110101764) and the Social Sciences & Humanities Research Council of Canada (435-2014-0256). Some of the material in this chapter is adapted from Maguire & Hardy (2013)

REFERENCES

Anastas, P. T. & Warner, J. C. (1998). *Green Chemistry: Theory and Practice.* Oxford: Oxford University Press.

Ash, J. S. & Smallman, C. (2008). Rescue Missions and Risk management: Highly Reliable or Over Committed? *Journal of Contingencies and Crisis Management,* 16(1), 37–52.

Beck, U. (1992). *Risk Society: Towards a New Modernity.* New Delhi: Sage.

Colborn, T., Dumanoski, D., & Myers, J. P. (1996). *Our Stolen Future: Are We Threatening Our Fertility, Intelligence, and Survival?—A Scientific Detective Story.* New York: Plume.

Cooper, K., Marshall, V., Vanderlinden, L., & Ursitti, F. (2011). *Early Exposures to Hazardous Chemicals/Pollution and Associations with Chronic Disease: A Scoping Review.* Canadian Environmental Law Association, Toronto, ON, Canada. <http://www.cela.ca> (accessed July 2013).

Environment Canada (2013). Environment Canada Research Projects. <http://www.ec.gc.ca/api-ipy> (accessed 17 July 2013).

Environment Canada & Health Canada (2008). *Screening Assessment for the Challenge Acetic Acid Ethenyl Ester (Vinyl Acetate Monomer) Chemical Abstracts Service Registry Number 108-05-4.* <https://www.ec.gc.ca/ese-ees/default.asp?lang=En&n=E41E17F4-1> (accessed July 2010).

EU (2007). *European Union Risk Assessment Report Draft 2007: Risk Assessment Vinyl Acetate CAS No. 108-05-4 EINECS No. 203-545-4.* Draft of 06/12/2007.

EU (2008). *European Union Risk Assessment Report: Vinyl Acetate CAS No. 108-05-4 EINECS No. 203-545-4.* <http://ec.europa.eu/health/ph_risk/committees/04_scher/docs/scher_o_108.pdf> (accessed 31 January 2011).

Fagin, D. (2012). The Learning Curve. *Nature,* 490(7421), 462–5.

Foucault, M. (1979). *Discipline and Punish: The Birth of the Prison.* Harmondsworth, UK: Penguin.

Gephart, R. P., Jr, Van Maanen, J., & Oberlechner, T. (2009). Organizations and Risk in Late Modernity. *Organization Studies,* 30(2–3), 5–20.

Government of Canada (2008a). *Chemicals Management Plan—Challenge Advisory Panel. Summary Report: March 28, 2008.* Ottawa: Government of Canada.

Government of Canada (2008b). *Chemicals Management Plan—Challenge Advisory Panel. Summary Report: From the Meetings held October 20 and 27, 2008.* Ottawa: Government of Canada.

Government of Canada (2009). *Call for the Nomination to the Challenge Advisory Panel.* Ottawa: Government of Canada.

Government of Canada (2010). *Order Adding a Toxic Substance to Schedule 1 to the Canadian Environmental Protection Act, 1999.* <http://www.gazette.gc.ca/rp-pr/p1/2010/2010-02-27/html/reg1-eng.html> (accessed July 2010).

Government of Canada (2013). *Chemicals and Plastics.* http://www.international.gc.ca/investors-investisseurs/sector-secteurs/chemicals-chimiques.aspx> (accessed 17 July 2010).

Hardy, C. & Maguire, S. (2016). Organizing Risk: Discourse, Power and Riskification. *Academy of Management Review,* 41(1), 80–108.

Hilgartner, S. (1992). The Social Construction of Risk Objects: Or, How to Pry Open Networks of Risk. In J. F. Short Jr & L. Clarke (Eds), *Organizations, Uncertainties, and Risk* (pp. 39–51). Boulder, CO: Westview Press.

Jasanoff, S. (1998). The Political Science of Risk Perception. *Reliability Engineering and System Safety*, 59(1), 91–9.

Li, C. J. & Jessop, P. G. (2004). Guest Editorial: Canada is Greener this Spring. *Green Chemistry*, 6, 51.

Macrae, C. (2007). *Interrogating the Unknown: Risk Analysis and Sensemaking in Airline Safety Oversight*. Discussion paper no. 43. Economic and Social Research Council Centre for Analysis of Risk and Regulation, London School of Economics and Political Science, London.

Maguire, S. & Bertels, S. (2012). Chemistry and Business that are Benign by Design: Leveraging the Canadian Chemistry Industry's Leadership in Sustainability. *Catalyst*, winter, 19–20.

Maguire S. & Hardy, C. (2009). Discourse and Deinstitutionalization: The Decline of DDT. *Academy of Management Journal*, 52(1), 148–78.

Maguire, S. & Hardy, C. (2013). Organizing Processes and the Construction of Risk: A Discursive Approach. *Academy of Management Journal*, 56(1): 231–55.

Maguire, S., Iles, A., Matus, K., Mulvihill, M., Schwarzman, M. R., & Wilson, M. P. (2013). Bringing Meanings to Molecules by Integrating Green Chemistry and Social Sciences. In International Social Science Council (Eds), *World Science Report 2013: Changing Global Environments: Transformative Impact of Social Sciences* (pp. 298–303). Paris: UNESCO.

Manley, J. B., Anastas, P. T., & Cue, B. W. Jr (2008). Frontiers in Green Chemistry: Meeting the Grand Challenges for Sustainability in R&D and Manufacturing. *Journal of Cleaner Production*, 16, 743–50.

Matus, K. (2009). The ACS Green Chemistry Institute: A Case Study of Partnerships to Promote Sustainability in the Chemical Enterprise. In National Academies Press (Ed.), *Enhancing the Effectiveness of Sustainability Partnerships: Summary of a Workshop* (pp. 263–92). Washington, DC: National Academies Press.

Mulvihill, M. J., Beach, E. S., Zimmerman, J. B., & Anastas, P. T. (2011). Green Chemistry and Green Engineering: A Framework for Sustainable Technology Development. *Annual Review of Environment and Resources*, 36, 271–93.

Nakayachi, K. (2000). Do People Actually Pursue Risk Elimination in Environmental Risk Management? *Risk Analysis*, 20(5), 705–11.

Phillips N. & Hardy, C. (2002). *Discourse Analysis: Investigating Processes of Social Construction*. Thousand Oaks, CA: Sage.

Phillips, N., Lawrence, T., & Hardy, C. (2004). Discourse and Institutions. *Academy of Management Review*, 29(4), 635–52.

Pike Research (2011). *Green Chemistry: Bio-based Chemicals, Renewable Feedstocks, Green Polymers, Less-toxic Alternative Chemical Formulations, and the Foundations of a Sustainable Chemical Industry*. Washington, DC: Pike Research.

Power, M. (2005). The Invention of Operational Risk. *Review of International Political Economy*, 12(4), 577–99.

Prüss-Ustün, A., Vickers, C., Haelfliger, P., & Bertollini, R. (2011). Knowns and Unknowns on Burden of Disease due to Chemicals: A Systematic Review. *Environmental Health*, 10(9), 1–15.

Slovic, P. (1998). The Risk Game. *Reliability Engineering and System Safety*, 59, 73–7.

SUBSPORT (2013). Specific Substances Alternatives Assessment—Perchloroethylene. <http://www.subsport.eu/wp-content/uploads/data/perchloroethylene.pdf> (accessed 30 July 2013).

Sutanto S. (2014). *Textile Dry Cleaning Using Carbon Dioxide: Process, Apparatus and Mechanical Action.* The Netherlands: Gildeprint.

Vinyl Acetate Council (2009). *Health and Environment (excerpt from the Vinyl Acetate Safe Handling Guide).* Washington, DC: Vinyl Acetate Council.

Wentz, M., Beck, K. R., Monfalcone, V. A., & Slivensky, R. D. (2001). Colorfastness of Fabrics Cleaned in Liquid Carbon Dioxide. *AATCC Review*, 1(5), 25–30.

WHO/UNEP (2012). *State of the Science for Endocrine-disrupting Chemicals.* Geneva/Nairobi: World Health Organization/United Nations Environment Program.

Wilson, M. P. & Schwarzman, M. R. (2009). Toward a New U.S. Chemicals Policy: Rebuilding the Foundation to Advance New Science, Green Chemistry, and Environmental Health. *Environmental Health Perspectives*, 117(8), 1202–9.

Woodhouse, E. J. & Breyman, S. (2005). Green Chemistry as Social Movement? *Science, Technology, & Human Values*, 30(2), 199–222.

7

Technoculture

Risk Reporting and Analysis at a Large Airline

Tommaso Palermo

> If they get into the whistle-blower line then they've gone too far; you don't
> need a whistle, we give them a whole orchestra to play with, the whistle's
> the last thing on our list.
>
> (senior manager, Safety Department, at Airline)

Enterprise risk management frameworks portray risk management as a
standardized process of risk identification, reporting, and control (see
AIRMIC, ALARM, & IRM, 2002; COSO, 2004; ISO, 2009). However, risk
identification, reporting, and control are multifaceted practices. How can
individuals understand what qualifies as a risk to be reported (Macrae, 2007a,
2007b; Weick & Sutcliffe, 2007)? How can organizations address the numerous
biases that inhibit the ability to discuss risks and failures (Kaplan & Mikes,
2012)? What is the right balance between the use of incentive structures that
recognize financial and legal liability for risk and adoption of 'no-blame'
cultures (Hood & Jones, 1996)? What are the consequences of 'speaking up'
in contexts that are subject to increased demands for public scrutiny (Power,
2007)? And how do executives react to 'bad news' (Simons, 1999)?

Organizations often address these issues of risk identification and escalation
by prescribing structural changes and by adopting new control technologies
such as whistle-blowing, oversight functions, formal values-based controls,
reporting and monitoring systems. Demands for improvement are also made
in terms of 'softer' elements such as corporate (risk) cultures and ethics (e.g.
Kaplan & Mikes, 2012; Power et al., 2013; Weick & Sutcliffe, 2007). This
chapter explores the relations between control technologies and organizational
culture and how their mutual interdependence influences the flow of information between front-line, staff functions (e.g. risk, compliance, internal audit),
and top managers. The focus of this chapter can be characterized in terms of

the following questions: when and how do (and can) people feel free to 'speak up' and report risks? What kinds of technologies and cultures enable risk reporting and analysis? How does their operation define specific ways of working with risk?

In the spirit of this volume, the chapter does not draw on a specific theoretical lens or body of the literature. The chapter rather provides an empirical account of riskwork within the Safety Department of a large airline company (anonymized here as Airline). As suggested in the chapter's epigraph, the Safety Department provides to members of staff 'a whole orchestra' to play with. Following a brief account of the data collection and research methods, the chapter begins by illustrating the practices that constitute such an 'orchestra'. Second, it develops the notion of *technoculture*, which aims to capture the way in which a specific notion of corporate culture becomes hardwired, materialized, and operationally expressed by reporting and other managerial systems. Third, the chapter shows how this notion of technoculture helps us to understand riskwork by drawing on two vignettes, which illustrate how safety data are captured, used, and acted upon.

METHODS

The author collected qualitative data from the Safety Department of a major airline company, headquartered in the UK and operating a wide range of national and international flights.[1] Data were gathered from face-to-face meetings with six members of the Safety Department (including the director, her deputy and four members of staff from three distinct teams) and from public documents such as corporate reports and media articles. Formal interviews were complemented by informal conversations with the director and other members of staff. Interviews with the director and her deputy were recorded and then transcribed, while detailed notes were taken during the other meetings (therefore, unless specified otherwise, all quotes in this chapter come from the two senior managers).

The headquarters of Airline were visited in two distinct periods of time (May 2013 and May 2014), thus providing a tentative sense of the longitudinal development of safety risk workstreams. The company visits also included comprehensive exposure to different office spaces, including the working environment of senior managers, managers and members of staff from different functions (e.g. safety, commercial, engineers), crew rooms and the

[1] Data collection was initially carried out in the context of a broader project on risk culture in financial organizations (together with Mike Power (LSE) and Simon Ashby (Plymouth Business School)).

corporate canteen. Moreover, it was possible to observe the functioning of the safety reporting system (with simulated data), a demonstration of the use of smart phone apps to access the internal reporting system, as well as a video related to the induction programme for new hires. Observation of such elements complemented data collected from interviews and documents. As a research strategy, the approach adopted reflects the spirit of calls for closer attention to the field within research on '(risk) work' in organization studies (Barley & Kunda, 2001).

Data collected from the company were also complemented by information obtained directly from senior representatives of the UK aviation regulatory agency. Two meetings took place in July and October 2014. The conversations focused on the regulation and oversight of safety risks within the airline sector. Finally, interview material was supplemented by an analysis of publicly available material such as policy documents and corporate presentations.

PRACTICES

Just Culture

The notion of just culture was reiterated several times in relation to the work done within the Safety Department. This notion has been articulated in prior work on safety and crisis management in relation to the way in which organizations handle blame and punishment, and how this can influence what gets reported (Reason, 1997; Weick & Sutcliffe, 2007). Weick and Sutcliffe (2007: 131) describe just culture as 'an atmosphere of trust in which people are encouraged, even rewarded, for providing essential safety-related information—but in which they are clear about where the line must be drawn between acceptable and unacceptable behavior'. One interviewee defined just culture in her own way as follows:

> Just culture is a culture whereby an individual can make an honest mistake or perhaps an omission but where wilful violations are not tolerated...Because you can't have a no-blame culture whereby I want X to tell me if he's made a mistake and I promise you if you've made a mistake I won't do anything, okay...That is not good in the interests of the individual, nor the individual's colleagues, nor the interests of the business; there has to be this *idea of justice*. And that means that we can have a *fair hearing*. [emphasis added]

So the just culture concept recognizes that Airline has responsibility to identify the causal factors of a safety event to reduce the risk of recurrence, and also acknowledges that human failures can be the root cause of an event. But it also recognizes that if individuals operate in line with the company's procedures, training, and experience, then the failure will not necessarily result in disciplinary sanctions. Just culture is strongly intertwined with attitudes to internal reporting that reflect confidence in the possibility of having what interviewees called a 'fair hearing'. As put by a senior manager:

> If it's been a genuine mistake, if it's been a genuine omission, okay and it's commensurate with your training and skill level, then we need to learn from it. We might retrain you, we might give you some additional support but you fear not.

Just culture, and its development, is related to organizational culture (interviewees mention the famous expression attributed to Edgar Schein: 'the way we do things around here'), and so-called 'soft' elements such as 'energy' and 'leadership', the quality and amount of 'dialogue' between employees and senior management as well as among employees themselves. One senior manager often made reference to the formation of a 'contract of understanding' between the employee, the company, and its senior management. Using her words, 'we want you to report, we need that information to make your environment safer...But for you to report you need to understand how we're going to behave'. The description of such a cultural contract echoes discussions of culture as ways of knowing and sensemaking. Paraphrasing Schein, the key question is not so much how 'we do things around here', but 'how we develop expectations around here' (Weick & Sutcliffe, 2007: 119).

But just culture is also based on physical processes and procedures that contribute to the identification of a risk, its reporting as well as understanding whether it's a 'genuine mistake' or 'a wilful negligent act'. In short, the systemic component of just culture consists of a number of reporting and monitoring technologies. The following sections focus on three such technologies that share a set of commonalities, namely a strong emphasis on encouraging internal reporting, the availability of large datasets, and the relevance of data analysis skills.

Safety Reporting

The Safety Reporting[2] (SR) system is a web application that is designed to engage all staff in safety management and incident reporting. It is a hub for reporting safety issues, which is capable of supporting various processes such as event investigation, risk assessment and analysis, and peer reviews. SR has more than 10,000 users and almost 30,000 reports were recorded in the year preceding the research. The purpose of the system is to allow personnel to report any safety matters and it is adjusted to the different areas of the

---

[2] The name of the application has been modified to maintain anonymity.

organization (e.g. pilots, crew members, and other personnel). The underlying philosophy is that any and all matters should be reported. As put by a senior manager:

> So each area of the organization has a dedicated report form on which they can report any safety matters, whether they're...you know, if I take the pilot example, the pilot will use it to report any incidents that occur or potential incidents that occur during their operation. He'll also report it for a trip hazard on the way into the office, he'll also use it if he was transferring from one airport to another in a taxi and the taxi driver was mad. So you know, they have these dedicated streams that are particular to each department.

Figure 7.1 provides an overview of the application functionalities and reporting process. All investigations start with an incident report filed by a member of staff (hereafter called the reporter). The system has pre-set event descriptors with over 2,000 combinations that can be chosen by the person reporting an event, while basic information is already automatically inserted (e.g. number of flight, crew members). The bottom half of the screen visualized by the reporter asks for details about the event type, which can be very granular. Let's suppose that a bird has hit the airplane. Crew members can access the reporting system remotely, where some details are already inserted (e.g. crew details). The reporter inserts information about the event type. Further questions will be selected by the system based on the input already given: for instance, the part of the plane that was struck, type of bird, estimated number of birds. The reporter can highlight whether some information should be treated as confidential in case further investigation arises. The reporter can also use a red flag process to alert management to a potential safety risk that needs attention. The management then decides if the red flag warrants immediate attention.

The report can be closed immediately depending on the investigator's judgement about the relevance of the risk event. Alternatively, the investigation can take more or less time depending on each case. In some cases explanatory reports can take several months as the investigators need to seek out help with operations, engineers, and other functional experts. Indeed, requests for peer reviews are frequent. Information from experts is collected, stored, and can be retrieved as needed in specific boxes within the system. The final report is sent out to various recipients who have been involved with the investigation. The investigator can decide which parts of the report to disclose, who can receive the report, and which sections the recipient would be able to see. If recommendations are raised by investigators, the reporter or other staff involved need to upload evidence that something has been done or the reasons why the recommendations were rejected.

Various reports can be flexibly created and published based on different parts of the investigation (e.g. descriptors, recommendations, actions, risk

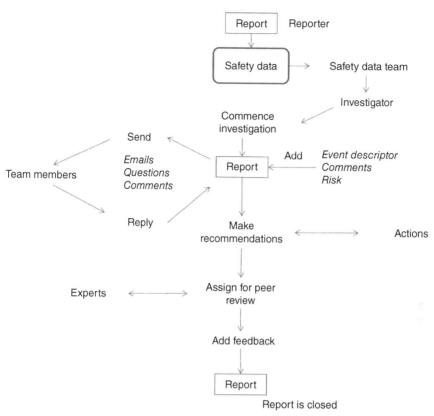

Figure 7.1. Safety reporting system at Airline

values). The system also provides a platform to interact with regulators. Investigators can do a print screen of different parts of the investigation and hand this material to the regulators. As put by one investigator: 'we just tell them, have a look yourself!'. The reports can be used as factual evidence that something is a recurring problem in a specific context (e.g. a 'bad' airport), and may require regulatory attention.

Flight Data Monitoring

Pilots' performance is also monitored in real time through a flight data monitoring (FDM) system. According to one member of the monitoring team, FDM aims to provide a 'non-punitive environment' to analyse data from black boxes. The investigations are carried out at central offices by a team of four people, all of whom have been active pilots in the past, an element that helps to add 'content and background' to the data analysis. As put by a member of the team, 'otherwise we would not have credibility' in conversations with flying pilots.

The analysis can be triggered by a pilot asking for it, by a safety report being filed, or by the monitoring team directly. Even if a pilot is not asking for it, the flight monitoring team should be able to start an investigation anyway. As put by one member of the team, 'the pilot needs to file a report if there is a reportable event', but the team revising the data 'would be able to pick up an anomaly anyway'. FDM is described as being not 'malicious' in intent, but the data basically enables the reconstruction of all the actions that have been taken by a pilot. Using the words of a member of the monitoring team, the system allows them to 'see if the pilot has done the right thing, for example in case of TCAS[3] if he was told to go down, did he actually go down?'.

The key skill according to the monitoring team's members is related to data analysis. For example, an investigation can relate to turbulence that is considered excessive. The monitoring team examines the data, which can be presented in different forms such as a spreadsheet or 3D visualizations of the plane's movement. If the problem cannot be figured out directly by the monitoring team, then the data is transferred to engineers. The opinion of engineers is normally sought anyway on the final document. The amount of information is significant, and a good investigator should be able to pick up the pieces of information that enable an explanation of the problem that has occurred, even if this information is not the most visible.

Fatigue Risk Management

The company has also developed a reporting process around fatigue issues, which since the early 2000s have been an increasingly prominent part of operational risk (e.g. including high risk events such as micro-sleep during critical phases of a flight). Fatigue risk management (FRM) is defined as a data-driven means of monitoring and managing fatigue-related safety risks to make sure that personnel are performing at an adequate level of alertness. Although there are regulations for FRM, an interviewee stated that 'the boundaries are thin…there are a number of things that can be done within or outside the rules'. For instance, a twelve-hour break can be interpreted flexibly as it can be taken at any time: 'but it is not the same twelve hours at night and twelve hours in the middle of the day'. Therefore, as illustrated by one senior manager, 'what [the Airline] did then was to challenge the regulator on the basis of academically accredited procedures and processes to say look, we think we can do this differently'.

The FRM system consists of several different components: an FRM policy; a crew fatigue reporting mechanism with associated feedback; procedures and

---

[3] A Traffic Collision Avoidance System monitors the airspace around an aircraft for other aircraft equipped with a corresponding active transponder, and warns pilots of the presence of other aircraft which may present a threat of collision.

measures for assessing and monitoring fatigue levels; procedures for investigating, and recording incidents that are attributable wholly or in part to fatigue; processes for evaluating information on fatigue levels and fatigue-related incidents, undertaking interventions, and evaluating the effects of those interventions; awareness training programmes; and, finally, a performance audit plan. Once again, internal reporting is the key trigger for fatigue-related investigations. The data is based on detailed reports filed by pilots and crew members (around 6,000 reports in the year preceding my research) which include elements such as details of current duty, previous duties, flying hours, night stops away from base, commute times, sickness records, and other so-called 'hassle' factors.

FRM team members see themselves as internal consultants and produce 'a huge amount of reporting every month' that aims to help decision-making, including for commercially sensitive issues such as flight scheduling. As in SR and FDM described above, the team aimed to encourage a reporting culture around fatigue risks. The availability of large samples of data was seen as crucial to identify specific stress points, such as certain airports that are at the centre of many routes and therefore can cause more problems with assembling crews. The FRM team analyses the data and tries to find the root causes, often through predictive models with the help of SR information. In contrast to other safety teams, most of the FRM team members do not have a background as flying pilots; 'being good with numbers' is instead the key skill required.

TECHNOCULTURE

The four discrete but related safety practices of Airline suggest a specific view of the relation between culture and control technologies, summarized by the motif of technoculture. Far from being a fully developed concept, technoculture may be useful in moving forward the theoretical and empirical study of how, where, and when risk management work takes place. Of course, 'technology' and 'culture' are topics that have been researched extensively in different ways and it would be overambitious to argue that a new compound word is self-evidently descriptive. In fact, the analytical distinction between culture and technology can be challenged in the first place. On the one hand, an organization can be seen as *being* a culture as opposed to *having* a culture (Alvesson, 2002: 24–9). According to this perspective, culture is not separable from other organizational properties, including technology. Rather, it permeates the entire organization and is reproduced in formal structures, administrative processes, strategic plans, and other, apparently technical, tasks and results-oriented activities. On the other hand, technology can be seen as a social product, rather than having a social impact once it is produced (Bijker et al., 1987). If one looks closely at those who work with technology

(e.g. engineers), technical, economic, scientific, social, and political considerations are intertwined right from the start of technology development (Callon,
1987). Apparently 'technical' phenomena are neither isolated nor static; they
are characterized by dynamic socio-technical networks that can vary in terms
of size and complexity, including multiple and various human and non-
human components (Hilgartner, 1992).[4]

Empirical studies have also shown how culture and technology are entangled with one another. It is possible to provide three examples where, similar
to Airline, technology refers not only to complex operations, but also to
technologies of control such as rules that guide decisions about risks, work
practices, procedural and hardware surveillance systems. The ethnographic
study carried out by Kunda (1992) in a US high-tech corporation (called Tech)
shows how corporate culture itself can be a technology of control. Multiple
communication circuits constantly promoted Tech's 'way of doing things',
defining not only required work behaviour but also rules for thoughts and
feelings. The historical ethnographic analysis carried out by Vaughan (1996)
on the *Challenger* disaster shows how the experimental character of the shuttle
technology coupled with group-based risk assessment processes, ad hoc hardware surveillance and measurement systems, and standardized rules for
decision-making across the organization resulted in a cultural tendency to
normalize technical anomalies (e.g. 'flying with flaws' at NASA). Finally, the
study carried out by Macrae (2007a, 2007b) on the work of safety experts in
the UK aviation sector suggests that the sheer complexity of airline operations
together with an appreciation of the limits of incident reporting technologies
contributed to the development of a distinct analytical culture characterized
by scepticism, humility, and caution. Safety people considered risk assessments to be the product of limited, and most likely flawed, knowledge and
therefore continually open to change.

In line with studies such as these, the concept of technoculture demands
that we avoid a dualism of technology and culture and that we explore the
practices where they are entangled with one another. It suggests that neither
culture nor technology are distinct features of the context in which safety
experts work, but they are manifested and co-produced in specific places and
times. Specifically, in this chapter, the expression technoculture is invoked to
identify and explore three coterminous features that characterize the entanglement of technology and culture in Airline: (1) the hard-wiring of cultural
values of safety into systems, processes, and other visible artefacts; (2) the
expansion of certain types of working interactions supported by reporting and

---

[4] Hilgartner (1992) uses the example of auto-based transport, which includes entities that
have physical existence such as tyres and engines, human subjects such as drivers and regulators,
and also less tangible elements such as traffic laws.

monitoring technologies; (3) the adoption of a business partnering approach by safety experts to build respect for safety values, people, and technologies.

Hard-wiring Culture

The just culture narrative is expressed in two mutually supportive pillars: on the one hand, a 'cultural contract' between senior management and employees; on the other hand, processes and systems. The practical functioning of safety practices suggests that just culture does not float around in a set of principles or corporate values; it gets hard-wired into control technologies. Reporting and monitoring systems embody the ambivalence of just culture that promotes an atmosphere of trust, in which people are encouraged to provide essential risk information that is not blameless. SR, for instance, is a highly forensic system that does 'not allow any corners to hide'. Staff members do not need to be 'good'; by and large, they are made 'good' by reporting and monitoring systems as the problems they report are likely to be picked up by the technology anyway. As put by one interviewee:

> And the way we do that is through two things; positive encouragement and leverage. And the leverage comes from the system and the system is geared… I liken it to a room with no corners…*you cannot hide anywhere* because there isn't a corner to hide in because the system drives that and it's auditable. [emphasis added]

Technologies of control such as SR, FDM, and FRM are not intended to be 'malicious' tools (a term used by a member of the FDM team) but rather should provide a non-punitive environment that encourages the reporting of any kind of issue. And yet, lurking in the background is the idea that issues will be picked up anyway through the system. As expressed by a senior manager in relation to the influence of technologies on just culture: 'from the pilot's point of view, they know everything's being watched, so that also in a subtle way helps them be honest'.

But senior managers stressed the difficulty to achieve control over individual actions through the use of monitoring technologies, incident reporting and investigation systems only. Just culture is also based on other 'soft' elements, including visible and sustained management attention to safety issues, which are the equivalent of the hard-wired FDM system put in place on the aircraft. These 'soft' elements can be materially traced in the organization, similar to the symbols, rituals, and other artefacts that are often associated with notions of corporate culture (Schein, 2004), and belief control systems (Simons, 1995). Interviewees continuously expressed the need for 'energy' and 'alchemy' on top of 'systems' by using metaphors and symbols that were cascaded down throughout the organization. For instance, the need for a full understanding of just culture from employees and regulators was explained through the use of examples that referred to academic research in anthropology.[5] Corporate presentations (both public and internal) referred to symbols, graphs, and diagrams elaborated in academic research (in particular by James Reason) in order to illustrate particular ways of thinking about culture in relation to safety and incidents.[6]

To summarize, just culture is hard-wired in a network of heterogeneous elements, ranging from monitoring systems to diagrams and metaphors. Each element is important, but it is their juxtaposition that makes just culture workable. Having either soft elements or monitoring systems only would not provide sufficient leverage, considering the complexity of operations and the variety of organizational roles (e.g. pilots, crew, non-flying members of staff). As put by a senior manager, when prompted to reflect on whether softer elements were superfluous in the presence of pervasive monitoring systems, 'I like to picture it as the image on the US dollar bill, you have the all seeing eye at the top of the pyramid looking into the organization, more a case of big "brothers" watching you, the eye (soft elements) and flight data monitoring (technology).'[7]

Interacting via Technology

A second characterizing element that emerges from Airline's safety practices relates to the interactive control style that they promote. Control technologies of Airline are designed to encourage interactions. This emphasis starts from the very broad approach taken to encourage the reporting of events by not imposing a materiality threshold. As put by a senior safety manager:

> Well the risk is as soon as you start trying to define what people should report and should not report they won't bother. So you're best to get them to report everything and then get clever how you sort out the chaff from the wheat...So we just say you know, just report everything.

---

[5] An example is related to the experience of indigenous people in Oceania, who witnessed the landing of planes and subsequently reproduced a rudimental airport waiting for airplanes to come and land. These people did not have a full understanding of how the airport/airplane system worked, although their attempt to reproduce the various components of an airport (e.g. runway, landing lights, control tower) was remarkable. In a similar way, a company would fail in safety management if people simply comply with the components of a safety management system without a full understanding of how these components add up to form a safe working environment.

[6] For example, I observed the use of a production vs. protection trade-off diagram, showing how the degree of protective measures must match the hazards of the productive operations; and also the use of the so-called Swiss Cheese model, which shows how risks can be mitigated by multiple types of defences which are 'layered' behind each other (see Reason, 1997).

[7] Email communication—November 2014.

SR's investigators suggested an increasing willingness to engage with the system, and certainly an increase in the usage of the system in the last six months. The firm that designed the system stated that Airline witnessed an increase by more than 50 per cent in incident reporting within a very short time of SR being deployed. As put by a senior manager, a crucial aspect of their job is 'to make it really easy for [employees] to report'. For this reason, staff can log into the SR system from almost anywhere.[8] Moreover, once a report is filed in the system, the SR application is designed to make it easier for investigators to ask their peers and experts to comment on or review their investigations and subsequently provide tailored feedback to the reporter.

But the interactive nature of safety work in Airline is not of interest simply because people are encouraged to report as much as possible. The technoculture of such an interactive style can be related to three specific features. First, the reporting technologies encourage an expanded view of the issues being reported, encompassing all sorts of seemingly minor things and maintaining open for investigation a multiplicity of risk objects (Hilgartner, 1992). As put by a senior manager:

> So the safety reports tell us what the reporter observed or thought happened and...might get a bit about why they thought it happened and we try and verify that through the investigation process. Flight data monitoring will tell you exactly what the aeroplane did but not why. Electronic training reports will tell you how a large group of people are likely to behave in a given non-normal situation. This will tell you about the reliability of equipment and there's a whole bunch of other stuff here, on-time performance, fuel, all components of that picture.

The initial piece of information travels from the actual place of an incident and is placed into a network of relations between elements that come from many other places, from distant materials, and faraway actors. A wide range of objects, besides senior managers and subordinates, safety and non-safety people, contribute to make control technologies interactive, stimulating reflections and raising further questions on a specific incident case. These elements not only contribute to form a more comprehensive view of what and why something happened. But they are also potentially transformed as part of an emerging socio-technical network around a specific safety issue (Hilgartner, 1992). Drawing on the previous quote, electronic training reports help to explain FDM information, which in turn add context to the reporter's perceptions of an event.

Second, the technology is designed to expand functionalities and working interactions. The technology is a vehicle for different types of touch points that occur between safety personnel and the rest of the organization. But the nature

---

[8] At the time of the second field visit in May 2014, the company was testing an app that will allow access to the system from people's personal devices.

of these interactions, though varied, has a specific common logic. SR is a forensic system, where everything done can be traced and where audit trails are preserved (i.e. the investigator can print different forms at different stages of the inquiry). The web-based application allows for the tracking of the report to the point of delivery, and is constantly verifying the robustness of the audit trail generated by each investigation. In so doing, the application is also disciplinary in the sense that it controls the workflow timings, for example with notifications on late responses approaching deadlines (although it also allows due dates to be reset as needed and request date extensions).

Third, interactions are frequent and mediated by reporting technology. This observation provides a counterpoint to previous research on management control systems and safety experts' work. Well-known research on interactively used control systems (e.g. Simons, 1995) emphasizes the importance of the big 'strategic' uncertainties that require face-to-face time in regular meetings between senior managers and subordinates. Interviews and direct observation at Airline show instead frequent interactions, which are mediated by the reporting technologies and are sustained by a relentless interest in small, and possibly trivial, things and massive archiving systems. Moreover, prior work on safety in the airline industry (e.g. Macrae, 2007a, 2007b) emphasizes the relevance of participative networks to cope with the perceived incompleteness of incident reporting data; investigators act as 'coordinating hubs' by informing others about signs of potential risks, requesting reviews and other information from specialists, and also forming temporary and distributed teams of experts. In Airline, the reporting technology seems to operate as a key 'coordinating hub', with a great deal of interaction which is not face to face, but enabled and mediated by technologies such as the SR system.

To summarize, just culture is hard-wired in a network of heterogeneous elements, which is a vehicle for different types of touch points and an expanded view of the issue being reported initially. Interaction is encouraged (i.e. easy access to reporting technology, absence of a materiality threshold), but mediated by reporting and monitoring technologies that contribute to control workflow timings and preserve an audit trail of what is being done. In such a context, what is the role of safety experts? This question will be addressed in the next section.

Business Partnering

The way in which organizational actors answer questions related to the area of responsibility of functional experts (risk managers in particular), and their position within the organization structure, has cultural implications, reflecting different values, norms, and assumptions around the way in which an organization sees and acts on risks (Power et al., 2013). Prior literature has explored the changing role of the risk manager in organizations (see Hall et al., 2015; Mikes, 2009, 2011; Power, 2007). On the one hand, risk managers can be technical experts of a sub-discipline of risk management (e.g. financial, safety, information technology risks). On the other hand, especially with the rise of a holistic conception of risk and risk management, risk managers can be seen as change facilitators and business partners. In the latter case, what matters are relational skills rather than 'technical' and abstract bodies of risk management knowledge.

In fact, the way in which such a business partnering role is exercised by functional experts such as risk managers is a phenomenon that awaits further research and critical assessment (see Chapter 12, this volume). In Airline, the hard-wiring of culture in control technologies and the expansion of working interactions via technology are interrelated with one aspect of business partnering: the ambition to build up respect for safety people and technologies. This ambition can be traced in two interrelated characteristics of the way in which personnel in the Safety Department work.

First, the personal background of safety staff is strongly related to the company's operations. There was a need to add what was called 'content and background' to analyse the safety data and to participate in business decisions. Business knowledge was a precondition for interaction with front-line and other staff functions in order to: understand which language to adopt for enhancing authority and credibility; become trusted business advisers; understand the outputs of reporting technologies. A range of informal techniques were used by the Safety Department in order to build respect and trust. Many of these involved facilitating peer-to-peer communication capability and providing a safe environment for people to act naturally and 'speak up' if there are problems. An example is provided in the following quote:

> We do things such as line-oriented safety audits and we put a trained person on the jump seat of the aircraft, he's not a training captain, he's not a manager, he's just one of their colleagues but we train him in observation. And they observe the flights against a threat in aero-taxonomy and we get a huge amount of information from that because what we're trying to do is observe the most natural behaviour we can of that pilot. As soon as we put a manager in there or a training captain, you're going to get their best behaviour. *You put their mate in there and you're more likely to get the nearest you can to what's happening day in, day out.* [emphasis added]

Second, safety personnel developed success stories about occasions where decisions supported by the Safety Department added value to the company. The precautionary logic of safety (e.g. to avoid people getting hurt) is intertwined with narratives of value creation and 'win-win' situations in terms of safety, costs, and business development. Stories of value creation are also based on the development of monitoring and reporting technologies. The design and implementation of the SR system is itself framed as a profitable investment for the company, besides the obvious benefits related to data collection and analysis. Instead of buying a product on the market, the decision was made to build the technology in partnership with a company working on mobile and web-based safety and compliance services. As put by one senior manager:

> So we decided what we had to do is to build our own system and so then we went back out to the market and said 'We want to build this system, who can help us?' And we found one company that said 'Oh yeah, we get it' and bothered to listen, a company called [name omitted] and so basically we entered a partnership with them whereby we provide the intellectual property around the design and they build the system. They then go off and sell the system to everybody and we get some of the royalties back.

This decision, according to senior managers, was characterized by 'lots of wins'. Besides benefits in terms of cost and design customization, supplier risk was also decreased and discounts were obtained from an insurance perspective since, as put by one senior manager, 'you're continuing to demonstrate risk management and giving them confidence'.

TECHNOCULTURE AND RISKWORK

As suggested in the introduction to this volume, the motif of riskwork encourages a focus on situationally specific forms of work. In line with this perspective, in this section I sketch two vignettes that aim to capture just culture in practice and the deeply intertwined relationship between culture and control technology. The vignettes provide short descriptions of situations (e.g. landing airplanes, opening doors) in which safety data were used to change current practices and behaviour. In line with the riskwork emphasis on work and 'normal' operations in risk management (see Introduction, this volume; Bourrier, 2002), the focus is on how members of Airline worked to change their and their colleagues' visions and cognitive maps in order to improve daily situations.

On Landing Airplanes

> Flight data monitoring data show landings outside the normal parameters. Is that risky? This really depends on the airport where the airplane has landed. The data shows that it's happening primarily in the summer on very long runways. It is likely that people are doing visual approaches as opposed to longwinded instrument approaches. There can be economical benefits and positive performance effects (e.g. reduced transfer time to the terminal buildings). There is no

immediate risk. But there is a latent risk that people get used to that behaviour. And, after a number of long landings, the model for a long runway may be unconsciously applied to a short runway. That is a problem. Behaviour has to be modified. Flight monitoring data people were taking photographs of Google satellite images and were overlaying on top of that the actual touchdown point on the runway where the aircraft was, and then sending this directly to the crew, saying: 'how do you feel about it?'.

This vignette reveals elements of the three features of technoculture sketched in the previous sections. First, the safety control and reporting technologies contribute to identifying the issue even in the absence of self-reporting. This is important as in complex organizations such as airlines risks are rarely self-evident (Macrae, 2007a). In fact, under certain conditions, a long landing may not be seen as a problem; on the contrary, it may have some beneficial consequences. As shown in the vignette, the risk materializes only under certain conditions (e.g. a short runway!). Yet there is a latent risk that the 'long landing' approach becomes the norm, and therefore is applied in the wrong context. As put by one interviewee, 'ideally what you want to do is, as that risk starts to emerge in the corner, you want to be able to go and address it before it materializes into something uncomfortable'.

Second, the vignette shows how an incident investigation is constituted by a number of different elements that come from many different places. Interactions are premised on capturing as much data as possible to extract patterns, trends, and correlations and to understand what may become a normalized form of deviance and thereby constitute a latent threat to flight safety. As put by one interviewee, the key aspect is the 'process of bringing context in all the time', by using data and interacting with front-line people and other functional experts. The reporting or identification of a long landing is only one component of a much larger information set that informs interactions between safety people and their colleagues. Triangulating different sources of data and analysing trends helps to understand where long landings are happening and to formulate assumptions about the underlying rationales (e.g. good weather, panoramic approaches to landing, fuel savings). Although there is an audit trail of the evidence being analysed, the investigation is not necessarily punitive, but aims to understand behaviour that may incorporate latent risks. Data-supported interaction helps to make clear why an issue such as long landing is important and needs to be addressed even if, in the first instance, it is not perceived as a risk.

Third, corrective actions suggest a business partnering approach that emphasizes 'mate-to-mate' conversations with the help of visual aids. Senior managers acknowledge that it would be easy to put a safety note out recommending that bad behaviour is to be avoided. But the same message can be conveyed with 'a sense of humour', not to shame people but making it obvious that there is something wrong with long landings. As put by one interviewee: 'It's not bossy, it's facilitative thinking you know, you're helping...you're taking people with you on a journey, this is the preferred modus operandi.'

In addition to communication methods and 'attention-grabbers' such as the above, the Safety Department relies on a network of liaison officers. Their goal is to facilitate peer-to-peer communication and increase the number and quality of touch points between safety and the front-line personnel. One senior manager said that 'their job is to...give people feedback as peer to peer, in confidence, to improve performance'. Interestingly, in a similar way to technologies of control such as FDM, liaison officers can be seen as a means of accessing the daily working practices of crew members. But they are also a way to enhance confidence and trust in safety workers: in short, to build respect for the Safety Department.

On Opening Doors

The doors of an aircraft have automatic escape slides so that if you open them in an emergency the slide automatically inflates. These automatic slides need to be disarmed when embarking passengers normally. If this is not done, there is a safety risk because if someone is standing on the steps and one of these slides explodes, it can hit the person with harmful consequences. A specialist was asked to break down the current task (the opening of the door under normal conditions) and understand why the safety risk may occur. The specialist and his support team designed a new task. The investment in having that specialist in to work on the task design was about £10,000. But every time the problem had occurred in the past, the company had to throw away the slide and buy a new one.

The safety risk illustrated in the vignette is perhaps more evident than the preceding one. If a problem occurs, then it is likely that someone has been injured and, at least, a material loss has occurred. In line with the chapter's motif of technoculture, this vignette shows how the reporting of safety events is only the starting point for a learning process which is premised on a relentless interest in data collection and analysis.

The reporting system showed that this problem had been occurring at Airline, although at a lower rate compared to the industry average. In this specific case, available data suggested a cyclical pattern. The occurrence of the problem decreased following a change in the procedure, but then tended to rise again for various reasons such as the intake of new hires. As in the previous vignette, the collection of data on the single 'fact' (problems with the opening of a door on flight X at airport Y on date Z) coexists with an aspiration to understand its underlying causes. Different sources of information are juxtaposed (e.g. incident reporting, new hires); interactions with colleagues from different functions take place, and external specialists are consulted.

The disciplinary element of technology (e.g. 'has someone made a wilful mistake?') is only one part of the story. Learning from the data is also crucial. In fact, the remedial actions are informed by a recognition of human fallibility. The company draws on a 'hierarchy of effectiveness' of safety measures, which ranges from redesigning a component (e.g. the door) to increasing awareness via communication campaigns. The benefits, costs, and uncertainty of alternative measures are taken into consideration: for instance, the redesign of a door is a massive cost, has large potential benefits, but also uncertainty as the problem may occur even with the redesigned door. As put by an interviewee: 'So right at the top is the design…Right at the bottom is a notice to crew to say "Don't forget to check you've disarmed the doors before opening them" and that's almost useless.'

Compared to the previous case, this vignette specifically illustrates the way in which an issue gets traction and is acted upon. Two elements emerge. The first involves a risk-based rationale. The company makes hundreds of flights a day, and the four doors of the airplane are opened twice per flight. Being a very routine job, even in the context of very low probability for the event to occur, the exposure is significant. The second element is related to the way in which safety experts can expand their organizational footprint. A general problem for functional experts such as risk managers is to justify the value of their recommendations (see Hall et al., 2015; Power, 2007; Power et al., 2013). The vignette suggests an explicit cost–benefit analysis related to the intervention recommended by the Safety Department. As put by one interviewee:

And the investment we made in having that person in to help us was probably about £10,000 but every time we blow a slide we have to throw it away and buy a new one. So we will have reaped the safety benefit and the direct cost and had less on-time performance impacts as a consequence because we're not having to wait for a new slide to be shipped in. So it's a win-win all round.

On this basis, this vignette reinforces the view that the partnering role of safety experts is not only based on relational skills, 'attention-grabbers', and liaison figures. It is also about developing a narrative of value-effectiveness through straightforward success stories. As put by one interviewee:

And if you're thinking about, you know, the upside of that in terms of the business, *well my example absolutely demonstrates the safety benefit, the direct cost benefit, the operational efficiency benefit* and that's what we're trying to do in this big programme. But it all fits in with this concept of a safety culture and learning culture and supporting culture and nurturing culture you know, just culture. [emphasis added]

CONCLUDING REFLECTIONS

In this chapter, I explored how technology and culture are co-produced and characterize specific kinds of riskwork in the aviation sector, namely efforts to promote 'speaking up' via risk reporting systems and subsequent analysis. The material collected from the Safety Department of a large airline company draws attention to the way in which a narrative is developed around the concept of just culture and how such a narrative is intertwined with control technologies.

The co-production of technology and culture is captured through the motif of technoculture, which expresses three themes: the hard-wiring of just culture into control technologies; the technology-supported expansion of working interactions; and business partnering to build respect for safety values, people, and technologies. Two vignettes related to routine events, such as landing airplanes and opening doors, add colour to the features of riskwork as technoculture. Specifically, we see the 'no corners to hide' dimension of just culture, but also its aspiration for a learning culture supported by granular data collection and analysis; we see the emergence of new, more or less cooperative, interactions across internal functions but also with external actors; we also see the development of narratives that reinforce the value-added role of the Safety Department, as well as 'attention-grabbers' and new communication lines in action.

This chapter started with a set of questions that stressed how risk reporting and analysis are riddled with ambiguities and contradictions: risks are not self-evident; reporters as well as the receivers of information are biased and fallible; and there is an inherent tension between the need for risk account-ability, financial and legal liability for risk, and the ambition to encourage risk reporting and 'speaking up'. Drawing on the technoculture concept, this chapter suggests that these tensions are addressed in practice by dynamic networks of heterogeneous elements, which stimulate and mediate inter-actions among safety and non-safety experts. Such socio-technical networks give expression to, rather than suppress, the ambiguities inherent in risk reporting and analysis. There is an encouragement to report that is not blameless; there is help and support from safety personnel, but also pervasive monitoring via systems and local networks of liaison officers; there is a focus on flying staff, but also recognition of other members of the organization and their potentially relevant role in just culture. Recent uses of the concept of organizational (risk) culture as 'the way we do things around here' stress shared understandings and solutions to common problems that can be engin-eered to achieve optimal solutions (see Power et al., 2013). On the contrary, technoculture recognizes, and even nurtures, the plurality of values and commitments that characterize riskwork.

In closing, it is appropriate to make one comment on the process of writing about organizational culture. Text about organizational culture like this chapter should be read in the context of the author's situation at the moment in which the text is developed (Kunda, 1992: ch. 6; Smircich, 1995; Yanow, 1995). Accordingly, it is important to understand that Airline was initially conceived as a comparator case in the context of a broader research project on risk culture in financial organizations (see Power et al., 2013). The aim was to obtain a point of contrast that could stimulate new questions and lines of thought. This specific circumstance influenced the shape of this chapter and the development of technoculture as an organizing concept. If the idea of technoculture plausibly describes features of practice in the aviation industry, it also provides many points of contrast with the financial sector. Examples of such points of contrast were: the lack of emphasis in Airline on formalized models that articulate different responsibilities over risk oversight and management; the remarkable degree of openness to the external world and respect for external advisers (including academic experts!); the lack of concerns about any dilution or capture risks (i.e. 'going native' problem); awareness that 'context is crucial' and the need for having time to reflect as much as to collect and analyse quantitative data.

So the appeal of technoculture in this chapter is shaped by the points of contrast with financial services organizations as much as by the data collected from Airline itself. There are certainly limitations to such an approach, such as a limited understanding of field-level practices in the aviation industry. However, data from Airline, and related reflections, help to transform culture from a 'tired answer' into an 'interesting question' (Smircich, 1995: 235). This is priceless for researchers confronted with an ever-expanding production of texts that point to culture as a black-box explanation of last resort, both for the financial crisis and other spectacular failures.

REFERENCES

AIRMIC, ALARM, & IRM (2002). *A Risk Management Standard*, pp. 1–17. <www.theirm. org/knowledge-and-resources/risk-management-standards/irms-risk-management-standard> (accessed 13 March 2016).

Alvesson, M. (2002). *Understanding Organizational Culture*. London: SAGE Publications.

Barley, S. R. & Kunda, G. (2001). Bringing Work Back In. *Organization Science*, 12(1), 76–95.

Bijker, W. E., Hughes, T. P., & Pinch, T. (Eds) (1987). *The Social Construction of Technological Systems*. Cambridge, MA: MIT Press.

Bourrier, M. (2002). Bridging Research and Practice: The Challenge of 'Normal Operations' Studies. *Journal of Contingencies and Crisis Management*, 10(4), 173–80.

Callon, M. (1987). Society in the Making: The Study of Technology as a Tool for Sociological Analysis. In W. E. Bijker, T. P. Hughes, & T. Pynch (Eds), *The Social Construction of Technological Systems* (pp. 83–103). Cambridge, MA: MIT Press.

Committee of Sponsoring Organizations of the Treadway Commission (COSO) (2004). *Enterprise Risk Management—Integrated Framework. Executive summary*, pp. 1–16. Committee of Sponsoring Organizations of the Treadway Commission. <www.coso.org/documents/coso_erm_executivesummary.pdf> (accessed 13 March 2016).

Hall, M., Mikes, A., & Millo, Y. (2015). How Do Risk Managers Become Influential? A Field Study of Toolmaking in Two Financial Institutions. *Management Accounting Research*, 26(1), 1–20.

Hilgartner, S. (1992). The Social Construction of Risk Objects: Or, How to Pry Open Networks of Risk. In J. F. Short & L. Clarke (Eds), *Organizations, Uncertainties and Risk* (pp. 39–53). Boulder, CO: Westview Press.

Hood, C. & Jones, D. (Eds) (1996). *Accident and Design: Contemporary Debates in Risk Management*. London: UCL Press.

ISO (2009). *ISO 31000:2009—Risk Management Principles and Guidelines*. <www.iso.org/iso/home/standards/iso31000.htm> (accessed 13 March 2016).

Kaplan, R. & Mikes, A. (2012). Managing Risks: A New Framework. *Harvard Business Review*, June, 49–60.

Kunda, G. (1992). *Engineering Culture: Control and Commitment in a High-Tech Corporation*. Philadelphia, PA: Temple University Press.

Macrae, C. (2007a). *Interrogating the Unknown: Risk Analysis and Sensemaking in Airline Safety Oversight*, pp. 1–18. London: Centre for Analysis of Risk and Regulation (CARR). <http://www.lse.ac.uk/accounting/CARR/publications/discussionPapers.aspx> (accessed 13 March 2016).

Macrae, C. (2007b). *Analyzing Near-miss Events: Risk Management in Incident Reporting and Investigation Systems*, pp. 1–24. London: Centre for Analysis of Risk and Regulation (CARR). <http://www.lse.ac.uk/accounting/CARR/publications/discussionPapers.aspx> (accessed 13 March 2016).

Mikes, A. (2009). Risk Management and Calculative Cultures. *Management Accounting Research*, 20(1), 18–40.

Mikes, A. (2011). From Counting Risk to Making Risk Count: Boundary-work in Risk Management. *Accounting, Organizations and Society*, 36(4–5), 226–45.

Power, M. K. (2007). *Organized Uncertainty: Designing a World of Risk Management*. Oxford: Oxford University Press.

Power, M. K., Ashby, S., & Palermo, T. (2013). *Risk Culture in Financial Organisations— A Research Report*, pp. 1–103. London: Centre for Analysis of Risk and Regulation (CARR). <www.lse.ac.uk/researchAndExpertise/units/CARR/pdf/Final-Risk-Culture-Report.pdf> (accessed 13 March 2016).

Reason, J. T. (1997). *Managing the Risks of Organizational Accidents*. Aldershot, UK: Ashgate.

Schein, E. H. (2004). *Organizational Culture and Leadership*, 3rd edition. San Francisco, CA: Wiley.

Simons, R. (1995). Control in an Age of Empowerment. *Harvard Business Review*, March–April, 80–8.

Simons, R. (1999). How Risky Is Your Company? *Harvard Business Review*, May–June, 85–94.

Smircich, L. (1995). Writing Organizational Tales: Reflections on Three Books on Organizational Culture. *Organization Science*, 6(2), 232–7.

Vaughan, D. (1996). *The Challenger Launch Decision: Risky Technology, Culture and Deviance at NASA*. Chicago, IL: University of Chicago Press.

Weick, K. E. & Sutcliffe, K. M. (2007). *Managing the Unexpected: Resilient Performance in an Age of Uncertainty*, 2nd edition. San Francisco, CA: Jossey-Bass.

Yanow, D. (1995). Writing Organizational Tales: Four Authors and Their Stories about Culture. *Organization Science*, 6(2), 225–38.

8

Conversation Stoppers

Constructing Consumer Attitudes to Risk in UK Wealth Management

Zsuzsanna Vargha

How can we ensure that banks offer consumers financial products according to their 'true' needs? This is the primary question financial services regulators ask ever more emphatically after the most recent financial crisis. The concern of UK regulation specifically has been to ensure appropriate services for ordinary consumers, embodied in the former Financial Services Authority's Treating Customer Fairly principles (FSA, 2006). More precisely, financial sellers in the UK must offer investments 'suitable' for their clients, in part by assessing the customers' so-called Attitude to Risk (ATR).[1] This is required since the 2007 implementation of the EU's Markets in Financial Instruments Directive (MiFID) Section 2 Article 19 (European Parliament & Council of the European Union, 2004).

This chapter analyses two contrasting forms of work in assessing customers' ATR based primarily on evidence from interviews and observations at a major UK financial firm. For a certain kind of *wealth manager*, risk preference emerges from the routine classifying work that constitutes financial planning while for *financial planners* in large retail banks, risk preference is the matter-of-fact result of a test to be plugged into the decision process. Despite these differences, in both cases ATR is not a pre-existing property of the consumer, to be extracted and matched with investments. Rather, it is a product of specific riskwork to construct ATR as a fact about the consumer which can become the object of regulation. This regulatory and managerial object—ATR—gains its 'facticity' to a large extent during the advising process in which it is assessed. How strong and durable a fact it becomes depends on the approach to assessing

---

[1] For space considerations, FactFinder financial planning tools have been omitted from this discussion.

and documenting it for review by quality controllers and regulators. Thus, in this setting, riskwork is entangled with regulatory work; the more auditable and demonstrable the nature of the riskwork, the stronger the regulatory fact that is produced about risk (risk preference).

The task of financial advisers is not so much to identify and contain risks, as is commonly the case in risk management, but as mediating agents of consumer finance, to match the supply and demand for risk in the retail market. The consumer's preference for risk—the ATR—must be correctly identified and matched to appropriate investment products. The assumption underlying the imperative to know a person's ATR is that consumers are incapable of establishing this as a fact themselves. But once elicited, the fact attaches to the person who, as governable subject, is transformed into an empowered decision-maker. Assessment is done in the name of, and for the benefit of, the consumer, while it is equally geared towards protecting the seller from regulatory sanction. This view of matching *risk* to *risk preference* at the individual level can in principle be scaled up to the level of the organization; the risk preference of retail investors is similar in nature and process of construction to the entrepreneurial notion of an organization's *risk appetite*.

THEORETICAL CONSIDERATIONS: FROM DECOUPLING TO RISKWORK

Common critiques of compliance practices see them as mere 'box-ticking' exercises or as 'decoupled' (Meyer & Rowan, 1977) activities which leave core practices unchanged. Similarly they can be seen as a form of 'risk colonization' (Rothstein, Huber, & Gaskell, 2006), where the original purpose of controlling a 'real' risk is diverted by layers of oversight. In contrast to viewing the risk preference assessment similarly as another futile regulatory exercise, this chapter takes the form and content of different ATR assessment styles seriously, following Sandholtz's (2012) detailed analysis of variation in adopting a new industrial standard into everyday operations. Sandholtz shows that in one department of a firm the standard became the methodical checklist imposed on previously unregulated work processes, while in the other it was intermingled with the already existing documentation practices.

Rather than assume a general trend of decoupling, then, we study the site of consumer financial regulation in the UK as a way to understand different ways of *coupling* firms and clients, as a result of 'light touch' regulation which does not specify rules of conduct. Gilad (2011) explored managerial compliance strategies responding to the FSA's broad principles of Treating Customers Fairly, or TCF (FSA, 2006). Such 'process-oriented regulation' (Gilad, 2011) permits firms to work out the details of how their processes comply. Depending on whether management saw TCF as in conflict with or aligned with their and the organization's identity, firms either simply re-described or substantially adjusted their operations to declare compliance with the principles.

By contrast, in the ATR cases examined here all participants understood their practices to be compliant. In fact, a characteristic of principles-based regulation is precisely that the regulator and the regulated often do not know in advance what will eventually be evaluated as compliant practice. Therefore, the notion of compliance and the study of managerial decisions to achieve compliance gives us a limited view. Our study focuses rather on the outcomes of compliance, the concrete compliance practices observable at the target site of regulation (here the encounter with the banking client), regardless of policy and managerial intention. By focusing on how financial firms and their clients discuss risk preference, we gain insight into the work of constructing ATR as a regulatory object.

The theoretical claim here is that historically people had not been consumers-with-risk-preferences. This argument is comparable to that made by Hilgartner about *risk objects*: to constitute risk, we make causal claims about certain objects that lead to harm (e.g. smoking causes cancer), as if these objects were pre-existing. Yet historical analysis shows that these risk objects as objects posing risk themselves come into the world as a result of new social and technical configurations (Hilgartner, 1992). Similarly, we can witness how consumers of financial products are also being 'made' through efforts to capture and act on their stated attitude to risk-taking.

RESEARCH METHODS

There are two main approaches we might follow to understand how individuals as bearers of risk preference are created: first, by tracing the genealogy of the practice; and, second, by observing specific situations in which risk preference is extracted from and attributed to individuals. For the purpose of this chapter, I focus on the latter, observing how advisers discuss risk preference with clients, drawing on an ethnomethodological and actor–network approach discussed in earlier work on financial advice in Hungary (Vargha, 2010). That earlier study provided insights into the broader technologies of mass interactions between advisers and clients, rather than taking a specific focus on risk preference.

The chapter draws on three types of data. First, fieldwork conducted between 2011 and 2012 focused on a UK wealth management firm (henceforth: Firm) and comprised interviews and participant observation. The Firm emphasizes the importance of face-to-face advice in wealth management. Several interviews were carried out with the company's then chairman, with multiple top managers (in IT and marketing), with several senior financial advisers, and with participants and managers of the extensive training programme at the firm: from executive director level to manager and trainer. Participant observation of the training of new recruits was carried out on multiple days. Participation included giving feedback on role-playing exercises and observing a discussion panel where junior advisers were invited to share their experiences with novices. In addition, a financial planning session was carried out with a senior adviser of the Firm, in which the researcher was the subject of financial advice. Interviews with advisers focused on their strategies of conducting face-to-face interactions with a client, allowing the topic of risk regulation to emerge from advisers' view of the work process, instead of framing it as a direct question about compliance. This gives us a better view of riskwork not as a stand-alone 'calculative' practice but as a feature of firm–client interactions.

Second, data on the wealth management Firm's style of riskwork to produce ATR were complemented with data on the dominant form of practice in consumer banking more broadly, based on multiple sources. Participant observation of a bank's financial planning session took place and was similar to the wealth management encounter above. The session was led by a 'financial planner' at a large UK bank's branch, again with the researcher as the subject of advice. Other sources comprised banking industry literature in the UK on ATR and risk preference more broadly, and a sample of UK banks' procedures to establish risk preference. The latter are primarily 'risk profiling tools' in the form of questionnaires, many of which are available online. The dominance of these tools in retail financial services was also established by the regulator (see below).

Third, the data collected directly from the 'regulated' entities were comple-mented by an analysis of regulatory documents from the UK Financial Services Authority 2006–12 (succeeded by the Financial Cunduct Authority). The use of these documents is twofold: on the one hand, they reveal the official regulatory approach; on the other hand, the regulator's review of industry practices and its reasoning for issuing large fines on select institutions, provides a window on prevailing styles of ATR riskwork in the retail banking sector.

REGULATION AND RISKWORK: ASSESSING CONSUMERS' ATTITUDE TO RISK

The following sections describe the empirically observed variation in producing the regulatory object 'Attitude to Risk'. The first section points to the paradigmatic view of risk preference in social science, which matches the regulatory approach. The second section discusses how principles-based regulation prescribes but does not determine riskwork. The third section introduces the dominant style of riskwork in UK financial services, the use of 'risk profiling tools', through the case of a large bank. The fourth section focuses on the riskwork observable in wealth management encounters with clients, and the ways of establishing ATR in that setting. The discussion section compares and interprets these findings.

The Social Scientific Background of Financial Regulation

The idea that individuals *have* inherent risk preferences is central to, and exported from, both economics and psychology and more broadly, the inter-disciplinary decision sciences. Encompassing economics, psychology, behavioural and neuroscience, this latter burgeoning area of research, primarily focusing on decisions under uncertainty, has developed on the assumption that risk preference is a natural attribute of the individual construed as an isolated decision-maker (for an overview, see Appelt, Milch, & Weber, 2011). Debate revolves around the experimental methods that most reliably 'elicit' risk preference (Charness, Gneezy, & Imas, 2013) and the sources of individual difference and contexts which influence resulting behaviour (Dohmen et al., 2011). Going further, the propensity for risk-taking has recently been attributed to tangible parts of the individual, namely brain activity made visible by magnetic resonance imaging (fMRI) techniques (Engelmann & Tamir, 2009). Consider this exemplary research question:

> [We] propose a way of assessing a person's inherent risk preference that factors out individual and situational differences in risk perception. We document that a definition of risk aversion and risk seeking as the preference for options *perceived* to be more risky or less risky, respectively, provides *the cross-situational stability to a person's risk preference* that has eluded more traditional definitions. (Weber & Milliman, 1997: 123, emphasis added)

Thus, while there is widespread understanding that risk-taking choices can be 'domain specific', so that individuals might make different risky decisions in, say, finance than in sport, these differences are nonetheless seen to be modulated displays of an underlying preference.

The UK's ATR regulation reflects this view of the individual as a carrier of an inherent risk preference. Indeed, the UK FSA has worked with economics experts in crafting its customer protection policies. Practitioners and regulated entities also seem to share this view when they opt for risk questionnaires, as analysed below. However, not all actors subscribe to this scientific baseline. More generally, the analysis of specific kinds of riskwork begins to shed light on how financial firms and their regulators may both import existing theories of risk preference and also create their own versions, as they construct the regulatory fact of ATR.

The Regulatory View: 'Suitable' Financial Advice Is Accountable

Assuming that risk preference is a given and knowable property of individuals, as UK regulators have, how can we extract it from consumers? The regulatory view has been permissive in this regard, provided the result is 'suitable' according to criteria which have continually evolved. A typical rendition of these broad criteria is as follows:

> The Conduct of Business sourcebook (COBS) 9.2.1R requires a firm to take reasonable steps to ensure that a personal recommendation, or decision to trade, is suitable for its customer. COBS 9.2.2R requires firms, among other things, to take account of a customer's preferences regarding risk taking, their risk profile and ensure they are able financially to bear any related investment risks consistent with their investment objectives. (Financial Services Authority, 2011b: 2)

The FSA also resorted to enforcing the risk assessment requirement by pointing to best and worst practices. For example, the *FSA Factsheet for Financial Advisers* gives the following example:

> Firm F had no clear policy on how ATR [attitude to risk] should be established; it used a scale of 1 to 10, without a clear definition of the categories. One adviser said he would deem 'low risk' to be between categories 1 to 3 and another adviser said he considered it to be between categories 1 to 4. (Financial Services Authority, 2011a)

Yet throughout its analysis of various cases, the regulator did not aim to legitimate certain methods over others: 'We do not prescribe *how* firms establish the risk a customer is willing and able to take or how they make investment selections' (FSA 2011b: 2). However, from the FSA analysis it is clear that standardized risk surveys and other 'risk profiling tools' were used at hundreds of financial firms between 2008 and 2010 and have come to dominate UK banks' approach to ATR. Furthermore, these risk profiling tools as implementations of consumer risk assessment fell short of the regulator's expectations of accountability. There has been a '[f]ailure to *collect and properly account for* all the information relevant to assessing the risk a customer is willing and able to take' (FSA 2011b: 3, emphasis added).

This criticism was highlighted in the specific case where the Financial Conduct Authority (successor of the FSA) fined the insurance company AXA £1.5m for its insufficient suitability and risk assessment practices in the wealth management and investment advisory arm (FCA, 2013). This fine reveals the evolving regulatory view on firms' methods and approach to ATR. A key 'failing' was the inadequate documentation of the assessment's circumstances. Furthermore, the questionnaire's risk categories were not clearly defined, often did not quantify how much risk was associated with them (e.g. 'some risk and some growth'), did not document how ATR was explained, and were not 'demonstrably suitable' for customers. Overall, the Notice of the AXA fine reveals how much the regulator requires an audit trail for the ATR process facing so much liberty in the form of assessment.

In what follows, two distinct approaches to establishing ATR, which have emerged from a detailed study of riskwork on the ground, are analysed [2]. On the one hand, the financial planners of large UK banks typically use risk profiling survey software (Figure 8.1) while, on the other hand, the high-status financial advisers at the UK financial Firm compose the risk preference figure from the consultation, from semi-formal idiosyncratic inquiry, and from graphs laid out by hand on paper. While the regulator seems to accept different ways of 'taking into account' risk profile and financial ability, we will see that these constitute radically different ways of thinking about risk preferences.

FINANCIAL RISK PREFERENCE AS THE RESULT OF A MULTIPLE-CHOICE TEST

Large retail banks do not seem to mind chunky, punctuated interactions and use standardized risk preference questionnaires. These have become legitimate parts of the planning infrastructure. Academic research in behavioural economics and psychology about risk tolerance has been channelled to practitioners in financial planning, partly to scrutinize the already existing practice of using risk questionnaires from a scientific perspective (e.g. Roszkowski, Davey, & Grable, 2005). Concurrently, third-party technology providers such as Finametrica and Morningstar have been delivering psychometric risk profiling tools to banks based on these insights (e.g. using the 'Byrne–Blake' questionnaire—see Byrne & Blake, 2012).

At one large UK retail bank, the meeting with a financial planner includes going over current income and expenses and savings plans, which is followed by an explicit risk survey: 'We do a psychometric questionnaire. Have you done it before?' The financial planner types the answers on a laptop. There are three key questions to answer:

1 Would you agree with emergency funds being three times the net income?

2 Life insurance for your child [calls child by name]—have you thought about it?

3 100 pounds can be spent differently [as an introduction to the questionnaire]

---

[2] Note the parallel discussion on the process of establishing 'risk appetite', a similar concept developed for entire organizations (Power, 2009).

Risk Profile Questionnaire completed for:

Zsuzsanna Vargha

The Risk Profile Questionnaire is designed to provide an indication of an individual's attitude to risk and reward. The questions asked and the answers given are detailed below.

In reviewing this questionnaire you should remember...
- There are no right or wrong answers
- Your initial response to the questions will normally provide the most accurate result
- Your risk profile may change over time and you should look to review this in line with your objectives

Question	Answers for Zsuzsanna Vargha
1. What amount of risk are you currently prepared to take with your financial investments in order to see higher returns? a. A small amount b. A moderate amount c. A large amount of risk d. A very large amount of risk	b. A moderate amount
2. To reach my financial goal(s) I prefer an investment which is safe and grows slowly but steadily, even if it means lower growth overall. a. Strongly Agree b. Agree c. In-between d. Disagree e. Strongly Disagree	c. In-between
3. If I picked an investment with potential for large gains but also the risk of large losses I would feel: a. Very Uncomfortable b. A little concerned c. Accepting of the possible high & lows d. Excited by the potential for gain	a. Very Uncomfortable
4. I need to feel that my money is secure and not at risk even if it means it doesn't grow as fast as it could. a. Strongly Agree b. Agree c. In-between d. Disagree e. Strongly Disagree	c. In-between
5. I find it interesting to explore investment opportunities for my money. a. Strongly Agree b. Agree c. In-between d. Disagree e. Strongly Disagree	c. In-between
6. When I consider investments that have an element of risk I feel quite anxious. a. Strongly Agree b. Agree c. In-between d. Disagree e. Strongly Disagree	c. In-between
7. I am looking for high long term investment growth. I am willing to accept the possibility of potential losses to achieve this. a. Strongly Agree b. Agree c. In-between d. Disagree e. Strongly Disagree	c. In-between
8. If I get bad financial news I will tend to worry about it more than most people would in the same situation. a. Strongly Agree b. Agree c. In-between d. Disagree e. Strongly Disagree	b. Agree
9. An investment that has the potential to make a lot of money usually also has a risk of losing money. If you had money to invest, how much would you be willig to place in an investment with possible high returns but an element of risk? a. All of it b. More than half c. Half d. Less than half e. None	c. Half

Figure 8.1. Risk attitude questionnaire at a large retail bank

The planner then states: 'We should establish how much risk you take with £100.' Indeed, the laptop on which responses to the previous questions have until now been entered is turned over to the client to fill out a questionnaire herself. The survey consists of nine multiple-choice questions. The client completes these on-screen one question at a time. After answering a question, the next one appears. Figure 8.1 shows the entire survey.

The survey offers up different imaginary situations to the client, revolving around the *feeling of risk*, without concrete financial values being mentioned. The phrasing that recurs most is 'feel', and qualifiers such as 'anxious', 'concerned', 'accepting', 'excited', 'interesting', 'worry', 'safe', and 'secure'. Survey research techniques are used, which test the robustness of the client's responses: questions are repeated in slightly reformulated ways to cross-check the validity of earlier answers. The completed survey and the score itself are stored in the bank's information system together with the client's profile.

The result is a single score between 1 and 5. In the post-FSA review environment, this score is treated with some care, as further questioning of the financial planner revealed. The bank's policy and the adviser's understanding suggest that they know that risk preference is not fixed. Risk survey data are not stored indefinitely and the information system prompts the survey to be retaken after a period. Nonetheless, updating the survey was regarded as being very advanced at the time, 'best practice' according to the FSA 2011 review. In addition to the bank's protocols, the financial planner had her own views on why risk preference may differ over time. She indicated that it can depend on the client's momentary 'mood', on their 'general outlook on life' (in an optimistic period) on 'current economic events' (crisis, upheaval) or on a changed life situation (unemployment, promotion, child). Consequently, the financial planner requests all clients who she meets to retake the survey after several months.

The potency of the score, the test result, lies in its portability and compatibility. Even though in exemplary cases the bank and the adviser may acknowledge that the score is not a fixed truth, it is still plugged into the advice process and ultimately shapes investment advice. The advice can always be shown (to regulators) to have been based on the single number derived from the questionnaire. As for clients, although the survey itself states that risk profiles may change, their own profile remains an expert product outside of their reach. Once completed, the questions and answers disappear into the laptop, showing only the result. Clients cannot review their profile or take it home as the survey is not printed for them.

The FSA recognized the dangers of governing advice based on the questionnaire's risk preference score only after these tools had become widespread. In its comprehensive 2011 industry review, it warned that questionnaires are sensitive instruments and the measure they yield is only as good as the methodology:

Where firms use a questionnaire to collect information from customers, we are concerned that these often use poor question and answer options, have over-sensitive scoring or attribute inappropriate weighting to answers. Such flaws can result in inappropriate conflation or interpretation of customer responses. (FSA 2011b: 3)

RISK PREFERENCE AS THE RESULT OF CONVERSATIONS ABOUT CURRENT ALLOCATION

In contrast to the previous example, experienced advisers at a major UK wealth management Firm seek to conduct uninterrupted interactions and interweave a client's life story and financial strategy fluidly, drawing conclusions from one to the other. Risk preference emerges from the details of 'graphical' planning work done with the client. Yet, this discursive–visual practice of 'discovering' risk preference led to a dispute between the Firm and the UK financial regulator regarding the very nature of consumer ATR and legitimate ways of evidencing it.

The wealth managers interviewed claimed that *interaction* was their area of expertise. They argued that financial planning is about forming relationships and cannot be formalized. During their encounters, clients come to trust the adviser and share their social–financial situation. Asked directly, clients will not disclose crucial family arrangements which may be material to the financial 'solutions' deemed appropriate for them (e.g. tax). Effectively, these wealth managers defend conversation as a better, and more accurate, truth-producing method than a contrived series of formal questions. In fact, the wealth managers imply that the paper trail and the formal sequence destroy the sharing process itself. Similarly, establishing ATR is not a discrete step for them: risk is established in the course of 'holistic' advising.

For an ATR assessment to become a regulatory fact, however, it has to be auditable. Pressure to *show* how much risk consumers were willing to take on, and to prove that the right amount of risk was sold to them, reflects a long-standing regulatory drive in the UK to improve and expand the 'audit trail' for financial advice. This drive was made clear in the 2013 fine of AXA discussed above. So a debate ensued between the Financial Services Authority (FSA) and the Firm about the proper way of assessing consumers' ATR.

The chairman of the Firm at the time explained that the 'FSA was worried that [the advisers] weren't going into this [into establishing the risk attitude] in enough detail'. In response, the Firm argued, among others, that 'people have multiple attitudes to risk, depending on which pot of money, or which point in time'. He gave the example of an entrepreneur who had been very risk-taking in the past but now that he'd made his money, he did not want to lose it. He is going to be risk averse. The FSA 'wanted to bring it down to a single number' to which the Firm objected.

What rounds out the Firm's reasoning is the overall view of the client relationship. The chairman's view was that the ATR measure was developed as a consequence of a 'bad stock market' which had elicited 'customer complaints'. In his words, what would typically happen is that an 'old lady writes "my investment is down by 18 per cent"', and this would trigger an investigation by the regulator into whether the financial adviser was mis-selling an investment product to someone who did not understand it, or was not willing to lose capital in the first place. Yet for the Firm, if an adverse investment outcome happens, it would take place within the larger flow of the long-term relationship. This is what he called 'reverse sell', the ability to demonstrate disinterest towards the client: 'If someone has £100,000 the good adviser does not get the client to invest it with the firm.' The adviser would explain that a fund must be set aside for 'emergencies—cash 25 [out of the 100]. A good adviser would say why not [make the cash reserve] 40, invest 60 with us.'

For negative scenarios the chairman explains that 'keeping in touch' is 'another element of interpersonal skill, especially when markets go down. Banks are bad at this, they have call centres', whereas the Firm's advisers 'hold their clients' hands in these times. You shouldn't pretend you know what the markets will do. If you pretend, it's pushy. If you are liquid enough, you last through.' The Firm's advisers thus take a 'longer-term view of markets'. The chairman cites figures of 95 per cent client retention rate against 87 per cent or less for banks. The Firm builds on family relationships, on servicing entire families and generations; another client pool is former CEOs. In the end, the wealth management Firm did have to adopt the single scale and number but the way the latter participates in the conversation is typically in a particular and fluid form. A senior adviser explains that 'We also do the risk attitude from 1 to 5, after the Assets, Liabilities, family' situation is laid out in the conversation.

In what follows, an exemplary case of how the Firm's advisers incorporated client risk preference is considered. The senior adviser's work exemplifies the Firm's approach to locating and documenting the risk profile within the advising process.

The adviser literally sketches the current financial assets of the client in pen and paper. The amount invested in each asset type is represented by a bar on a chart, from safe to risky asset types on the horizontal axis. For example, 1 is 'Cash' (£250,000), 2 is 'Home' (£1.75 million), 3 is 'Shares' (£1.5 million). The pattern of the resulting bar chart tells the adviser the pattern of the client's risk habits. This is contrasted with what the client *says* about his or her own risk-taking behaviour. He may describe himself as a risk-taker in the conversation, yet when the charts are drawn up, it turns out that he keeps most of the money in very liquid and low-yield assets.

From this visual statement of existing allocation, the adviser gleans both the implicit risk preference and the foundations on which to build the long-term financial strategy. The adviser's priority is to 'make sure that there is a cash emergency fund (not having to sell when the asset is down)'. This form of risk insulation comes up in other conversations as well.

Moving from this visually revealed risk attitude (coordinate system) to the pie charts of investment fund choice takes place by calculation on the sheet of paper, with pencil again. The adviser sees his role as a guide who can navigate 'tax efficient' and long-term solutions once the client's long-term life goals have been made clear: 'I direct them—I recommend to put this money from shares into this "tax box".' This navigation of the client is based on the graph sketched and the calculations performed in front of them using pen and paper to demonstrate the savings to be had. The ATR comes into play primarily by means of a pie chart, which is within a circumscribed part of this long-term strategy. The Firm offers its clients several types of fund portfolios which, in the advisers' understanding, correspond to different views on risk.

At this point in the process, the adviser explains, the client and he will together consider a 'mixture of our funds depending on attitude to risk. We go through the actual mix [offered in the brochure], and the client might say, if they know those funds a bit, that "oh, I don't want the Property" [real estate funds]…then we take it out and swap it for a different fund.' This is a commitment since previously the advisers did not recommend specific fund mixes. Moreover, the firm 'guarantees the advice', which means that they guarantee its suitability to the client's profile.

Apart from the investment fund portfolios, where ATR is typically used, it is assessed for other types of investments, to account for *lateral* variation across asset types. The training staff of the Firm's recruitment programme explained this clearly. Echoing the Firm's view presented by the chairman on the variegated nature of risk preference, the trainers remind participants that 'the client could have a different Attitude to Risk for retirement than for investment. For retirement it may be higher!'—meaning that the client may want to take higher risks with savings invested for retirement than for 'regular' invested money. Thus, the adviser may not be able to assume how the client relates to all asset types. This is slightly different from the life-cycle argument made above, that ATR may vary over time. This argument highlights that at a certain point in time, ATR may vary across different investment types.

The visual methods that advisers develop show great breadth, yet they reflect the Firm's approach to ATR as something emerging from the advising conversation. Another adviser draws what she calls 'my circles', a 'visual aid' with which clients 'can see the weightings or shortfalls' of their plans. In this outcome-oriented planning exercise, a series of circles are drawn on a sheet of paper to signal the client's financial goals (e.g. the ultimate 'Target income' of

£50,000 at retirement), arranged from short term to long term, and different 'pots' of money associated with them. The client's existing funds and debts are in some of them; these are complemented with the necessary funds for achieving the target long-term lifestyle. This method has been so successful that '90 per cent of clients ask for a photocopy [of their circles page]'.

The ATR is embedded in this process, as this adviser, too, picks out the relevant information about the client's relationship to risk from the flow of conversation and her circles graph. Indeed, common to both advisers, the graphical devices have precedence in establishing the risk attitude. This adviser emphasizes that clients' views of their risk-taking propensity is often different from what their asset allocation shows. 'People tell you lots of info without realizing that they're telling it to you. A client would say "I'm cautious" but... invested in emerging markets, or another would say, "I'm adventurous"...but everything is in cash'.

The Firm's advisers are required, after the extensive face-to-face discussion with the client, to send a so-called suitability letter to the client summarizing their discussions, providing an analysis of their financial situation, and formulating recommendations for financial decisions. The assessments and recommendations are not merely based on the face-to-face conversation but are also supported by very detailed records, which the client must previously submit to the adviser. The recommendations, in turn, can be very general and not directed at specific products at this stage.

DISCUSSION

The work of assessing consumer risk preference has specific characteristics relative to other types of riskwork. ATR regulation acts on the individual but implicitly requires them to *manage* his or her own risks—not eliminate them. Whereas individuals are commonly the objects of safety-oriented regulation aiming to protect them from harm, profit-oriented enterprises are founded on risk-taking. Regulating consumer risk preference has brought the two perspectives together, constructing in practice the 'entrepreneurial' subject of finance (Langley, 2006; O'Malley, 2000).

To emphasize how unusual it is for risk management to operate at the individual level, consider a few thought experiments. It is hardly imaginable, for example, that consumers be asked to state their risk tolerance to nuclear background radiation and select their place of residence accordingly, or to reveal their preference for levels of bisphenol A in their water bottles and be offered the types of plastic bottles which match those levels. In contrast, *levels* of risk tolerance are implicitly established when it comes to deciding between alternative medical interventions. The doctor explains the different treatments and operations to the patient, their chances of success and chances of complications. It is the patient's responsibility to evaluate how much risk she is willing to take and accordingly to choose the course of treatment (e.g. mentioned by Douglas, 1992: 14). However, even in this familiar and well-scrutinized setting we do not see a procedure to establish the patient's own risk attitude to medical events, in the way we do with the on-the-spot extraction of financial risk preference.

In the financial regulator's formulation, this responsibility for individual, as opposed to organizational, risk management emerges as the consequence of a market process. Consumers of financial services are buying risk and hence they must have preferences for risk, which must be matched with the risk of the product. How this regulatory view of risk is enacted in practice was the subject of this chapter, focusing not on the 'matching' of clients with products but on the prior process of establishing their ATR.

On the one hand, in organizations that emphasize relationship-building, we found that risk preference is less taken for granted within a complex and long-term view of clients. On the other hand, in highly formalized encounters with mass clients as in UK retail banks, mandatory and quantifiable assessments of risk preference become part of the bureaucratic procedure. Preference is firmed up, processed, and referenced in a relatively straightforward way. This finding is consistent with earlier work on mass-personalized banking encounters (Vargha, 2010).

Correspondingly, two different approaches to the elicitation of risk prefer-ence emerge. First, there is *scenario-based* risk preference, where the ATR software's survey questions create hypothetical and abstract scenarios of decision-making, often without financial values (see Figure 8.1). Second, there is *revealed* risk preference, where the client's current assets are mapped implicitly from the safest (cash) to the riskiest investment. With a few add-itional questions the adviser makes an inference from the current revealed distribution of assets, sketched out as a graph on a sheet of paper, to an idea of what the risk preference might be.

Both risk preference techniques produce truths about the consumer in the Foucauldian sense, as they claim to unearth the risk properties of consumers, albeit in a compliant way. The large retail bank's financial planner lets the client play an experiment on herself, to lure her inherent relationship to risk into the open. The wealth management advisers listen to the client's own narrative and watch for the revealed risk preferences emerging from the hand-drawn graphs. These truths about the client are formatted differently, too. The risk questionnaires ask about attitude to money in the abstract, as a neutral object, while wealth managers recognized that people do not relate to all money equally and neutrally. While the regulator has pressed for systematic and detailed measurement of risk preference, the Firm held that individuals do not have a single risk preference; it varies according to 'which pot of money' they are considering. In their advising process, advisers thus try to access the 'mental accounting' (Thaler, 1999) and 'earmarking' (Zelizer, 1997) habits of consumers, whereby people separate and keep track of money from various sources (salary or inheritance) and spend them according to their values (e.g. 'windfall income should not be used for daily expenses'), giving meaning to their relationships (a favourite nephew might get more inheritance).

In a similar way to the construction of *risk objects* (Hilgartner, 1992), consumers-with-risk preference are also constructed as realities brought into the world. This takes place at the junction of several things: regulation which recognizes the importance of risk preference, procedures that establish risk preference, and decisions that follow from a certain risk preference. In the end, consumers increasingly 'have' a risk preference expressed in the ATR. However, as the different modes of riskwork above demonstrated, this process is not yet a fully stabilized one; there are continuing controversies about how to find out risk preference and what it is exactly that one finds out.

Thus, these two examples exhibit different views of the customer which surface in the calculative habits of ATR assessments: the more mechanical retail model is focused on transactions and on finding cost-effective ways to handle large numbers of customers. Tight cost control translates into seeing customers as a calculable, quantifiable mass. The model of the private bank, of wealth management, is intensively focused on the relationship and sees the latter essentially as not quantifiable. Advisers are not pressured to cost their engagements with clients. In contrast, the standardized, generic, and automated ATR assessment at the retail bank aids cost-efficient handling of the required task. Wealth managers push back against such quantification, based on a (nonetheless) calculative view that expects the relationship to yield results in the long term. This approach only works, they say, if customers are not mass-processed. This reaffirmation of the business model resonates with Gilad's finding about organizational identity and compliance. When process-oriented regulation is perceived as a threat to identity, that is, to 'members' intersubjective perception of the central and enduring attributes that distinguish their organization from similar entities', firms engage in the 'reframing of regulatory expectations into existing businesses' discourses and methodologies' (Gilad, 2011: 312).

As emergent compliance practices, however, it is the scenario-based assessment that has been perceived as most readily fulfilling the regulator's requirements for systematic, consistent, documented, and hence auditable measures. From the regulatory perspective, sketching the assets in pen and paper is not only less standardized and less auditable, but it is also more ambiguous. These sketches are at the same time an integral part of the personalized *selling* technique (see the effect of hand-drawn product demonstrations in Vargha (2011)). Sitting with the client and sketching the situation requires listening to the client, and advisers recognize that listening is an important part of selling. Although in principle an assessment of risk profile from the presentation of current assets might be acceptable, the process of arriving at such a presentation mixes selling and assessment to an indistinguishable degree. From the regulatory viewpoint, even with their shortcomings, the risk profiling surveys have stronger facticity.

The close study of 'formal' and 'informal' variants of consumer financial riskwork suggests two important themes for further discussion: how the market negotiates regulation, and the effect on identity.

The Boundary between Markets and Regulation

While riskwork originates in, and is closely tied up with, regulation work, it is also embedded in market processes in which financial advisers close deals. But this is not a simple tension between market activity, which demands risk-taking, and efforts to divert harm and catastrophe. Rather, the work of producing the ATR requires various actors to reflect on and struggle over where economic *value* is being produced in the process, for both the regulated entity, and the object of regulation—the consumer.

First, there is a struggle between the regulators and the regulated to place value on certain parts of the financial advising relationship and not on others. The regulated firms try to defend the fluidity of interaction as part of the business model and as a better risk tool for regulation. Second, when this is not successful, the encounter itself *changes* as advisers blend the rules of the state into their work and start owning the new documentary methods of audit (this includes the FSA's *Key Facts* document). Yet the risk preference survey is an ambiguous device embodying both 'state' and 'market'. The boundary between the firm and the regulator *becomes* blurred in the encounter between client and firm. It is no longer clear what is the firm and what is the FSA, and whose intentions are being executed or enforced, especially when it comes to the devices which have been inserted in a joint effort. The risk survey is often produced in-house by the firm, it does not make reference to regulation (as opposed to other documents), and has become embedded in the financial advice process as a self-evident step in the giving of proper advice.

Ironically, *the more the regulator is present* in the encounter, *the more ambiguous the encounter becomes.* The more that documentation is explained by the adviser as being 'required by regulation', the more it raises the question for the client as to whether this is a potentially dangerous encounter. Both parties are aware that the encounter is under state regulation, because of the forms that must be brought into the meeting and filled out, and agreed to. Only a complete lack of documentation would signal status and trust.

Third, studying the work of managing risk at the sales interface, one client at a time, shows the problematic project of risk-matching for the neo liberal consumer. The theoretical challenge is to take governmentality apart into its specific processes, to show more precisely how the governing of individual consumers is taking place (Barry, Osborne, & Rose, 1996). The UK approach to consumer financial protection rests on the acknowledgement that consumers have different needs and preferences, yet as natural propensities, these are out of consumers' control. Thus, it is the expert's responsibility to bring the client's risk preference to the surface and connect products 'correctly' to it. With an emphasis on the *suitability* of advice, this risk management framework envisions that the risk of product and consumer are separate, isolated, constant, and assessable entities that must be matched by the intermediary. After this matching moment, however, *responsibilization* (Miller & Rose, 1990) takes full effect as the legal responsibility devolves to the consumer to accept the outcomes that come with his/her risk profile.

In post-crisis financial regulation, this kind of accounting transparency for risk preference potentially 'has unintended effects such that the making visible starts to change that which is rendered transparent...transparency works back upon those subject to it in ways that are often counterproductive, or at least far exceeds the passive image of a simple making visible' (Roberts, 2009: 958). Based on Judith Butler's theory of 'giving an account of oneself', Roberts goes on to suggest that we should not be asking for such responsibilization of consumers because of 'the impossibility of a self that is fully transparent to itself (and therefore others)' (2009: 958). Exploring the performative, and potentially counterproductive effects of ATR accountabilities would be a next step in the study of consumer financial protection.

Identity Effects: Risk Assessment as 'Truth-Producing Practice'

The by-products of riskwork, of fabricating the regulatory object—the consumer's Attitude to Risk—are in fact accounts of the self, potentially shaping consumer identity explicitly or implicitly. The customer is at the boundary of the organization and needs to be attached to the organization. Mechanisms of attachment between customers and products have been recognized as key to markets (Callon, Méadel, & Rabeharisoa, 2002), and what we see here is not only relational attachment but also how risk, in the form of ATR, attaches clients to the organization itself and mediates their relationship with it. Riskwork in financial advice specifies *how*, under what terms, and into which categorizations the client might be brought into the system of the organization, as a subject in risk preference assessment. ATR acts as a gateway through which customers pass, and based on their 'diagnosis', their entry to the organization is negotiated.

The subject learns about herself in the sales encounter, which turns out to be a psychodynamic process, albeit in different ways in the two cases. The on-screen or online multiple-choice surveys bear the scientific influence of experimental psychology and test risky decision-making in hypothetical situations, with a single score as their result. ATR emerges not from interaction with an expert but through the act of the customer filling out the questionnaire. In the advice situation, risk preference is summoned to appear with the help of the device. The task of the survey is to unearth the underlying truth about the client. The result will be a documented ATR with a single value, often between 1 and 5, accompanied by an adjective such as 'cautious'.

The 'test' thus turns into a *technology of the self* (Foucault et al., 1988) that produces the truth of the investor personality. Completing the questionnaire, finding the best answers among the multiple choices offered, is a process of working on the self. The risk information is built by the client, the test result must be shared with her according to the FSA regulations, and she is informed that the investment choices must be within the risk range corresponding to that number. While the wealth management Firm's approach could also be seen as a technology of the self, it cannot be exercised alone. The adviser must always be present to guide the exploration of a client's existing way of life. In contrast, the standardized risk questionnaire is a stand-alone technology with which to discover the self, by oneself. It is decoupled from the adviser, and we can witness its online proliferation in the form of self-assessment tools. In both cases, the risk device used may ultimately affect how consumers view themselves henceforth. Yet there could be a significant difference between the two modes of riskwork in terms of the 'self' that clients walk away with. This is a topic for further research.

At the same time, the risk score serves as a bureaucratic audit tool—due to its more organized (electronic) documentation, the retail bank version of ATR achieves more 'regulatory facticity'. The established risk preference is documented by the information systems of the bank, and is materialized through its paths 'inside' the organization. It constitutes evidence of compliance and as such, it participates in *audit trails* (Power, 2015). ATR becomes a stable regulatory and organizational fact despite the understanding that risk preference changes over time and that the test must be repeated and earlier results overwritten or discarded. The survey's process of attachment to the organization by risk constitutes consumers as the good economic subjects expected by neo-liberal regulation: they become actors who *have* and *know* their own risk preference, and are therefore capable of carrying out economic decisions, which are understood to be inherently risk-based.

CONCLUSIONS

Many directions arise for future research and in conclusion we touch on those related to individual and organizational identity. First, risk preference can gain 'facticity' as it moves from the client through the organization, to the regulator, the media, and other places, independent of clients' engagement with it. Formalized risk profiling tools seem to have stronger 'facticity' while we can be less conclusive about the other method. A question to explore is the role of 'audit trails' (Power, 2015) in producing facts about risk, in the organization.

Second, there are likely to be side effects of producing this fact, namely effects on consumers, as mentioned above. Is the production of ATR a Foucauldian technology of the self, an exercise of self-examination with lasting effects on consumers' identification and market actions, or is it understood to be a purely bureaucratic practice by all parties? Our hypothesis is that even if it is merely a bureaucratic exercise, consumers' curiosity is kindled and know-ledge of the self produced, with potentially lasting effects. It follows that the account of oneself generated by this riskwork has to be reconciled to, and negotiated with, one's already existing self-image.

Third, what are the links between risk to the consumer and risk to the organization? How do banks in practice link the individual risk profiles and their overall management of organizational risk? For example, if the bank discovers, through its compliance practice of documenting clients' ATR, that it is significantly exposed to high risk-taking clients, does this information feed into the Enterprise Risk Management framework? There is also the question of correctness: what happens if ATR is determined 'wrongly' and consumers are sold the wrong products, that is, how do banks take into account the risks of mis-selling due to their own ATR procedures?

Fourth, this leads us finally to the question of organizational risk manage-ment. More research is needed to understand the parallel mechanisms, and actual linkages between, individual 'risk preference' and organizational 'risk appetite' (on the latter see Power (2007). We do not simply mean managers' view of risk-taking (e.g. March & Shapira, 1987), but rather, the process of establishing the 'risk appetite' of the organization as part of enterprise risk management (Rittenberg & Martens, 2012). This question relates to the scalability of governmental rationality, as Foucault suggests, to different economic units. Even if there is no direct link between individual risk prefer-ence and organizational risk appetite as novel governing concepts, we can expect to see issues of identity negotiation around 'risk-taking' at the organizational level of risk management which are similar in kind to those experienced by individual consumers.

REFERENCES

Appelt, K. C., Milch, K. F., & Weber, E. U. (2011). The Decision Making Individual Differences Inventory and Guidelines for the Study of Individual Differences in Judg-ment and Decision-Making Research. *Judgment and Decision Making*, 6(3), 252–62.

Barry, A., Osborne, T., & Rose, N. S. (1996). *Foucault and Political Reason: Liberalism, Neo-liberalism and Rationalities of Government*. London: UCL Press.

Byrne, A. & Blake, D. (2012). *Investment Risk and Financial Advice*. London: Vanguard Asset Management.

Callon, M., Méadel, C., & Rabeharisoa, V. (2002). The Economy of Qualities. *Economy and Society*, 31(2), 194–217.

Charness, G., Gneezy, U., & Imas, A. (2013). Experimental Methods: Eliciting risk Preferences. *Journal of Economic Behavior and Organization*, 87, 43–51.

Dohmen, T., Falk, A., Huffman, D., & Wagner, G. G. (2011). Individual Risk Attitudes: Measurement, Determinants, and Behavioral Consequences. *Journal of the European Economic Association*, 9, 522–50.

Douglas, M. (1992). *Risk and Blame: Essays in Cultural Theory*. London and New York: Routledge.

Engelmann, J. B. & Tamir, D. (2009). Individual Differences in Risk Preference Predict Neural Responses During Financial Decision-Making. *Brain Research*, 1290, 28–51.

European Parliament & the Council of the European Union. (2004). Directive 2004/39/EC of the European Parliament and of the Council on Markets in financial instruments EU: Official Journal of the European Union. <http://eur-lex.europa.eu/legal-content/EN/TXT/PDF/?uri=CELEX:32004L0039&from=EN> (accessed March 2016).

FCA (2013). *Final Notice to Axa Wealth Services Ltd* London: Financial Conduct Authority.

Foucault, M., Martin, L. H., Gutman, H., & Hutton, P. H. (1988). *Technologies of the Self: A Seminar with Michel Foucault*. Amherst, MA: University of Massachusetts Press.

FSA (2006). *Treating Customers Fairly—Towards Fair Outcomes for Consumers*. London: Financial Services Authority.

FSA (2011a). *FSA Factsheet for Financial Advisers: Improving the Quality of Your Advice Process—Assessment of Customer Needs*. London: Financial Services Authority.

FSA (2011b). *Guidance Consultation—Assessing Suitability: Establishing the Risk a Customer Is Willing and Able to Take and Making a Suitable Investment Selection*. London: Financial Services Authority.

Gilad, S. (2011). Institutionalizing Fairness in Financial Markets: Mission Impossible? *Regulation & Governance*, 5(3), 309–32.

Hilgartner, S. (1992). The Social Construction of Risk Objects: Or, How to Pry Open Networks of Risk. In J. F. Short & L. Clarke (Eds), *Organizations, Uncertainties and Risks* (pp. 39–53). Boulder, CO: Westview Press.

Langley, P. (2006). The Making of Investor Subjects in Anglo-American Pensions. *Environment and Planning D: Society and Space*, 24(6), 919–34.

March, J. G. & Shapira, Z. (1987). Managerial Perspectives on Risk and Risk Taking. *Management Science*, 33(11), 1404–18.

Meyer, J. W. & Rowan, B. (1977). Institutionalized Organizations: Formal Structure as Myth and Ceremony. *American Journal of Sociology*, 83(2), 340–63.

Miller, P. & Rose, N. (1990). Governing Economic life. *Economy and Society*, 19(1), 1–31.

O'Malley, P. (2000). Uncertain Subjects: Risks, Liberalism and Contract. *Economy and Society*, 29(4), 460–84.

Power, M. (2007). *Organized Uncertainty: Designing a World of Risk Management*. Oxford: Oxford University Press.

Power, M. (2009). The Risk Management of Nothing. *Accounting, Organizations and Society*, 34(6–7), 849–55.

Power, M. (2015). Organizations and Audit Trails. Paper presented at the 'Thinking Infrastructures' workshop, Copenhagen Business School, 1 October.

Rittenberg, L. & Martens, F. (2012). *Enterprise Risk Management: Understanding and Communicating Risk Appetite (Thought Leadership in ERM)*. COSO. <http://www.coso.org/documents/ERM-Understanding%20%20Communicating%20Risk%20Appetite-WEB_FINAL_r9.pdf> (accessed March 2016).

Roberts, J. (2009). No One Is Perfect: The Limits of Transparency and an Ethic for 'Intelligent' Accountability. *Accounting, Organizations and Society*, 34, 957–70.

Roszkowski, M., Davey, G., & Grable, J. (2005). Insights from Psychology and Psychometrics on Measuring Risk Tolerance. *Journal of Financial Planning*, 18(4), 66–77.

Rothstein, H., Huber, M., & Gaskell, G. (2006). A Theory of Risk Colonization: The Spiralling Regulatory Logics of Societal and Institutional Risk. *Economy and Society*, 35(1), 91–112.

Sandholtz, K. W. (2012). Making Standards Stick: A Theory of Coupled vs. Decoupled Compliance. *Organization Studies*, 33(5–6), 655–79.

Thaler, R. H. (1999). Mental Accounting Matters. *Journal of Behavioral Decision Making*, 12(3), 183–206.

Vargha, Z. (2010). Technologies of Persuasion: Personal Selling and the Making of Markets in Consumer Finance. Ph.D. dissertation, Department of Sociology, Columbia University, New York.

Vargha, Z. (2011). From Long-term Savings to Instant Mortgages: Financial Demonstration and the Role of Interaction in Markets. *Organization*, 18(2), 215–35.

Weber, E. U. & Milliman, R. A. (1997). Perceived Risk Attitudes: Relating Risk Perception to Risky Choice. *Management Science*, 43(2), 123–44.

Zelizer, V. A. R. (1997). *The Social Meaning of Money*. Princeton, NJ: Princeton University Press.

9

Risk and Routine in the Digitized World

Brian T. Pentland

Our personal and business computing systems are continually becoming more sophisticated, distributed, networked, and layered. At the same time, they are increasingly intertwined with everything we do. We use our digital devices to communicate, collaborate, and compete, anywhere and anytime. Digitization has a lot of benefits, but if these systems are out of control, a lot of things can go wrong, from loss of data (Finkel & Heavey, 2014) to loss of life (Dobson, 2004). As a result, individuals and organizations invest considerable time and money into managing the risks related to digitization.

Digitization provides an interesting arena in which to examine how we think about and manage risk. The benefits of digitization arise, to a great extent, from new interconnections and the positive externalities induced by having a larger number of participants sharing the same platform (Rochet & Tirole, 2003). Our digital connections allow us to bridge geographic and social worlds in innumerable ways. At the same time, many of the risks associated with digitization, such as malware and hacking, are exacerbated by new interconnections. While particular benefits and risks may seem obvious, these benefits and risks are interdependent in ways that are sometimes difficult to anticipate or understand.

Digitization is also interesting because it tends to blur familiar boundaries and distinctions, such as work and home, people and things, front- and back-office, public and private. We routinely use a variety of digital devices, such as computers, tablets, and smartphones at home, at work, and in between. These may be our own personal devices, used for our own personal purposes, or they may be owned and maintained by an organization and used for organizational purposes. Quite often, these distinctions are blurred, when we bring our own devices to work, or update our Facebook status from the office. In responding to an email or texting a photo to a friend, the devices themselves can be seen as actors in their own right (Latour, 2005), as digitization tends to blur the distinction between us and our things. Conventional distinctions between front office and back office are somewhat blurry, as well. With cloud-based services and user-configured platforms (such as smartphones), we have become our own system administrators. Security experts talk about 'lines of defense' in networks (Djenouri, Khelladi, & Badache, 2005), but this metaphor implies that the threats are outside and that it is possible to identify a boundary.

In practice, it seems increasingly difficult to draw clear lines, and it is hard to know what we are defending against. We see and hear a constant stream of news and media about identity theft, hacking, cyber-terrorism, and more, but there is a diversity of opinion about how serious and how likely any particular digital risk may be (Pew Research, 2014). Some argue that exaggeration and fearmongering are being used to bolster sales of security-related products and services, and to advocate for increased government surveillance and control. If so, it seems to be working well. The economic scale of the effort devoted to analysing, mitigating, and managing digital risk would be difficult to estimate because much of this effort is a taken-for-granted part of other activities (e.g. entering and updating passwords). Nevertheless, the Gartner Group estimates that worldwide spending on information security reached $71.1 billion in 2014 and will continue to grow substantially. The US Bureau of Labor Statistics lists over 75,000 people with the job title 'Information Security Analyst' as of 2012. However, as I will argue here, everyone involved in using digital technology, in any capacity, is engaged in managing risk at least part of the time.

In this chapter, I invite the reader to step back from any particular risk and consider the broader landscape of digital risk from the perspective of organizational routines: recognizable, repetitive patterns of interdependent action carried out by multiple actors (Feldman & Pentland, 2003). This perspective embodies what Knorr-Cetina (1981) would call *methodological situationalism*, because the emphasis is on situations and collective patterns of action, rather than individual actors assessing the risk of individual actions. The routines perspective is relevant because information technology and organizational routines are deeply intertwined (D'Adderio, 2008; Leonardi, 2011); whenever you are looking at one you are almost inevitably seeing the other. Given the increasingly interconnected, interdependent nature of digital technology, organized patterns of action are a central aspect of working in a digitized world.

The chapter begins with a brief discussion of organizational routines. While routines are often cast in opposition to rational action, they can be well adapted, efficient, and safe in stable, familiar contexts (Cohen et al., 1996). However, the digital arena is not stable. It is constantly changing and routinized patterns of action are likely to be problematic. The next sections of the chapter provide examples of how routine courses of action can lead to unexpected results and unanticipated risk. These examples highlight the need for a way of conceptualizing digital risk that takes into account the multiplicity of possibilities and their interdependence. As a step towards addressing this need, the chapter concludes by summarizing the examples mentioned here in a 'narrative network' (Pentland & Feldman, 2007). While any representation entails some simplification, the narrative network allows a more inclusive perspective on routinized patterns of action.

ROUTINES AND RISK

The concept of an organizational routine was introduced as a response to an overly rational model of organizational decision-making (Cyert & March, 1963). Thus, the basic idea of an organizational routine stands in contrast to the familiar paradigm of rational decision-making (Simon, 1979). In that paradigm, decisions are made by individual decision-makers, with rational calculation as the ideal standard against which decision processes are evaluated. Rational calculation continues to be a familiar basis for official representations of risk assessment (see Chapter 1, this volume), so it makes a useful point of reference for explaining how the routines perspective is different.

Until recently, the term 'routine' was usually used as an adjective to indicate a behaviour that might conform to a standard operating procedure (SOP) or a pre-established set of rules. For example, economic literature often refers to 'routine work' (Autor & Dorn, 2013). In the extreme, such behaviour might be completely habitual or mindless (Ashforth & Fried, 1988). In current organizational theory, the term 'routine' is used to refer to repetitive patterns of interdependent action (Feldman & Pentland, 2003). This action-centred paradigm embodies a basic shift away from the more traditional actor-centred paradigm that characterizes rational actor theory and behavioural decision theory (Pentland & Hærem, 2015). The routines perspective emphasizes interdependence between actions, the involvement of multiple actors, and the adaptation of action patterns over time, through repetition rather than calculation. The focus is on the actions, rather than the actors. This shift in perspective provides a unique vantage point for thinking about risk.

Actions Occur in Interdependent Patterns

The classic approach to decision-making treats each decision (or action) as independent. Each decision (or action) is separate from other decisions (or actions). If we view actions as part of a routine, then each action occurs as part of a course of action, or in response to other actions. They are not independent. Consider, for example, the decision to subscribe to a cloud-based file-sharing service like DropBox or GoogleDocs. This decision might occur in the context of a project where a group of people (colleagues, co-workers, family members, or friends) need to share documents. If someone suggests that everyone should subscribe to the service, everyone usually does. This illustrates how the benefits of digitization often flow from greater connectivity and interdependence.

Then, to get the file-sharing service to work correctly, you might discover that you need to change the settings on your network firewall. This change will allow remote devices to access and update files on your computer. In this scenario, the decision to change firewall settings could be the result of a request to contribute a chapter to an edited book, or a family project to make an album of holiday photos for the grandparents. The decision to change your firewall settings and potentially expose yourself to risk would not stand alone. It is part of the collaboration. In general, it seems likely that decisions to change security settings or upgrade software are usually not taken in isolation; they become necessary as a result of some other decision or action. This illustrates the counter-point: that the risks of digitization are often the result of increased connectivity and interdependence.

Work Involves Multiple Actors

The file-sharing example also illustrates that there are multiple actors in any meaningful work process. Because our actions are interdependent, my actions are usually enabled or constrained by the actions of others. For example, we all need to subscribe to the same cloud-based service and share the right folders. What appears to be 'my decision' could be heavily influenced by the course of action that my unseen colleagues are collectively enacting. The extension from single to multiple actors is what makes the pattern of action 'organizational' as opposed to individual; it does not need to occur in the context of a formal organization. It seems more appropriate to think of it as situational (Knorr-Cetina, 1981).

Also, it is important to note that the 'multiple actors' in a routine are often non-human (e.g. a cellphone, a website, a router, a workflow system, or a cloud-based collaboration tool). These actors can in effect 'make decisions' and take actions that are just as real and essential to the overall routine as the actions of the human actors. For example, the firewall mentioned in the previous example is an active device; it can examine every incoming and outgoing connection request and data packet. It uses rules to decide what traffic is allowed to get through. The inclusion of non-human actors is well established in actor–network theory (ANT) (Latour, 2005), and in the theory of organizational routines (D'Adderio, 2008), but stands in contrast to traditional perspectives that are focused on individual human decision-makers.

Adaptation Rather Than Calculation

Early conceptions of organizational routines characterized them as 'mindless' and automatic (Ashforth & Fried 1988), and that is certainly a fair description for many routines (Rice & Cooper, 2010). However, contemporary theory suggests that within a collective pattern of action, there may be a mixture of heuristic processing and rational calculation (Pentland & Hærem, 2015). Either way, routines are generally adapted to the context in which they were formed (Cohen et al., 1996). Contextual adaptation is a natural product of path dependence (Schulz, 2008): if an action pattern was successful in the past, it provides a precedent for future actions. Thus, routinized action patterns are like ruts in the road—we tend to follow the most common path (Cohen, 2007), and that path usually keeps us safely on the road.

While routinized, heuristic decision-making is often regarded as inferior to rational calculation, Gigerenzer (2000) argues that at the individual level, this is the mechanism that makes humans smart. Routines result in excellent outcomes as long as they are performed in the same context in which they were formed. So, drinking well-water without treatment or purification may be a perfectly safe routine in some locations, but risky in others.

Of course, repetition is a critical dimension of this phenomenon. When you and your family drink well-water day after day, year after year, you are relying on the safety and purity of the source. As long as the world is stable, the routine pattern of action is safe. But in exceptional situations, such as fighting forest fires (Weick, 1993), routine patterns of action can be disastrous. In his classic analysis of the actions of a team of 'smokejumpers' at the Mann Gulch fire, Weick (1993) argues that the best survival strategy involved improvisation, rather that routine. While Weick (1993) uses the term 'routine' as roughly synonymous with 'standard operating procedure', the point is clear: in novel situations, routines can fail. Subsequent to that disaster, the US Forest Service updated its training and equipment; they adapted their action patterns to deal with more severe situations.

The processes through which routines form and adapt is a topic of ongoing research, but the original insight remains valid: in a stable context, we can engage in repetitive patterns of action without the need for deep, calculative analysis. In a stable world, routinized action can be fine-tuned to take on an acceptable level of risk. For example, when we are driving on a familiar road, we can drive a little bit over the speed limit without getting a ticket and without getting in an accident. On an unfamiliar road, it may be difficult to know what speed is safe. The analogy with driving is particularly appropriate, since the words 'rut', 'route', and 'routine' all have the same etymological basis.

CHALLENGES OF THE DIGITAL ARENA

There are several features of the digitized world that tend to problematize our familiar 'ruts in the road':

1 Small actions can have big consequences. For example, installing or uninstalling software can change important functions or settings. These changes are often as simple as ticking a little checkbox, so they are easy to miss and easy to get wrong.

2 There is often considerable uncertainty about the effects of particular events or actions. For example, if you get an unfamiliar warning message, does it indicate a serious problem or not? Should you open a port on a firewall to allow outside network traffic to enter? More generally, how can we tell which settings are really important?

3 In a networked world, there are a large number of actors. We engage in routinized patterns of action with an increasingly numerous and obscure set of other actors. Some of the actors are human, but many are not, and it is increasingly difficult to discern the difference.

4 As the layers of software grow in number and complexity, it seems more likely that we will discover hidden threats: so-called 'zero day' security threats. The term 'zero day' refers to a previously unknown threat for which anti-virus or anti-malware software is not yet available.

5 New software changes the function and character of its host. The change may be small or large, subtle or obvious, benign or malignant. An upgraded device is no longer the same device. Yet, if the device is incorporated into our routines and continues to function, we usually act as though it has not changed.

6 Frequent changes tend to exacerbate all of the other problems because they make it difficult to know how the computer works. Thus, while automatic updates are often intended to reduce risk (by improving security and reliability), they may have the opposite effect if users get confused, change settings, or don't understand how the new code works.

In fairness, digitization also has a number of potentially positive influences, but the list seems short by comparison. For example, it enables automated controls and continuous monitoring (Kuhn & Sutton, 2010). However, the seemingly endless stream of security breaches suggest that at present, these controls are not sufficient (for an up-to-date list of significant data loss events, see <http://www.datalossdb.org>).

The constant change in the digital arena stands in contrast to other arenas where threat mechanisms are more knowable and stable, at least in principle. For example, with infectious diseases or chemical toxins (such as heavy metals or bisphenol A), there may be uncertainty or controversy about how the pathogen affects humans or other species (Chapter 6, this volume). The controversy can go on for years, but, if a consensus can be reached, it becomes possible to evaluate the risk of alterative scenarios, set standards for exposure, and so on (Chapter 1, this volume).

The high level of interconnectedness in the digital arena is also distinctive. In principle, assessments of probability and impact of relevant events (and subsequent outcomes) can be used to estimate risk by summing across the events, but this assumes that the events and outcomes are independent. If the consequences of familiar patterns of action are unpredictable, or invisible, but highly interconnected, then it becomes difficult to assess risk. In many respects, the situation is similar to the argument that Perrow (1984) made in his classic analysis of 'Normal Accidents'. People who are operating a complex, tightly coupled technology are faced with a situation that may be beyond their ability to understand. But instead of nuclear power plants, we are operating smartphones and videogame consoles. In the sections that follow, I will offer some examples to illustrate this more clearly.

Should I Click on That?

We all receive messages that contain attachments and links. The obviously fraudulent messages involving financial windfalls from Nigeria are easy to recognize and avoid. But when you get an official-looking message that seems to be from your bank, or a friend, you might not stop and think. With careful social engineering, it is fairly easy to construct messages that will entice people to take the bait.

Merely opening an email is unlikely to cause an infection, but when we click on a link or open an attachment, that is a different story. Those actions can authorize a program to run. The details of what that program may be authorized to do are not always clear (e.g. open a network connection? Copy a file? Install another program?). It depends on settings that we may (or may not) understand, and that may (or may not) be adequate to protect us.

Should I Subscribe to That Service?

A next step beyond the simple click is to subscribe to a new service. Leaving aside the details of what information to provide (do you give your real name, birthdate, gender, etc.?), the basic question is whether to subscribe or not. At a minimum, you must subscribe to the services offered by your employer, your government, your financial institutions, healthcare providers, insurance companies, cellphone vendors, airlines, and so on. Each of these entities delivers a set of routinized, digitized services that you or your family needs to use from time to time. In addition, if your professional identity requires some digital presence, you probably need to subscribe to social media sites, such as LinkedIn, Facebook, Twitter, and so on.

There are lots of services competing for our subscription and our attention. For example, a service called ResearchGate recently infected Michigan State University. I say 'infected' because ResearchGate relies on a viral marketing mechanism to gain subscribers. They use publicly available information about authorship to identify and invite your co-authors, people who have cited your papers, and so on. Based on this information, they solicit your subscription and ongoing participation. They may have infected your university, as well. They seem to be preying on our desire, as academics, to increase our 'impact'. I cannot tell if they provide a useful service or not, but it seems as if my personal 'impact factor' grows if I participate more. Should it be part of my routine to update ResearchGate every time I publish a working paper? And should I invite all of my colleagues to subscribe? It is difficult to assess the risks and benefits.

Like ResearchGate, the rapid adoption of cloud-based services is a 'viral' phenomenon, at least in part. Like a biological infection, the use of services such as DropBox and GoogleDocs tends to spread by social contagion: if your colleagues, family, co-workers or class-mates use the service, you need to use it, as well. Their routines become your routines. The positive externalities associated with common routines on a common platform are an important part of their value (Rochet & Tirole, 2003).

However, many users may not be aware that their services have services. Many social media platforms use APIs (application program interfaces) to connect to other platforms in order to increase their functionality. The point here is that one action (subscription) can set in motion a rather complex set of automated actions and interactions that will continue to occur, periodically, for the (un)foreseeable future. For example, our service providers may sell information about us to others as part of their business model. While these behind-the-scenes transactions are governed by privacy policies and statute, accidental or unintentional disclosures are not. At the very least, these transactions distribute our information more broadly, opening up additional opportunities for trouble.

Rules versus Routines in the Back Office

Organizations use frameworks, such as CoBIT 5.0, ISO27000, and PCI DSS2.0 to help guard against security breaches and other kinds of failures (Williams, Hardy, & Holgate, 2013). These frameworks include large numbers of rules, but rules need to be translated into routines before they have any practical effect (Reynaud, 2005). For example, there is a sophisticated standard for payment card security (PCI DSS 2.0); it specifies how information about credit and debit card transactions should be transmitted, stored, and encrypted.

These rules are intended to guard against fraud and loss of data, among other things.

In spite of these rules, there can be holes in the system. For example, there have been a series of large data loss incidents at North American retailers in recent years. One of the most visible was the security breach at Target, which occurred during the holiday shopping season. Target operates over 1,700 large retail stores in the US, and consistently ranks in Fortune Magazine's list of the World's Most Admired Companies. On 19 December 2013, Target confirmed that their systems had been hacked, and that the US Secret Service was investigating. As the facts emerged, it became clear that over 40 million payment card records had been stolen, along with personal information on 70 million individuals (Risen, 2014). The information systems security team at Target apparently received specific warnings about an impending data breach but did not act on them (Finkle & Heavey, 2014). It is not clear from published sources, but the new intrusion detection system does not seem to have been fully integrated into their actual work routines. Since news of the Target breach became public, we have seen other prominent examples: Home Depot, JPMorgan Chase & Co., and Sony Entertainment, to name a few.

So, even at trusted retailers, who are technically in compliance with all applicable rules, our information is not necessarily secure. These transactions can result in rather severe problems if they pass through a location that has been compromised. Shoppers think they are just paying for their items, as usual. In fact, if they are paying at a point-of-sale terminal that has been compromised, they are also giving their personal information to an organization that will put it up for sale on the black market, along with millions of others.

Layers of Risk in the Digital Architecture

The example of data loss from a retail transaction highlights another basic issue about digitization: we rely on the integrity and controls of the systems we use. Consider the so-called 'Heartbleed' security threat, which affected encrypted Internet traffic. Internet security pundits sounded the alarm: 'Heartbleed has the potential to be one of the biggest, most widespread vulnerabilities in the history of the modern web' (Warren, 2014). The threat seemed to be severe because it had gone undetected for about two years, and it affected the encryption mechanism used for so-called 'secure' websites (https). The Heartbleed threat was believed to be particularly serious because it not only affected websites, it affected *routers* and other kinds of network infrastructure (Fung, 2014):

Over a dozen Cisco products or services are thought to be vulnerable to Heartbleed, the company confirmed Thursday. The list includes videoconferencing products and a mobile client for Apple's iOS, among others. In addition, the Wall Street Journal reported Thursday that the Heartbleed bug extends to products made by Juniper Networks.

The discovery of Heartbleed exemplifies two problems. First, it is a rare but rather dramatic example of a so-called 'zero-day' event that affected Internet infrastructure. Usually, security flaws are limited to particular software platforms or applications. Second, it demonstrates that the difficulty in assessing digital risk is compounded by the fact that in a modern, networked environment, there are many layers of software running on each 'host'. On the Internet, data passes through an unknown, ever-changing set of hosts. In principle, each layer on each host is vulnerable, at least to some extent. To address this concern, sensitive Internet traffic is encrypted. When we see a connection to a site with a valid certificate using 'https', it means that the packets being routed over that connection are encrypted end to end. Virtual private networks (VPNs), the backbone of the modern distributed enterprise, operate on the same basic technology. In principle, as long as the endpoints are secure, the hosts along the way don't matter. It is not clear whether the Heartbleed threat has resulted in actual data loss or not; organizations do not necessarily report such events, and an intrusion of this kind might go undetected, since it would affect network traffic 'outside' the normal organizational boundary. For the purposes of this discussion, it highlights the fact that it is difficult to be aware of all the risks that exist in the digital arena (Rettig, 2007).

CONCEPTUALIZING RISK IN THE DIGITAL ARENA

The preceding examples demonstrate some of the challenges posed by an arena that is rapidly changing and highly interconnected. To understand risk in the digital domain, we need to find a way to represent risks that arise from interdependent activities and technologies. One possibility is the narrative network (Pentland & Feldman, 2007), a framework that was originally introduced as a way to describe technologically enabled patterns of action. The narrative network provides a concise way to describe the central tendency in patterns of action, as well as the variety (Cohen, 2007). Each node in the network is an action or event that is part of the routine. The ties between the nodes represent sequence. With adequate data, the ties can represent the relative frequency of what event typically happens next, like a transition matrix. This makes it useful for quantitative analysis. In this respect, it is similar to a decision tree, except that it captures the possibility of loops and the nodes can include any kind of action, not just decisions.

There is a simple, qualitative interpretation, as well. Each node in the network is an event: a piece of a story. The ties represent the sequence of events: the connection from one event to the next. Thus, one can 'read' the stories in the network by following along from node to node. Instead of just capturing one event, or one story, placing the events in a network provides a concise way to represent a large number of possible stories (or narratives).

Thus, a narrative network provides a way to represent the problem we face in assessing digital risk: what patterns of action are most likely, and what are their possible consequences? Given an event that has just occurred, it indicates the probability of what might happen next. If one can attach values to the paths, as well as probabilities, then the network is similar to a decision tree. It provides a way to compare the expected value of alternative paths. Therefore, it is a useful way to think about risk. Imagine, for example, that you have been invited for an evening out with your friends. To get there, you could drive or take the subway. Over the course of the evening, you might do some drinking. Knowing your friends, you might do quite a bit. Then, you will need to get back home. Will the subway still be running? Will one of your friends have a car? Even a simple night out can generate a large network of possibilities, and each path in the network can be interpreted as a possible story for the evening. If one wants to avoid stories that end with jail time, it is wise to think ahead.

We can use the narrative network representation to compare alternative perspectives on digital risk. For example, risk in the digital arena is sometimes understood by analogy with infectious disease: computers get viruses. Earlier in this chapter, I used this analogy to describe the 'viral' spread of social media and file-sharing services. This analogy makes a useful starting point because it captures some aspects of the digital arena fairly well. A simple narrative network for biological infection is shown in Figure 9.1. This network only includes the pathways, not the probabilities or values.

When a biological organism becomes infected with a disease, a number of different scenarios may unfold. First, the disease may or may not have symptoms. If it does have symptoms, and the disease is diagnosed, there may be an effective treatment and a quick path to recovery. If undiagnosed or untreated, the condition may improve on its own, it may linger indefinitely, or it may lead to death. To understand the risk to the individual, one needs to understand the probability and consequences of each scenario. With many kinds of diseases, there is also a significant possibility of transmission. To understand the risk of the disease to a population, one needs additional information about contagion and the resistance of different segments of the population. Naturally, the interaction patterns of the population members will influence the rate of contagion. From the point of infection (see top of Figure 9.1), to the ultimate outcomes (cure or death, at the bottom of Figure 9.1), the typical paths through the network are straightforward. Each path through the network tells the story of a typical disease progression.

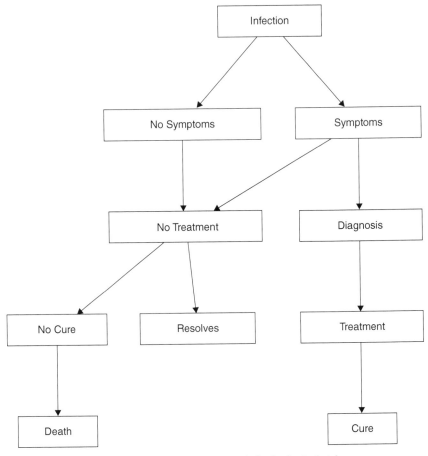

Figure 9.1. A narrative network for biological risk

With a computer virus (or other kinds of malware), the situation is similar in some respects. Digital viruses cause digital diseases and they can spread quickly over a network. The infection may be diagnosed and treated, leading to full recovery. If undiagnosed, however, it continues to pose a threat to the host, and may also pose a threat of transmission. Anti-malware services use this metaphor to help to track and report the seriousness of newly discovered threats.

However, in the digital arena, the number and variety of possible pathways is much larger. Figure 9.2 shows a narrative network based on the scenarios mentioned in this chapter. It extends Figure 9.1 by distinguishing between actions taken by 'you' (no shading), the end user, and actions taken by 'others' (shading). This distinction blurs in some cases (e.g. did you 'lose' your password, or did others 'steal' it?). The assignment of agency (or blame)

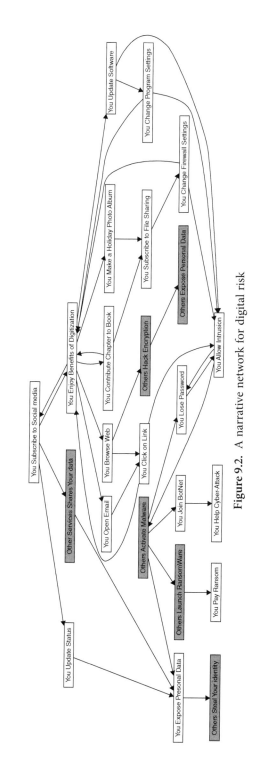

Figure 9.2. A narrative network for digital risk

may be an interesting issue, but it is less significant than the overall complexity of the network.

By comparing Figures 9.1 and 9.2, we can see that the medical analogy fails to capture some significant aspects of the phenomenon. First of all, in the digital arena, the threat is usually not sickness or death. The object-at-risk (or value-at-risk) is usually information, money, or something more abstract, such as privacy or reputation. Second, since a computer is an active device, malware can be programmed to perform all kinds of different functions. It can do more than just infect the host. For example, it can perform tasks like recording keystrokes (e.g. passwords) and sending them to a remote host. It can also transform your computer into a weapon. Infected computers form 'bot-nets' that can be used to provide a service for attacking others. Third, computers can be programmed to attack their owners through so-called 'ransom ware'. Ransomware is a kind of malware that takes control of your computer and your files and holds them hostage. If you pay the 'ransom', you supposedly get your computer and your files back. Getting infected with ransom-ware initiates a recognizable pattern of action, but it is not based on collaboration. In all these cases, your computer becomes an active participant in a recognizable pattern of interdependent action that is, at least to some extent, outside your control.

Another difference with the biological case is that other agents can be actively involved in targeting you or your organization. These are sometimes referred to as advanced persistent threats (APTs), to signal that they are continually adapting and escalating (Pew Research Center, 2014). National governments may be among the most advanced and persistent purveyors of cyber-threats and cyber-defence. As a result, this arena may be more aptly characterized as a strategic game (i.e. war), rather than biological transmission of a pathogen. While some argue that the level of threat is easily exaggerated because it makes a dramatic story, none would argue that these threats are non-existent (Pew Research Center, 2014).

In principle, assessments of probability and impact of relevant events (and subsequent outcomes) can be used to estimate risk by summing across the events along each possible pathway. In making this computation, the benefits of digitization would need to be balanced against the risks. Every pathway has benefits and risks. The risk of a negative outcome may be very low on any particular pathway, but we traverse these paths many times a day (opening email, clicking on links, sharing files, updating our status, and so forth). Further, by constantly sharing, updating, and subscribing, we expand the set of pathways exponentially (Hærem et al., 2015). We are making the game more complicated, increasing the likelihood of what Perrow (1984) would call normal accidents. Like a game of chess, it is difficult to see more than a few moves ahead. Unlike a game of chess, however, we are usually not concentrating on how each of our moves may create opportunities for our opponents (who, in the digital arena, are generally unknown and unseen).

The narrative network may provide a tool for improving on our natural tendency to follow the ruts in the road. If we mark the negative outcomes, the narrative network can be interpreted as a kind of risk map. Jordan and Jørgensen (Chapter 2, this volume) describe techniques used to estimate and manage risk in project management by mapping the severity and likelihood of particular risks. In this approach, each risk is treated somewhat separately, with its own coloured map. In contrast, a narrative network provides less information about any particular risk, but it shows them all together, along with other activities. By displaying the sequential connections between actions, it may provide a way to visualize and navigate the pathways that lead towards (or away from) particularly risky or undesirable outcomes. Used proactively, it could actually serve as a map.

DISCUSSION

Routinized patterns of action are a ubiquitous part of the social world. In his theory of structuration, Giddens (1984) placed routinization at the centre. As digitization continues to transform business and our personal lives, the routines perspective helps us to think in terms of action patterns (rather than just individual decisions). I would suggest two key insights.

First, routines foster an increasingly complex technological world. While it may seem counter-intuitive to say so, routines drive change. In some of the examples mentioned (e.g. collaborating via Dropbox or GoogleDocs), collaboration drives the adoption of the new technology. When a friend or colleague invites us to collaborate, we subscribe. The spread of social media operates along the same lines. The use of services like ResearchGate, LinkedIn, and Twitter depend on norms of reciprocity (you endorse me, I endorse you; you follow me, I follow you). It's monkey see, monkey do; we imitate and replicate patterns of action. We enrol others in the routines supported by the platform, which in turn builds subscribers for the platform. In doing so, we build interdependence between our actions. We can think of this as a process of infection, but that fails to capture the advantages we gain for those connections. If we think of the new connections as new potential pathways—new possibilities for interaction—then it is clearer that each pathway can have benefits and risks.

Second, at the same time, routines reduce our chances of adapting to that changing context. This is because routines are also a well-known source of inertia; they tend to be resistant to change (Cohen et al., 1996). The resistance to change is functional, as long the routine is well adapted to a stable context. Routines allow participants to get their work done without rethinking or re-evaluating the course of action (Cohen et al., 1996). When well adapted, routines are source of efficiency. To a great extent, routinized behaviour is inevitable; we tend to follow the ruts in the road, not necessarily by rational choice, but because it is the easiest way to roll.

Furthermore, routines are especially unlikely to adapt when the context is changing in ways that are difficult to see or predict. Learning requires feedback about consequences, and a focal 'learner' (or system, or subsystem) that is able to act on that feedback. These conditions do not necessarily hold for organizational routines. Rice & Cooper (2010) offer an extensive analysis of why dysfunctional routines persist, even in relatively stable situations. In rapidly changing situations, where information about consequences is obscure, it is hard to see how functional adaptation is possible. In a world where our routine activities are carried out in conjunction with an array of digital actors, each click, each connection, each subscription, each authorization, and each upgrade can potentially change the context of subsequent actions. Our actions are networked, but the connections are difficult to see.

A simple-minded alarmist, like Chicken Little, would certainly conclude that the sky is falling. Perhaps, but I think a more realistic description is that it is *hard to tell* if the sky is falling (see Perrow, 1984). It may be falling in some places (or not), but our vision is not good enough to tell *which* places. The same factors that make risks difficult to detect also make them difficult to *control*. To address this concern, we need to devise better ways to describe, visualize, and think about risk in a context that is constantly changing as a result of our own (in)actions and the (in)actions of others.

The vocabulary of organizational routines, which focuses on patterns of action as the unit of analysis, provides one way to describe the effects of digitization on our work and personal lives. Our actions are more connected and interdependent than ever. Our action patterns are collective, but not necessarily collaborative. Because the technical details are constantly changing and highly consequential, it is difficult to write anything of lasting value on this topic. But that is exactly the point: it is the intersection between our very human routines and our very digitized world that makes a challenging arena for riskwork. By helping us to see connections between actions, narrative networks may offer a better and more dynamic visualization of risk than traditional risk maps.

REFERENCES

Ashforth, B. & Fried Y. (1988). The Mindlessness of Organizational Behaviors. *Human Relations*, 41(4), 305–29.

Autor, B. & Dorn, D. (2013). The Growth of Low-skill Service Jobs and the Polarization of the US Labor Market. *American Economic Review*, 103(5), 1553–97.

Cohen, M. (2007). Reading Dewey: Reflections on the Study of Routine. *Organization Studies*, 28(5), 773–86.

Cohen, M., Burkhart, R., Dosi, G., Egidi, M., Marengo, L., Warglien, M., & Winter, S. (1996). Routines and Other Recurrent Action Patterns of Organizations: Contemporary Research Issues. *Industrial and Corporate Change*, 5, 653–98.

Cyert, R. & March, J. (1963). *A Behavioural Theory of the Firm.* Englewood Cliffs, NJ: Prentice-Hall.

D'Adderio, L. (2008). The Performativity of Routines: Theorising the Influence of Artefacts and Distributed Agencies on Routines Dynamics. *Research Policy*, 37(5), 769–89.

Djenouri, D., Khelladi, L., & Badache, N. (2005). A Survey of Security Issues in Mobile ad hoc Networks. *IEEE Communications Surveys*, 7(4), 2–28.

Dobson, J. E. (2004). The GIS Revolution in Science and Society. In S. Brunn, S. Cutter, & J. Harrington Jr (Eds), *Geography and Technology* (pp. 573–87). Berlin: Springer.

Feldman, M. S. & Pentland, B. T. (2003). Reconceptualizing Organizational Routines as a Source of Flexibility and Change. *Administrative Science Quarterly*, 48(1), 94–118.

Finkel, J. & Heavey, S. (2014). Target Says It Declined to Act on Early Alert of Cyber Breach. <http://www.reuters.com/article/2014/03/13/us-target-breach-idUSBREA2 C14F20140313> (accessed 11 April 2014).

Fung, B. (2014). The Heartbleed Situation Just Got a Lot Worse. It Also Affects Routers. <http://www.washingtonpost.com/blogs/the-switch/wp/2014/04/10/bad-news-heartbleed-now-also-affects-routers-and-networking-equipment> (accessed 11 April 2014).

Giddens, A. (1984). *The Constitution of Society: Outline of the Theory of Structuration.* Berkeley, CA: University of California Press.

Gigerenzer G. (2000). *Adaptive Thinking: Rationality in the Real World.* Oxford: Oxford University Press.

Hærem, T., Pentland, B. T., & Miller, K. D. (2015). Task Complexity: Extending a Core Concept. *Academy of Management Review*, 40(3), 446–60.

Knorr-Cetina, D. (1981). Introduction: the Micro-Sociological Challenge of Macro-Sociology: Towards a Reconstruction of Social Theory and Methodology. In Knorr-Cetina, K. and Cicourel, A. (Eds), *Advances in Social Theory and Methodology: Toward an Integration of Micro- and Macro-sociologies*, (pp. 1–47). New York: Routledge & Kegan Paul.

Kuhn, J. & Sutton, S. (2010). Continuous Auditing in ERP System Environments: the Current State and Future Directions. *Journal of Information Systems*, 24(1), 91–112.

Latour, B. (2005). *Reassembling the Social: An Introduction to Actor-Network-Theory.* Oxford: Clarendon Press.

Leonardi, P. M. (2011). When Flexible Routines meet Flexible Technologies: Affordance, Constraint, and the Imbrication of Human and Material Agencies. *MIS Quarterly*, 35(1), 147–67.

Pentland, B. T. & Feldman, M. S. (2007). Narrative Networks: Patterns of Technology and Organization. *Organization Science*, 18(5), 781–95.

Pentland, B. T. & Hærem, T. (2015). Organizational Routines as Patterns of Action: Implications for Organizational Behavior. *Annual Review of Organizational Psychology and Organizational Behavior*, 2, 465–87.

Perrow, C. (1984). *Normal Accidents: Living with High Risk Technologies*. New York: Basic Books.

Pew Research Center (2014). Cyber Attacks Likely to Increase. 29 October. <http://www.pewInternet.org/2014/10/29/cyber-attacks-likely-to-increase> (accessed 11 April 2014).

Rettig, C. (2007). The Trouble with Enterprise Software. *MIT Sloan Management Review*, 49, 21–7.

Reynaud B. (2005). The Void at the Heart of Rules: Routines in the Context of Rule-Following: The Case of the Paris Metro Workshop. *Industrial and Corporate Change*, 14, 847–71.

Rice, R. E. & Cooper, S. D. (2010). *Organizations and Unusual Routines: A Systems Analysis of Dysfunctional Feedback Processes*. Cambridge: Cambridge University Press.

Risen, T. (2014). FTC Investigates Target Data Card Breach. <http://www.usnews.com/news/articles/2014/03/26/ftc-investigates-target-data-breach> (accessed 11 April 2014).

Rochet, J. C. & Tirole, J. (2003). Platform Competition in Two-sided Markets. *Journal of the European Economic Association*, 1(4), 990–1029.

Schulz, M. (2008). Staying on Track: A Voyage to the Internal Mechanisms of Routine Reproduction. In M. Becker (Ed.), *Handbook of Organizational Routines* (pp. 228–57). Cheltenham, UK: Edward Elgar.

Simon, H. A. (1979). Rational Decision Making in Business Organizations. *American Economic Review*, 69(4), 493–513.

Warren, C. (2014). Why Heartbleed Is the Ultimate Web Nightmare. <http://mashable.com/2014/04/09/heartbleed-nightmare> (accessed 11 April 2014).

Weick, K. E. (1993). The Collapse of Sensemaking in Organizations: The Mann Gulch Disaster. *Administrative Science Quarterly*, 38(4), 628–52.

Williams, S. P., Hardy, C. A., & Holgate, J. A. (2013). Information Security Governance Practices in Critical Infrastructure Organizations: A Socio-Technical and Institutional Logic Perspective. *Electronic Markets*, 23(4), 341–54.

10

Doing Institutional Riskwork in a Mental Health Hospital

Véronique Labelle and Linda Rouleau

As one of the key risks faced by healthcare systems, patient safety has been the focus of a growing number of studies (Macrae, 2008). The way that this particular type of risk has been managed in healthcare organizations owes a lot to publications, such as *To Err Is Human* (Kohn et al., 1999), which increased awareness of medical errors and which has led to several forms of patient safety legislation in Western countries. This legislation resulted in the development of structures, mechanisms, and particular risk management roles within, and at the interface of, healthcare organizations (Wiig and Lindøe, 2009). Furthermore, such regulations increased the active participation of diverse actors at the organizational level, such as leaders (Clarke et al., 2007), board members, healthcare professionals, operational personnel, technical specialists, and line managers (Macrae, 2008), patient safety officers (Denham, 2007), and also patients (Davis et al., 2007; Hovey et al., 2010; Quirk et al., 2005). In other words, it can be said that regulatory changes at the macro level intend to make every member of the healthcare organization a risk manager and a key player in risk management (Smiechewicz, 2009). However, although much has been said about knowledge management and accident reporting by healthcare professionals (Barach & Small, 2000; Currie et al., 2008, 2009; Waring & Currie, 2009), and the participative potential of such reporting systems (Macrae, 2008), we still know very little about the practices whereby multiple actors manage safety risks in their day-to-day work in healthcare organizations.

In order to fill this gap, we propose to follow the 'turn to work' in organizational and management theory (Phillips & Lawrence, 2012), to study how the work of managing risks is accomplished in the organizational daily life of a mental health hospital. This turn to work refers to 'widespread scholarly engagement with new forms of work that involve individuals and organizations purposefully and strategically expending effort to affect their social-symbolic context' (Phillips & Lawrence, 2012: 223). Phillips and Lawrence's review (2012: 224) of various forms of work currently being studied in the literature shows that these new research streams all describe actors as they are engaged in a purposeful effort to change, model, and transform some aspect of their context. This effortful work does not imply unconstrained agency, but is rather embedded in the social–symbolic structures it aims to affect.

This turn to work can be connected to the notion of 'risk work' as conceptualized by Horlick-Jones (2005: 293) and described by him as 'situationally-specific risk-related practices'. Riskwork takes place in encounters with risk (Hutter, 2005; Hutter & Power, 2005) at different levels and may involve a variety of forms of effort (Labelle & Rouleau, 2016). This chapter examines the day-to-day risk-related practices of multiple actors in a psychiatric setting in order to better understand how riskwork both contributes to, and seeks to resolve tensions between, safety and patient autonomy philosophies of care. In other words, the analysis will provide insights into the challenge of keeping everyone safe while enabling patients to make their own decisions and to be considered as teammates in the risk management process.

The chapter is organized as follows: first, we present the case study and the methodology used for gathering and analysing the data. Then, we describe the four forms of riskwork that have been identified in this research, namely techno-scientific, regulative–normative, political, and interpretative. Third, we discuss how the dynamic relationships between these different forms of riskwork reveal the tensions between safety and patient autonomy philosophies and enable them to be collectively addressed.

RISK MANAGEMENT IN A QUEBEC HEALTHCARE SETTING

The research took place in a psychiatric setting offering specialized (evaluation and treatment, hospitalization, and intensive follow-up) and ultra-specialized (services offered to people presenting complex health issues which require specific expertise) mental health services. The specificity of the case can largely be attributed to the unique place that the organization holds in Canada's history and Quebec's collective imagination. As one of the largest mental health institutions in the country, it has witnessed 140 years of mental healthcare evolution. The organization has around 400 beds inside the hospital, 1,500 places in intermediary and residential resources, and a total of 2,000 employees. Overall, it offers specialized care for 10,000 people every year.

In risk management matters, the organization is not a neophyte. Since 1992, when it became a participant in the Accreditation Canada programme, the organization has had an internal risk management policy. Nowadays, the organization's risk management structure is framed by the province's Bill 113, which, among other requirements, mandates the reporting and disclosure of incidents and accidents and the creation of a risk management committee in each healthcare organization. The bill also requires healthcare organizations to participate in the Accreditation Canada programme. Quality and safety issues are also addressed in various committees, often multidisciplinary, that allow dialogue between clinical and non-clinical advisers, clinical and non-clinical managers, clinical professionals, as well as patients and their advocates. Indeed, over the last few years, patients have been increasingly involved in their care plan, but also in the organization's projects and activities. With innovative initiatives such as the patient–partnership programme, which recognizes patients as partners in care and research, and a patient–citizenship orientation, which promotes patient autonomy, the organization is heading towards a more inclusive and open form of mental healthcare. However, this direction of change causes tension in the way risks are managed because efforts to increase patients' autonomy often mean taking more risks for both patients and staff.

Even though the risk management activities are part of a broader integrated quality programme and are decentralized throughout the organization's quality committees, there is nevertheless a core committee, called the risk management committee, which monitors and assesses risk management efforts and coordinates risk management activities across the organization. This core team reports directly to the board and the director general. Its composition has to respect the requirements to represent employees, patients, and contractual parties. Its mandate is to develop and promote ways to: identify and analyse incident and accident risks, such as falls, medication-related events, aggression, and runaways; ensure patient safety; offer support to accident victims and their families; put in place a surveillance system and a local registry of incidents and accidents; raise awareness about risk management; and, finally, identify measures to prevent the recurrence of incidents and accidents, as well as further control measures if needed.

The unique history of the organization and the development of its risk management vision and practices, tightly coupled with its efforts towards patient autonomy, justify the choice of this unique case (Yin, 2009). Psychiatric settings provide unique challenges for engaging in risk management studies at the organizational level, since the communal nature of psychiatric wards also involves the 'need to protect vulnerable patients from other patients; patients, property, and staff from unwanted outsiders; patients from themselves; and, at times, the public from patients' (Bowers et al., 2002: 428). Such a context highlights the variety of actors that take an active part in day-to-day risk management efforts, including patients who are far from being passive actors in the area of risk management on psychiatric wards (Quirk et al., 2005; Ryan, 2000).

METHODS

Data Collection

Data were collected by the first author for a period of seventeen months, from January 2012 to May 2013. The key informant, the assistant to the director general, provided the author with an office, which she shared with the patient–partnership research team. She had the chance to visit different care units, including seclusion rooms. In addition, she was given a tour of recent changes in the unit settings, designed to improve safety. Being 'inside the walls' to observe risk management practices gave her the opportunity to have numerous formal and informal conversations with staff and patients regarding the organization's activities. These conversations were valuable in acquiring a deeper and more comprehensive view of their involvement in the everyday life of the organization, and also for obtaining both contrasting and compatible views on safety issues and initiatives. Two sources of data collection were privileged: observations and interviews.

Observations

The fieldwork involved the observation of committees and work groups since risk management was decentralized and took many forms across the organization. First, committees where risk management and safety issues were a central preoccupation were selected: the risk management work group, the risk management committee and the vigilance and quality committee. In order to make sense of risk management in relation to the general orientations and activities across the organization, CEO and board of director meetings were also observed. Second, in order to include the collaborative nature of risk management in our observations, three committees working on specific types of risks were targeted, namely the seclusion and restraint protocol committee, the fall prevention committee, and the medication error prevention committee. Access to the emergency planning committee was also permitted. Third, the users' committee and the patient–partnership committee were observed in order to understand the user's role and the patient autonomy orientation.

Overall, more than sixty meetings were observed. During these observations, special attention was paid to interactions between actors when risks were identified (in a proactive or reactive manner), accidents reported and solutions debated. Rather than focusing solely on patient safety as a specific category of risk, we also paid attention to non-patient aspects of healthcare safety such as occupational safety, since worker and patient safety should be looked at with equal interest as key characteristics of organizational safety

(Goodman, 2002). Furthermore, in mental health settings, aggression risks are quite common and they are also increasing in hospitals in general (Bowers et al., 2002). These particular risks were very frequently part of discussions about patient safety. Finally, observing these committees was crucial to our study since they revealed the rich nature of discursive work about risks in the form of 'producing, distributing, and consuming texts' (Maguire & Hardy, 2013: 232) about what is considered as a risk in the organization.

Interviews

Forty interviews were conducted with members of the committees observed. Committee members were chosen using a combination of two sampling strategies. First, members were chosen based on 'methodological groupism' which targets social groups and their conventions as units of analysis (Kaghan & Lounsbury, 2011: 75). Four categories of participants were formed and represent the diversity of the committee members: clinical and non-clinical advisers (6A), clinical and non-clinical managers (22 M), five clinical professionals (5 CP), patients and their advocates (7 P). Second, committee members who participate in or seem to be aware of risk management discourses and guidelines were privileged. Here, the sampling strategy used is 'milieu sampling' in the sense that we targeted the work environment[1] (Pires, 1997: 32) of risk management.

Data Analysis

The data collected were analysed recursively in three distinct phases according to the principles proposed by grounded data analysis (Strauss & Corbin, 1998). The first phase involved hybrid coding. In this phase, we worked with *initial coding* to generate tentative and provisional themes (Saldaña, 2009: 81). We also used *process coding*, because it generates themes indicating action (Saldaña, 2009: 77). More specifically, each description of events related to everyday risk management was coded in order to identify actions. This allowed us to get a better sense of what is done when actors deal with risk in their everyday work. We also programmed our coding to give us the opportunity to compare the results between types of actors. Although we found a lot of variations in the everyday work of our informants, we were still able to reach a level of saturation when we noticed that every coding could fit in one of the first order constructs (Strauss & Corbin, 1998). The second phase consisted of generating meaningful categories of riskwork. This phase also allowed us to identify patterns between the riskwork accomplished by different

[1] Free translation of 'univers de travail'.

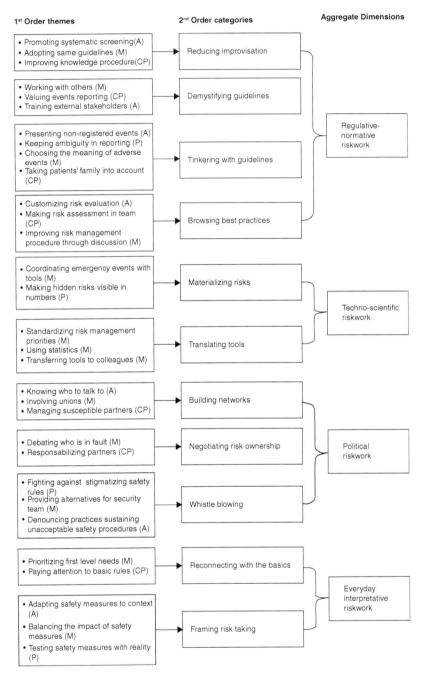

Figure 10.1. Data structure

types of actors. The third phase consisted of linking and integrating these categories of riskwork to show the relationships between them by comparing these categories with examples of riskwork described in the literature. We applied the same analytic strategy to the two data sources and we applied constant comparison between what was observed and the ongoing analysis. Figure 10.1 presents our data structure.

Results

The data analysis reveals that clinical and non-clinical advisers, clinical and non-clinical managers, clinical professionals, and patients and their advocates engage in four forms of riskwork, namely: regulative–normative, techno-scientific, political, and interpretative. Each of these forms of riskwork groups a set of purposive efforts by a diversity of actors. We will now describe these forms of riskwork and provide representative quotes from the variety of actors who deal with risk in their activities. This description will help us to illustrate how each of these forms of riskwork both activate and resolve the tensions between safety and patient autonomy philosophies.

REGULATIVE–NORMATIVE RISKWORK

Regulative–normative riskwork refers to the regulation-based efforts of actors to affect the way safety risks are managed. When faced with safety risks, actors have to consider a multitude of laws, norms, rules, and guidelines. One purposive effort accomplished in this form of riskwork consists in *reducing improvisation*. As the following observation shows, improvisation is equated with a lack of skill and the answer to this problem is the enforcement of official protocols.

> CLINICAL ADVISER: The problem here is falls, it seems we often just go with our feelings. People do not always apply the protocols, they don't always evaluate well. We are not being systematic enough and we absolutely must train people. There has to be systematic screening.
>
> MANAGER 2: Yes and we should really involve research in this.

Reducing improvisation consequently means that managing risks is not based solely on personal judgement, but does not completely discard it:

> NON-CLINICAL MANAGER: Like everywhere else, you used to make a judgement that was less framed and structured, that was good for the most part, but it was a personal judgement on the risks, while now, everyone has the same guidelines. (interview)

The specific combination of normative elements that actors have to consider is 'situationally-specific' (Horlick-Jones, 2005), in the sense that a clear identification of risk jurisdiction is hard to make, even more so in the heat of an emergency situation, so regulative–normative riskwork requires patience and a long-term vision. Indeed, a second purposive effort is *demystifying guidelines*. A very large number of conversations related to the different ways in which the quantity of accident reports, which are at the core of the patient safety regulation regime, could be increased:

> CLINICAL MANAGER: The more time goes by, the more it's accepted in the hospital, the more it's clearly understood; sure there is still some minor resistance at times, but we know where it is and it has always been in the same place. By being there, being present, by having worked with managers…There has been training for reporting, the training sessions are going well and are being given more and more frequently. (interview)

The riskwork of demystifying guidelines is prompted by active or passive resistance to incident reporting. Reporting is controversial because it increases scrutiny and fear of blame (Storey & Buchanan, 2008). In contrast to the airline industry where the technology registers problems even if pilots do not report them (see Chapter 7, this volume), hospitals have to work on trust to get people to declare and generate an accurate picture of incidents and accidents. Such work is primarily (but not exclusively) done by non-clinical advisers (or risk managers), who are chiefly responsible for promoting these guidelines and who gradually establish trust, as a 'keystone of patient safety' (Firth-Cozens, 2004) by reminding people of the non-punitive and confidential nature of incident and accident reports. Far from trying to apply norms in a mechanical way, the actors we observed were often *tinkering with guidelines*. Surprisingly, this tinkering was done by trying to find ways to go beyond normative requirements instead of resisting them:

> NON-CLINICAL ADVISER: In terms of risk management, we will look at events that are not registered (in the provincial registry of adverse events). We present them anyway.
> PATIENT ADVOCATE: So there is a thin line between what is considered or not?
> NON-CLINICAL MANAGER: No, no, it is very clear, but as an organization, we decided that we should look into these adverse events.
> PROFESSIONAL: It is also very important for the patients' families. (observation)

Although regulators drive local action on risks, primarily by making those risks visible to people who are obliged to act on them (Reason, 1997 in Macrae, 2008: 64), our results showed that even the statistical representation of data was tinkered with.

> We changed the national registry guidelines a little bit. In order to give an accurate view of our reality, we present data differently in terms of categories.

For instance, they identify falls, medication, treatment, diagnostic tests, diet, equipment, buildings, abuse, aggression, harassment, transfusion, other and undetermined. That's what we were presenting, but there were categories that were hidden in others, like runaways and escapes. These are our top four, but they didn't stand out, so we decided to present it differently to meet our own needs. (non-clinical adviser, interview)

Another example of *tinkering with guidelines* has to do with the specificities of a mental health setting. In the case of infection control and prevention, there are strict procedures to follow in case of an influenza outbreak.

> But what do you do when the patient doesn't want to stay in his room? There is an influenza outbreak, but he is starting to become agitated…we won't put him in the isolation room. Maybe we will let him out for thirty or forty minutes with a mask. We have to deal with that. We don't want to put him in isolation and find out that we impacted his treatment negatively. We manage risks, but we have to be very imaginative…we didn't have procedures for mental health settings, so we built them up along the way. (interview with clinical adviser)

The procedure that is referred to in this quote was so innovative that the team was invited by their professional association to share their challenging experience and how they created a new way to manage infection risks.

Finally, regulative–normative riskwork is also accomplished by *browsing best practices* to find out how others found solutions to the same patient safety issues:

CLINICAL ADVISER: That organization does a personalized risk evaluation for every patient with their team. For instance, they decide that letting the patient keep his clothes on is an acceptable risk. [in restraint situations]

PROFESSIONAL: I find it very interesting that the team risk assessment led them to avoid restraint. (observation).

While best practices on falls risk assessment were discussed, we observed that clinical and non-clinical advisers did not see eye to eye at first in terms of risk assessment best practices for the assessment of fall risks. Although they agreed on the importance of 'writing things down', the non-clinical adviser was in favour of using elaborate assessment procedures and forms, while clinical advisers raised concerns about deskilling if such methods were used. In other words, intuition had to be preserved, but clear procedures were needed to keep track of the treatment and to avoid, for instance, using restraint chairs excessively.

TECHNO-SCIENTIFIC RISKWORK

As the result of modernization programmes in healthcare, risk regulations take for granted the transferability of tools and techniques from other sectors such as aviation for reporting and learning systems (Barach & Small, 2000; Helmreich & Davies, 1997; Macrae, 2008). *Techno-scientific riskwork* refers to this growing interest in technological and scientific-based ways to identify, assess, and deal with safety risks. During the fieldwork for this study, we observed frequent efforts towards *materializing risks*, in the form of graphs, tables, reports, and other visual media. As a clinical manager says: 'We should see with statistics if there is a causal relation between the growing number of falls and the decline in the use of restraints' (observation). This quote shows that graphs and statistics can be considered as bureaucratic 'roadmaps' that help to prioritize actions and projects (see Chapter 2, this volume). In order to do something about risks, actors have to represent them in a concrete way. We saw the use of such visual media multiplying almost exponentially during the fieldwork. The organization even hired a technician dedicated to producing them. Throughout the meetings, through its multiple materialized forms, risk became more than mere sensemaking, it became a boundary object (Star & Griesemer, 1989) that reconciled the efforts of actors from different backgrounds and occupational positions.

Furthermore, efforts towards *translating tools* were observed. Since tools designed for other industries are imported into the healthcare sector actors have to find ways to adapt them to the complexity of healthcare settings that are making efforts to achieve a more integrated and organization-wide approach to quality and risk management (Callaly et al., 2005). The following discussion on the evaluation of an event management tool illustrates such translation:

CLINICAL MANAGER: Could it be also used for clinical [purposes]? because we could use it to coordinate our activities?

NON-CLINICAL MANAGER [*about a coordinating tool for emergency events*]: At organization X, they already have it and it is possible to separate technical and clinical guard. It uses geomatics. There is a map...for instance, if a patient runs away, you could mobilize a large number of people at the same time...it would be far more efficient than a walkie-talkie. (observation)

Another tool was created collaboratively with other organizations. We witnessed the presentation of the tool to the local risk managers' work table and participants agreed that the tool was impressive. An adviser suggested it would be a good idea to use it for clinical purposes:

Back then, the prioritization of projects and risk management was done solely based on people's experience. They [three other organizations] want to standardize a prioritization process using risk management for the entire region. We are a part of that and we started to use it here. We were ripe for a more formal process and there is a strong tendency toward risk management. (interview with non-clinical manager.)

This tool was originally developed for the management of risks related to the hospital's buildings. However, it was customized to include patients' needs and patient safety guidelines, as another manager involved in the project explained:

> I established a risk criteria: what's the effect on the patient. For instance, I rated 1 for a loss of treatment or for the loss of life or a prolongation of treatment. A rating of 2 was the prolongation of recovery or a few injuries and so on...I also calibrated the criteria's ability to meet patient safety guidelines, which were not well adjusted at first. (interview with non-clinical manager)

These managers were able to provide the organization with a customized risk management tool that could be used for other purposes; they innovated by integrating impacts of different risks on patients; and they shared that innovation with the other organizations involved in the project.

Such efforts were made towards finding a more scientific and technological way of dealing with safety risks for the entire organization. Translating tools may seem to be similar to materializing risks in the sense that they both refer to what Power (2004: 53–4) calls 'the ambition to measure everything' with 'rational calculation and modelling'. While materializing risks concerns the retrospective aspect of risk management, in the form of reporting systems (Currie et al., 2008), translating tools refers to the prospective approach in which the occurrence of risk is predicted (Battles et al., 2006).

Although these tools are evaluated by various actors, non-clinical managers and advisers were most closely associated with techno-scientific riskwork, often followed by clinical managers, who tried to find ways to adapt such technologies and scientific methods to clinical activities. In sum, we can say that techno-scientific riskwork is based on more or less complex tools shared and shaped by different actors across the organization to fit specific risk management needs.

POLITICAL RISKWORK

The multiplicity of rules and normative guidelines, and pressure for enforcement, lead to calls for greater transparency. Thus, regulative–normative riskwork stimulates *political riskwork*. Such work refers to interest-based motivations (Horlick-Jones, 2005) and 'political behaviors' (Currie et al., 2008: 370) between different actors around safety risks. The literature on patient safety highlights the political aspects of risk management by focusing on knowledge management and transparency, which are both perceived as a threat to the medical professional's autonomy. Although our informants indicated that there was some resistance to knowledge sharing and transparency, and not exclusively on the part of doctors, our results show the use of purposive efforts in *building networks* in order to overcome at least part of the issue. Indeed, these efforts are made primarily by clinical and non-clinical advisers, since their interventions cut across many teams, units, and departments. To improve the management of patient safety risks, they need to know what is happening, but they are well aware that accident and incident reports don't tell the whole story, as actors also 'interact with indigenous risk practices and mentalities' (Fischer & Ferlie, 2013: 31). They have to elaborate strategies and make allies to overcome such resistance to transparency. Since the local complaints commissioner has a legal power that advisers don't have, she was often mentioned as a valuable source of information that would be very difficult to access otherwise:

> The complaints commissioner helps me a lot to know what is happening, because sometimes, people don't let me in as easily as they do her. It depends on what you're dealing with...Sometimes, things happen and we learn about it long after...you have to know who to talk to, to get the information. (interview with clinical adviser)

Another example involves one of the most important safety issues in mental health settings, which is the risk of aggression. Indeed, aggression could cause harm to staff as well as other patients or the patient himself. In this particular case, the lines between patient safety and occupational safety were often blurred. In order to make staff adopt a new training programme aimed at managing aggressive behaviour, the union had to be convinced, since there was resistance to abandoning the programme that was already in place:

> Not everyone was happy with it. Some people didn't believe in it as much. From the start, it was important to involve our unions, [to ask] do you agree to that? We have places where we give training and we have some minor difficulties, but we know that we'll bring up these difficulties, to find solutions with our union partners. (interview with non-clinical adviser)

Since the lines were often blurred between occupational safety and patient safety, actors were forced towards *negotiating risk ownership*. Reporting of events made such political riskwork quite visible. Indeed, a single event often involved more than one department and reporting responsibilities. In addition, post event investigations were either debated or duplicated between emergency measures and risk management, or between risk management and occupational health and safety.

A further example involved two technical departments and their relation to patient safety risks. As a non-clinical manager regarding windows inspection said:

> After we wash the windows, and there are a lot of them, there is a protocol to follow to ensure that security locks are put back in place afterwards. There was a bit of confrontation between technical services and hygiene and sanitation teams. Nobody wanted to be blamed for neglecting a defect during inspection. Everyone

started to blame each other until we sorted things out and found common ground. (interview with non-clinical manager)

Even the patients were called upon to *own* their risks as the following observation shows:

> There is a debate on the title of the pamphlet, which is making people aware of their role in safety throughout the organization. One professional says: we have to emphasize the responsibility of the patients. They don't just have rights, they have responsibilities too. Sometimes, there are some who won't take responsibility. They act in unacceptable ways and they blame it on the illness. We really must say that they also have a responsibility in safety. (observation)

Negotiating risk ownership was always a core preoccupation when patient safety risks were addressed, because, as one informant said during a debate on medication error prevention measures: 'but if we put too many people in charge, there is no one in charge anymore and we lose the possibility to ask for accountability'.

Finally, *whistle-blowing* became a kind of riskwork for both patients and professionals in relation to each other. Above all other issues, aggression by patients was the most controversial and politically charged of all safety risks addressed during our research. For that reason, one adviser told us: 'In this place, restraint measures are the bonds of war.' Indeed, requirements to decrease the use of restraints made many people uncomfortable and others truly alarmed by the fact that alternatives were safer for the patient, but more dangerous for the staff. While staff blew the whistle about the absence of panic buttons or understaffing of units, which put professionals at risk, patients and patients' advocates were tired of hearing that patients were dangerous, violent, or 'lunatics'. An example of whistle-blowing by a patient in relation to measures taken to reduce safety risks is illustrated in the following observation:

> A patient [showing a picture on a PowerPoint slide]: 'I went to the gym [inside the hospital] and look what I saw! I was so mad! This is clearly stigmatizing, like I'm going to throw a piece of equipment at someone or something!' The sign said that no patient would be admitted in the gym without authorization and without being accompanied by a responsible person. After she complained, the sign was immediately removed.

Such examples show that political riskwork is not performed solely by doctors or powerful actors. There is a strong collective aspect to the management of safety risks and a variety of actors are trying to serve their own interests or the interests of those they represent. Instead of binary power struggles between doctors and nurses (McDonald et al., 2005) or between managers and doctors (Currie et al., 2008), results show complex relationships revolving around the management of safety risks.

EVERYDAY INTERPRETATIVE RISKWORK

Because there are always tensions between groups, actors engage in what we call *interpretative riskwork*—i.e. efforts based on the lived experience of actors to affect the way safety risks are managed. First, we observed that actors accomplish interpretative riskwork efforts by *reconnecting with the basics*. With the development of knowledge management systems and the increasing number of committees required by patient safety regulations, multiple actors have to debate and discuss issues that they never experienced first-hand or rarely encounter in the case of top management. Consequently, actors, including patients, put effort into sharing everyday experiences of safety risk issues, but also into sharing how they experience the solutions put in place:

> You know, the patient is thirsty...what are we doing to make sure he can go to the bathroom? There are a lot of questions, it is really interesting. For example, patients told us that when they are restrained, they lose track of time and become agitated, so they asked if it was possible to put a clock in the isolation room. While we get lost in big theories and think about complicated solutions, they really bring us back to basics. (interview with non-clinical manager)

Instead of merely stimulating knowledge about safety risks, *reconnecting with the basics* allows different participants to share how they experience safety risks and confront them.

Interpretative riskwork is also accomplished by *framing risk taking*. A recurring theme stemming from the data analysis was the importance of 'balancing rights and risks' (Robinson et al., 2007). During our fieldwork, we witnessed an intensification of discussions about the need to establish a new organizational culture that ceased to see patients as dangerous to themselves or others. One major initiative that raised safety concerns for both patients and staff was the unlocking of bathrooms in the common areas of the organization. During the process, top management multiplied opportunities to attach a positive connotation to this initiative. It became a strong symbol of commitment from the organization to change the way safety risks were managed. However, these efforts were not limited to rhetoric or cognitive framing. It was also about proposing a collective experience. The following discussion during a committee meeting shows that the experience with bathrooms was used to evaluate other possibilities to remove devices that were once considered important safety measures.

ADVISER: I did an investigation of the stairwells to see how the wooden boards are positioned. I discovered that they were put there after a suicide. We are now wondering if we can remove them safely.

MANAGER: It is obvious that we have to ensure safety, but how far can we go?

PROFESSIONAL: We are not in the same context now. In the case of the bathrooms, it was a major situation, but this is not necessary.
ADVISER 2: When we unlocked the bathrooms, it went well.
PATIENT: And in the context of full citizenship, it is important not to stigmatize.

Another example is shown in the following interview. After someone committed suicide by throwing himself out of the window in another organization, a non-clinical manager mentioned a discussion during a meeting of the local risk managers' work table on whether or not all windows should be locked. Participants agreed that they were not willing to lock everything to reduce safety risks to a minimum. One participant said around this discussion:

> Being in this hospital doesn't mean I'm suicidal and going to throw myself out the window. If it is not in the person's diagnosis, why would I lock all the windows with screws everywhere? It's easy to say, we lock everything…you also have to consider comfort. If I lock every window, it is going to be so hot that people will suffocate, because we don't have air conditioning. We are not in prison here…It would not make any sense to unlock access to units, but at the same time lock all the windows. (interview with non-clinical manager)

As we can see, interpretative riskwork is performed by a variety of actors and aims to shape perceptions, interpretations and values, which are all part of a broader collection of symbols built around patient safety risks. These elements are at the core of what the literature on patient safety identifies as a patient safety culture (Bagian, 2005), but a closer look at the everyday lived experience of actors gives us the opportunity to look at risk issues with fresh eyes and avoid the usual categorization of what is dangerous or what is best for the patients and staff. The specificity of psychiatric settings calls for us to pay attention to 'balancing the safety and security of patients, staff and the public, while respecting the rights and choices of individual patients' (Bowers et al., 2002, in Quirk, Lelliott, & Seale 2005, 86), which requires going beyond establishing a safety culture. In other words, our results show that risk management is no longer about keeping patients and staff safe at all costs, but more about finding ways to humanize it. Our observations showed that interpretative riskwork was able to provide ways to do that.

DISCUSSION AND CONCLUSION

In this chapter, we proposed to follow the 'turn to work' (Phillips & Lawrence, 2012), to investigate how riskwork is accomplished by multiple actors. By exploring efforts related to safety risks in a psychiatric setting, we found that advisers, managers, professionals, and patients and their advocates engage in four forms of riskwork, namely: regulative–normative, techno-scientific, political, and interpretative. Besides this general finding, five others that emerged from the analysis need to be mentioned. First, it is worth noting that even though each form of riskwork is mainly accomplished by one specific group of actors, all actors participate in every form of riskwork. For example, patients are not only involved in interpretative riskwork as might at first be assumed, they are also engaged in other forms of riskwork. By being present on different committees, they are increasingly participating in regulative–normative and techno-scientific riskwork. Like other actors present, they are socialized into using technical risk language and statistical representations of safety risks. The same can be said about non-clinical managers. While we would think that they would be more invested in techno-scientific riskwork, they also perform political and interpretative riskwork.

    Second, our findings showed that these forms of riskwork are interrelated and constitute different layers of the riskwork accomplished simultaneously in organizational day-to-day risk management, even though they appear to be essentially different. For instance, regulative–normative riskwork is closely linked to techno-scientific riskwork, since safety regulations and guidelines also provide toolkits, inspired by other industries, for organizations to manage safety risks. Once actors become familiar with common tools, they find ways to further their use by a variety of departments and actors. Since regulative–normative and techno-scientific riskwork increase scrutiny and transparency, they become the grounds from which political riskwork can be performed. Interests and resistance related to safety risks are made apparent, which in turn become the basis for interpretative riskwork, because actors have to find common ground from which to manage safety risks despite these tensions.

    Third, our analysis revealed that the riskwork we identified as interpretative seems to be the most neglected one in the literature to date. In patient safety literature, participation in reporting systems seems to be one of the main roads to patient safety. Our data showed on the one hand that the knowledge, transparency, and circulation of safety information put forward by such systems can also be achieved by other means, such as forums where actors can share stories and opinions about how the management of safety risks impacts their everyday life in the organization. On the other hand, our data showed that efforts towards safety are not incompatible with new ways of managing safety risk. As the results demonstrated, interpretative riskwork goes beyond mere political interests to propose a mosaic of what form and level of risks actors are willing to take and which safety measures correspond to their beliefs and values. In other words, feeling safe and actually being safe can be made compatible with feeling and being considered as an active partner in risk management decisions.

    Fourth, the fine-grained analysis of these data helped us to see clearly how each form of riskwork is embedded in what we will call here 'carriers' of stability and change at the organizational level. For instance, routines seem to play an important role in the production and reproduction of regulative–normative riskwork. Our results showed that this form of riskwork aims to transform tacit ways to manage safety risks into an explicit and repetitive form of best practice. However, our data also pointed to the fact that this approach cannot altogether override improvisation and situated judgement. In fact, we could say that regulative–normative riskwork calls for the reflexive, rather than automatic, embedding of rules in routines. Indeed, (echoing Chapter 12, this volume), we contend that: 'In order to close the expectations gap, risk managers need first and foremost commitment from others in the organization to accept a relevant and situationally contingent version of risk management, tailored to their needs.' If actors are expected to comply, they need to feel that the guidelines they apply reflect their needs, but also their values and philosophy regarding risks.

Tools, equipment, and technologies are of prime importance in techno-scientific riskwork. More than insignificant objects, their meanings can vary across time and space, as Scott (2008) would have said for institutional carriers. When accident statistics are presented to different groups, they carry different meanings dependent on which question is asked at the exact moment a particular group consults them. The same can be said of elaborate calculative tools, which, as we saw, are translated by users. Such tools can be seen as impregnated with 'an institutional residue that shapes how artifacts are constructed, used and understood' (Kaghan & Lounsbury, 2013), and therefore, become 'an occasion for structuration' (Scott, 2008: 145).

Regarding political riskwork, we showed that social connections between organizational actors could be collaborative or confrontational and that alliances are crucial. For example, advisers might only have the power to make recommendations and have to associate with actors who can provide them with the information they need. Building informal networks can also help to avoid the worst effects of 'crowding out' by techno-scientific artefacts, such as risk maps (see Chapter 2, this volume).

Interpretative riskwork is symbolic, in part involving work to 'cast issues in a particular light and suggest possible ways to respond to these issues' (Campbell, 2005: 48–9, in Scott, 2008: 141). Our results revealed how a simple clock as a temporal device could both make the restraint experience easier for patients and show a non-clinical manager that preventing the escalation of possibly dangerous behaviour could be simpler than he thought. We also showed how symbols of the mental health stigma, such as security devices and locks, were used to provide a new way of managing safety risks. In fact, we could say that different forms of riskwork also constitute 'practices of valuation' (see Chapter 5, this volume) by putting forward specific and often competing sets of values every time risks are discussed or acted upon. In this way, members of the organizations are able to tackle the tensions arising when efforts towards patient safety threaten patient autonomy and vice versa.

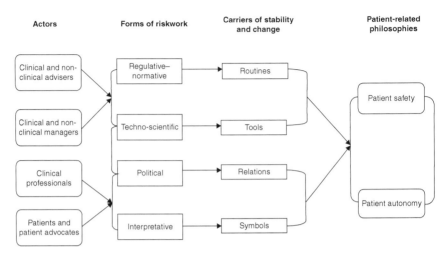

| Actors | Forms of riskwork | Carriers of stability and change | Patient-related philosophies |

Figure 10.2. Forms of riskwork and the tensions between patient safety and patient autonomy philosophies

Fifth, these results allowed us to propose a model for explaining how riskwork contributes to activate and resolve the tensions between safety and patient autonomy requirements that are made explicit and are addressed collectively. As shown in Figure 10.2, different actors conduct different forms of riskwork, although as we already mentioned, each form of riskwork is not performed exclusively by just one group of actors. As we explained, clinical and non-clinical advisers, along with clinical and non-clinical managers are more invested in regulative–normative and techno-scientific riskwork. As carriers of these forms of riskwork, routines and tools provide common ways to manage safety risks, but also provide actors with a more formalized and codified way to know and assess safety risks before making a decision about the level of risk they are ready to tolerate for themselves and the patients. Here, local references are created, as well as a collective memory about the way things should be done, regardless of actors' compliance with regulatory requirements.

Clinical professionals, and patients and their advocates, who are mainly but, as mentioned, not exclusively, accomplishing political and interpretative riskwork through relationships and symbols, are confronting values, experiences, and perceptions about managing safety risks. These forms of riskwork embody the means for staff to express their need to feel safe when accomplishing their daily tasks while also providing the means for patients to express their need to feel empowered. The relationships built and the symbols constructed, enable actors to deal with issues related to patient autonomy and to the way safety risks are managed.

It is through this dynamic between these different forms of riskwork that the tensions between safety and patient autonomy philosophies are made explicit and collectively addressed. Consequently, these riskwork efforts, through their respective carriers of stability and change, provide the opportunity to uncover slightly problematic situations regarding safety risks, but also unacceptable situations, such as abuse or unaddressed threats. Riskworkers can then have a say about the kind of organization they want to work and live in according to 'what is held as of value and why' (see Chapter 5, this volume).

Moreover, it is through these forms of riskwork that the blending of seemingly conflicting philosophies of patient safety and patient autonomy is carried out in the day-to-day work of these actors. Indeed, when routines and technologies are inadequate to address the conflicting philosophies, relationships and symbols are drawn upon. In turn, when relationships and symbols are utilized, routines and tools are often translated in accordance with available resources. Put differently, we suggest that when advisers, professionals, managers, and patients perform one form of riskwork or another, they also activate or resolve the tensions between the two philosophies underlying the risk management in this psychiatric setting.

The theoretical model advanced in this chapter shows how riskwork can reconcile the philosophy of safety and patient autonomy inside the organization. In short, the efforts of managers, advisers, professionals, and patients and their advocates are more than a mere change in managing risk culture; they also contribute to organizational change. We suggest that these forms of riskwork might also be a powerful trigger for the diffusion of innovation at the field level. By uncovering tensions between safety requirements and the specific needs of patients, but also by adapting risk management to the daily challenges faced by the actors, these forms of riskwork help us to rethink the needs of mental health and long-term care settings in terms of resources that increase quality of life, instead of trying to eliminate dangers at all costs.

REFERENCES

Bagian, J. P. (2005). Patient Safety: What Is Really at Issue? *Frontiers of Health Services Management*, 22(1), 3.

Barach, P. & Small, S. D. (2000). Reporting and Preventing Medical Mishaps: Lessons from Non-medical Near Miss Reporting Systems. *BMJ: British Medical Journal*, 320(7237), 759.

Battles, J., Dixon, N., Borotkanics, R., Rabin-Fastmen, B., & Kaplan, H. (2006). Sensemaking of Patient Safety Risks and Hazards. *Health Research and Educational Trust*, 41(4), 1555.

Bowers, L., Crowhurst, N., Alexander, J., Callaghan, P., Eales, S., Guy, S., McCann, E., & Ryan, C. (2002). Safety and Security Policies on Psychiatric Acute Admission Wards: Results from a London-wide Survey. *Journal of Psychiatric and Mental Health Nursing*, 9(4), 427.

Callaly, T., Arya, D., & Minas, H. (2005). Quality, Risk Management and Governance in Mental Health: An Overview. *Australasian Psychiatry: Bulletin of Royal Australian and New Zealand College of Psychiatrists*, 13(1), 16.

Campbell, J. L. (2005). 'Where Do We Stand?' Common Mechanisms in Organizations and Social Movements Research. In G. F. Davis, D. McAdam, W. Richard Scott, & M. Zald (Eds), *Social Movements and Organization Theory* (pp. 41–58). New York: Cambridge University Press.

Clarke, J. R., Lerner, J. C., & Marella, W. (2007). The Role for Leaders of Health Care Organizations in Patient Safety. *American Journal of Medical Quality*, 22(5), 311.

Currie, G., Humpreys, M., Waring, J., & Rowley, E. (2009). Narratives of Professional Regulation and Patient Safety: The Case of Medical Devices in Anaesthetics. *Health, Risk & Society*, 11(2), 117.

Currie, G., Waring, J., & Finn, R. (2008). The Limits of Knowledge Management for UK Public Services Modernization: The Case of Patient Safety and Service Quality. *Public Administration*, 86(2), 363.

Davis, R. E., Jacklin, R., Sevdalis, N., & Vincent, C. A. (2007). Patient Involvement in Patient Safety: What Factors Influence Patient Participation and Engagement? *Health Expectations: An International Journal of Public Participation in Health Care and Health Policy*, 10(3), 259.

Denham, C. R. (2007). The New Patient Safety Officer: A Lifeline for Patients, a Life Jacket for CEOs. *Journal of Patient Safety*, 3(1), 43.

Firth-Cozens, J. (2004). Organizational Trust: The Keystone to Patient Safety. *Quality and Safety in Health Care*, 13, 56.

Fischer, M. D. & Ferlie, E. (2013). Resisting Hybridisation between Modes of Clinical Risk Management: Contradiction, Contest, and the Production of Intractable Conflict. *Accounting, Organizations and Society*, 38, 30.

Goodman, G. R. (2002). Safety Throughout the Hospital. *Health Forum Journal*, 45(3), 6.

Helmreich, R. L. & Davies, J. M. (1997). Anaesthetic Simulation and Lessons to Be Learned from Aviation. *Canadian Journal of Anaesthesia*, 44(9), 907.

Horlick-Jones, T. (2005). On Risk Work: Professional Discourse, Accountability, and Everyday Action. *Health, Risk & Society*, 7(3), 293.

Hovey, R. B., Morck, A., Nettleton, S., Robin, S., Bullis, D., Findlay, A., & Massfeller, H. (2010). Partners in Our Care: Patient Safety from a Patient Perspective. *Quality & Safety in Health Care*, 19(6), e59.

Hutter, B. (2005). 'Ways of Seeing': Understandings of Risk in Organizational Settings. In B. Hutter & M. Power (Eds), *Organizational Encounters with Risk* (pp. 67–91). Cambridge: Cambridge University Press.

Hutter, B. & Power, M. (2005). 'Organizational Encounters with Risk: An Introduction'. In Hutter, B. & Power, M. (Eds), *Organizational Encounters with Risk* (pp. 1–32). Cambridge: Cambridge University Press.

Kaghan, W. & Lounsbury, M. (2011). Institutions and Work. *Journal of Management Inquiry*, 20, 73.

Kaghan, W. N. & Lounsbury, M. (2013). Artifacts, Articulation Work, and Institutional Residue. In A. Rafaeli & M. Pratt (Eds), *Artifacts and Organizations: Beyond Mere Symbolism* (pp. 259–78). Mahwah, NJ: Psychology Press.

Kohn, L. T., Corrigan, J. M., & Donaldson, M. S. (Eds), (1999).*To Err Is Human: Building a Safer Health System*. Washington, DC: National Academy Press.

Labelle, V. & Rouleau, L. (2016). The Institutional Work of Hospital Risk Managers: Democratizing and Professionalizing Risk Management. *Journal of Risk Research*, Published online, DOI: 10.1080/13669877.2016.1147488.

McDonald, R., Waring, J., & Harrison, S. (2005). 'Balancing Risk, That Is My Life': The Politics of Risk in a Hospital Operating Theatre Department. *Health, Risk & Society*, 7(4), 397.

Macrae, C. (2008). Learning From Patient Safety Incidents: Creating Participative Risk Regulation in Healthcare. *Health, Risk & Society*, 10, 53.

Maguire, S. & Hardy, C. (2013). Organizing Processes and the Construction of Risk: A Discursive Approach. *Academy of Management Review*, 56(1), 231.

Phillips, N. & Lawrence, T. B. (2012). The Turn to Work in Organization and Management Theory: Some Implications for Strategic Organization. *Strategic Organization*, 10(3), 223.

Pires, A. (1997). Échantillonnage et Recherche Qualitative: Essai Théorique et Méthodologique. In J. Poupart, L.-H. Groulx, A. Laperrière, R. Mayer, & A. Pires (Eds), *La Recherche Qualitative: Enjeux Épistémologiques et Méthodologiques* (pp. 113–69). Boucherville: Gaëtan Morin.

Power, M. (2004). *The Risk Management of Everything: Rethinking the Politics of Uncertainty*. London: Demos.

Quirk, A., Lelliott, P., & Seale, C. (2005). Risk Management by Patients on Psychiatric Wards in London: An Ethnographic Study. *Health, Risk & Society*, 7(1), 85.

Reason, J. T. (1997). *Managing the Risks of Organizational Accidents*, Aldershot: Ashgate.

Robinson, L., Hutchings, D., Corner, L., Finch, T., Hughes, J., Brittain, K., & Bond, J. (2007). Balancing Rights and Risks: Conflicting Perspectives in the Management of Wandering in Dementia. *Health, Risk & Society*, 9(4), 389.

Ryan, T. (2000). Exploring the Risk Management Strategies of Mental Health Service Users. *Health, Risk & Society*, 2(3), 267.

Saldaña, J. (2009). *The Coding Manual for Qualitative Researchers*. Los Angeles, CA: Sage.

Scott, W. R. (2008). *Institutions and Organizations—Ideas and Interests*. Los Angeles, CA: Sage.

Smiechewicz, W. (2009). ERM 2.0 Makes Everybody a Risk Manager. *Financial Executive*, 25(3), 61.

Star, S. & Griesemer, J. (1989). Institutional Ecology, Translations' and Boundary Objects: Amateurs and Professionals in Berkeley's Museum of Vertebrate Zoology 1907–39. *Social Studies of Science*, 19, 387.

Storey, J. & Buchanan, D. (2008). Healthcare Governance and Organizational Barriers to Learning from Mistakes. *Journal of Health Organization and Management*, 22(6), 642.

Strauss, A. & Corbin, J. (1998). *Basics of Qualitative Research: Techniques and Procedures for Developing Grounded Theory*. 2nd edition. Thousand Oaks, CA: Sage.

Waring, J. & Currie, G. (2009). Managing Expert Knowledge: Organizational Challenges and Managerial Futures for the UK Medical Profession. *Organization Studies*, 30, 755.

Wiig, S. & Lindøe, P. H. (2009). Patient Safety in the Interface between Hospital and Risk Regulator. *Journal of Risk Research*, 12(3), 411.

Yin, R. K. (2009). *Case Study Research, Design and Methods*, 4th edition. Thousand Oaks, CA: Sage.

11

Affective Overflows in Clinical Riskwork

Michael D. Fischer and Gerry McGivern

The terms 'clinical' and 'risk management' are commonly associated with rational detachment and cold, objective calculation, emotionally removed from the subjective experience of dealing with sickness, injury, and death. In contrast, we suggest that emotion and affect are integral to the work of managing clinical risk, often involving the intimate handling of human subjects and their embodied subjectivities. Dominant ideals of clinical risk management obscure these emotional–affective dimensions and what we describe below as 'affective overflows' in the 'heat' of day-to-day risk management (Dolan & Doyle, 2000; Godin, 2004; Hirschhorn, 1999). In day-to-day clinical practices, emotions are materially entangled with the micro-technologies and devices of risk management in its routine practices, habits, and scripts (Fischer & Ferlie, 2013; Power, 2011). Indeed, these practices reveal an informal and more 'indigenous' practice of clinical 'riskwork', in which risk technologies and devices are tactically deployed, refashioned, or undermined (Fischer, 2012; McGivern & Ferlie, 2007; McGivern & Fischer, 2010; 2012; Nicolini et al., 2011; Waring, 2005).

The interaction between people and material objects—sociomateriality—is of growing scholarly interest (Cetina & Bruegger, 2000; Orlikowski & Scott, 2008; Star & Griesemer, 1989) and regarded as an intrinsic feature of everyday working practices. Less attention though, has been paid to the way emotions, passions, fantasies, and desires shape and 'animate' this world of material objects. For example, in his manifesto for relational sociology, Emirbayer (1997: 311) advocates exploring 'culture and collective emotions' and notes that 'the study of transpersonal emotional flows has remained seriously underdeveloped'.

Studies of emotion within organizations generally consider intra- and inter-subjective emotion operating within and between individuals and groups (Fineman, 2008; Gabriel, 1995, 1999), often elusively (Courpasson & Thoenig, 2010; Morrill, 1995; Roberts et al., 2006). However, emotions are inherently connected with desires, values, and fantasies—and readily caught up with material objects. These 'affective intensities' (Massumi, 2002; Thrift, 2008) confer emotional meaning and attachment to objects, which are 'reworked' as they come into and out of mental focus, and are continuously shaped and remade through changes in everyday practice.

This affective dimension of risk management work has previously been suggested across diverse fields, including in studies of financial traders, accountants, and auditors (Fenton-O'Creevy et al., 2007, 2011, 2012). For example, Guenin-Paracini et al.'s (2014) ethnographic study of a large audit firm found that risk was associated with the emotion of fear, which shaped accountants' thoughts and use of techniques during audit processes. Similarly, Boedker and Chua's (2013) study of a major corporation found that both affect and rational calculation generated energy and collective action as an 'affective technology' tied to circulating accounting practices and devices:

> A flow of emotional energy that travels in networks of technology, people, images...technologies are important because they distribute and circulate affect in action nets...Affect flows from non-human devices to people and back again...its circulation via technology...act[ing] as a node in a network of affect production. (262–3)

From this perspective, the affective dimension of organizational life involves shared 'intensities', which circulate between subjective and material 'realities', *affecting* subjective experience and emotions, rather than necessarily emanating from them (Navaro-Yashin, 2012; Wetherell, 2012). In contrast, previous empirical research (Fischer, 2008), has found that 'indigenous' risk systems are more strongly imbued with intersubjective dynamics and meanings. However, these (and all risk systems) have a tendency to acquire a public trajectory: what begins as a latent risk representation may become an object of formal risk management (Castel, 1991; O'Malley, 2004; Power, 2007).

In this chapter, we focus on clinical risk management in mental healthcare as an exemplary case of the submerged dynamics of indigenous risk systems. Understanding the (necessarily) more intersubjective and embodied aspects of extreme cases can reveal dynamics that are present, if less visible, in other contexts (Eisenhardt, 1989). To bring our material to the fore, we draw from longitudinal ethnography (Fischer, 2008) of a specialist health service for the treatment of a high-risk patient group (people with personality disorders).

We suggest, first, that practising healthcare elicits a mix of positive and negative emotional feelings connected with handling and being accountable for the care of other people—their bodily experiences, transformations, illnesses, and sometimes death. In classic studies, such as Menzies-Lyth's (1960) psychoanalytic study of nurses' defensive mechanisms, anxiety appears as a diffuse and generalized explanation of these experiences. However, this overlooks a more complex picture in which diverse subjective experiences are bound up with one another.

Such 'intersubjectivity' involves connections folded into human experience (Mitchell, 2000; Mitchell & Aron, 1999). Crapanzano (1992, 2006) describes the experience of intersubjectivity as an 'interlocutory drama' that connects us with others—mediating our experiences of ourselves and others. There is 'nothing irrational, nothing even fictive about the scene...in its experience, in its description...Both the scene and...objective reality are subjectively experienced' (Crapanzano, 2006: 398). As this suggests, intersubjective experiences can tend to be emotional 'dramas' filled with expectations, meanings, and desires, which are continuously improvised and which unfold in often surprising and unpredictable ways. Such dramatization arises in many contexts involving emotional investments in the work of managing risk, but especially so in 'human service organizations' where there are expectations of balancing the desire for healing and care, with the wish to be protected from harm.

Second, these dramas become entangled with material possessions, tools, and artefacts. Indeed, we argue that intersubjective experiences involve a material focus, involving people as well as non-human objects. Influenced by anthropology, human geography, and cultural theory, the scholarship on affect tends to focus on the so-called 'affective intensities' of physical objects, institutions, and buildings, as though such objects themselves produce 'affects' on humans (see Massumi, 2002; Thrift, 2008). However, this chapter suggests a different starting point for these intersubjective aspects in the context of clinical riskwork (for other intersubective accounts of affect, see Navaro-Yashin, 2012; Wetherell, 2012). We argue that material objects do not have the 'solidity' they may appear to have, but are being continuously brought into being and shaped as part of the 'making' of risk. As we describe below, devices and technologies that appear as background context in one moment can become dramatically 'real' in the heat of a crisis or near-miss. Risks and their material representations thus reflect and 'embody' subjective experiences and projections that produce *affects* during incidents and crises.

Finally, we argue that during dramas and crises, affective flows between indigenous and formal systems may become affectively 'heated' (Fischer & Ferlie, 2013). As Callon (1998) argues, in such conditions 'everything becomes controversial', creating 'overflows' which can escalate, producing new risk objects and eroding arrangements for containment through expert framing. Indigenous clinical riskwork reveals processes of 'organizational becoming' (Tsoukas & Chia, 2002) that are inherently caught up in affective interactions between human subjects and the material objects, devices, and technologies with which they work. We explore how complaints and whistle-blowing affectively 'inflame' incidents, producing heated interactions that 'overflow' (Callon, 1998) beyond the technologies and devices intended to contain and manage them.

Overall, the chapter suggests that affective investments in the work of clinical risk management produce an 'affective economy' in which risk objects, technologies, and devices circulate. Whereas in 'cool' conditions risk management may proceed along intended decision pathways (Callon, 1998), when affect is added, interactions between relational and formal risk management systems create turbulent flows (Fischer, 2008, 2012), with repercussions for those invested and involved in the field. As the case of mental health personality disorder services discussed below shows, affective flows and the tendency for overflows are intrinsic aspects of clinical risk and its management.

PERSONALITY DISORDER AS A RISK OBJECT

The healthcare context is of general interest because technical, rational–analytic prescribed guidelines and standardized practices are blended with traditional clinical judgements, a 'felt' sense, and an idealized empathic engagement with patients. For example, the ideal of 'a good bedside manner' has become increasingly a focus of medical training and professional standards. Thus there is a potentially paradoxical dual trajectory within healthcare, being on the one hand technocratic in orientation and on the other hand involving informed patient choice and empathic engagement with patients.

The subfield of psychiatry is an ideal case for exploring this dual trajectory and the 'felt' emotional aspects of healthcare. In part, this is because psychiatry pays more attention to patients' cognitions, emotions, and subjective experiences than other medical subfields, but also because technical treatment emphasizes relations and 'therapeutic alliances' between patients and clinicians over pharmacological or physical interventions. Formal organizations also play a significant and visible role in psychiatric healthcare in the sense that organizational responses to clinical crises and risk management become the 'front stage' for risks which emerge from professional and patient communities that may be more or less attuned to the lives and experiences of their participants. 'Difficult to manage' personality disorders provide an opportunity to study clinical risk management as it unfolds in the space between front and back stage, where emotional–affective indigenous clinical work interacts with risk systems but also, ultimately, with public policy issues.

A number of high-profile homicides in the late 1990s, committed by people with mental illness, heightened public concern about the perceived risks presented by people with severe mental disorders. Determined to tackle the dangers presented by people with such disorders, the UK government put public protection at the centre of its mental health policy (Department of Health & Home Office, 1999, 2000). It proposed legislation to allow the indefinite detention of people with severe mental disorders, based on presumed risk to the public. What particularly exercised UK government attention, were the risks presented by people with severe personality disorders.

While medical psychiatry often considers severe personality disorders as untreatable, the realization that some people with these conditions were dangerous brought this issue into the political spotlight.

Shortly after the UK 1997 general election, Michael Stone—a convicted psychopath—was arrested for the double homicide of Lin Russell and her 6-year-old daughter, Megan. Her other daughter, 9-year-old Josie, had been left for dead with severe head injuries. The event produced public shock and outrage. A public enquiry attributed blame to severely flawed systems of risk management by mental health services (which had released him into the community after assessing his condition as untreatable).

While managing risk of violence or self-harm in personality disorder patients has been a longstanding concern in mental health services and prisons, such rare but high-profile cases of homicide in the 1990s, committed by people with either severe personality disorders or schizophrenia, drove the UK government to introduce a National Service Framework for Mental Health. Public protection from 'dangerous people' became a policy priority and the new Labour government (Department of Health, 1998) produced a comprehensive mental health strategy covering topics ranging from promoting 'healthy communities' to ensuring the secure incarceration of people with severe mental illnesses, considered to be of greatest risk to others. A National Service Framework (Department of Health, 1999b) set out new statutory responsibilities for assessing and handling patients, differentiating and managing patients deemed to be at high risk of violence or self-harm (Department of Health & Home Office 1999; National Institute for Mental Health in England, 2003).

A Care Programme Approach (CPA) was developed as an interagency administrative framework for assessing, planning, coordinating, and reviewing care plans (Department of Health, 1999a). The CPA specifies arrangements for multidisciplinary, multiagency meetings requiring crisis and contingency plans, handover arrangements between agencies, recording and sharing records, and formally reviewing plans. These requirements are managed by named key workers—usually nurses or social workers—who are responsible for coordinating and administering the framework. The new arrangements were overseen by statutory 'clinical governance' arrangements assigned to hospital boards as an accountability framework for assuring systematic standards of care, transparency, reporting, and care improvements. The boards were formally responsible for auditing their CPA framework on an annual basis.

However, unlike patients with physical disorders, the engagement of people with personality disorders with a system like CPA can be difficult, even when patients actively seek help. People with personality disorders tend to engage erratically with care programmes, often dropping out of treatment. High levels of emotional vulnerability prompt some to seek help only when they are in a state of crisis, often threatening suicide, or following self-harm. Although relatively few treatments for personality disorders have been found to be effective, an influential report (Reed, 1994) argued that the democratic therapeutic community (DTC) model had been shown to be more promising than other existing models of treatment. The DTC model involves full-time immersion in an intensive, demanding, and psychologically challenging programme for up to a year. The Department of Health commissioned a national DTC service consisting of three communities, along with well-resourced outreach teams operating across district mental health services.

Methods and Data

Our empirical focus in what follows is based on a four year ethnographic study (Fischer, 2008) of interorganizational relations between one of the DTCs and external agencies in health services, social care, high-security hospitals, and prisons. One author (Fischer) had professional links to the DTC and studied its clinical work and wider engagement across three UK inner-city conurbations and a rural area. During an initial two-year phase, he explored care coordination and the transition of patients between agencies. In a second phase, his empirical research concentrated on the DTC itself and its relations with a broader set of government agencies, including national commissioners and the Department of Health. Participant observations (195 hours), seventy-six in-depth formal interviews (1.5–2 hours in duration), and informal interviews (over a period of seven years) were triangulated against clinical, management, and policy texts collated during the study.

MANAGING RISK IN LOCAL MENTAL HEALTH SERVICES

In the first case, drawn from an inner-city hospital, we see various ways in which psychiatrists and clinical psychologists attempt to prevent risk escalation by handling cases of personality disorder behind the scenes, drawing on emotional–relational techniques rather than formal organizational processes. Practitioners' sensitivity to patients' emotions is generally regarded as a valuable tool, providing insights into possible reactions or escalation of problems. Handling their patients, their own reactions, and colleagues' emotions is an everyday aspect of psychiatrists' and clinical psychologists' work.

> I don't like working with angry, antisocial men, they freak me out. I am irrationally uncomfortable with them and probably just not empathic. And I worry about bumping into them in the street, that they will come and track me down…you hear of therapists being stalked by patients. And the other thing which freaks me

out is that they are often very charming and you just feel: Jesus, I am getting sucked in here! They have done horrendous things to people and yet they are actually being quite nice, saying you are really helping me. (clinical psychologist)

Doctors were thrashing around trying to find out what was the matter with me. And I was telling them but they didn't hear...All my suicide attempts were because nobody was listening to me, everyone got caught up in all of this self-harm stuff and seemed to think that was more serious than the real problem, which they just ignored completely, even though I was desperate. It was making me feel even more suicidal. (patient)

As one psychiatrist describes, emotional relations can spread and quickly escalate, especially where there is risk of harm.

They create massive anxiety—my colleagues come running, terrified because the patient's talking about self-harm. These patients know our anxieties; they know how to engage the doctor, because that doctor is scared for his professional life, frightened about presiding over a patient who kills themselves. They test you, they will say, 'oh doctor I feel suicidal'; and they look you in the eye to see how you react. I feel dead anxious too. But it means we always act defensively, we end up admitting them [to hospital] because we have to be seen to be doing something, when sometimes doing nothing or putting responsibility back to the patient might be the best course of action. (consultant psychiatrist 1)

As we find in this example, emotions tend to readily flow between human subjects and systems of risk management, which can become articulated in various and contradictory ways within organizational settings. These include administrative and technological responses that tend towards diffusing risks (such as continuous observation and forcible detention of patients under mental health legislation) as well as clinical responses that may seek to elicit greater patient responsibility.

Interactions between professionals and patients thus tend to be mediated by responses to actual clinical risks (first order, acting in the patient's best interests to prevent harm) and systems of formal risk management (second order risks, arising from challenges to the risk management system).

Professionals get their fingers burnt because these patients challenge the system and get detained for their own safety. And the whole thing becomes increasingly confused, because the patient fights to come out and you end up restricting them even more, trying to stop them from hurting themselves, rather than addressing any underlying psychopathology. You feel, well, I have taken over a very difficult patient and have ended up being backed into a corner, with the patient detained. And the nursing staff are all divided and are up in arms screaming at you, and the patient seems to be deteriorating, and I am trapped. What do I do next? It is very, very difficult. (consultant psychiatrist 2)

Far from these formal risk management systems (including responses, such as physical detention or pharmacological sedation) being experienced as 'cold', clinical, or organizational technologies that are external to emotional exchange, emotion becomes embroiled within this risk system, attaching itself to the technologies and materials of risk management. Such intersubjective entanglement with technologies can further intensify emotional reactions and clinical risk. For this reason, experienced practitioners often seek to manage personality disorder patients invisibly, outside of formal risk management systems. Although not formally visible, handling intersubjectivity and emotional reactions through private engagement increases the scope for clinically embedded risk management.

So we find professionals working in a semi-autonomous capacity, managing clinical relations unencumbered by formal risk management arrangements. We see such clinical riskwork as mediating between formal and informal risk management systems. Indeed, especially for many experienced clinicians, working with difficult patients takes place through an informal and indigenous risk system, out of sight of the formal risk systems, and often the wider clinical care system. As one community psychiatrist described it, his personal style was like a 'warm bath' which his patients tended to want to stay in for long periods. He kept in touch with one long-term patient who visited him ('like an old friend') several years after he had moved to a different country. More commonly, however, clinicians described striving to provide psychological 'containment' for personality disorder patients, relying more on a therapeutic alliance rather than interventions, and attempting to insulate them from the wider clinical and risk systems.

> The service is not set up to cope with personality disorders, they end up being disliked and labelled as time wasters, it makes them worse and more entrenched. I would never refer anyone with a personality disorder to the rest of the team. Anyone who I would see as personality disorder will inevitably stay (just) with me. (consultant psychiatrist 3)

This illustrates the dynamic tension between indigenous and formal risk systems. In the case of personality disorders, such tensions are not exceptional incidents requiring an emergency response, but are part of the everyday tensions and signs of trouble that practitioners are vigilant about—steering between informal and formal risk management as part of everyday work.

These tensions become particularly salient when localized trouble escalates to formal complaints or whistle-blowing involving external parties. One medical director described how his staff attempted to manage a patient through more informal out-patient care—rather than run the risk of her repeating a pattern of escalating self-harm by admitting her to hospital. But this backfired as this patient attracted the attention of authorities:

> [she] presented very dramatically, standing on the edge of a motorway bridge, blocking traffic...police helicopters out and everything...she actually fell from the bridge and was badly injured. The police were traumatized by it and released a lot

of damaging information to the press…big newspaper headlines—a hatchet job. No mention of the fact that she had had months as an inpatient, she was being managed through a seven days a week care plan, involved in all sorts of therapies. There were [Members of Parliament] involved, the authorities demanding weekly statements on what was happening. (medical director)

As Callon (1998) suggests, the local handling of risk in complex and relationally 'volatile' cases such as this may produce 'overflows', shifting the focus from first order risks to the risk management systems. Whereas such escalation can increase tensions within formal (and reputational) risk management arrangements, this may be in direct conflict with the handling of clinical risks. As our medical director describes it:

[our hospital] lawyers said if we had been in the coroner's court, it would have been very difficult to convince a jury of peers that [treating such a high-risk patient as an outpatient] was a sensible plan. You have to understand the risks of doing things that seem crazy but are in the patient's long term interests. (medical director)

In other words riskwork can *produce* risk as emotions run high, producing affective flows and overflows beyond formal risk management systems. In this sense, in the case of complaints and whistle-blowing, the risk management system may become 'heated' through this emotional economy of risk. This can create pressure to develop more elaborate informal and relational riskwork practices to contain this 'heating' process.

For instance, a multidisciplinary care team became divided over whether they should work with a patient who some believed posed a risk to children. Unable to resolve the conflict internally, their manager referred the issue to the hospital CEO:

It was really destructive and created a big split in the team. The service wasn't geared up for dealing with this level of risk. We were never going to meet his needs but just compound his frustration and further increase his risky behaviour. There was a real deadlock. Eventually it was resolved because this man was excellent at complaining, flagging up deficits in our service to the highest echelons, it made everybody really anxious. In the end, our CEO and the director of social services ended up having weekly (counselling) sessions with him. It was incredibly bizarre! (head of psychology)

While such indigenous clinical risk management work is often invisible to formal risk systems, it is an important aspect of clinical work. The dynamics of emotional entanglement between people and risk systems and technologies produce unexpected flows and overflows to other parties, altering usual decision path dependencies. In the next section, we explore how 'materiality' operates as part of this emotional economy of risk.

THE DTC: SHIFTS BETWEEN INFORMAL AND FORMAL RISKWORK SYSTEMS

The Democratic Therapeutic Community (DTC) system had been identified as one of the few successful clinical treatments for personality disorders (Reed, 1994), involving an intensive re-socialization programme of full-time residential treatment over a period of twelve months. The DTC was run using a complex set of rules and a structured timetable of group work designed to 'slow incidents down' so that they could be discussed and 'worked through' over time (often several days), before making decisions and taking action.

Risk assessment and management were seen as the principle therapeutic task, requiring all current and prospective DTC members to learn to recognize and understand their own emotions and those of others, as a means of handling the potential for risk escalation. Indeed, patients were seen as more effective and accurate assessors of clinical risk than clinical staff, and they generally had a strong personal investment in keeping the DTC 'a safe space'. Accordingly they played a significant role in running the DTC (the elected 'Top Three' patients jointly led the day-to-day running of the community, together with a senior team of doctors, psychologists, and nurses), as well as clinical decision-making, voting on who should be admitted to, or discharged from, the unit.

The DTC's rules were democratically determined, interpreted, and occasionally amended, based on long-established principles of democratization (the full community of patients and staff make clinical and management decisions throughout the day through democratic voting); communalism (all members are required to participate in the life of running the community, such as cleaning and preparing meals); permissiveness (members are expected to interact authentically and to 'surface' problem issues and behaviours); and reality confrontation (members are expected to learn and take responsibility for the impact of their behaviour on others) (Rapoport, 1960). Meetings of the full community could be called at any time of the day or night to manage emerging incidents or crises until the following scheduled community meeting.

Emphasis was placed on patients identifying and managing risks within the community. The DTC ran a daily timetable of small and large group activities from morning until late evening, in which all patients and staff were expected to fully participate, as the DTC's model of therapeutic treatment and its core technology for identifying, assessing, and managing clinical risk. Outside of formal group activities, members were expected to take any concern or issues to Top Three who, together with staff, would decide whether to call an emergency meeting of the full community, or to provide informal support until the next scheduled meeting. As one therapist described it:

> If the culture of enquiry is not carried by residents, it becomes something that the staff are left to do. And when questions come from staff rather than residents, we are accused of being too psychotherapeutic [and] making residents feel vulnerable and abused. The longer [this] goes on, the less communication takes place, and momentum builds for things to take place behind the scenes.

A major aspect of this collective riskwork was the process of selecting and 'constructing' risks, which often develop through a rather fragmented and accidental clustering of events. For instance, a heated altercation developed during a daily community meeting between Simon (patient) and John (a senior therapist), triggered by a comment that Simon interpreted as a 'put-down'.

> Simon explodes in anger, protesting that John's got it in for him—he's always on his case...another exchange promptly follows. Simon mutters [ambiguously] 'if you think you can do that, think again'. John, visibly flushed and agitated, protests that Simon's 'threat' is completely unacceptable: 'we don't do that kind of thing in here, it's not on'. Frustrated, Simon storms out of the unit...feeling provoked by John and 'sick of being controlled'. (extract from fieldnotes)

As members tried to work out how to make sense of what John perceived as Simon's 'threat', there was uncertainty and effort in constructing this as a risk. Few had noticed much of the interaction between the two. Overall, the community was sympathetic to Simon feeling 'picked on' by staff. Some clinicians seemed uncertain as to whether Simon's comment was intended as a threat. John looked awkwardly for reassurance from colleagues, and seemed even less certain about his interpretation after the meeting. Perhaps he had just overreacted? Yet in a subsequent staff debriefing, John's continuing emotional reaction to the exchange persuaded the staff team that Simon should face the consequences of his aggressive outburst.

After speaking with staff, Top Three called an emergency meeting of the community which (after much debate) voted to technically 'discharge' Simon from the unit. However, under the DTC's structured system of rules, they allowed him to request a temporary twenty-four-hour 'sleeping-in extension' to renegotiate his membership of the community. While formally suspended from the community, a condition for renewing his temporary extension was his willingness to review his perceptions, behaviour, and attitude, in the daily community meetings. Members were, in turn, required to assess his commitment to the community and the risks he presented to himself and others, and to review and vote on his extension every twenty-four hours. They finally elected to reinstate him as a community member after the maximum permitted extension of seventy-two hours.

Such risk reviews were conducted as part of the daily community meetings, which were ritualistic and formalized in tone. Led by the 'Top Three' patients, the proceedings followed a structured agenda, recording 'missed groups' (patients were considered to have 'suspended themselves' if they missed three groups), reviewing 'referred meetings' (emergency meetings with patients 'at risk'), noting rule-breaking, feeding back unstructured leisure time, and planning meals and cleaning rotas. An elected secretary minuted the meetings in detail and then read the minutes (at length) in a morning community meeting the next day. Meetings involved frequent votes for decision-making based upon a set protocol: a five-minute open discussion, followed by a proposal from the chair, a call for objections, and then a vote based on a show of hands (both staff and patients are required to vote). Two 'tellers' finally counted and recorded votes for, against, and abstentions.

> The meeting is very formal [ritualized], starting with a name-round 'for the visitor'. There was a reading of the previous day's very detailed minutes and notes of discussion, which seemed verbatim...This was listened to in silence, with an almost religious respect...It felt the reading was being received like a sacred text in a monastery. (extract from fieldnotes)

Although a central part of the DTC's functioning, the content of these meetings and their minutes were treated as confidential and formally invisible to the wider CPA and clinical governance requirements. As a record of community events, rather than individual patient case notes, they were not shared with outside agencies. In line with the DTC treatment model (as a group-based model in which there is no individual therapy) staff did not record separate case notes of clinical care.

Importantly, however, this approach to assessing, planning, and reviewing care was translated into how the DTC contributed to its formal CPA requirements. When producing written reports for outside agencies, patients were involved in assessing each other's risk, determining their future care needs, and (usually, but not always with a clinical staff member) providing jointly produced accounts of their treatment. The DTC insisted upon patients attending their interagency CPA meetings to contribute to the assessment, planning, and review process. Often to the surprise of other agencies (who tend to treat the CPA as an administrative exercise), DTC patients also brought along one or more other patients with the intention of supporting them.

> The client wrote her own assessment report, saying she was just about to leave and how well she'd done. We don't know what goes on because the DTC gives you very little information. And so the client comes to the CPA meeting with this report and her agenda. I am like, *what*? Clients don't have agendas—we tell them! So that's all been quite threatening for some staff, especially the psychiatrists. And we've had to walk a real tightrope with this client, trying to explain you can't just

walk in and demand all these things from services, because when you do, they just cut you off. (social work manager)

The DTC's collective methods for identifying and creating risk objects can be seen as an elaborate and embedded 'indigenous system' of clinical riskwork that is strongly based on relational forms of risk management. Whereas not all risks were necessarily brought into the DTC's community meetings (incidents take place in private, in the evenings, and sometimes outside of the community) this system was designed to be responsive and 'concertina-like' in bringing clinical riskwork closer to the underlying uncertainty and flux of possible and actual incidents in patients' everyday lives. For example, a request to Top Three for 'floors and doors' would result in a rota of patients sleeping on the floor or remaining awake outside the bedroom of a patient feeling vulnerable, to provide active support through the night. In keeping with this indigenous system, the textual representations of these risks was recorded and recited as confidential community minutes that remained invisible to, and unaudited by, formal risk management procedures.

AFFECTIVE OVERFLOWS INTO THE POLICY DOMAIN

A critical incident produced a significant change in the way the DTC and its hospital board handled clinical risks. A former DTC patient murdered his partner, several weeks after being discharged from the community. Health authorities reacted by instigating a 'root and branch' comprehensive risk assessment of the entire service to bring the DTC 'in line' with the working of other psychiatric units. The hospital board commissioned specialists in forensic psychiatry to conduct an inquiry, emphasizing actuarial (statistics-based) models of risk prediction, rather than the DTC's model of clinical judgement. New formal risk management arrangements required regular staff audits and upward reporting of risks, such as 'ligature points' (physical features that could provide a noose for strangulation). Arrangements included formally recording and reporting discussions with patients, including 'advice on clinical risks' and discharge planning. Hospital managers challenged the idea of patients' equal participation in the CPA process, insisting that clinical authority should override patient opinion.

The introduction of these new formal risk arrangements heightened DTC members' emotional reactions (of bereavement, guilt, and self-blame) to the homicide, and added to anxiety about what some staff perceived to be a 'witch-hunt' as they '[waited] for the finger of blame to be pointed'. However, they also disrupted the DTC's indigenous risk management system, as staff adopted a more procedural mindset. Patients perceived this as a betrayal of the DTC's democratic methods.

A key change was the manner in which risks were identified and materially represented within the DTC, shifting from open and exploratory practices of 'slowing things down' to a more 'heated' process of rapidly identifying and formally reporting risks. For example, widespread drug and alcohol use within the DTC was discovered one night after a violent disturbance (a patient 'lost it' and started throwing furniture), to which police were called. Anxious to reassert clinical authority, the DTC clinical team immediately discharged several patients who they believed to be directly responsible, and insisted that remaining patients formally consent to random drug and alcohol testing by local police. During the morning's community meeting, DTC leaders introduced hospital consent forms that they handed to patients, passing them between each other in silence. A few patients ran from the room in tears. Most of those remaining signed the forms, reluctantly consenting to the police taking random samples of their saliva, urine, blood, and hair at any time of day or night.

> I'm struck by the seemingly draconian and legalistic consent form...The clinical director is taking advice from the drugs liaison police. Afterwards, junior staff disagree about the new arrangements: 'we are far too reactive, we really undermine the residents...constantly checking up on them and it's really not helping'...But DTC leaders insist their decision is not going to be reversed. (extract from fieldnotes)

Staff feelings of anger, resentment, and betrayal by increasingly 'untrustworthy' patients were integral to the way that these risks were perceived and constructed. Among patients, these new arrangements were experienced not as neutral 'technologies' but as emotionally and morally laden, and with a perceived wish to blame and punish.

Instead of community meetings operating as a 'safe space' for surfacing and exploring emerging risks, they became points of tension between formal and informal risk systems.

> It's like a prison stand-off...trying to psyche each other out. Who's going to break first? Who's going to be able to stay silent the longest? The most powerful people are the ones who say nothing. (patient)

During a routine community meeting 'visited' by senior hospital managers, for instance, they suspected that two patients were in a sexual relationship, which was discouraged, rather than prohibited, according to DTC rules. Afterwards the senior managers insisted that the clinical director should stop their relationship, if necessary by threatening the pair with immediate discharge.

> We said to the clinical director: look, you need to do something to stop it. These people should be concentrating on their therapy...A lot of work had to go on

from here to say have you counselled those individuals, have you recorded that
you have counselled [them], and have you advised the different agencies.
(hospital manager)

With escalating disturbance developing 'behind the scenes' among patients
and in confrontations with staff, clinical identification and upwards reporting
of risk (through daily risk reports) produced an increasingly 'heated' sense of
conflict—with the unintended perverse consequence of increasing substantive
(first order) and constructed (second order) risks.

> There is not one community here—there are two. I really don't trust staff.
> You can't call it a community when you can't talk with them about anything…you
> can't call it democratic. (patient)

> The past months have been hell…a complete lack of trust…There was no
> protected time, no retreat…it's like a year in Beirut. (patient)

An important dimension of risk escalation within and beyond the DTC is its
repercussions within the clinical setting. The dynamics of overflow were
significant beyond the setting, in terms of reshaping wider perceptions of
risk and especially notions of what constitutes the relevant risk object to be
managed. However, these perceptions and reactions also shaped how clinical
risk was managed internally and, as we have seen, how clinicians and managers orientated themselves to handling an increasing range of circulating risk
objects. As one senior manager commented, this sense of progressively tense
risk negotiations between patients, clinicians, and managers tended to
reinforce the confusion and 'heat' in the risk management system.

> I deliberately don't get close to operational delivery. You can see other…directors
> getting pulled in and you can see how all-consuming it is. So I have tried to keep a
> bit of a distance so I can try to help them think logically. There's been an awful lot
> of emotion for them. It is really like being in a total institution—you give your
> whole life to that service. (hospital manager)

Indeed, such tensions were further fuelled by the DTC senior managers'
sensitivity to wider reactions as uncertainty about the risk management
arrangements caught the attention of the national commissioners who
'didn't understand the model, acted highly emotionally [and] upped the ante
even more…It makes the Board anxious, it really does' (senior executive). As
one official commented, the DTC was perceived as 'poisonous…the atmosphere is so intense that people just get fried up. I have never…faced that
degree of hostility. It is the only organization that (the national commissioners)
agreed never to meet single-handed' (senior official).

    Although such wider reactions are important and interesting in illustrating
the dynamics of overflow in risk management systems, the most salient aspect
for our analysis were their local effects upon the DTC, in particular the
amplification of perceived threats arising from second order risk management.

Officials lost confidence in the service, and ultimately closed all three units (even though they had received a positive, independent evaluation (Fiander et al., 2004)). Significant factors in this closure process were the affective tensions that were mobilized within and beyond the DTC and expressed in its system of clinical risk management.

> I'm astounded at the failure...to support the place. We end up with the service collapsing because it did was what it was asked to do...politically, there were some 'shenanigans'...and the thing collapsed. There is a serious underestimation of the dynamics of these [interorganizational] relationships and how they work. (senior official)

DISCUSSION AND CONCLUSIONS

The cases of the hospital setting and the DTC environment analysed in this chapter point to how affective components of clinical riskwork may be influenced by intersubjective relations within 'ordinary' clinical practice. We suggest that this is an underexplored area that may rebalance previous studies of emotional reactions evoked through formal risk management systems (Fischer & Ferlie, 2013; McGivern & Fischer, 2012). Furthermore, future studies should take a 'sociomaterial turn' in order to understand the 'back stage' dynamics of clinical risk management, as an important yet under-researched aspect of risk management technologies. In conclusion, we suggest three implications for the future analysis of the routines and 'facticity' (Power et al., 2009) of everyday risk management and its inherently emotion-laden character.

The Intersubjective Dynamics of Affective Flow in Everyday Clinical Work

First, the cases in this chapter show how the intersubjective dynamics and tensions of staff–patient relations necessarily bring affect and risk together. Patients and staff attempt to engage but often end up talking past each other: staff 'got caught up in all of this self harm stuff and seemed to think that was more serious than the real [clinical] problem'. Indeed, staff tend to be strongly affected by this interrelationship, producing a sense of affective contagion. Their perceptions of possible or actual danger connect interpersonal tensions and reactions within the clinical interaction, with implied or actual threat of risk technologies being (potentially) invoked. In this sense, staff experience being 'made to feel' tensions that are both intersubjective in relation to particular patients yet simultaneously relate to the risk management systems.

This suggests that formal risk technologies are not somehow separate from, but are intrinsically bound up with these staff–patient interactions, and embedded in routine clinical assessment, treatment, and rehabilitation. Clinical risk is thus constructed and experienced as threatening and potentially overwhelming.

Invoking and Using Risk Technologies Is Affectively and Morally Laden, Entailing Local Material Effects

Second, the DTC case reveals how texts, devices, and material technologies are an essential part of the clinical interaction. These are powerfully brought into play as part of the risk management process, increasing forms of relational control (sometimes referred to in clinical settings as 'relational security'), and shifting power dynamics in ways that may exacerbate tensions. They may function as part of a self-regulating system creating potential 'cooling' and regulating effects, or possibly produce 'heating' dynamics that exacerbate tensions (Fischer, 2012). Our point is that these risk technologies are brought into play as already affectively laden with institutional and clinical meanings, and acquire further meanings and influence as particular relationships develop.

For example, our analysis of Simon's 'threatening behaviour' in the DTC, reveals an emergent process of risk identification within micro-level interactions. Whereas the community's perception of actual risk was initially hesitant and uncertain, it was shaped and transformed through a sequence of staff and community meetings and voting rules—a core DTC method for assessing and discussing risk management. As risk identification technologies, these initial meetings and procedures strengthened the idea of risk within the clinical interaction, helping to fuel emotional reactions and the perception of Simon as presenting a risk of harm. Once this risk object was collectively formed, the DTC then proceeded to treat it according to the well-established rules of the formal risk management system.

This collective production of risk objects involves individual patients being actively constructed as risky or at risk. In the case of Simon, the patient reaction and resistance/defiance added further weight to the collective emerging sense of threat, which was seen as justifying the risk management response, even when some staff doubted the accuracy of the original assessment. So we suggest that, whereas risk management may be designed to cool problems, its effects in practice may be to increase a sense of threat, fear, and blame, potentially increasing tensions within the specific setting.

These insights from the DTC setting are consistent with Douglas's (1992) broader thesis that risk is tied to emotions, affect, and moral values, with associated dimensions of fault and blame acting as rhetorical resources. She shows how risks are selected by groups and evaluated in terms of their potential consequences as political, aesthetic, and moral matters. Indeed, we have empirically shown how, in a range of different clinical contexts, participants fear the operations and effects of risk technologies often more than actual risks (McGivern & Ferlie, 2007; McGivern & Fischer, 2010, 2012). These risk technologies may thus produce the unintended consequence of motivating clinicians to cover up issues connected to actual clinical risk because they are anxious about being blamed and scapegoated.

How Affect Overflows through Risk Management Systems—the Container Becomes the Uncontained

Finally, in this chapter we have shown that, when 'heated', intersubjective emotions affect and can overwhelm risk management systems designed to contain them, producing escalation and overflows. Following Callon (1998) we suggested that such systems can become the conduit for escalation as risk moves beyond the original settings, increasing the difficulties of containment. We also found that heated interpersonal conflicts arising between patients and clinicians (Fischer & Ferlie, 2013; McGivern & Fischer, 2012) or between medical professionals (McGivern & Ferlie, 2007) may lead them to construct cases of clinical risk which then escalate to become a source of further risk. In this sense, risk objects shift beyond patients as staff, managers, and risk technologies themselves become the objects of risk. This process has a dynamic fluidity that influences and reshapes the 'solidity' of risk devices and technologies. Mundane processes, devices, and inscriptions alter meanings and uses, shaping experiences and perceptions of organizational dynamics beyond the original sites of risk. As we have described in the case of the DTC, affective overflows in riskwork may at times overwhelm managerial and policy arrangements for risk management, resulting in the decline and even collapse of clinical services.

REFERENCES

Boedker, C. & Chua, W. F. (2013). Accounting as an Affective Technology: A Study of Circulation, Agency and Entrancement. *Accounting Organizations and Society*, 38, 245–67.

Callon, M. (1998). An Essay on Framing and Overflowing: Economic Externalities Revisited by Sociology. *Sociological Review*, 46(S1), 244–69.

Castel, R. (1991). From Dangerousness to Risk. In G. Burchell, C. Gordon, & P. Miller (Eds), *The Foucault Effect: Studies in Governmentality* (pp. 281–98). Chicago, IL: University of Chicago Press.

Courpasson, D. & Thoenig, J.-C. (2010). *When Managers Rebel*. Basingstoke, UK: Palgrave Macmillan.

Crapanzano, V. (1992). *Hermes' Dilemma and Hamlet's Desire: On the Epistemology of Interpretation*. Cambridge, MA: Harvard University Press.

Crapanzano, V. (2006). The Scene: Shadowing the Real. *Anthropological Theory*, 6(4), 387–405.

Department of Health (1998). *Modernising Mental Health Services: Safe, Sound and Supportive*. London: Department of Health.

Department of Health (1999a). *Effective Care Coordination in Mental Health Services: Modernising the Care Programme Approach*. London: Department of Health.

Department of Health (1999b). *National Service Framework for Mental Health: Modern Standards and Service Models*. London: Department of Health.

Department of Health & Home Office (1999). *Managing Dangerous People with Severe Personality Disorder: Proposals for Policy Development*. London: HMSO.

Department of Health & Home Office (2000). *Reforming the Mental Health Act: Part II, High Risk Patients*. Cm5016-II. London: Stationery Office.

Dolan, M. & Doyle, M. (2000). Violence Risk Prediction: Clinical and Actuarial Measures and the Role of the Psychopathy Checklist. *British Journal of Psychiatry*, 177(4), 303–11.

Douglas, M. (1992). *Risk and Blame: Essays in Cultural Theory*. London: Routledge.

Eisenhardt, K. M. (1989). Building Theories from Case-Study Research. *Academy of Management Review*, 14(4), 532–50.

Emirbayer, M. (1997). Manifesto for a Relational Sociology. *American Journal of Sociology*, 103(2), 281–317.

Fenton-O'Creevy, M., Lins, J. T., Vohra, S., Richards, D. W., Davies, G., & Schaaff, K. (2012). Emotion Regulation and Trader Expertise: Heart Rate Variability on the Trading Floor. *Journal of Neuroscience, Psychology, and Economics*, 5(4), 227–37.

Fenton-O'Creevy, M., Nicholson, N., Soane, E., & Willman, P. (2007). *Traders: Risks, Decisions, and Management in Financial Markets*. Oxford: Oxford University Press.

Fenton-O'Creevy, M., Soane, E. Nicholson, N., & Willman, P. (2011). Thinking, Feeling and Deciding: The Influence of Emotions on the Decision Making and Performance of Traders. *Journal of Organizational Behaviour*, 32(8), 1044–81.

Fiander, M., Burns, T., Langham, S., & Normand, C. (2004). (DTC) *Replication Study —Clinical Progress & Health Economic Strands Integrated Final Report*. London: St George's Hospital Medical School, University of London.

Fineman, S. (Ed.). (2008). *The Emotional Organization: Passions and Power*. Malden, UK: Blackwell.

Fischer, M. D. (2008). An Ethnographic Study of Turbulence in the Management of Personality Disorders: An Interorganisational Perspective. Ph.D. thesis, Imperial College London, University of London, UK.

Fischer, M. D. (2012). Organizational Turbulence, Trouble and Trauma: Theorizing the Collapse of a Mental Health Setting. *Organization Studies*, 33(9), 1153–73.

Fischer, M.D. & Ferlie, E. (2013). Resisting Hybridisation between Modes of Clinical Risk Management: Contradiction, Contest, and the Production of Intractable Conflict. *Accounting Organizations and Society*, 38(1), 30–49.

Gabriel, Y. (1995). The Unmanaged Organization: Stories, Fantasies and Subjectivity. *Organization Studies*, 16(3), 477–501.

Gabriel, Y. (1999). *Organizations in Depth: The Psychoanalysis of Organizations*. London: Sage.

Godin, P. (2004). 'You Don't Tick Boxes on a Form': A Study of How Community Mental Health Nurses Assess and Manage Risk. *Health, Risk & Society*, 6(4), 347–60.

Guénin-Paracini, H., Malsch, B., & Paillé, A. M. (2014). Fear and Risk in the Audit Process. *Accounting, Organizations & Society*, 39(4), 264–88.

Hirschhorn, L. (1999). The Primary Risk. *Human Relations*, 52(1), 5–23.

Knorr Cetina, K. & Bruegger, U. (2000). The Market as an Object of Attachment: Exploring Postsocial Relations in Financial Markets. *Canadian Journal of Sociology*, 25(2), 141–68.

McGivern, G. & Ferlie, E. (2007). Playing Tick-Box Games: Interrelating Defences in Professional Appraisal. *Human Relations*, 60(9), 1361–85.

McGivern, G. & Fischer, M. D. (2010). Medical Regulation, Spectacular Transparency and the Blame Business. *Journal of Health Organization and Management*, 24(6), 597–610.

McGivern, G. & Fischer, M. D. (2012). Reactivity and Reactions to Regulatory Transparency in Medicine, Psychotherapy and Counselling. *Social Science and Medicine*, 74(3), 289–96.

Massumi, B. (2002). *Parables for the Virtual: Movement, Affect, Sensation*. Durham, NC: Duke University Press.

Menzies Lyth, I. (1960). A Case Study in the Functioning of Social Systems as a Defence against Anxiety: A Report on a Study of the Nursing Service of a General Hospital. *Human Relations*, 13(2), 95–121.

Mitchell, S. A. (2000). *Relationality: From Attachment to Intersubjectivity*. Hillsdale, NJ: Analytic Press.

Mitchell, S. A. & Aron, L. (Eds) (1999). *Relational Psychoanalysis: The Emergence of a Tradition*. Hillsdale, NJ: Analytic Press.

Morrill, C. (1995). *The Executive Way: Conflict Management in Corporations*. Chicago, IL: University of Chicago Press.

National Institute for Mental Health in England (2003). Personality Disorder—No Longer a Diagnosis of Exclusion: Policy Implementation Guidance for the Development of Services for People with Personality Disorder. London.

Navaro-Yashin, Y. (2012). *The Make-Believe Space: Affective Geography in a Postwar Polity*. Durham, NC: Duke University Press.

Nicolini, D., Waring, J., & Mengis, J. (2011). The Challenges of Undertaking Root Cause Analysis in Health Care: A Qualitative Study. *Journal of Health Service Research and Policy*, 16, 34–41.

O'Malley, P. (2004). *Risk, Uncertainty and Government*. London: Glasshouse Press.

Orlikowski, W. J. & Scott, S. V. (2008). Sociomateriality: Challenging the Separation of Technology, Work and Organization. *Academy of Management Annals*, 2(1), 433–74.

Power, M. (2007). *Organized Uncertainty: Designing a World of Risk Management*. Oxford: Oxford University Press.

Power, M. (2011). Foucault and Sociology. *Annual Review of Sociology*, 37(1), 35–56.

Power, M., Scheytt, T., Soin, K., & Sahlin, K. (2009). Reputational Risk as a Logic of Organizing in Late Modernity. *Organization Studies*, 30, 301–24.

Rapoport, R. N. (1960). *Community as Doctor: New Perspectives on a Therapeutic Community*. London: Tavistock.

Reed, J. (1994). *Report of the Department of Health and Home Office Working Group on Psychopathic Disorder*. London: Department of Health and Home Office.

Roberts, J., Sanderson, P., Barker, R., & Hendry, J. (2006). In the Mirror of the Market: The Disciplinary Effects of Company/Fund Manager Meetings. *Accounting Organizations and Society*, 31(3), 277–94.

Star, S. L. & Griesemer, J. R. (1989). Institutional Ecology, 'Translations' and Boundary Objects: Amateurs and Professionals in Berkeley's Museum of Vertebrate Zoology, 1907–39. *Social Studies of Science*, 19(3), 387–420.

Thrift, N. J. (2008). *Non-representational Theory: Space, Politics, Affect*. London: Routledge.

Tsoukas, H. & Chia, R. (2002). On Organizational Becoming: Rethinking Organizational Change. *Organization Science*, 13(5), 567–82.

Waring, J. (2005). Beyond Blame: Cultural Barriers to Medical Incident Reporting. *Social Science and Medicine*, 60(9), 1927–35.

Wetherell, M. (2012). *Affect and Emotion: A New Social Science Understanding*. Los Angeles, CA: Sage.

12

The Triumph of the Humble
Chief Risk Officer

Anette Mikes

In the wake of the 2007–9 financial crisis, continuing corporate debacles, and ongoing corporate governance calls for the appointment of chief risk officers (CROs) and risk management committees, it is particularly important to understand what role risk officers do or may play. The compliance imperative requires banks to implement a firm-wide risk management framework complete with analytical models for measuring and controlling quantifiable risks. In addition, corporate governance guidelines advocate the 'business partner' role for risk management. In this context, the question becomes: how do senior risk officers strike a balance between the roles of 'compliance champion' and business partner?

The practitioner literature on risk management promotes the view that the CRO should focus on developing fruitful interactions between risk managers and the organization's managerial and executive layers (Economist Intelligence Unit Limited, 2010); for example, by adopting the role of 'strategic business advisor' (KPMG, 2011: 27). The rising visibility of enterprise risk management (ERM) and risk managers in organizations reflects the reconfiguration of uncertainty into an area of management (Power, 2007), which places demands on the risk manager to be a proactive assessor and communicator of uncertainty, capable of operating as a partner to business decision makers rather than as a reactive control agent.

Risk managers seem to be riding a favourable tide, with regulators, standard setters, and emerging professional associations advocating their value. More and more companies have appointed CROs over the last decade and surveys demonstrate that the proliferation of senior risk officers is ubiquitous.[1] While

---

[1] A recent survey (Accenture, 2013) of a diverse sample of 446 large organizations (46 per cent were in financial services; others were in the utilities, healthcare, life sciences, and government sectors) found that the presence of a CRO or equivalent senior risk officer was 'near-universal', with 96 per cent of the respondents having one in 2013 (up from 78 per cent in 2011). However,

only a minority of respondents tend to treat the ERM framework of the Committee of Sponsoring Organizations (COSO) of the Treadway Commission (Committee of Sponsoring Organizations of the Treadway Commission, 2004) as their blueprint and many do not follow any particular standard or framework,[2] surveys generally agree that the percentage of companies embracing ERM (that is, reporting that they have 'an ERM framework and/or an ERM policy') has reached the 'critical mass of 60%' (Deloitte, 2013; RIMS & Advisen, 2013). Putting their money where their mouth is, companies are increasing their spending on risk management and many plan to keep doing so.[3] Yet the jury is still out on ERM's actual value added. According to a 2013 survey carried out by RIMS, risk managers varied widely in their satisfaction with their progress (RIMS & Advisen, 2013), while a survey of C-suite executives found that fewer than half were convinced that their organization has an effective risk management programme (KPMG, 2013).

At best, such evidence tells us that organizations vary widely in their design, implementation, and use of risk management practices and tools. At worst, risk management (or the appointment of CROs) is a fad, gobbling up more resources without closing the all-too-evident 'expectations gap' (Power, 2007) between what companies hope risk management can do and what actual risk management functions have generally been able to do.

This chapter focuses on two companies in which the risk management staff defined and brought about their own version of risk management. Having traced the evolution of these two risk management functions, their apparatus (tools and processes), and their relationships with the rest of the organization, I was struck, first, by the apparent success of these CROs at making risk management a seemingly inevitable part of organizational life. Over the years, they developed new tools that seamlessly linked up with the work of business managers, creating the impression that the real work of risk management took place in the business lines and was carried out by employees. Yet the risk managers (or rather, the risk function managers) retained a certain amount of connection to these practices,

surveys less focused on regulated industries suggest that the acceptance of CROs (and formal risk-management functions) could be much less widespread—31 per cent in global firms (Beasley et al., 2010) and even lower in non-regulated US organizations.

[2] A 2013 survey of 1,095 risk managers (RIMS & Advisen, 2013) suggests that 22 per cent of companies adopted the COSO framework, 23 per cent embraced the ISO 31000 standard, and 26 per cent do not follow any particular framework in defining their 'enterprise risk management' practices.

[3] A global survey of 1,092 respondents from diverse industries, carried out in late 2012 (KPMG, 2013), found that the level of investment in risk management as a percentage of total revenues had grown in the past three years, with 66 per cent of respondents expecting that proportion to rise in the next three years.

which enabled them to demarcate risk management as their expertise and *raison d'être*.

Second, I was intrigued by the paradoxical attitudes displayed by these CROs towards their own work: they appeared to be both tremendously confident and also surprisingly humble. Surrounded by corporate governance advocates, regulators, consultants, and certified risk professionals with a vested interest in telling them what risk managers should do and be, they nevertheless had the confidence to steer away from the emerging conventional wisdom, the risk management standards and guidelines, and the consultants who advocated them. They both took on the challenge of developing the idea of risk management and its apparatus themselves. And at the same time, they displayed a lot of humility, by acknowledging failures, struggles, and imperfections and by regarding their work as unfinished.

Third, these CROs sensed that the excessive and uncritical use of certain kinds of risk management vocabulary and technology could harm rather than further their cause. Irritated by the proliferation of abstract vocabulary emanating from risk management standards, these CROs tried to learn and speak the language of the business. By co-creating risk tools and a sparse risk vocabulary with those who would be expected to use them, these CROs created what I call 'risk talk'—an organizational discourse about risk issues ranging from task-related problems and perceived organizational weaknesses to concerns about resource planning—so practical that managers didn't even know they were speaking it.

Finally, these CROs operated extremely frugally. With only one or two full-time staff, they played the role of facilitator of risk talk and kept their resource requirements to a bare minimum. They planned no further investment in risk management and did not ask for increases in their formal authority or decision rights. Towards the end of the research horizon, the role of the CRO was structurally demoted at both companies—becoming one or two steps further removed from the CEO in the reporting hierarchy—yet the organizational reach and influence of these CROs remained intact.

Thus, the two case studies document what might be called the triumph of the humble CRO (in these particular settings) over the advocates of giving risk managers ever more autonomy, visibility, and resources. It is the triumph of ordinary risk talk and a commonsensical apparatus over ever-more-sophisticated risk models and off-the-shelf IT programs that promise a comprehensive and sophisticated display of risks.

In the next section, I briefly describe the case sites and my research process. Second, I outline the evolution of the risk apparatus and describe the work of risk management ('riskwork') at the two companies. Third, I describe the CROs' efforts to develop risk tools and a common language for risk talk, with the effect of democratizing risk management, and turning it into a form of organizational therapy. Fourth, I illustrate the mix of confidence and humility that characterized the attitude of these CROs towards their own creations. I also describe how these CROs kept their span of control narrow and even came to accept less formal authority, while (somewhat counterintuitively) widening their span of support.

THE CASE SITES AND RESEARCH PROCESS

Electroworks, a major Canadian power utility, operated in an industry in which lack of operational reliability could lead not only to financial and asset damage but also to human injury and death. The provincial regulatory agency had capped the price that Electroworks could charge, while also requiring it to lead conservation initiatives that would reduce future revenues. Electroworks had to manage a complex web of conflicting interests—the agendas of government ministers, regulators, consumers, environmental groups, aboriginal ('first nation') landowners, and the capital-market debt-holders that had subscribed to the company's C$1 billion bond issue. I started fieldwork at Electroworks in spring 2008. Through twenty-five interviews, I aimed to reconstruct the history of ERM at Electroworks from its consultant-led introduction through its transformation to its current inevitable, yet still evolving state.

Magic Toys was a large, family-owned toymaker, operating in a highly competitive, fast-paced industry which essentially produces and markets 'fashion for kids'. Most of the company's annual sales came from new product launches, which elevated the importance of product development and innovation. The firm's primary customers were the global retailers who distributed children's toys. Serving these retail chains with accurate and timely deliveries and ensuring fast shelf-turnover were of paramount importance in Magic Toys's business model, which aspired to 'world-class' marketing and distribution capabilities. In this context, risk management's role was to assist the smooth delivery of new product lines and to 'prepare the company for uncertainty'.[4] I started fieldwork there in 2012 and, through forty-four interviews with risk function managers and business executives, I tried to sketch the evolution of risk practices from 'form-filling' to an established, actionable, and consequential part of the annual planning exercise.

---

[4] Internal document, 'Version 2.0 /15 March 2012'.

THE EVOLUTION OF THE RISK MANAGEMENT APPARATUS

Origins

Early in 1999, in preparation for listing on the Toronto stock exchange, the Electroworks board of directors decided that the company should implement ERM, in compliance with listing requirements.[5] They hired a succession of four consulting firms which (in the words of the later CRO) 'all came through doing ERM-type stuff. They would come in. They would do risk interviews. They would do risk maps. They would charge a quarter of a million dollars and deliver a nice report. But nothing happened. There was no knowledge transfer.' After this false start, the CEO and CFO asked the head of internal audit, Robert Lewis,[6] to 'take on ERM', with very little directive but with a sense of need conveyed by the board and the listing requirements. Trained as an accountant and originally hired from the banking industry to be the head of internal audit, Lewis had little expertise in any of the day-to-day challenges faced by Electroworks line-workers, engineers, lawyers, and customer service managers. He saw risk management as both a challenge and a development opportunity for his internal audit function. He realized that he had the opportunity to define what risk management was to be and what his own role as CRO was to be:

> Initially I said, 'No, I don't think I should take it on. I think there's a conflict of interest, because of my audit role, but let me think about it. I'll sleep on it and get back to you tomorrow.' So I went home and I thought about it and I guess my feeling was that before the consultants, nothing had happened in the risk domain. Now, after the consultants had left, nothing was happening. And while it might be a little bit of a conflict, I felt, well, it might be fun. I'll give it a shot, but I'll run it as a completely separate product line.

Lewis established a 'Chinese wall' to separate his internal audit and risk management roles. He hired two staff members (from outside the internal audit function) for the facilitation of risk workshops, record keeping and the subsequent production of risk reports. Thus records of the risk workshops could be kept confidential and separate from internal audit assessments and no one besides Lewis was involved in both activities. He had the habit of signalling which hat he was wearing by actually appearing in meetings with a baseball cap carrying either an 'Internal Audit' or an 'ERM' label.

In contrast to Lewis, the CRO at Magic Toys, Carl Hirschmann,[7] had spent his entire career in the company as a financial controller. The notion of risk

---

[5] Although Electroworks eventually abandoned its listing plans, ERM remained.
[6] Pseudonym.   [7] Pseudonym.

management came to him as an out-of-the-blue request from his boss, the CFO, in 2007. At the time, Magic Toys was recovering from a serious crisis that saw high staff turnover and the appointment of the company's first-ever outside CEO (a former McKinsey consultant). As part of the recovery, the board requested that the company should adopt risk management best practices. Like Lewis, Hirschmann initially refused to take on the role: 'I said, "No, because that's a compliance job and I don't want to spend the rest of my career doing compliance. Forget it. I don't have the patience for it".'

Note that both Lewis and Hirschmann were initially inclined to turn down the CRO role because they were worried about polluting their existing roles with 'dirty work'—tasks apparently incompatible with their claimed identities (Hughes, 1951; Morales & Lambert, 2013). While Lewis was concerned about 'a little bit of a conflict'—that is, compromising his status and independence as the company's internal auditor—Hirschmann felt that the compliance image of risk management carried less prestige than his current role.

However, realizing that they were in a position to bargain about the exact nature of the CRO's responsibilities, both men ended up defining the role for themselves. Hirschmann's story continues:

> The next day, the CFO came to my office and said, 'What would it take?' So I went to his office on the following Monday—I spent most of the previous weekend reading about risk management—and I said, 'I want risk management to be proactive. I want to run a strategic process. I want to focus on value creation more than value protection. I don't want to do compliance validation all the time.' And the CFO said, 'Yeah, go ahead'.

By embracing a focus on 'value creation' and the 'strategic process', Hirschmann was not only constructing a new organizational role, but was also engaged in 'identity work' (Morales & Lambert, 2013: 230), positioning himself as a strategic contributor rather than a compliance actor.

Hirschmann's next realization was that, at Magic Toys, many of the risk areas defined in the available ERM frameworks were already monitored and managed by specific functions. In an internal memo, he declared:

> Operational risk is handled by planning and production. Employee health and safety is OHSAS 18001 certified. Hazards are managed through explicit insurance programmes...IT security risk is a defined functional area. [The finance department] covers currencies, hedging and credit risks. And [the legal function] is actively pursuing trademark violations...Only strategic risks aren't handled explicitly or systematically.

Rather than positioning the would-be risk management function as an umbrella function for all of these risk areas, Hirschmann chose a niche—strategic risk—and called the new function strategic risk management. Hiring only two employees, he searched for meaningful opportunities and for tools that would contribute to the management of the business. The staff groups dedicated to riskwork at the two companies were decidedly small: this was possible because of the CRO's careful selection of risk tasks that did not overlap with other control functions. In other words, risk teams may be small when other areas also engage in riskwork. For example, ERM-relevant compliance work and the handling of specialist risk issues require the technical expertise of well-established staff groups (such as the finance function) or that of the business lines.

Timelines

Over time, Lewis introduced a three-phase ERM programme, consisting of *risk workshops, biannual risk updates*, and *risk-based resource allocation* that was linked to the annual planning process. Table 12.1 presents a timeline to summarize this evolution.

Initially, riskwork at Electroworks was manifest in the proliferation of risk management workshops in which participants evaluated 'risk impact', 'probability of risk occurrence', and 'control strength' (in order to get a sense of

Table 12.1. The evolution of the risk function at Electroworks

	1999–2000	2000–4	2004–2
Facilitators of riskwork	Consultants	CRO; risk team of 2 and investment-planning department	CRO; risk team of 2
Fora for risk talk	Consultants' interviews with managers	Workshops; one-to-one interviews; annual planning and resource allocation debates	Workshops; one-to-one interviews; annual planning and resource allocation debates; black swan workshops
Risk tools	Consultants' risk assessment templates	In-house risk assessment templates (for workshops and investment proposal evaluation); headline news updates for interview discussion; biannual corporate risk profile reports	As before, plus in-house template for black swan evaluation
Frequency of formal risk meetings	4 projects carried out by different consulting firms	40–50 risk workshops; biannual risk updates (interviews); annual planning (with involvement of investment-management department)	5–12 risk workshops; biannual risk updates (interviews); annual planning (investment-management department not involved); biannual CRO presentation to the full board; ad hoc black swan workshops (from 2008 on)

'residual risk'). The workshops achieved a consensus assessment on each of these dimensions by repeated and anonymous voting, with intermittent discussions, facilitated by a risk officer ('workshop facilitator'). Once the management team had assessed risks and controls, the risk officers prepared a risk map—a two-dimensional rank-ordered chart of 'residual risks'.

Twice a year, in January and July, Lewis and his team prepared a corporate risk profile report, summarizing the principal risks facing the organization, for the executive team (biannual risk updates). He also presented the report in person to the audit committee and, from 2004 onwards, to the entire board of directors.

To prepare for the final phase of the ERM process (risk-based resource allocation), the investment-planning department and the risk management team jointly developed templates for allocating resources. Engineers (challenged by the investment-planning department) had to evaluate their risk management proposals in terms of cost and the severity of the risk that their programme aimed to mitigate. They calculated a 'bang for the buck' index to show the risk reduction per dollar spent and ranked the investment programmes accordingly. By 2004, the engineering teams and top management were both sufficiently fluent in risk and cost assessments that they were able to do without the investment-planning department and it was dissolved. Yet the risk management team and the practice of risk-based resource allocation remained.

In 2008, responding to the global financial crisis and a worldwide concern with systemic risks and 'black swan' events,[8] Lewis and his team initiated so-called 'black swan workshops', a separate process to focus executives' and board members' attention on low-probability high-impact events that were not normally discussed in risk workshops and the biannual risk updates. These discussions used a new template, asking directors to consider the 'velocity of the underlying trend' and the company's perceived 'resilience' to such events. Lewis described these workshops as 'more a thought experiment than a risk workshop'. They were held on demand (but at least annually). Insights were fed back into the company's disaster recovery plans.

The timeline in Table 12.2 summarizes the evolution of the risk management processes and apparatus at Magic Toys.

Noting that Magic Toys was a project-focused organization, with each project leading to a new product release or a process improvement, Hirschmann defined risk at the project level—as 'a change which negatively impacts our ability to achieve our targets and goals with the strategies and initiatives defined'[9]—and gave managers a list of examples ('loss of consumer affinity; loss of major customer; changes in the competitive landscape; loss of integrity; major supply chain disruptions').

---

[8] A 'black swan'—a term popularized by Taleb (2007)—is an event, positive or negative, that is deemed improbable yet would have massive consequences.
[9] Internal document, 'Version 2.0 /15 March 2012'.

Table 12.2. The evolution of the risk function at Magic Toys

	2006–8	2009	2010–12
Facilitators of riskwork	CRO plus risk team of 1	CRO plus risk team of 2	CRO plus risk team of 2
Fora for risk talk	Risk and opportunity identification	Risk and opportunity identification; ad hoc scenario exercise (failed)	Risk and opportunity identification; regular scenario planning
Risk tools	Spreadsheet tool for risk and opportunity identification; biannual ERM report	Spreadsheet tool for risk and opportunity identification; biannual ERM report; scenarios (external Davos scenarios)	Spreadsheet tool for risk and opportunity identification; biannual ERM report; scenarios (internally generated)

Hirschmann's first deliverable to the Magic Toys board was a fifteen-page report on the strategic risks as assessed by the business lines, including a two-page 'bullet list and a single chart'. The report was based on a spreadsheet that Hirschmann developed for interviewing managers and collecting strategic risk information from them.

The board reports were updated biannually. In between, Hirschmann and his team introduced scenario planning, not only to help managers 'prepare for uncertainty' but also to periodically reassess the 110 risks they had collectively logged in the risk spreadsheet. After an initial trial and disappointment, a redesigned and more relevant scenario exercise took root and, by 2012, had become an integral part of the Magic Toys planning process.

RISK TALK

Lewis acknowledged that the risk assessment process at Electroworks was subjective, not 'scientific'. Yet the risk workshops were an instant and enduring success, as explained by one risk officer (the workshop facilitator):

> Our original ambitious plan was to do twelve risk assessments a year. The senior executive team embraced the approach so enthusiastically that one year we did sixty different risk assessment workshops. My role was to help executives tell their bosses about the risks they faced and how they were mitigating those risks. We helped them make judgements about the adequacy of the mitigating actions proposed and taken.

The risk team realized that, in order to make the risk assessment discussions relevant, the tools (risk assessment templates) had to be seen as relevant, too. They asked senior managers, who had accountability for a particular set of objectives (for example, financial or regulatory), to review and approve the related risk-impact scales annually. Thus, the CFO defined and reviewed the financial scale, the chief regulatory officer reviewed the regulatory scale, and so on. In the end, the resulting tool (called the 'Objectives-Impact Matrix') represented every business function's understanding of the various shades of impact that risk events posed to their objectives, in parallel with others' readings of the same impact. The tool was essentially a multi-language impact-assessment manual that everyone concerned could read from their own perspective.

The immediate contribution of the multidimensional risk assessment tool was the democratization of risk management: employees with very different backgrounds and expertise could participate in risk talk.

Having co-created, with the business lines, the language of risk assessments, Lewis also co-opted business managers in setting the agenda for the risk workshops. Prior to each workshop, Lewis's risk team informally polled participants and drew up a list of sixty to seventy potential risks or threats to the business or project being discussed. They emailed the list to the participating management team, asking them to choose the ten most critical risks facing their business or project. Based on these choices, the risk team narrowed the list down to eight to ten risks to be discussed.

In order to prepare the biannual risk updates, Lewis interviewed the top thirty to forty executives. According to Lewis, these discussions were driven by managerial concerns:

> I take the one-page strategic objectives, the news update,[10] and the summary of the previous risk assessments to all interviews, so the context is clearly set. Then I pull out the empty risk-profile template and ask what had changed, what is new. The risk assessments could change because of the mitigation steps taken, or because of external changes in the environment. Some people grab the template and start filling it out on the spot. Others will literally shut their eyes, put their feet up on the desk and tell me what is worrying them.

All three phases of ERM at Electroworks channelled risk information vertically and horizontally throughout the company, enabling executives and employees to develop a shared understanding of what risks the company faced and what had to be done about them. Indeed, by 2008, Lewis noted that the workshops had helped participants understand their own risks in the context of those faced by others:

> Magic occurs in risk workshops. People enjoy them. Some say, 'I have always worried about this topic and now I am less worried because I see that someone else is dealing with it or I have learned it is a low-probability event.' Other people

---

[10] A brief report containing headlines and summaries from the press, selected by the CRO on the basis of their relevance to risk discussions at Electroworks.

said, 'I could put forward my point and get people to agree that it is something we should be spending more time on because it is a high risk.'

By highlighting the risks to the company's diverse objectives, the Objectives-Impact Matrix also invited a kind of pluralism into risk talk by opening the door to dissonance and conflict. In the face of this pluralism, however, risk talk offered the 'talking cure' (Holt, 2004), by allowing managers to 'shut their eyes and put their feet up', and vent their worries. The 'magic' was not only an emerging organization-wide understanding about strategy and its problems, but also its conduct as a form of organizational therapy (Holt, 2004).

The constant visibility of the company's multiple, conflicting objectives also brought home to managers the need to prioritize these objectives and, if necessary, agree to trade-offs. In the annual resource-allocation meetings and in the board discussions that followed, managers were forced to agree, for example, that—for better or worse—in the next year or investment period they had to bear down on an asset-improvement objective, perhaps at the expense of environmental safety or customer service priorities. Risk talk in the resource-allocation discussions and in board meetings made such prioritizing necessary and explicit.

By now, participants were using a new vocabulary. It was a specific—yet, to them, unobtrusive—risk talk, which allowed them to voice their concerns more precisely. Lewis permitted himself a broad smile as he recalled what he considered to be his team's ultimate achievement:

> The management team got so familiar with coming to workshops and understanding what the scales were and how to vote that it just became part of their language to the extent that they started to do some of the stuff on their own and now the big thrill for me is when I go to a management meeting and they're discussing all of the ERM terminology about residual risk and mitigation…It's just great to see and they understand each other and they're really speaking a common language.

In his policy document (written for the board), Hirschmann insisted that Magic Toys' 'Strategic Risk Management (SRM) processes are defined to largely comply with the ISO 31000 standard'. He deliberately referenced the International Standards Organization as an external source of credibility that managers recognized and associated with their own standards of manufacturing excellence. Yet he departed from ISO 31000 as he was defining SRM at the project level (rather than at the enterprise level).

He also recognized that the extensive ERM vocabulary emanating from ISO 31000 was counterproductive: 'Initially, we came [to managers] with a lot of risk management jargon and got thrown out of the door. Nobody understood what we said. I learnt quickly that it's important for us risk managers—my team—that we speak the language of the business. We want to make it as simple and intuitive as possible.'

Hirschmann recruited a former project manager, Lynne Matte,[11] and set out to explain the *raison d'être* of risk management to project managers in their own language. In series of such meetings, Hirschmann and Matte jokingly agreed that 'a project is a dream with a deadline' and explained, 'Our starting point is that our task is to make you shine. Whether you fail or succeed with the project is your responsibility. But we have some tools and an approach and a process that can help you succeed, even if the world turns out to be different from what you have hoped for.'

Hirschmann and his team 'chased' project managers for risk updates twice a year, using the risk register (an Excel spreadsheet) as the channel of communication. But they also had the power to convene senior managers to discuss strategic issues and their implications for the company:

> Every now and then—that is, every time we change strategic direction—I gather people—specialist people, mostly senior, mostly directors, senior directors, and a couple of VPs—to discuss: with this strategic initiative, what do you see from your perspective? Tell me all about the risks that say, 'Okay, now we can't go to Asia, or we have to go to Asia in a different way than we thought we would'. Then I update my risk database based on that.

As Hirschmann's risk inquiries became ubiquitous, managers came to expect them and began proactively sharing risk information with the risk team. Hirschmann recalled, 'When something happens, like in the case of the Icelandic ash cloud or the tsunami in Japan, at least fifteen people emailed me to say, "Do you have this in your risk database?"'

In 2009, Hirschmann and his team, wondering what further support they could provide to the business, convened a senior managers' meeting to discuss the implications of a set of four strategic scenarios, based on the megatrends defined by the World Economic Forum in 2008 for the Davos meetings. Hirschmann's report on those discussions ended up 'in the bottom of everybody's drawer, because nobody could relate to the scenarios that we [had] done'.

Having learned from that experience, Hirschmann redesigned the scenario process to allow managers to generate scenarios based on their own worries, with the risk team providing mere suggestions for the 'dimensions of uncertainty' that managers can pick from and freely add to. He also initiated scenario discussions to explicitly support business managers in preparing their annual plans. In the scenario sessions, managers listed the issues they had to contend with under each scenario, then prioritized them according to their likelihood and their speed of emergence. The sessions never concluded without an hour-long discussion of 'act' issues: managers had to agree explicitly on who would do what by when about the fastest-emerging, most likely issues.

---

[11] Pseudonym.

Hirschmann considered the introduction of the 'fifth hour' (and the inclusion of the 'act issues' in the annual business plans) as the turning point: 'And that was it. That final discussion makes sure that the "act issues" are actually acted upon. It was a hint given to us from two members of our [top management]. Then it just became part of the business planning process.'

In 2013, scenario planning became part of the Magic Toys business-planning process. Twenty-three scenario sessions were held that year, involving 19 top managers and over 200 other employees and affecting 21 three-year business plans. The heads of three business areas chose to deploy scenario planning upfront, as an 'inspiration' to their regular planning process, while the others held these sessions *ex post*, as a form of 'resilience testing'. Hirschmann reported that the scenario-planning sessions helped the managers collectively identify 136 'act issues' and 80 'prepare issues', which resulted in adjustments to the 'Must-Win Battles' and 'How to Win' sections of the 21 business plans.

Scenario planning, linked to the business-planning process, channelled risk information vertically and horizontally throughout the company, enabling executives and employees to develop a shared understanding of what risks the company faced and what had to be done when and by whom. As in Electroworks, risk talk also allowed a form of organizational therapy: 'without aspirations to control activity, but with aspirations to provoke insight' (Holt, 2004: 266) into the uncertainties being faced, the scenario sessions allowed managers to express and discuss their worst fears, as happened in the session I observed when a senior director raised the issue of the uncertainty of demand projections in a new market:

> We are about to invest billions...in infrastructure over there. And we want to keep all our manufacturing in-house. What if we're to invest in all this and then we just have the same market [demand] that we have today? It just wouldn't pay for us. As a company, I would say we're much better at scaling up than scaling down.

This insight then generated a reflexive debate about an organizational weakness, eventually leading to suggestions as to how to counter it.

It is noteworthy that a key condition for risk talk to become seemingly inevitable at both companies was its linkage to the planning process. This can be attributed to the way both CROs initially defined their own jobs and bargained for the ability to take part in, set the tone of, and shape strategic discussions.

CONFIDENCE

Lacking the formal qualifications and domain expertise with which to engage Electroworks engineers at risk assessment workshops and resource-allocation meetings, Lewis and his team acted as facilitators. But they did their homework in response to the board's request for an ERM process; they spent four months 'reading everything we could about it: publications by the Conference Board of Canada, by Tillinghast Towers Perrin, the Australian Standard 4360,[12] articles and many books'. In the end, Lewis decided to 'do it [his] own way':

> There has been a lot of bad literature, a lot of bad consultants; a lot of people were going down the wrong road. [ERM consultants] would charge us [a fortune] to do something they probably did the week before for some other company. In the end, I concluded ERM can be so simple and so logical were it not for the many people who seek to complicate it.

His espoused practice of ERM required three people ('three personality types'):

> The first one is someone to make it happen. That's me. Okay, somebody who will push down doors, is driven, and has the credibility and authority to open doors and make it happen. The second is a nice, charismatic personality who people enjoy working with. And that was [the workshop facilitator], an absolute charmer. A super-nice guy, good-looking, charming, very knowledgeable, who became a very good [workshop] facilitator. The third one is a person with an analytical mind who can manage the vast quantities of data [collected at the workshops]. You don't find those characteristics in the same person, so I teamed them together.

He consciously departed from conventional wisdom by deciding to 'just start running workshops':

> The theory says go on, train and educate people on ERM by going and giving presentations. My answer to this was, No, no, no, you have to run workshops; that's the way you get others involved, engaged, and that's how they learn, not by sitting through a PowerPoint.

By 2003, ERM at Electroworks was sufficiently established that Lewis could judge it a success and confidently enter the wider ERM discourse by publishing articles and book chapters on his company's ERM practice. Publicizing his approach to ERM was part of his campaign against 'people who seek to complicate' ERM, but it also reassured the company's management team and board of directors that 'we were ahead of the game and our regulator was so impressed with [our ERM] that they are going to take and mandate it for everyone else [in the industry] to do it this way'.

Having examined several software packages and attended consultants' presentations on risk databases, Hirschmann concluded that 'finding the right one [for Magic Toys] was rather difficult'. He ended up developing his own Excel spreadsheet ('I've used Excel since 1984, I know how to do it'), which was

---

[12] Standards Australia (2004).

maintained and updated by one of his team members, based on written or spoken input from 'risk owners'.

Hirschmann continuously wheedled and cajoled business managers to send updates on risks and actions. He never used fiat and never referenced the ERM policy documents; he appeared permissive and lenient but at the same time, the downside consequences of not responding were implicit in his communications. He described one instance when a late response cost a manager holiday time to catch up with his risk reporting:

> I told him [the risk owner]: 'I need to know what you're doing'. He said, 'Sure, how do we do this most easily?' I say, 'Most easily, I've sent you the risk and I've sent you the template I'm using for updating mitigations. Who is doing what and why do we think it works? It's a questionnaire.' And he said, 'Okay. When do you need it by?' I say, 'Well, I can get the report out two or three days after you're done, so you decide.' The day before Christmas, he said, 'I didn't get to do it yet. Is it okay if I do it after Christmas?' I said, 'Sure, but we have to send the report to the board by [early January], and that would be demonstrating that you are not in control of something we think you are controlling so...' After Christmas, he admitted that he spent three hours filling in templates in his holiday, to give me that feedback by January, so we can have it in the updated report.

Hirschmann made it clear to everyone that his responsibility was the design and facilitation of the SRM process—not more, not less. He pushed back on a request for quarterly risk reports from a board member on the grounds that 'ours is a seasonal business. We have half the turnover the last ten weeks of Christmas, the majority of the rest around Easter. It doesn't make sense to make a first and third quarter report.' When the same board member insisted on quarterly reporting, Hirschmann stood his ground and persuaded the CEO that it would be 'a waste of time'. The board member yielded.

Having facilitated the preparation of the biannual risk report, the risk team did not remain entirely silent. In the report, there was a section devoted to 'what the Strategic Risk Management Office believes'. Here Hirschmann could be explicit and challenging:

> In the latest report I just sent out in June [2013], I put in the comments that this year may be the first one since 2005 that we will not meet our targets. I had the CFO on the phone as soon as he saw the draft, telling me, 'Our target is 11% sales growth. That number is not in jeopardy.' And I said, 'Sorry, John, I don't agree. It is in jeopardy. I didn't say we won't make our targets. I said we may not make our targets. In fact, I think it's in serious, severe jeopardy. We are growing, but year-to-date, we had an 8% growth on consumer sales, and you want to make it 11% by high season? That's not a done deal. By no way.' He still disagreed with me, but allowed me to send it to the board. Next, I had the VP-marketing on the phone. I had to explain that I ran my Monte Carlo simulation on our budgeted and year-to-date figures and what that means to them: 'Guys, you are getting late for the party, but yet you are still cruising at 40 mph on the highway. Why not take more

risks, speed up to the 70 you are allowed to drive, if that will more likely take you to the party in time.'

Over the years, Hirschmann formulated a view of risk management that emphasized its enabling rather than its constraining aspect. He put this in writing in a series of papers and book chapters co-authored with a business-school academic. Contradicting the corporate-governance advocates and guidelines that considered risk management as a 'line of defence' in the internal control landscape, Hirschmann emphasized that the role of the risk management function was to support—rather than control—managers:

> I think one of the places where the traditional risk managers in other companies have problems is that they emerged—they come from a control environment, internal audit or something like that. That means that when they walk in the door, you see them as internal audit coming and checking you up. We do not come from that part of the business. We've never been into that. Actually, until a couple of years ago, we never had an internal audit function. But we're coming with a license to ask questions that help them succeed. Because, well, SRM may be a part of controlling, but it's actually a part of supporting.

HUMILITY AND FRUGALITY

While Lewis's risk team remained small, as per his original vision (one person providing authority, one workshop facilitator, and one data manager), it influenced much of the organization though workshops, the annual planning, and the biannual updates. Lewis and his team were quick to acknowledge that despite their perceived successes, their full vision for ERM had not been accomplished and perhaps never would be. Lewis summarized his 'theoretical dream' as the 'risk dashboard': a software-enabled, computerized version of his risk reports, accessible anytime by any senior manager, providing up-to-date and fast graphic displays of all risk information, summarized into colourful risk maps and top-10 risk lists, with drill-down capability into individual items. But Lewis was conscious that Electroworks did not have the 'systems', skill set, or 'culture' to implement such a model.

   Upon Lewis's retirement in 2012, Electroworks did not recruit a new CRO. The previous workshop facilitator, Larry White,[13] became director of ERM (and no longer reported directly to the CEO, but to the treasurer). Unlike many ERM advocates, White did not perceive this seeming demotion of the risk function as a weakness:

----

[13] Pseudonym.

Lots of consultants, lots of people speak at conferences about the importance of a top-down-driven risk function, supported by the CEO. I think that's actually a vulnerability. You cannot do ERM by fiat. I do not need the CEO to say to our guys, 'Every six months you must do a risk workshop with [White] and I want to see the report'. But a good way for the CEO to support ERM is in the way she asks questions. Ours would say [to the business manager]: 'Okay, I've got your plan. How could this go wrong? What are your risks? You're not sure? Well, you know, there is this guy over here—Larry White—who can help you figure it out. Why don't you go and see him, because he'll help you figure that out. Then you can come back to me and we can make this decision.' So risk management gets pulled into the business because there is a vacuum to fill, as opposed to me imposing myself—or somebody on my behalf imposing me—on them.

At Electroworks, the risk function's span of control (in terms of resources, decision rights, and formal authority) remained narrow and even shrank over time. However, the willingness of the CEO and the business lines to participate in risk talk made up for that. Bringing about that wide span of support via the proliferation of a practical, business-relevant risk process and vocabulary was the risk team's key achievement.

At Magic Toys, Hirschmann faced a number of debacles as he built his own risk management tools and processes. He noted that 'the first couple of databases didn't work, the third one did'. This trial-and-error approach characterized the development of the scenario process, too. After the initial disappointment, Hirschmann was ready to admit to senior managers that the exercise had failed due to the lack of any 'follow-through or action'. Despite this acknowledgement, one of the senior managers expressed support, which catalysed further development of the tool:

> In early 2011, I got to talk by coincidence with [a senior manager] over a cup of coffee and we got to talk about these scenarios and he said, 'You really have something good about this scenario discussion—quite great. Why didn't it work?' I said, 'I really don't know. I understood it didn't work and I accept that it didn't work, but I really don't know why.' He said, 'Try to figure it out. See if we can make it work.' And I went back with that and said to myself over and over, 'Okay, why didn't it work?' and contemplated why it didn't work and eventually, I found out where the flaw was: the ownership of the scenarios.

From then on, Hirschmann and his team insisted that in the risk discussions, whatever tool was used to channel them, managers had to 'keep their thunder'. He explained:

> Managers hate to be told what to do...and the higher the organizational level, the more the resentment. So by letting them run the show and by limiting scenario planning to a half-day workshop for each team, we got the proverbial foot in the door.

The risk team also made it clear that their role was merely facilitating, not advising. Lynne Matte, who was a former project manager, had to fight her natural inclination to become more directive: 'As a risk manager, you should never take over [the discussion]. Even if you know the solution, keep your mouth shut.' Hirschmann added: 'It's their decision, it's their perception, it's their risk. If I started to advise or correct them, I would start owning the stuff and I can't do that.'

Hirschmann saw risk management as 'common sense' and emphasized 'understanding the business and the industry'. He was careful not to take any credit for the business's successes. Noting that Magic Toys did eventually exceed its 2013 sales targets, he concluded:

> There is a benefit to knowing whether you are taking the right amount of risk. You need to be able to take chances, but you need to know how many chances you can take. We grew 25 per cent last year. I can't take the credit for that, but I pushed the ball. I told every manager who was willing to listen that we found that we were not taking enough risk. In the end, we were able to shift product sales and suddenly we were the winners because we had the products and we got more shelf space. We more than doubled our shelf space at Walmart. And with 200 million people through the stores every week, that matters. I am not part of corporate management [top management] and I cannot take credit for any of this. Risk management is a very, very small part of the success we've had.

Despite his humble rhetoric of simplicity and common sense, Hirschmann created a risk function that had the ears of the board and senior management. This remained the case even when a reorganization left the CRO with a reporting line to the treasurer (who then reported to the CFO). Though formally the CRO was four steps removed from the board of directors, by 2013 he had established a process that shaped the discussion of every business plan and the biannual board meetings.

Hirschmann commented that his careful positioning of the role provided him with seemingly frugal resources and a team of only two. In fact, in both companies, it seems that the risk teams were small not so much out of humility, but because other areas (internal audit, other staff functions, and the front lines) did some of the work, such as compliance, that the risk team might have done in other companies.

Despite the frugality of resources (or perhaps *because* of it), both teams enjoyed a wide span of support, which Hirschmann described as follows:

> I get all the support and all the time I need. If I want to go on training or to a conference, I get the funding. I have all the resources I need. I have the right to focus on strategic risks only. I don't do insurance. I don't do vendor risk management or anything like that. Other people are doing that.

Hirschmann also built an invaluable relationship with the fourth-generation owner of the family-held firm, who had just been appointed to the Magic Toys board:

> I benefit from the fact that I know the guy since he wore diapers, literally. He's a young guy, he's 32, he is just coming in and he wants to be a good owner and a good part of the board of directors. And he sees a risk-management approach as the best way he can add value to the board of directors because…it gives him a point of entry to say, 'Okay, what about this? What about that?' Then he can add positively to the discussion.

By mentoring the young owner, Hirschmann added another layer of significance to his role. He was becoming influential in the manner of the *éminences grises* of a bygone era, operating behind the scenes in an unofficial capacity of his own making.

DISCUSSION AND CONCLUSION

This chapter tracked the evolution of the role of two CROs and the tools and processes they implemented. While their companies are in very different industries (one is a power company, the other is a toy manufacturer), both embraced the concepts and tools of ERM. Over a number of years, risk management in both firms evolved from a collection of 'off-the-shelf', acquired tools and practices into a tailored and seemingly inevitable control process. The chapter investigated the CRO's role in bringing about these transformations.

The CRO at Electroworks, by facilitating continuous risk talk in workshops and face-to-face meetings over a period of ten years, orchestrated the creation and proliferation of a new language for the business (that of risk management) and established processes that regularly convened business people from diverse places and hierarchical levels to discuss issues of concern. At first, the value—and even the validity—of risk talk was far from self-evident to the business managers. It took a long time to become manifest in, for example, assessments on a scale of 1 to 5 of 'impact and likelihood of risk' and formally documented in risk maps and 'lists of top-10 risks'. The contribution of the CRO and his small team was to co-opt the business in the creation and use of risk talk. By merely providing a few rudimentary concepts and a minimal risk vocabulary, the CRO was able to get business people to fill in gaps in meaning. He was also able to get business people to add the rules of use. For example, he would delegate the definition of '1–5 impact scales' to those business managers able to make sense and use of them. The final test of the acceptance of risk talk was its formal linking to resource allocation in the annual budgeting process, which gave risk management permanence, significance, and an air of inevitability.

The second case, seemingly quite different, focused on a CRO who initially tried but failed to create significant and permanent linkages between a conventional ERM tool (a risk database) and the business lines. After a period of search, he settled on a less conventional risk-identification tool—scenario planning—and facilitated its transformation, over a period of five years, from an ad hoc future-gazing exercise to widely accepted risk talk that had become a seemingly self-evident element of the annual business planning process.

We see that the role of the CRO may have less to do with packaging risk management tools and marketing them to business managers than with facilitating the creation and internalization of a specific type of risk talk as a legitimate, cross-functional language of business. The risk management function may be most successful when it resists conventional and conflicting demands to be either close to or independent of business managers. Instead, by acting as a facilitator of risk talk, the CRO can enable the real work of risk management to take place not in the risk management function, but in the business lines.

In both companies, facilitation required considerable humility of the CRO, manifest in limited (and even decreasing) formal authority and meagre resources. Their skill was to build an informal network of relationships with executives and business managers, which allowed them to resist being stereotyped as either compliance champions or business partners. Instead, they created and shaped the perception of a role which was of their own making: neither reactive, nor proactive, it was a reflexive practice and a careful balancing act between keeping one's distance and staying involved.

This analysis suggests that calls for increasing investments in risk management and for the formal inclusion of senior risk officers in the C-suite might be misguided. In order to close the expectations gap, risk managers need first and foremost to secure a commitment from others in the organization to accept a relevant and situationally contingent version of risk management, tailored to their needs.

Another challenge for managers and practitioners is to engage with regulators and corporate-governance advocates in the spirit of a 'new politics of uncertainty'—questioning 'standardized models' of risk management, and distancing themselves from 'an industry of managerial and auditor certifications, and...layers of pseudo-comfort about risk' (Power, 2007: 201). Thus risk management would become a mechanism for envisioning or simply venting future fears, paving the way towards more dialogue, experimentation, and learning.

The key to the humble CRO's success is therefore not so much the ability to go beyond the compliance role or to turn into a business partner, but the ability to bring about consequential risk talk where it matters—in the business lines, helping those who carry out the real work of risk management.

REFERENCES

Accenture (2013). *Accenture 2013 Global Risk Management Study: Risk Management for an Era of Greater Uncertainty*. London: Accenture.
Beasley, M., Branson, B., & Hancock, B. (2010). *Report on the Current State of Enterprise Risk Oversight*. AICPA and North Carolina State University.
Committee of Sponsoring Organizations of the Treadway Commission (COSO) (2004). *Enterprise Risk Management Framework*. New York: American Institute of Certified Public Accountants.
Deloitte (2013). *Global Risk Management Survey, Eighth Edition: Setting a Higher Bar*. London: Deloitte.
Economist Intelligence Unit Limited (2010). *Risk Management in the Front Line*. London: EIU.
Holt, R. (2004). Risk Management: The Talking Cure. *Organization*, 11, 251–70.
Hughes, E. C. (1951). Mistakes at Work. *Canadian Journal of Economics and Political Science*, 17(3), 320–7.
International Standards Organization (ISO) (2009). *ISO 31000:2009, Risk Management—Principles and Guidelines*. Geneva: International Standards Organization.
KPMG (2011). *Risk Management: A Driver of Enterprise Value in the Emerging Environment*. London: KPMG.
KPMG (2013). *Expectations of Risk Management Outpacing Capabilities—It's Time for Action*. London: KPMG.
Morales, J. & Lambert, C. (2013). Dirty Work and the Construction of Identity. An Ethnographic Study of Management Accounting Practices. *Accounting, Organizations and Society*, 38, 228–44.
Power, M. (2007). *Organized Uncertainty—Designing a World of Risk Management*. Oxford: Oxford University Press.
RIMS & Advisen (2013). *2013 RIMS Enterprise Risk Management (ERM) Survey*. London: RIMS.
Standards Australia (2004). *AS/NZS 4360:2004 Risk Management*, 3rd edition. Sydney: Standards Australia Publications.
Taleb, N. (2007). *The Black Swan: The Impact of the Highly Improbable*. London: Allen Lane.

Postscript

On Riskwork and Auditwork

Michael Power

The different contributions to this volume show how the everyday management of risk in organizations is entangled with processes of representation. Demortain (Chapter 1) begins the collection by analysing the conscious efforts of a diverse group of experts to build an abstract representation of the risk management process. It became a standard which has been widely diffused and hugely influential. Jørgensen and Jordan (Chapter 2), Hall and Fernando (Chapter 3), and Boholm and Corvellec (Chapter 5) all provide detailed accounts from the field about how risk maps and related devices, such as registers and risk indicators, are created and used by different organizational actors. The non-executive directors in Zhivitskaya and Power's (Chapter 4) exploration of risk oversight are concerned in part about how their role in challenging executives might be represented in committee minutes, which the regulator will read and use to evaluate them. The two CROs in Mikes' (Chapter 12) account of their strategies for improving risk management utilize devices for representing risks in workshops, even though their overall strategy is more interactive and conversational. Vargha (Chapter 8) studies how the 'attitude to risk' of consumers of financial products is itself produced, how advisers use different technologies of representation to capture and construct such attitudes, and how these representations contribute to the formation of client identities as rational consumers of financial products. Maguire and Hardy's (Chapter 6) account of the discursive work in the regulation of the Canadian chemicals industry implicates different models for representing and measuring hazard and exposure. Both Labelle and Rouleau (Chapter 10), and Fischer and McGivern (Chapter 11), detail the effects of accountability requirements on the representation of clinical risk. And Palermo (Chapter 7) focuses centrally on the cultural significance of a reporting system for capturing and representing safety-relevant data.

So, in broad terms, the chapters in this book collectively suggest that when we examine the organizational life of risk management at the level of specific practices, we find that risk and representation are intertwined. In managing risk, organizational actors are constantly engaged in the work of representing it.

From a philosophical point of view, this comingling of risk and representation is readily understandable and even unsurprising. Risks are contingencies or future possibilities which have not yet crystallized into events. As non-real possibilities, they literally do not exist and cannot be seen until they are represented and processed in apparatuses for their management (Power, 2013, 2014). When a disaster happens, it is no longer a risk. It has crystallized as an event. The event may be a sign of other possible future events, and may create new risks, but the event as an actuality is no longer a risk strictly speaking. On this view the unreality of risk in the future can only be made real and actionable in the present by being somehow captured and represented. Risks must be inscribed in models, maps, and in metrics.

This philosophical necessity of the representation of risk in risk management has a sociological correlate. When we look closely at risk management in the field as the different authors have done in the preceding chapters, we see that practices are littered with *artefacts*, many of which contain and inscribe representations of risk. What anthropologists have always known, and is at the heart of the 'material turn' in organization studies, is that artefacts of different kinds play a key role in shaping practices (see Carlile et al., 2013; Orlikowski & Scott, 2008). For example, documents and records like risk maps are known to be important artefactual mechanisms through which agents contribute to, and sustain, organizational structure and enable organizations to perpetuate themselves through time. All the contributions to *Riskwork* suggest how the empirical study of risk management as it happens requires research analysts to pay close attention to the variety of artefacts for representing risk and their effects on human actors. As Jørgensen and Jordan demonstrate in their chapter, risk maps are not neutral mirrors of risk; they are not passive 'intermediaries' of risk information in Latour's sense (2005). They must be studied as potentially powerful 'mediators' and actors in their own right whose non-human agency shapes organizational and individual attention to risk.

Building on the centrality of artefacts for representing risk, this postscript to the volume poses a number of questions that might inform a future programme of research. In what ways are the artefacts for representing risk connected to other organizational artefacts? How, if at all, do they connect to wider organizational infrastructures of accountability and performance management, and what are the effects of these connections? Elsewhere (Power, 2007) I have suggested that risk management has become a dominant 'language' of account-giving and recent developments in corporate governance in the United Kingdom have done nothing to weaken this claim (see FRC, 2014). Others have argued that risk management protocols are transformed within climates of blame and heightened accountability (Hood, 2011) which create 'timid' organizations (Hunt, 2003). In such settings organizational actors seem always to be managing two risks—both the so-called real or 'first-order' risk and also the 'second-order' or *institutional risk* of being blamed, both individually and organizationally (see Pidgeon et al., 2003; Rothstein et al., 2007).

Yet making a distinction between first- and second-order risks to characterize this phenomenon is itself problematic. Reputational risk, which we might ordinarily label as a second-order risk, has in fact become a primary preoccupation of many organizations in recent years (Power et al., 2009). Furthermore, institutional theories teach us that organizations routinely seek to acquire and maintain institutional legitimacy, so that so-called 'secondary' risk management or blame avoidance is hardly exceptional. However, if the primary–secondary distinction is rather tired, it is nevertheless important to remember why it was appealing in the first place, namely because it provided a simple characterization of an organizational environment in which the management of institutional legitimacy was becoming more explicit and self-conscious. The distinction, for all its imperfections, reminds us that the management of risk is entangled with institutional frameworks which pose their own risks to individuals and organizations (Rothstein et al., 2007). Indeed, it also reminds us, as does Demortain (Chapter 1), that risk management frameworks are institutional norms which demand conformity.

This neo-institutionalist agenda within risk management has been, and continues to be, rich and promising. However, it has tended to be unspecific about the mechanisms of this entanglement at the level of work processes and their dynamics. One way to have a better grasp of these dynamics is to pay more systematic empirical attention to the arrangements of organizational artefacts, namely the infrastructure for representing and organizing the work of risk.

As noted in the introduction, this volume makes a modest contribution to the broader so-called 'turn to work' which is evident in organizational studies in general. The twelve preceding chapters have all in different ways focused on the work context of risk management, on the many struggles and activities conducted in the name of risk. But within these efforts in each chapter another systematic theme has also become visible, albeit in an undeveloped way, namely 'an artefactual turn' with an emphasis on material devices for the representation of risk and their wider function in networks of *accountability*. To develop this theme a little further we need the assistance of routines theory.

ROUTINES AND ARTEFACTS

In recent years scholars have paid increasing attention to the internal structure of routines, positioning them as more dynamic in nature than static concepts of habituated action suggest (Feldman, 2000; Feldman & Pentland, 2003). For example, Pentland and Feldman (2005) analyse the internal dynamics of routines into two moving parts. Any routine is animated by an abstract understanding of how it should work and its purpose. They call this the *ostensive* dimension, an example of which would be a standard operating protocol. This is distinct from the specific, local *performance* of the routine by organizational agents. Feldman (2000) argues that these two components interact dynamically in sequences whereby organizational plans are realized in specific actions which lead to outcomes, a refinement of ideals and back to plans again. This loop characterizes a continuous feedback process—akin to micro-structuration—between formal and enacted knowledge.

However, there is also a third important element of organizational routines, namely artefacts: 'Artefacts such as work logs and databases can...provide a convenient archival trace of the performance aspect...keep track of work processes, [and] may be used as indicators of performances' (Pentland & Feldman, 2005: 796–803). D'Adderio (2011) extends this line of reasoning even further by arguing that the artefactual dimension of routines is not simply a neutral mirror of a routine and is not merely a substitute for imperfect human memory. Rather artefacts are also mediators in Latour's (2005) sense mentioned above. They play a key role in constituting the meaning and conduct of the routine itself. Artefacts embody the 'habits, intentions, and rationales held by the agencies by which they have been created' (D'Adderio, 2011) and will shape the way organizational agents enact routines. These artefacts are 'entangled in a thick web of organizational relationships' (D'Adderio, 2011: 215) which may constitute a distinctive 'socio-technical agencement' in its own right.

These studies of organizational routines and of the central role played by artefacts are highly suggestive of how we might think about, and approach, the analysis of risk management practice. From a positivistic and somewhat normative point of view, we may be naturally inclined to ask what the risks facing an organization are, and whether it manages them well or badly. This is of course a very sensible preoccupation for scholars and practitioners alike and is not to be derided. But the turn to artefacts suggests a different analytical agenda which might loosely be labelled constructivist.[1] It can be defined in terms of the following indicative questions: what is the infrastructure of artefacts through which risk is routinely identified, communicated and acted on? How do these artefacts have agency in shaping both the risks which

---

[1] It could be argued that this constructivist agenda can contribute normatively to 'better' risk management practice, allowing practitioners to reflect on their systems of representation of risk. This potential contribution is variously termed 'reflexivity' or 'double-loop learning'. In my experiences of eleven years as a director of financial services firms in the United Kingdom I have observed, albeit anecdotally, that senior practitioners tend to be natural constructivists rather than naive positivists as they are often portrayed.

routinely get attention and the form of that attention? How do these artefacts connect to systems of individual and organizational account giving? Put simply, these questions imply that a great deal of riskwork is done by non-human actors—the artefacts of risk management.

This research agenda for risk management does not necessitate the abandonment of a functionalist frame of analysis for artefacts such as risk protocols, but it requires that this functionality be 'bracketed' for the purpose of analysis. After all, as Gawande's (2010) celebration of the checklist as the embodiment of accumulated knowledge and expertise argues, real lives are saved by pilots and surgeons using well-designed checklists. In these cases the artefact of the checklist is close in space and time to those making decisions and performing actions to manage flight safety and surgical risk respectively. Following the checklist mitigates the risk of human error, imperfect memory, and unnecessary variation in the performance of a critical task and its consequences for life. Nothing could be more real or more positively functional for practical outcomes as this mundane artefact. This is the persuasive power of Gawande's thesis.

And yet even in this worthy example, the checklist is a more complex artefact than it first appears. First the form of the checklist often has a distinct forensic history, usually emerging from post-accident investigations and analyses. Second, the checklist as artefact may not have an organizational life solely for the benefit of *in situ* pilots and surgeons. It may persist as a record of what was done and be checked by others to determine compliance with good practice or, indeed, as part of an investigation. In short, the checklist may exist in a *system of linked artefacts* which make the actions of the pilot and surgeon visible and accountable to others—hospital and airport managers, investigators, regulators, and so on. In short, it is part of an *audit trail*.

If risk is only known through its representations in artefacts like checklists and risk maps, the distinction between primary and secondary or institutional risk outlined earlier must now be recast as one between different kinds of artefactual representation of risk, which may themselves only vary by degree as I suggest further below. On the one hand, there seem to be artefacts like Gawande's checklists which are directly *performative* in the management of risk. In Pentland and Feldman's terms these artefacts embody a clear ostensive purpose which trained operatives are highly motivated to enact—they are constitutive of standard operating procedure. On the other hand, there seems to be a class of artefacts which are systematically organized to build up *accounts* of performance or permit *forensic* ex post investigation of performance. These artefacts have a different organizational trajectory from the first kind; they can move very far from the routines with which they are associated and become aggregated as performance representations which are stored and subject to further analysis.

Although such a distinction between two classes of artefact is theoretically plausible, the empirical difficulty is that, as we see even in the case of checklists, an artefact may often have *both* performative and forensic aspects to varying degrees. Many artefacts sit at the boundary between the management of the risk and systems for performance accountability and this mingling of what we might call their performative and forensic aspects generates further critical questions, such as: under what conditions do organizational actors pay more attention to the forensic role of risk management artefacts than to those which are performative? What might be the consequences of such a shift? Could these consequences, understood broadly as the risk of accountability crowding performativity, themselves be represented within the risk management system?

If these and related questions make sense, they suggest a programme of empirical study in risk management which builds on the insights of routines theory. A first step would be to map the 'system of artefacts' which constitutes risk management.

MAPPING ARTEFACTS IN RISK MANAGEMENT

To be clear about the argument so far, it is not being denied that risks are real in the sense that when they crystallize bad things happen and there are real effects. As Mary Douglas said of her own cultural theory of risk: 'the argument is not about the reality of dangers; but about how they are politicized' (Douglas, 1992: 29). In terms of the present argument, we might substitute the word 'represented' for 'politicized' with the same intent. And for this reason the risk representations which direct organizational attention and decision making can, and often do, end up being inadequate. There is a reality which eludes and disappoints our efforts to represent it and these failures set in motion a search for new and better ways of representing risk.

Take the example of the *systemic* risk of the financial system. While the danger existed and was conceptualized as a risk prior to the financial crisis, the dominant representation was in in terms of the financial strength of individual banks. A huge amount of costly activity—*riskwork*—was focused on the production of solvency representations and related capital issues at the level of the *individual* firm with the implied assumption that if the sum of financial organizations were individually sound, then the system was sound (Haldane, 2009). But the interconnectivity risk associated with the wholesale inter-bank market was much less prominent and was poorly represented, leading one senior practitioner to describe the financial crisis as an 'intellectual failure' (Turner, 2009). So, following the height of the financial crisis a great deal of effort has been undertaken to correct this failure and to represent bank interconnectedness and its associated risks, involving new kinds of models and analysis.

Whether systemic risk is 'real' or not is a question of interest only from a certain philosophical point of view. What is of more interest is how the danger of systemic collapse has a history (Özgöde, 2011) in which it has transitioned from one system of representation to another, with a corresponding change in the riskwork and associated systems of artefacts. In Hilgartner's (1992) terms, we could say that the risk object of systemic risk always existed in some sense, but it has now been 'emplaced' in a new sociotechnical network for representing and intervening in it. As analysts, we should not rush to judge whether this is an improvement or not, although as citizens and taxpayers we rather hope so. Instead, we can usefully document the new contours of systemic risk management in terms of changes in the system of artefacts for its representation and control, and thereby understand more about the dynamics relating actions in the name of risk management and their modes of representation.

The 'system of artefacts' perspective on risk management being proposed is as much methodological as substantive. It requires a close analysis of specific artefacts, the routines that they constitute and their connectivity with other artefacts and routines. Connections may arise because of the 'movement' of an artefact itself, or by some kind of transfer, manually or digitally, of the traces of performance contained in the artefact. Thus, checklists can be stored or transferred for possible inspection, or the data they contain—if any—can be summated and transferred to another artefact.

More generally, the system of artefacts approach recognizes that organizational actors who engage in the routine management of risks are also producing artefacts whose trajectory constitutes the 'regulated life' of an organization. Human actors may or may not be fully cognizant that what they are doing will become a performance representation to be evaluated by others inside or outside the organization. Their riskwork may leave a trace in an artefact which may in turn be integrated with other similar traces, and which allows that riskwork to be checked. To put it another way, such traces may make the work of risk management *auditable*; riskwork at the granular level may therefore often implicate *auditwork*.

Yet how strong is the influence of this so-called logic of auditability, instantiated in a connected system of artefacts, on the routine actions that make up risk management, and what might be its effects? This is a matter for further empirical enquiry. In mapping the artefacts involved in risk management, we would need to look at the strength and shape of such connections. Gawande's checklists may in fact only be very loosely coupled to wider forensic processes in the organization; they exist to be used *in situ* to guide action rather than to collect traces of action. In other words, they have strong local performativity but are weakly connected to artefacts within the accountability system. In contrast, a divisional risk register may be tightly coupled to artefacts in an organizational-wide performance management system and exist to gather data for comparative analysis and evaluation.

ANALYSING AUDITWORK WITHIN RISKWORK

Does the tail of accountability and possible blame wag the dog of risk management? Are organizational agents excessively focused on managing the risk to themselves and their reputations, constructing defendable audit trails which may actually increase overall risk? There is a general awareness of this issue by both scholars and by those who work in regulation and risk management. However, borrowing the 'artefactual turn' from routines theory encourages scholars to move beyond general assertions of 'blame avoidance', 'reputation management', or 'legitimation strategies' in characterizing the side effects of accountability for risk management. This perspective strengthens the analytical and empirical focus on how artefacts are active in shaping both attention and action in the risk management space. In concluding this post-script and the volume as a whole, such an 'artefactual turn' within risk studies anticipates a potential empirical programme focused on the dynamics of what I call 'auditwork' within riskwork. The spirit of this potential programme is suggested by the following five thematic points of inquiry:

1 *Sequence*: do the representations of risk in artefacts primarily *precede* the performance of risk management actions or do they exist to record actions which have happened?

2 *Allocation of time*: how much time do organizational actors spend in performing the management of risk actions as compared to producing representations of those actions?

3 *Editing*: are the representations of risk management actions significantly edited *after* those actions have been taken?

4 *Storage*: are the artefacts for representing risks immediately discarded after their use to orient action or are they stored for accountability purposes?

5 *Standardization*: are artefacts for guiding risk management standardized to make operating protocols easy to understand by actors or primarily to enable collation and aggregation and connection to other artefacts?

The answers to these questions in specific empirical settings may not always be clear-cut, and the questions themselves are far from perfect and need refine-ment and development. But they help to define a space of investigation bounded by two ideal typical configurations of artefacts. The first ideal type corresponds closely to Gawande's checklist: the artefact precedes the risk management action; the actors are engaged 100 per cent in performing actions guided by the checklist; they do not edit the checklist in use; the checklist may be immediately discarded after use or it may be retained for future local use only; it is standardized for cognitive reasons but not for collation and performance representation purposes.

The second ideal type speaks to the concerns of many risk management commentators about the so-called 'risks of risk management'. It provides further structure to critical constructs such as 'risk listing' (Boholm & Corvellec, Chapter 5), 'box-ticking' and 'secondary' risk management. In terms of the simple list of artefact-oriented questions, this pathology can be characterized in the following way: representations of risk are only loosely related to actions and are largely ex post and historic; their construction consumes operator time; they are subject to continuous editing; they are stored for possible later inspection; they are standardized in a way which permits collation and aggregation. In this ideal type, we might say that this 'auditwork' 'crowds' the riskwork. Furthermore, in the forensic world of this ideal type, the surgeon's or pilot's *use* of a checklist does not exist in an institutional sense unless a trace is left behind which can be checked by others.

Building on these ideal types, we can begin to imagine a dynamic process relating them to each other, and how there might be a change in organizational risk management practices which reflects a drift from the first to the second ideal type. In such a case, we would expect to see that the work of representing risk management becomes a specialized activity itself. Organizational actors imagine they are managing risk but over time their work consists in managing the multiple representations of risk. In short, risk management becomes increasingly constituted by a logic of auditability (Power, 2007) which values storable traces of actions and legal ideals of precision in the representation of actions. If this dynamic or something like it exists, it is hardly a surprise that we are disappointed from time to time.

Equally, a dynamic in which the second ideal type dominates is neither inevitable nor ubiquitous, as Gawande's study of checklists suggests. The actors depicted in the various chapters of this volume are all working hard to resist this second ideal type, sometimes consciously sometimes implicitly. They are both engaged in the effortful work of managing risk and also in efforts to keep auditwork somehow in its place. Yet, they inevitably inhabit an organizational world of representations, of artefacts. There is no risk management without artefacts but, as suggested above, artefacts may be more or less connected to wider systems of accountability. For example, the risk map is both an artefact which enables project communication about risk and also something which solidifies into an accounting artefact in an accounting system. We may wish to peel away the pure riskwork from the polluting effect of accountability systems but, as long as risk is mediated by artefactual representations of it, this is likely to be impossible.

Finally, an essential tension between action and representation exists at the heart of all organizational routines. It gives them their dynamic properties and this is especially true for the routines that constitute risk management practices. Situated human actors navigate the so-called 'risks of risk management' posed by a world of artefacts and as analysts we have an opportunity to observe their skill and effort, sometimes resisting and sometimes succumbing to a logic of auditability which can be pervasive and powerful. While this volume provides a body of evidence about the effortful nature of riskwork in many different settings, routines theory provides the conceptual apparatus and empirical sensibilities to take this agenda further.

REFERENCES

Carlile, P., Nicolini, D., Langley, A., & Tsoukas, H. (Eds) (2013). *How Matter Matters: Objects, Artifacts and Materiality in Organization Studies*. Oxford: Oxford University Press.

D'Adderio, L. (2011). Artifacts at the Centre of Routines: Performing the Material Turn in Routines Theory. *Journal of Institutional Economics*, 7(2), 197–230.

Douglas, M. (Ed.) (1992). *Risk and Blame: Essays in Cultural Theory*. London: Routledge.

Feldman, M. (2000). Organizational Routines as a Source of Continuous Change. *Organization Science*, 11, 611–29.

Feldman, M. & Pentland, B. (2003). Reconceptualizing Organizational Routines as a Source of Flexibility and Change. *Administrative Science Quarterly*, 48, 94–118.

FRC (2014). *Guidance on Risk Management, Internal Control and Related Financial and Business Reporting*. London: Financial Reporting Council.

Gawande, A. (2010). *The Checklist Manifesto: How to Get Things Right*. London: Profile Books.

Haldane, A. (2009). *Rethinking the Financial Network*. London: Bank of England.

Hilgartner, S. (1992). The Social Construction of Risk Objects: Or, How to Pry Open Networks of Risk. In J. F. Short & L. Clarke (Eds), *Organizations, Uncertainties and Risk* (pp. 39–53). Boulder, CO: Westview Press.

Hood, C. (2011). *The Blame Game: Spin, Bureaucracy and Self-Preservation in Government*. Princeton, NJ: Princeton University Press.

Hunt, B. (2003). *The Timid Organisation: Why Business Is Terrified of Taking Risk*. Chichester, UK: Wiley.

Latour, B. (2005). *Reassembling the Social*. Oxford: Oxford University Press.

Orlikowski, W. & Scott, S. (2008). Sociomateriality: Challenging the Separation of Technology, Work and Organization. *Academy of Management Annals*, 2(1), 433–74.

Özgöde, O. (2011). The Emergence of Systemic Financial Risk: From Structural Adjustment (Back) to Vulnerability Reduction. January. <www.limn.it/issue/01>.

Pentland, B. & Feldman, M. (2005). Organizational Routines as a Unit of Analysis. *Industrial and Corporate Change*, 14, 793–815.

Pidgeon, N. E., Kasperson, R. K., & Slovic, P. (Eds) (2003). *The Social Amplification of Risk*. Cambridge: Cambridge University Press.

Power, M. (2007). *Organized Uncertainty: Designing a World of Risk Management*. Oxford: Oxford University Press.

Power, M. (2013). The Apparatus of Fraud Risk. *Accounting, Organizations and Society*, 38(6/7), 525–43.

Power, M. (2014). Risk, Social Theories and Organizations. In P. Adler, P. du Gay, G. Morgan, & M. Reed (Eds), *The Oxford Handbook of Sociology, Social Theory and Organization Studies: Contemporary Currents* (pp. 370–92). Oxford: Oxford University Press.

Power, M., Scheytt, T., Soin, K., & Sahlin, K. (2009). Reputational Risk as a Logic of Organizing in Late Modernity. *Organization Studies*, 30(2/3), 165–88.

Rothstein, H., Huber, M., & Gaskell, G. (2007). A Theory of Risk Colonization: The Spiralling Regulatory Logics of Societal and Institutional Risk. *Economy and Society*, 35(1), 91–112.

Turner, A. (2009*). Forward by the Chairman. Financial Services Authority Business Plan 2009/10*. London: Financial Services Authority.

Index

Printed and bound by CPI Group (UK) Ltd, Croydon, CR0 4YY